Framing a Lost City

Dear Catherine,
Thank you for your
Support!
much love,
Amy

Joe R. and Teresa Lozano Long Series in Latin American and Latino Art and Culture

Framing a Lost City

Science, Photography, and the Making of Machu Picchu

AMY COX HALL

University of Texas Press ⟡ Austin

Requests for permission to reproduce material from this work should be sent to:
Permissions
University of Texas Press
P.O. Box 7819
Austin, TX 78713-7819
utpress.utexas.edu/rp-form

⊗ The paper used in this book meets the minimum requirements of
ANSI/NISO Z39.48-1992 (R1997) (Permanence of Paper).

Library of Congress Cataloging-in-Publication Data

Names: Hall, Amy Cox, author.
Title: Framing a lost city : science, photography, and the making of
Machu Picchu / Amy Cox Hall.
Description: First edition. | Austin : University of Texas Press, 2017. |
Includes bibliographical references and index.
Identifiers: LCCN 2016054039
  ISBN 978-1-4773-1367-1 (cloth : alk. paper)
  ISBN 978-1-4773-1368-8 (pbk. : alk. paper)
  ISBN 978-1-4773-1369-5 (library e-book)
  ISBN 978-1-4773-1370-1 (non-library e-book)
Subjects: LCSH: Machu Picchu Site (Peru) | Peru—Antiquities. | Anthropological
ethics. | Peruvian Expeditions (1912–1915) | Yale Peruvian Expedition (1911) |
Yale Peruvian Expedition (1912) | Bingham, Hiram, 1875–1956. | Photography—
Moral and ethical aspects—Peru—Machu Picchu Site.
Classification: LCC F3429.1.M3 H35 2017 | DDC 985/.37—dc23
LC record available at https://lccn.loc.gov/2016054039

doi:10.7560/313671

For Kirk

Contents

List of Illustrations **ix**

Acknowledgments **xi**

A Note on the Text **xv**

Introduction: Seeing Science **1**

Sight

1. Epistolary Science **25**

2. *Huaquero* Vision **49**

Circulation

3. Latin America as Laboratory **69**

4. Discovery Aesthetics **86**

5. Picturing the Miserable Indian for Science **114**

Contests

6. The Politics of Seeing **137**

Conclusion: Artifact **164**

Notes **183**

Reference List **241**

Index **261**

List of Illustrations

Figure 1.1. *Ayer y Hoy*, Sergio Langer, 2008.   **xvii**

Figure 3.1. Hiram Bingham with his camera, 1912.   **70**

Figure 3.2. An untitled lantern slide, hand-tinted by W. C. Ives in Mystic, Connecticut, for use in Bingham's illustrated lectures, 1911.   **78**

Figure 3.3. Two panoramic photographs in expedition photo album, 1912.   **83**

Figure 3.4. "The Ruins of the Ancient Inca Capital, Machu Picchu," Hiram Bingham, 1912.   **84**

Figure 4.1. "Bird's-Eye View of Machu Picchu (During Clearing) and the Urubamba Canon," Hiram Bingham, 1912.   **96**

Figure 4.2. "A Good Mule Road in Southern Peru," Hiram Bingham, 1912.   **98**

Figure 4.3. "The Altar of the Chief Temple of Machu Picchu," Hiram Bingham, 1912.   **99**

Figure 4.4. "The Best type of Indian Workman: Southern Peru," Hiram Bingham, 1912.   **100**

Figure 4.5. "A Typical Cuzco Indian Mother and Baby," Luther T. Nelson, 1912.   **102**

Figure 4.6. Untitled, *Ilustración Peruana*, 1912.   **108**

Figure 4.7. Untitled, *Ilustración Peruana*, 1912.   **109**

Figure 5.1. Untitled photographs, labeled "F," taken by David Ford, c. 1915.   **120**

Figure 5.2. Plate 2 from H. B. Ferris, *Anthropological Studies on the Quichua and Machiganga Indians.*   **126**

Figure 7.1. *Grupo en Machupichu*, Cabrera Brothers, 1940.   **165**

Figure 7.2. *Turista en Aguas Calientes*, David Salas, 1955.   **166**

Figure 7.3. *Los Turistas*, Marcel Velaochaga, 2007.   **175**

Figure 7.4. *Los Prisioneros*, Marcel Velaochaga, 2007.   **176**

Figure 7.5. Advertisement at a Cuzco bus stop, 2008.   **180**

Acknowledgments

Grants from the Fulbright Program, the National Science Foundation, the University of Florida's Center for Latin American Studies, and Amherst College funded this research. Much of chapter 5 was written while I was in residence at the Hambidge Center for Creative Arts and Sciences in Rabun Gap, Georgia. The quiet time there was invaluable for the development of that part of the book. Without this support, the multisite and multiyear research required for this book would have been impossible. I am grateful for the permissions granted by Sergio Langer and Marcel Velaochaga to publish their work in this book. Their art has helped me think through my own ideas.

Having worked on this project for longer than I care to admit, I am indebted to many people, some of whom are mentioned here.

The University of Florida provided an eclectic mix of faculty and graduate students who broadened my thinking in ways I only now realize. I cannot thank Brenda Chalfin and Florence Babb enough for their enduring enthusiasm for this project and for their encouragement. Glenn Willumson expanded my interest in photography and was a uniquely talented mentor and teacher whose courses and comments improved my thinking and my writing. Stacey Langwick's course on the anthropology of science helped me reconsider my approach to history and anthropology. I am grateful to Michael Moseley for his insights into Peruvian archaeology and for his good humor. Mark Thurner carefully read early drafts of this work and pushed me to incorporate historical arguments and Peruvian historiography more deeply.

Peer support has been vital to the completion of this book, and I wish I had recognized the importance of this earlier in my life. My cohort at the

University of Florida offered friendship and opened my eyes to perspectives from Latin America that I hadn't previously considered. Scott Catey read countless drafts of initial grant proposals as well as subsequent chapters; "Epistolary Science" owes much to his comments. Lauren Fordyce was a supportive listener who understood the challenges of pursuing an academic career. Finally, Juan Carlos Callirgos helped me navigate life in Peru both past and present. I am grateful for his dependable friendship, support, close readings, and chapter consultations. I cannot thank him enough.

Although my training is primarily in cultural anthropology, the research for this book is historical. In the United States, I reviewed all the archival material held in the Yale Peruvian Expedition Papers and the Bingham Family Papers in Yale University's Sterling Library's Manuscripts and Archives. The research assistants were extraordinarily helpful and informative, even mailing me materials when I was no longer on campus. I examined US State Department correspondence at the National Archives, and archival materials and photographic albums at the National Geographic Society. Renee Braden at the National Geographic Society was a true gem. After many, many years of trying to view the photo albums of Hiram Bingham's expeditions, she finally made it happen. I am so thankful that she took time out of her extraordinarily busy schedule to facilitate the visit.

In Lima, Peru, I worked in a number of public archives, including the Museo Nacional de Arqueología, Antropología e Historia del Perú; the Archivo General de la Nación; the archive at the Ministerio de Relaciones Exteriores del Perú; and the Instituto Riva-Agüero, which holds a repository of newspapers and illustrated magazines from the early 1900s as well as the papers of Albert Giesecke, Mejía Xesspe, and the Zapata/Arias-Schreiber collection of articles on the defense of monument patrimony. At the former Instituto Nacional de Cultura, I examined the papers of Luis Eduardo Valcárcel. I also visited the collections at Lima's Pontificia Universidad Católica del Perú and the National Library, which has holdings of newspaper runs and illustrated magazines such as *Actualidades, Variedades, Prisma, El Perú Ilustrado*, and *El Correo de Peru*. I am humbled by the trust and goodwill the librarians and archivists showed me.

In Cuzco, Peru, I examined the regional archive and library, along with the photographic archive, Fototeca Andina, at the Centro de Estudios Bartolomé de las Casas. There, the librarians helped clarify some of the factual errors on the photographs held in the archive, making sure I wasn't led astray. I visited other archives, such as the Sociedad Geográfica of Lima, where I found no documents, but whose historic location was evocative of the faded elegance of a bygone era. I also visited personal archives and met with people such as Luis Figueroa Yábar, the well-known filmmaker of the Cuzco school and son of the artist and photographer Juan Manuel Figueroa Aznar, who shared his documents, photographs, and memories with me.

The Latin American Collection at the University of Florida was an incredible resource that I often took for granted. The Frost Library at Amherst College has been a superior example of what can happen with care, interest, and resources at a university library. They were and are amazing.

I am fortunate to have supportive and kind colleagues in the Department of Anthropology and Sociology at Amherst College. Deborah Gewertz, Chris Dole, Vanessa Fong, Nusrat Chowdhury, Jerry Himmelstein, Ron Lembo, Leah Schmalzbauer, and Hannah Holleman welcomed me and gave me thoughtful guidance and support. I am especially grateful to Deborah and Leah for their encouragement and their advice on publishing. I also thank Austin Sarat for making me feel like I belonged at a place like Amherst and for approving last-minute research and travel money. My students at Amherst College and UNC-Charlotte helped me become a better teacher and, in the process, a better scholar and writer.

In Peru, countless people assisted me with archives and bureaucracies, and also with life. I am grateful to them all. In particular, Mariana Mould de Pease welcomed me into her home and shared her ideas, papers, and perspectives. She is a treasure. Jorge Flores Ochoa offered his time and his insights with me over many years. Leylys Gutierrez invited me into COLITUR and encouraged tour guides to speak to me about their experiences at Machu Picchu. This part of the research was a welcome relief from the chill of reading rooms.

I also owe special thanks to the beautiful Castellanos family for inviting me to be a part of their family. Diana Castellanos's friendship continues to be a source of great joy and support for me.

Reviews by Christopher Heaney and Walter Little helped clarify and deepen the argument of this book. I am grateful for the time and care they showed in their reviews and for their enriching suggestions, all of which have improved the book. Kerry Webb was a thoughtful and diligent editor who guided the book seamlessly through the process from review to publication. I appreciate immensely how she believed in this project. Kip Keller was an extraordinary copy editor. I am in awe of his skill.

Finally I would like to thank my family. My mom, while not understanding the purpose of my chosen profession, was supportive nonetheless. My father read drafts of my research and has always encouraged me to keep writing. I wrote my dissertation while pregnant with my first daughter and began teaching while pregnant with my second. In retrospect, I have no idea how that was possible, but it must have had something to do with the sweet love, admiration, and excitement they showed me. They are joys that continue to give me sense and a place in the world.

The book is dedicated to Kirk, my spouse. I have no idea how you continued to be supportive. Thank you for extending such grace.

A Note on the Text

Technically, the 1911 expedition was the only one officially called the Yale Peruvian Expedition. Subsequent expeditions were called the 1912, and then the 1914–1915, Peruvian Expedition under the Auspices of Yale University and National Geographic Society. Gilbert Grosvenor, the director of the society and editor of *National Geographic Magazine*, often mentioned to Bingham that when the expeditions were discussed publicly, the society felt that it did not get the credit it deserved. I have nonetheless chosen to refer to all three expeditions as Yale Peruvian Expeditions for simplicity's sake and because this is how they are typically known.

Figure 1.1. *Ayer y Hoy*, Sergio Langer, 2008. This image is taken from the Sunday magazine insert *Somos* in *El Comercio*, the largest daily newspaper in Lima, Peru. The cartoon, a comment on conquest, appeared in 2008. The cartoonist satirizes tourists laden with cameras, provoking us to think critically about the practice of tourism. I also read it through the lens of this book, somewhat literally, thinking that the cartoonist might be suggesting, as I do, that photography is a tool of conquest and is as potent as a rifle—perhaps more so because the shots keep getting fired, the bullets never ceasing to circulate. Courtesy of the artist.

Seeing Science

It [Machu Picchu] is far more wonderful and interesting than Choqquequirau. The stone is as fine as any in Cuzco! It is unknown and will make a fine story.
HIRAM BINGHAM TO HIS WIFE, JULY 26, 1911

Nearly twenty years ago I first visited Machu Picchu as a backpacker hiking the Inca Trail. I arrived in Cuzco, looked around, talked to a tour agency, negotiated the price, booked my trip, and left the next day with a hodgepodge of tourists from the UK, Australia, and the United States. On the day we made the arduous climb to Huarmiwañusqa (Dead Woman's Pass, 13,770 feet), the porters carried tourists' belongings stacked five feet high across their backs. I marveled at their strength and agility as they ran up the mountain in rubber sandals, but I lamented the obvious inequality. Having insisted on carrying my backpack, I arrived at the top proud of my accomplishment, but sensed that the situation was less clear, since the porters seemed disappointed at not being paid to carry my pack. After three days of hiking, we arrived to Machu Picchu, where a new guide told us, in incomprehensible English, about the area. I walked up Huayna Picchu, taking in the breathtaking views from the jutting spire of this young mountain and admiring the elegance of a perfectly placed hamlet.

Today this scenario is less likely to occur. Tourists must schedule their adventure, booking the trip to Machu Picchu months in advance. Hiking the trail is regulated by Peru's Ministry of Culture, and camping sites are limited to those overseen by a few approved tour operators. Tourists can no longer decide spontaneously to hike up Huayna Picchu, but instead need to make a reservation and pay a separate entry fee. Prices have skyrocketed.

In 1983, Machu Picchu was named a UNESCO World Heritage Site. In 2007, the site was deemed a wonder of the modern world. Over a million tourists visited Machu Picchu in 2014.[1] In 2015, a round-trip tourist ticket on the train from Cuzco to Aguas Calientes cost $90–$398. The entrance fee for the park, including a visit to Huayna Picchu and the Temple of the Moon, which were previously included in the entry fee, was 152 Peruvian soles, or approximately $47, for non-Peruvian adults. To visit only Machu Picchu cost 128 Peruvian soles, or $40. Peruvians continue to be able to visit Machu Picchu on Sunday for free, but even with the reduced admission, the cost of a visit is out of reach for most Peruvians. Both a source of foreign capital and the linchpin to a national identity that unites people into the imagined collective called "Peruvian," Machu Picchu has become a logo as powerful as Nike's swoosh.

Scholars believe that Machu Picchu was a royal estate or retreat for the Inca Pachacuti, the ninth Sapa Inca, who ruled from 1438 to 1471. At the time of his death, the Incan Empire was at its apogee, stretching from northern Ecuador to Chile, including what is today Peru, Bolivia, and northern Argentina. After the Spanish conquered the Inca, Machu Picchu retreated from view. It wasn't until 1911, when Hiram Bingham, a historian at Yale University, took its picture, that Machu Picchu began its path to celebrity. A photograph first made Machu Picchu famous, helping transform the place into a lost city discovered, an Andean utopia found. The place has not been the same since.

This book is about seeing. More specifically, it is about Hiram Bingham's three expeditions to Peru, which took place from 1911 to 1916, and the role of visualizing technologies in fashioning knowledge about nations, peoples, and the past as national patrimony.[2] If nothing else, Hiram Bingham and the Yale Peruvian Expeditions (1911, 1912, 1914–1915) represented Machu Picchu and Peru to the world. They made maps, displayed antiquities, took pictures, wrote books and articles, and gave illustrated lectures. Their words and images framed a place from a specific vantage, one that placed it in a dominant domain of visibility.[3] Discovery narratives, which often focus on Bingham's heroism or antiheroism, tend to eclipse this fact. And yet, what we know about Machu Picchu, the most iconic example of Peruvian heritage, derives from, or is couched in terms set by, the Yale Peruvian Expeditions' imagining and framing of that specific geographic site. It seems that Machu Picchu does not speak without speaking to Yale first.[4] This book examines what Hiram Bingham chose to observe and how he observed it, to explicate the ways in which Machu Picchu was made, not only by the Incas, but also by expeditionary science in the first part of the twentieth century.

In 1978, Edward Said published *Orientalism*. The text marked a turning point in scholarship about the ways in which the Other has been seen and represented and how power is imbricated and circulated through seemingly innocuous fields.[5] Since the book's publication, paintings, photographs, novels, museums, art, and travel writing have all been examined for the ways in which peoples and nations have been fashioned, invented, and negotiated by outsiders.[6] Over the last two decades, work in science and technology studies (STS) has focused on the processes by which representational fields ground authoritative and universal knowledge.[7] No longer viewed as a direct reflection of nature, the pursuit of scientific knowledge with technological instruments has instead been shown to be constitutive of it.[8] Images are key actors not only in the formation of individual and group identities but also in the production of scientific knowledge.[9] More than an exegesis on stereotypes, this body of scholarship is an examination of how seeing and representation by certain situated subjects craft powerful narratives that calcify into facts and knowledge, subjugating the Other into authoritative structures of visibility. Ways of seeing fashion truth.

If science is a term that describes the acquisition of knowledge about the physical and natural world through observation, then engaging those practices of observation is critical for furthering our understanding of the construction, veracity, and historicity of knowledge. As Lorraine Daston and Elizabeth Lunbeck point out, "Observation educates the senses, calibrates judgment, picks out objects of scientific inquiry and forges 'thought collectives.'"[10] This book examines the scientific and expeditionary practices and technologies that constituted such observations, and thus how publics came to understand Machu Picchu as a discovered lost city.[11] In so doing, this book parses the composition of Machu Picchu vis-à-vis the entanglements of science, instruments of knowledge, and racialized discourses about Peruvian histories and peoples, which ultimately transformed the site into a lost city and national patrimony.[12]

STS and Expeditionary Science

At first, Hiram Bingham and the Yale Peruvian Expeditions seemed unlikely candidates for the inflection and reliance on research produced under the rubric of science and technology studies. Although Bingham was an explorer and considered himself and the expeditions to Peru to be scientific, STS in academia has tended to focus on either science produced before the twentieth century or scientific technology such as medical imaging devices, computers, and superconductors.[13] Physics and biomedicine, particularly the study of the body and work in clinical settings, have been privileged over expeditionary science in science studies scholarship.[14] Furthermore, trying to link STS to explorers has proved confusing and at times counterintuitive. From a popular standpoint, science and scientists conjure an image of white coats, glass beakers, pharmaceuticals, and computers. Drawing on science studies to examine expeditionary practices made sense to me but seemed to be contradicted by the very label itself. Bingham's expedition and his findings did not seem scientific enough.

While Bingham felt that he produced scientific findings through mapmaking, geographic work, and osteology, these did not come to the forefront as the primary or important outcomes of the expeditions. No inventions, laboratories, or devices arose from the three Yale expeditions to Peru. Moreover, archaeology, which one might assume was the main scientific practice used in uncovering Machu Picchu and learning about its past, was not conducted on the three tours. None of the members of the three expeditions to Peru were thoroughly trained in archaeology. Bingham was trained in history, and his teams typically consisted of a geographer, an osteologist, a naturalist, and a topographer as well as several young assistants. Although the expeditions' topographic maps continue to be used by explorers today and Bingham is credited with locating Vitcos, where Manco Inca ruled until he was assassinated by the Spanish, Bingham's legacy does not readily read as scientific.[15]

A possible reason for this is that during the time of Bingham's expeditions, science was less specialized than it is today. Educated people dabbled in science. Illustrated lectures by explorers, including Bingham, or nonprofessional scientists were common.[16] For example, Bingham was a member of the Cosmos Club, an all-male society whose members needed either to have done "meritorious work in science, literature or the fine arts" or simply to be cultivated in those fields.[17] The pursuit of science for the expeditionary teams was science-*cum*-history-*cum*-adventure-*cum*-industry. The blurring of these pursuits demonstrates the anachronism of these labels in the early twentieth century when the romantic-scientific aura of the explorer established in the nineteenth century was still very much alive. This is not to say that science did not play a significant role in the facilitating, legitimizing, and carrying out of the expedition. Without the sheen and the technologies of the scientific expedition, the Yale cohort would have produced a rather different legacy. Indeed, it was precisely the frame of science that guaranteed Bingham and the expeditions' long cultural legacy in Peru and the world at large.

Trained as a historian, Bingham might be best characterized as an explorer and collector with a scientific purpose.[18] As the first professor of South American history at Yale, he sought to develop exciting and relevant questions that built on previous scholarship. He then methodically attempted to answer those questions, hoping to contribute to something beyond individual experience, enriching civilization's knowledge. The expeditions expanded on previous, long-standing expeditionary pursuits such as cataloguing, naming, and collecting, but also subtly shifted what came to constitute science.

Bingham's two most prolific scientific practices on his 1911 expedition were mapmaking and photography. Both were continued on subsequent trips. Collecting remains figured extensively on the second and third expeditions, and that practice has left a lasting impression on both the politics of the expedition and Bingham's reputation. Initially, however, the majority of expeditionary practice in 1911 was executed through measuring and making pictures. Photographic technology and the reproduction of images played a significant role in the formation of Machu Picchu, helping standardize views based on select criteria, ultimately marking locations, people, and things as lost then found.

In 1911, Peru was compared with other nations, and found wanting. Racial and moral categories were used to rank nations on scales of industrialization and civilization. Ricardo Salvatore suggests that during this period, "South America became a 'continent of opportunity' and also a land of 'lost cities' and 'ancient glories,' a contradictory synthesis of future market opportunities and current backwardness."[19] Peru's desire for parity in the community of nations was part of the zeitgeist in which nations strove to become modern, and for many elite Peruvians, Bingham's expeditions were considered a way to fashion a nation out of colonial ruins.[20] Transnational infrastructures, scientific pursuits, and national images all worked to constitute a discursive complex that was characterized as modern: a mental outlook accompanied by a specific institutional order.[21] That order informed the three expeditions and shaped how choices were made, and actions defined, to translate a place into a scientific discovery of a lost city of global import.

Science, however, was not only an attitude and outlook of modernity, but also one whose instruments and inscriptions shaped the political space as much as it did its subjects. Modernity referred not only to the economic structures of life,[22] but also to its mechanical forms of reproduction, which began in Peru in the late 1800s and came into sharp relief around the time of Bingham's expedition.[23] Indeed, it was through photography that Machu Picchu became "known to the world."[24] Thousands of photographs were taken over the course of the three expeditions, five hundred of Machu Picchu alone.[25] The act of taking photographs, along with the selection, circulation, and manipulation of images and diagrams to global and national publics, uniquely shaped Machu Picchu into an internationally recognized site and a Peruvian national icon. Although local understandings of the area now known as Machu Picchu existed before Bingham's expeditions, global and national meanings of Machu Picchu continue to be traced to the ways in which the site was imagined and packaged in the early 1900s.

Thinking about the Yale expeditions to Machu Picchu offers an opportunity to examine not simply its own making but also the story of Peru in the twentieth century and how it is inextricably bound up in a tale of global proportions. The abandoned archaeological site stands at the center of Peru's colonial past and its postcolonial future, speaking volumes about modernization, development, race, indigeneity, long histories of scientific expeditions, photography, US-Peruvian relations, tourism, and national identity. Through an examination of seeing and visibility as they relate to Machu Picchu, this book aims to contribute insights to broader questions about the coupling of science and modernity and the forces of nation making in the twentieth century. Pictures do not simply represent people or objects, but want something and act on the viewer.[26] The following chapters closely examine the ways in which visualizing technologies were used to set the Andean landscape into a specific, particularly modern formation.

Vision and Scientific Expeditions in South America

Many scholars have examined how science as a global discourse, metonym of empire, and powerful practice circulated in the New World in the eighteenth and nineteenth centuries.[27] Charles de La Condamine's expedition in 1735 to South America sought to catalogue and categorize resources. This mission, coupled with the publication of Carolus Linnaeus's *The System of Nature* (1735), led to global-scale meaning being constructed through the descriptive apparatuses of natural history.[28] Collections for

European botanical gardens and natural history museums served as objects of scientific inquiry and as evidence of conquered geography.[29]

In contrast to La Condamine's texts, which categorized the Americas as accessible, recognizable, and collectible, Alexander von Humboldt's accounts of his expeditions presented South America as an overwhelming spectacle of nature awaiting conquering.[30] Humboldt was not interested in filling taxonomic gaps, but sought encompassing laws of nature within apparent chaos and an uncertain future.[31] He measured, collected, and illustrated. He brought instruments (forty-two on his trip to Venezuela) and paper, scales, tools, and vials for storing seeds.[32] He returned with sixty thousand specimens, and his drawings changed the way people saw the Americas.[33] The images were an aesthetic achievement, rich in color and detail, but also a scientific one, since they allowed others to witness the marvels of Latin America without ever leaving Europe.[34]

By the mid-nineteenth century, scientific exploration in South America began to include research in ethnography, which broadly included collecting antiquities, excavating for remains, and conducting works in anthropometry and physiognomic typing.[35] Fresh methods and perspectives bolstered knowledge of a "new" America through graphics and illustrations.[36] Works such as *Antigüedades Peruanas*, by Mariano Eduardo de Rivero and Johann Jakob von Tschudi (1851), exemplified a Humboldtian tradition of seeing the landscape directly, even if it was through the eyes and representations of the explorer.[37]

British and Anglo-American explorers followed in the footsteps of their French and Spanish predecessors in exploring the Peruvian interior, too.[38] Sir Clements Markham's 1852 voyage to Cuzco and subsequent book, *Travels in Peru and India* (1862), and Ephraim George Squier's US-government-sponsored Peruvian expedition and resulting *Peru: Incidents of Travel and Exploration in the Land of the Incas* (1877), were landmarks in a burgeoning literature. Bingham's South American expeditions (1906–1907, 1908–1909, 1911, 1912, 1914–1915) were rooted in this trajectory.[39]

Squier, in particular, marked a turning point for modern Andean studies.[40] Like other nineteenth-century explorers of South America, he had a philosophy of vision that was statistical and quantitative. Science involved the display of items such as skulls or potsherds as "populations" whose patterns could be measured, and meanings generalized.[41] To meet the demands of modern science, Squier brought along a compass, measuring line, pencil, and camera.[42] Photography was central to his science, and his writings were an extended travel narrative with mapping and images.[43]

Although Bingham's interest in Peru drew on Squier's research and was piqued by Adolph Bandelier's *The Islands of Titicaca and Koati* (1910), his research agenda was influenced most by Clements Markham. Markham wrote several books that shaped Bingham's conception of Peru, including *Cuzco: A Journey to the Ancient Capital of Peru* (1856),[44] *Travels in Peru and India* (1862), *A History of Peru* (1892), and *The Incas of Peru* (1910). Although Markham's scholarly aim was to learn about the Incas and their origins,[45] his travelogues are a mix of adventure, historicity, and industry consulting.

In *A History of Peru*, Markham's narrative begins with the era of the Incas and ends with an analysis of the republic. Concluding his book are four chapters on Peru's situation at the time: "People of Peru," "The Literature of Peru," "The Trade of Peru," and "The Wealth of Peru." In these chapters, Markham describes the promise of Peru as a nation, outlining the problems and possibilities for Peru's future industrial development. Like Peru's early geographers, who saw their discipline as an opportunity to exploit natural resources for development,[46] Markham saw Peru's potential, particularly when it came to its diverse climate and abundant resources.[47] Specifically, Markham envisaged Peru's development into a modern nation as coming from the benefits of international commerce with Britain, which dominated South America's interior trade at the time.[48] Markham concluded, "It may, therefore, be accepted when the means of traffic, in the Peruvian Montana, is fully developed, and steamers are running on all the navigable rivers, that a very extensive and lucrative trade in India rubber will be developed and maintained."[49] He called for new trade routes connecting Cuzco to Brazil, as well as for the building of infrastructure to harness Peru's enormous wealth in natural resources.

Markham's books are replete with admiration for Peru's distant past as well as hope for its promising future. In *A History of Peru*, Markham commended the country on its blessed nature and representation of "every clime." He concluded the book by writing that if Peru's two great needs, immigration and peace, were met, "there may still be a bright future in store for the long suffering children of the sun."[50]

At that time, scientific exploration in Peru focused on "ancient civilizations" and human antiquity.[51] Explorers, influenced by the publication of Charles Darwin's *On the Origin of the Species* (1859), had become generally interested in questions about deep history, human origins, speciation, and the peopling of South America.[52] Study of present-day Andean populations had not achieved the same status as the investigation of antiquities. This disparity was due in part to the continued conceptualization of Peru's indigenous populations as "epigones incapable of contributing to the understanding of Inca greatness."[53] Instead, explorers such as Squier and Markham examined the Peruvian nation's imagined past civilizations through the glorified lens of the Inca "race."

Representations such as Squier's photographs and drawings of the Ti-wanaku ruins materialized and naturalized this historical schism through further temporal distancing.[54] Objects became monumentalized and thereby underwrote Peru's bifurcated national history. Peru's dead golden age ultimately became its future through a dismissal and obscuring of the present. In fashioning a modern Peru out of its Incan past, the process of nation building constructed and shaped a national identity.[55] Such an emphasis on antiquity and the privileging of the Inca reiterated the Spanish-Creole schema of Peru's glorious native past versus its miserable Indian present.

This bias was directed at Peru by Peruvian antiquarians as well as foreigners. Spurred by a global interest in classical Roman antiquities, Lima's Geographical Society and the Cuzco Science Center were formed by Peruvians to study Peru's so-called ancient past.[56] Collecting brought prestige, taste, and class to the collector, but also continued to produce living Quechua speakers as relics, downfallen antiquities themselves.[57] The collecting of Incan symbols was as much cosmopolitan as it was patriotic but remained deeply racialized and bifurcated, even within Peru by Peruvian collectors.[58]

Bingham saw South America's present condition as problematic and thought that science was an avenue to improve conditions. In 1906, he was working on a history of the South American wars of independence and on biographies of José de San Martín and Simón Bolívar. Because of a lack of trustworthy sources, Bingham found the project unsustainable and shifted his goal. He became interested in the battles that Bolívar fought at Carabobo (in present-day Venezuela) and Boyacá (in present-day Colombia). Since descriptions of the battles were "very meager," he sought to experience the place for himself, studying the country where Bolívar lived and fought, visiting the most important scenes of the battles, and exploring the route of "his most celebrated campaign."[59] In retracing the marches and battle scenes, Bingham hoped to ascertain the obstacles overcome by the liberating army and to contribute to knowledge about Bolívar and the conditions within which these two famed battles were fought. Rather than a mere traveler's tale, his "scientific work" would offer some "observations of use in geography and ethnology."[60] Dr. Hamilton Rice, who had previously explored from Quito to Pará by way of the Napo and Amazon Rivers, was a fellow of the Royal Geographical Society. He accompanied

Bingham, often being called into service to remedy local medical maladies and perform surgeries. The two-person team took along books, maps, tents, surgical equipment, surveying instruments, and guns, all of which passed freely through customs without examination.

Bingham's account of the trip, *The Journal of an Expedition Across Venezuela and Colombia, 1906–1907: An Exploration of the Route of Bolívar's Celebrated March of 1819 and of the Battle-Fields of Boyacá and Carabobo* (1909), reads as a coming-of-age memoir and is replete with Bingham's musings and inner thoughts. In the text, Bingham is the master of all that he sees, acting as the anointed translator and knowledge broker for future travelers through his many scene settings: descriptions of buildings, paintings, landscapes, and even a bit of curiosity directed at the natural world.[61] Photographs of buildings, landscapes, and people, for the most part unidentified, are interspersed throughout the text to act as evidentiary proof to the written word.[62] The images visualize his movement through the landscape, marking rivers, plazas, mountains, and the people he encounters. His observations about the moral character of people are rooted in the racial categories of the time and supplemented with photographs of nameless types such as "a Yaruro Chief."[63] Although there are humorous parts in the book, such as an incident of the team being swindled,[64] the book does not shed light on Bolívar or the battles. Instead, it is about Bingham and one Anglo-Saxon's (his term) observations about reasons for the backwardness of the countries and the lack of foreign capitalist investment.[65]

Following that experience, he attended the First Pan-American Scientific Congress, held in Santiago, Chile, in December 1908.[66] He first sailed to Rio de Janeiro and made his way to Argentina in order to explore the historic trade route between Buenos Aires, Potosí, and Lima. He went overland into Cuzco, Peru. This exploration was recounted in *Across South America: An Account of a Journey from Buenos Aires to Lima by Way of Potosí* (1911).

Like *Journal of an Expedition*, *Across South America* begins with descriptions of buildings, roads, racial types, architecture, and commerce. The text includes further conjecture about the economic development of Peru and South America generally, advancing his perspective on the importance of investment in ports, railroads, and transportation for national economic growth. He speculates about the reasons, including climate and "race history," for the lack of unification of the governments and nations of South America.[67] Bingham writes: "Like my journey across Venezuela and Colombia this [trip] taught me to feel anew the stupendous difficulties that lie in the way of advancing South American civilization."[68] He concludes with an appraisal of South American traits and behaviors, including manners, styles of speech, and lack of honesty, suggesting that while South America inherited "racial antipathies" and was not yet as civilized as the United States or Europe, it was improving. Citing the fact that the South American countries received their independence nearly fifty years after the United States did, Bingham's narrative situates South America within an evolutionary and industrialist paradigm with the United States as the apex of modernity. He concludes by noting that an honest appraisal of South America (such as his) was necessary to build confidence and, therefore, trade relations: "There is not the slightest question that there is a great opportunity awaiting the American manufacturer and exporter when he is willing to grasp it with intelligent persistence and determination. South America is ready to take American goods in very large quantities as soon as we are ready to take time to give attention to her needs."[69]

By the time of Bingham's arrival in Peru in 1911, South America had become a field of interest for diplomatic policy and for US business interests.[70] Foreign capital was used to purchase land, mineral concessions, and exportation rights in Peru. Peru's economic policy became increasingly aligned with external capital interests, and exploration by foreigners was welcomed.[71] Like Squier and Markham, Bingham saw Peru as a nation offering historical insight and economic potential if the present could be overcome. Grounded in the historical schism between Peru's perceived glorious Incan past and its miserable native present, Bingham's expeditionary practices produced materials that circulated with various ends, including civilizing in the name of industry and modernity.[72]

Bingham entered a Peru that was deeply divided and unequal, politically and economically.[73] A small segment of society held most of the property as the hacienda system, already in place in the late nineteenth century, expanded.[74] The economy relied on exports and foreign capital for investment and development, which led to further monopolies in agriculture, mining, and wool production.[75] Such consolidation meant a crisis for common property in rural communities as communal lands and smallholdings were squeezed.[76] Cuzco at the time was a city "dominated by a minority composed of a few hundred large and medium sized landowning families, a handful of bourgeoisie with a mentality of industrialization and a circle of foreign or Arequipeña merchants that easily exploited the needs of all."[77] The middle class hardly existed, and the remainder of the population lived in the countryside.

To survive and grow, haciendas relied on exploitative labor practices that were deeply racialized. Indeed, without the labor available from indigenous communities, the haciendas would not have existed.[78] Many used *enganche*, a legal system of labor recruitment wherein laborers were coerced through advance payment to work for a set amount of time.[79] Such a system, which preyed on the most marginalized, was replicated in abusive hierarchical labor arrangements.[80] Others in the highlands relied on "free labor" wherein people worked on a hacienda in exchange for being allowed to pasture their animals or produce their own crops on the land.[81] Haciendas on the coast also relied on sharecropping (*yanaconaje*) performed by workers from the Andes, often without contracts or specified arrangements.[82] Moreover, Lima elites relied on an Andean *gamonal* system, wherein local political bosses could rule as they pleased in exchange for their support of the national government.[83] However, *gamonales* were creative in their appropriation of national political discourse, often using it to reinforce their own power.[84] Characterized by dislocated peasants, migrant workers, and corporate elites, the system was paternalistic, coercive, and violent.[85] In April 1911, a few months before Bingham's arrival in Peru, a general strike, the first in Peru's history, was held to protest such abusive labor practices.

Bingham's expeditions to Colombia and Venezuela, and his trip from Buenos Aires to Lima, framed South America as a repository for potential scientific and historic discoveries. Yet underscoring the interest in scientific work was a civilizing narrative. Drawing on early twentieth-century racial paradigms, Bingham made observations and drew conclusions about the economic and political trajectories of South American nations.[86] Bingham's efforts were multidirectional: his expeditionary science sought to foster and expand US business interests, contribute to scientific knowledge, and make a name for himself. For the three Yale Peruvian Expeditions, he continued along this trajectory, traveling roads built to facilitate trade from the area's haciendas,[87] and relying on a labor pool coerced by local elites who believed in the promise of science to spur national development. Eventually, Machu Picchu, the discovered lost city, became a marvelous possession in its own right, even though it was never really lost and wasn't a city.[88]

The 1911 Yale Peruvian Expedition

In *Across South America*, Bingham wrote about his visit to the ruins of Choqquequirau and reviewed some of the reasons why it was referred to as the "Cradle of Gold."[89] Bingham concluded that Choqquequirau was not a "Cradle of Gold" or "a temple or a treasure house." Rather, it was, he suggested, originally a fortress defending the valley of the Apurímac, a place where life was strenuous.[90] The sighting of Choqquequirau, however, fostered his interest in further exploration: "The interesting question remains: Was this the ultimate refuge of the last Inca"?[91]

Manco Capac, the last Incan ruler, took refuge from the Spanish conquerors in a place referred to as Vilcabamba. Based on the writings of Father Antonio de la Calancha[92] and the early geographers Antonio Raimondi and Mariano Paz Soldan, many believed that the legendary refuge of Vilcabamba was Choqquequirau. Bingham was doubtful. He concluded the chapter on Choqquequirau in *Across South America* by noting that although Raimondi might be correct, he would need additional proof: "Until some one shall have explored the present village of Vilcabamba and its vicinity, I am inclined to the opinion that Choqquequirau was merely a fortress."[93] Returning to explore the area became one of the rationales for the 1911 expedition. More importantly, however, this trip provided experience, know-how, and connections for the future 1911 expedition.

At Choqquequirau, Bingham uncovered caves with large rocks blocking their entrances. In them he examined decaying bones, a practice that was performed extensively on the three subsequent Yale expeditions.[94] A military accompaniment and letters of introduction smoothed his movement through the country. Being seen as a scientist won him support from industry and government, including free transport on the railroad and free entry at customs. As Bingham described the Pan-American Congress in *Across South America*, the meeting was less about the content of science than the opportunity for socializing.

On Bingham's 1909 trip to Peru, he also met men who would assist him in the future. Juan José Nuñez Valdivia, who eventually became the prefect in Cuzco, encouraged Bingham to visit Choqquequirau and then accompanied him on the trip.[95] Later, Bingham gave him a plaque thanking him for all his help on the expeditions.[96] Bingham also met Cesar Lomellini, an Italian merchant who resided in Cuzco, on this trip. Lomellini later provided Bingham with needed supplies and information. He visited Lima's Geographical Society for maps and met the Peruvian president, Augusto Leguía. The Peruvian historian and archivist Carlos Romero, spurred by the presence of Bingham at Choqquequirau, wrote his own report of the ruins, which detailed that the lost city was in the valley of the Urubamba, not the Apurímac.[97] This report would eventually find its way to Bingham.

Thus, the proposal for Bingham's 1911 Yale Peruvian Expedition was rooted in a long history of scientific exploration of South America, the knowledge and contacts he acquired during his initial South American experiences, and an outlook that framed Peru as a nation in need. The 1911 expedition sought to map a cross-section of a large portion of the Andes to ascertain how deep into the jungle the Incas had carried their civilization. The team would also make maps, climb and measure the height of Mount Coropuna, and study the depth of Lake Parinacochas.[98] Members of subsequent expeditions would continue to survey the area and make maps, scout and excavate ruins, measure and photograph Peru's Quechua-speaking population, work with the Bureau of Plant Industry of the US Department of Agriculture to study agricultural systems and crops, and collect specimens of birds, fish, and skeletal remains. The expansiveness of the 1911 expedition and its interdisciplinarity were thought worthwhile, since the branches of science represented might intersect and help one another.[99] Ultimately, the search for the lost city of the last Incan capital had a magnetic effect, uniting publics for support in both Peru and the United States while underscoring Peru's potential.

The 1911 expedition was made possible by Bingham's family money, Yale University's granting of academic leave, volunteers, and corporate sponsorship; subsequent expeditions were financed primarily by the National Geographic Society, Yale, and Bingham. Peruvian actors and transnational elites, however, should not be discounted. The government granted Bingham free entry for all expedition goods, a military accompaniment, permission to excavate, and free shipment of all materials within the country. In addition, Bingham consulted with local elites about the whereabouts of ruins, and stayed at local haciendas during the expeditions. Although Bingham's ability to ship materials out of Peru was constrained on subsequent expeditions, he was allowed access and entry to the Andean countryside during each visit. He relied on local labor, incentivized through monetary compensation or threats, to help excavate and clear sites. The science of the expeditions united a wide array of actors and was international in scope.

Alberto Flores Galindo suggests that the idealized depiction of a pre-Hispanic past, referred to as an Andean utopia, has acted as the organizing principle and discursive frame for a variety of national projects in Peru.[100] This view of the Incan past, emerging after the sixteenth century, was memorialized as an era free from disorder, hunger, and exploitation. It was a time when ancient Peruvians, imagined through their Incan ancestors, ruled.[101] The search for remains of the Incan past motivated Bingham,

Yale, and National Geographic, but also Peruvian intellectuals and elites as they sought not only to understand the past and provide an alternative to the present, but also to invent and discern a national future.[102]

The first Yale Peruvian Expedition lasted from late June through December 1911. On May 25, an advance party set sail with the equipment. Bingham and the rest of the party left on June 8. On June 24, Bingham climbed two thousand feet to Machu Picchu, accompanied by Melchor Arteaga and Sergeant Carrasco, the team's military escort.[103] A son of a farmer who made his home at Machu Picchu then accompanied Bingham to the ruins. Bingham spent a few hours at the site.[104]

Once back in the United States, Bingham made plans to return to Peru. He set sail on May 18, 1912, to conduct further work in and around Machu Picchu. He remained in Peru until late November. The final expedition began in the spring of 1914 and lasted through 1915. The first expedition was primarily taken up with survey work, mapping, and mountain climbing. The second expedition, which was quickly organized following the success of the first, centered on the excavation and mapping of Machu Picchu and its environs. The third expedition included further survey work, additional mapping of the area, and the collection of a large number of specimens. The third expedition also included more cultural work, which was primarily conducted by Bingham's assistant, Osgood Hardy. Hardy's tasks included learning Quechua and studying indigenous feasts and beliefs. Physicians on the last two expeditions took anthropometric measurements and photographs of the local population, and conducted health investigations.

After seeing Machu Picchu in 1911, Bingham initially surmised that it could be the "cradle of Inca civilization." Taking his cue from Markham, Bingham had set out to find the post-Conquest refuge known as Vilcabamba, the lost city of the Incas. Nonetheless, the supposed presence of "three windows" at Machu Picchu (the actual location of the three windows of the Inca origin story was later identified to be in nearby Ollantaytambo) led Bingham to speculate that he had discovered the birthplace of the Incan Empire. In his initial article for *Harper's Magazine*, Bingham wrote: "In the mean time it seems probable that Machu Picchu, discovered while on a search for the *last* Inca capital, was the *first*, the capital from which the Incas started on that glorious career of empire that eventually embraced a large part of South America."[105] This initial, "first and last" narrative of Machu Picchu responded to the long-standing scientific search for the Incas' origins and the romantic narrative of their heroic fall to the Spaniards.

Scientific Discoveries

Upon returning to the United States after the first expedition Bingham referred to his discovery of Machu Picchu as "scientific." This delineation was not insignificant. By claiming to have made a scientific discovery, Bingham gained recognition as an explorer who illuminated an amazing example of history. He also gained stature within an elite group of men. To discover something of scientific merit was to make a contribution to universal knowledge, not merely to explore or go on an adventure. This framing was due in part to at least three factors. First, the site was inhabited and farmed during Bingham's discovery. Second, across one of Machu Picchu's rocks was the signature "Agustín Lizárraga" and the date 1902.[106] Third, Bingham had paid someone to guide him to Machu Picchu. To situate the discovery as scientific meant that Bingham not only saw the place, as so many others before him had done, but also made a contribution that surpassed existing knowledge.

In Bingham's first published account of the discovery of Machu Picchu, he wrote: "It [Machu Picchu] was known to a few people in Cuzco, chiefly residents of the province of Convención, that there were ruins, still undescribed, in the valley of the Urubamba. One friend told us that a muleteer had told him of some ruins near the bridge of San Miguel."[107] Bingham went on to say that while en route to Machu Picchu, the expedition team reached a hut where they were treated hospitably: "Several good-natured Indians welcomed us and gave us gourds full of cool, delicious water, and a few cooked sweet-potatoes. All that we could see was a couple of small grass huts and a few terraces, faced with stone walls. The pleasant Indian family had chosen this eagle's nest for a home. They told us there were better ruins a little farther along."[108] Bingham admitted in the article that he had heard vague rumors about the ruins from friends and that Machu Picchu must have been previously known, because the French explorer Charles Wiener referred to the ruins in his text *Pérou et Bolivie* (1880).

In Bingham's pocket field journal, he initially credited Agustín Lizárraga with the discovery: "This place discovered in 1902 by Lizarraga. The people have lived here four years, planted cotton and vegetable and ruins on andenes. 3 huts now occupied. Climate seems to be good — . . . corn, sugar cane . . . tomatoes, currants, beans, potatoes. An Intihuatana stone near top of works. Much fine stone work. *Some* very large stones. Best windows I have ever seen. Many horses."[109] In his 1930 account, Bingham wrote about Wiener's unsuccessful attempt to visit in 1875 and then that Lizárraga "had been treasure hunting on these forest-clad slopes at least ten years before our visit to this cave."[110] Although Bingham referred to Lizárraga as the discoverer in his first articles and speeches, and even in *Inca Land* (1922), the presence of Lizárraga's signature faded until, in his final version of the story, *Lost City of the Incas* (1952), Bingham claimed to have found the site himself.[111]

Mariana Mould de Pease, a Peruvian writer and intellectual, has strongly contested Bingham's fame as discoverer of Machu Picchu. Although she refers to Bingham as the first traveler to visit the sanctuary of Machu Picchu and the first tourist, Mould de Pease argues that José Gabriel Cosio[112] in 1911 became the first Peruvian to visit Machu Picchu as scientist, writing his own Anglo-style travel memoir.[113] In several of Cosio's publications, he likewise repudiated the notion of Bingham as discoverer of the ruins.[114]

Mould de Pease views the signature of Agustín Lizárraga seen by Bingham on the walls of Machu Picchu as a sign of Machu Picchu's "Peruvianess."[115] For Mould de Pease, positioning Bingham as the discoverer has initiated a history of Machu Picchu as a place dedicated to foreign visitors. The fact that a local boy led Bingham to the site further fuels her desire to deemphasize and demythologize Bingham and the other expedition members as discoverers. Mould de Pease calls for a Peruanization of the site and its meaning, arguing that a new history must be written, this time from the perspective of Peru. This perspective must focus on the Peruvians who participated in making Machu Picchu famous and on the importance the area had for its inhabitants; it should not prioritize tourism over other uses.[116] In 2002 a group presented a motion to the Peruvian Congress calling on it to officially recognize Agustín Lizárraga, Gabino Sanchez, and Enrique Palma as discoverers of Machu Picchu because their names had been written on its rock walls in 1902.[117]

New scholarship further contests Bingham's claim to be the discoverer of Machu Picchu. A German engineer named J. M. von Hassel made maps of the area as early as 1874, and Augusto Berns, an engineer working for Southern Peruvian Railways, had attempted to extract riches from the area with his sawmill before Bingham's expedition.[118] Building on this, Mould de Pease contends that Bingham knew of Machu Picchu before his arrival in Peru in 1911 and was duplicitous, even conspiratorial, in claiming to have discovered the site.[119] Albert Giesecke, whom Bingham had invited to accompany him to the ruins, originally said that Bingham was lucky in finding Machu Picchu. Later, in a radio address to Club Cuzco on February 15, 1945, Giesecke changed his story, saying that he had told Bingham about the ruins.[120] Even the *New York Times* joined the debate over who really discovered Machu Picchu, asking in a 2008 headline, "Was a Lost City Ever Lost?"[121]

As more people weigh in on whether Bingham was the discoverer, the hunt for a true discoverer perpetuates the notion that Machu Picchu was found by an Anglo male. The notion that Quechua speakers had inhabited the area long before any of those discoverers arrived on the scene continues to be elided. The racialized myth of discovery continues without a larger contextualization of the individuals, networks, and infrastructure that facilitated the Yale Peruvian Expeditions. Precisely what Bingham did to transform the act of seeing Machu Picchu into a discovery has been ignored.

Craig Owens writes about the debate between the art historian Meyer Schapiro and the philosopher Martin Heidegger over a pair of boots painted by Vincent Van Gogh.[122] In *The Origin of the Work of Art*, Heidegger claims that the boots in Van Gogh's painting are a pair of peasant woman's shoes. Challenging Heidegger, Schapiro asserts that the shoes are the artist's, which therefore transforms the painting into a self-portrait. Citing Derrida, Owens writes that there is no disagreement between Schapiro and Heidegger. The two men are in perfect agreement because both are asking the same questions: To whom do the shoes belong? Whom do the shoes represent?

The search for Machu Picchu's real discoverer mirrors the question over the old boots in the painting. By replacing Bingham with a different heroic figure, Mould de Pease and countless others who have sought to debunk and demythologize Bingham all ask the same question: who discovered Machu Picchu? The answer is always the same: a mythic figure whose presence frames a place through the negation of others, all while perpetuating the notion of a lost city waiting to be found. That Bingham was not alone in his expeditionary achievements continues to be overlooked. Such questions seem to typify the long history of imperial and national narratives.[123] Bingham did not discover Machu Picchu. Rather, the allure of science, an elite industrial transnational social network, nationalist dreams, and a camera first imagined and then produced Machu Picchu as a discovery—the lost city trope eternally circulating anew.

Bingham did make the area known to a huge number of people. But his work was a reshaping, not an unearthing. Before Bingham's photographic parade, the archaeological site was used for farming and pasturage. People who inhabited the area had their own imaginings, meanings, and purposes for the area. Instead of referring to himself (or Cosio or Berns or von Hassel) as a discoverer *of* something, which implies the presence of a preexisting entity, all its shape and meaning lifted out of the ground whole, perhaps a more accurate description of Bingham would be a discoverer *for* something—tourism, sightseeing, economic development, photographic adventure, scientific inquiry, local identity. This book attempts to write the doing, the activity, the politics, and the work that was initially involved in making Machu Picchu into a lost city found—an artifact in all senses of the word.[124]

This book is not a story about the heroism or antiheroism of Hiram Bingham. The focus is not whether Hiram Bingham was a great explorer initially motivated to explore Peru by sexist competitive jealousy,[125] or whether Albert Giesecke first informed him of the whereabouts of Machu Picchu. This isn't a biography of Bingham or the men who accompanied him on the expeditions. Other books do a far better job of trying to gain insight into the personality of Bingham.[126] Instead, this book examines the practices and technologies of the expedition and how these transformed a place into a "discovery."[127] Thus, this book tracks how Machu Picchu was invented as a discovery and how the topos of lost cities captivated the world.

Seeing, Circulation, Contests

On the goals of historical anthropology, Brian Axel writes: "Rather than the study of a people in a particular place and at a certain time, what is at stake in historical anthropology is explaining the production of a people and the production of space and time."[128] The contributors to the volume *Anthrohistory* likewise abandon the idea of a total history in favor of examinations of specific concepts and ontologies.[129] Rather than viewing history as reconstruction, the authors propose to trace signs of things unfolding over time, emphasizing the in-between. Working in these generative margins of knowledge, what others have referred to as boundary work,[130] is the task of the historical anthropologist.

This book emphasizes the intricate details of how science makes its objects. The first two chapters examine how the 1911 expedition was initially conjured and seen. Chapter 1 looks at how the expedition was imagined, developed, navigated, and deployed, all through letters. Letter writing was, in effect, a foundational expeditionary practice, negotiating and conjuring a lost city. The materiality of the letters suggests that it was not simply the ideas espoused in them but also their tangibility that made them instrumental in the outcomes of the expeditions. The chapter details the success of letter writing by documenting the myriad donations received from corporations and wealthy industrialists and the ways in which the letters facilitated entry and access to the Peruvian countryside. Tracking the names of the correspondents reveals how a powerful network took shape, one that ultimately empowered Bingham to see.

Chapter 2 examines the expeditionary practices of collecting. In 1911, Bingham and the Yale Peruvian Expedition team first sighted Machu Picchu. On the team's return visits to Peru (1912 and 1914–1915), it mapped, excavated, and photographed the Andean region around Cuzco. The legacy of the expeditions includes its collections: exotic animals, books, antiquities, and, most significantly, skeletal remains. This chapter examines the collecting practices of the expeditions to suggest that the objects collected as well as the technologies and practices used in collecting helped fashion Machu Picchu into a lost city that was scientifically discovered by Bingham.

Drawing on evidence such as expedition circulars and reports to understand how collecting was accomplished on the three tours, this chapter demonstrates how the expedition relied on prospecting by paid local laborers, accompanied by state-sponsored coercion, to iterate the notion that science had a sovereign claim on objects that might contribute to the accumulation of its knowledge. Ultimately, the reenvisioning of Machu Picchu as a vestige of the glorious Inca race and a scientific discovery was materialized and initially evidenced through its collected objects. Photographs made public this reenvisioning.

The next three chapters focus on the ways in which initial scientific imaginings were materialized as representational facts that moved. Chapter 3 details the origins of the photographs of Machu Picchu, particularly the foldout panorama that appeared in the *National Geographic Magazine*'s iconic April 1913 issue, "In the Wonderland of Peru." The photographs were taken during a period when the camera was viewed as a scientific instrument that could capture data objectively. Although Bingham considered photography a primary scientific technology because it allowed team members to bring back material evidence of discoveries, the analysis presented in this chapter demonstrates that the use of the camera during the expeditions was a negotiated and disciplined practice. Kodak cameras were not simply taken out of their cases and used. Rather, their use was fraught with difficulty not only because of the cameras' users, but also because of the complicated technology and the fickle Andean climate. Thus, presenting Machu Picchu as a lost city that was discovered by the Yale expedition involved a particular configuration of human and nonhuman actors and practices that stabilized the so-called facts created by the expedition.

The National Geographic Society partially sponsored the 1912 and 1914–1915 Yale Peruvian Expeditions. In exchange for its sponsorship, the society was granted rights to all the expeditions' photographs. The first major public display of expeditionary photographs came in "In the Wonderland of Peru," which included 244 illustrations. Images from this issue were subsequently reprinted in newspapers, magazines, and traveling exhibitions worldwide. This chapter addresses the ways in which the framing of the initial photographic images of Machu Picchu was shaped by scientific, commercial, and national desires and designs. It examines not only how the magazine issue was carefully crafted by the editor of *National Geographic* to privilege photography as the primary means to convey information about Machu Picchu and Peru to readers, but also how this photographic meaning was unstable when circulated. Through a reading of the images and text of "In the Wonderland of Peru," and its selective translation in the popular Peruvian illustrated magazine *Ilustración Peruana*, this chapter examines how the notion of a discovered lost city was translated in Peru.

On the second and third expeditions, physicians conducted anthropometry on the Quechua-speaking population of Peru. Anthropometry, a popular science in the late nineteenth and early twentieth centuries, sought to address debates on racial origins through the collection and comparison of body measurements and categories such as age and sex. Bodies were mapped in an effort to scientifically situate subjects within an evolutionary paradigm that held Caucasian bodies as superior. Along with calipers and meter sticks, photography was integral to the science and collection of anthropometric data. Frontal and profile images of each subject were taken, and medical maladies such as massive goiters were documented. Unlike the images appearing in *National Geographic*, anthropometric photographs were not widely circulated. Chapter 5 examines the practice of anthropometry on the expeditions to suggest that the same race-inflected categorization that sustained practices such as the collection of antiquities also made possible the collection of native bodies through photography. In effect, there could be no glorious Incan past, with its accompanying vision for a future utopia, without the degenerative indigenous present to overcome.

Chapter 6 concludes with an examination of the conflict surrounding Bingham and Yale in Peru. In 1912, Yale and Hiram Bingham sought a ten-year concession from the Peruvian government to allow them the rights for exclusive removal of archaeological objects. This concession and Yale's presence became highly controversial. By the time of the final expedition, Peruvian national politics had shifted, and the removal of Peru's ancient past through what was considered the robbing of its ancestral grave sites became hotly contested, eventually culminating in an injunction to halt excavations. This final chapter charts the negotiations, failed concession, and concerted efforts to stabilize Machu Picchu as an object not of science but of Peruvian patrimony, suggesting that the right to see or frame was paramount to consolidating a national identity around historic Incan objects.

SIGHT

CHAPTER I

Epistolary Science

The officials of the Royal Geographical Society, and Sir Clements Markham,
who probably knows more about Peru than any living geographer, have assured
me that the region which we propose to explore is in great need of scientific
exploration. In fact they speak of it as one of the most interesting jobs that
remain to be done.
HIRAM BINGHAM TO HUNTINGTON SMITH, JANUARY 11, 1911

One of the pleasures of working in an archive is reading letters. The Yale
Peruvian Expedition Papers and the Bingham Family Papers are housed at
Yale University's Sterling Library. Bingham's papers include scrapbooks
full of newspaper cuttings, miscellaneous images, reports and articles
written by team members, and other documents related to the expeditions. The majority of the collection, however, consists of letters. Like
much of Yale's campus, the historic reading room, established in 1938,
pays architectural homage to European enlightenment and liberal study.
Entering the elegant wood-paneled room, with its high ceilings and handful of researchers seated at long communal tables, conjures personal fantasies of intellectual pursuit and collective contemplative study. What letters are they reading? Whose lives are they thinking about? Surrounded
by this display, one's sense of Machu Picchu's making begins.

The correspondence of the Yale Peruvian Expedition Papers includes
typed and handwritten letters as well as calling cards and postcards.[1] The
small rectangles of card stock with invitations to places like the Cosmos
Club, in Washington, DC, spark curiosity into the privileged frameworks
that Bingham accessed. Did he go? What was it like? What did he wear?
What did he drink? Who was there? With whom did he converse? Filed
in chronological order, the letters create suspense as the reader witnesses

the slow emergence of Machu Picchu and the crafting and crumbling of Bingham's reputation.

Although Bingham often dictated his correspondence to one of his secretaries, who typed the letters in carbon, some are penned in Bingham's hand. Prices and equipment were negotiated with Kodak; dreams were shared and disappointments tempered with the National Geographic Society; accounting figures and donations were calculated and settled with Yale's treasurer. Through the letters, one glimpses the negotiations and unfolding of the expeditions to Peru. These negotiations were not simply about defraying costs or managing personnel. They were also work in the purposeful imagining and practice of the expedition. Through all of them, Bingham and the dream of discovery were in play. Read together, they form a telling conversation—incomplete but evocative and illuminating.

Reading the letters painstakingly organized by Yale's archivists sheds light on the extensive cultivation in Machu Picchu taking root. Photography, a Tiffany heiress, the draw of ancient civilizations, Christian missionary pasts, and the thrust of finance and industry early in the twentieth century indelibly mark the ephemera and thus the site.[2] Machu Picchu is hewn through the banal reminders and logistical scaffolding seen on seemingly inconsequential slips of crispy, wafer-thin sheets of hospital blue. The correspondence not only conveys information about the benefits of Bingham's expedition and its practices—where they went, what they saw, and who did or did not join them—but also demonstrates the making of Machu Picchu as a discovery. In the letters, one witnesses social conventions of writing, exclusionary class hierarchies, the promise of privilege, philanthropy, the pursuit of antiquarianism, perceived thefts of national patrimony, racism, nationalism, logics, and relationships that ran the spectrum from friendship to enmity. From these letters, Machu Picchu and Hiram Bingham take shape, emerging not in totality, but dunelike, shifting, each letter massaging the narrative into a quintessential story of the early twentieth-century. The letters are not simply reflections of history. They are history.

This chapter examines letter writing as a constitutive practice of scientific ordering. Although Bruno Latour and Steve Woolgar famously tracked how facts became constituted in a closed laboratory setting, Bingham's expeditionary science in the laboratory of Latin America was less contained.[3] Bingham cultivated an extensive and expansive network of individuals and corporations to sponsor and support the expedition through letters. Letters were sent to interlocutors as close as nearby Mystic, Connecticut, and to places as far afield as England and Peru. Although letter writing is not typically considered a scientific practice, in this case it acted as one, forging not only a social network that validated and supported the expedition, but also an observational trajectory and meaningful framework for the discovery of a lost city. Besides making visible the network that translated Machu Picchu,[4] focusing on letter writing demonstrates the value of letters to the expedition as material objects in their own right.

Letter writing is a social practice and an act of communication exhibiting conventions of proper prose and civility.[5] Letters, however, also act as instruments of imagination and power, nurturing and expanding social space, gathering a collective of witnesses. The epistles of the Yale Peruvian Expedition demonstrate the bounded and privileged social network that participated in the initial imagining and subsequent witnessing of Machu Picchu, and also how that collectivity and such imagining was shaped. Through words or their absence, the letters conjure the experiment of the Andes within a proscribed and privileged social space. Through letter writing, the Andes, the Incas, and, ultimately, Machu Picchu were prefigured as geography, nation, and history in need of a scientific experiment. Through letters, agency was enacted.[6]

Important Scientific Work to Be Done

The importance of letters to science is not new. The "Republic of Letters" is a term used to describe a network of intellectuals during the seventeenth and eighteenth centuries who shared ideas and scientific papers through letter writing.[7] Voltaire, for example, penned some eighteen thousand letters, which acted as a vehicle for expanding an intellectual community, but also for resolving tensions and achieving authority, all through an ethos of politeness.[8] The reports that circulated during this period were rich in circumstantial detail and allowed readers to imagine, or virtually witness, an experimental scene that they did not actually see. The reports also acted as an instrument to enlarge the community witnessing the experiment, which in turn created a public that aided in constituting authentic knowledge and matters of fact.[9] Like scientific papers, Bingham's letters networked an expanding group of people, involving them in what would ultimately become one of the world's best-known and most visited heritage sites.

Although Bingham's epistolary verve was not as great as Voltaire's, he shared ideas, queries, and solicitations for assistance through letters. Unlike reports, however, the letters acted as key instruments in negotiating the grounds for the eventual experiment, informing and shaping expeditionary practice and outcomes. These negotiations were intellectual as well as social, since specific people and businesses were enrolled in the project through the crafting of a sellable vision of Peru and of a purpose for the Yale Peruvian Expedition. Before intrepid savants could find Machu Picchu from afar, it had to first be imagined as lost. Such imagining work prepared a foundation for the ways in which Machu Picchu came to have life globally.

In 1909, Julio C. Tello, who would become one of Peru's most celebrated archaeologists, sent Bingham, via a shared contact, Roland Dixon at Harvard University, a copy of a paper written by Carlos Romero (1909).[10] The paper discussed the ruins of Choqquequirau, which Bingham had recently visited, and suggested that the lost city of the Incas was named Vitcos and was located near Pucyura.[11] Bingham did not immediately act on this information, and instead spent the summer writing and enjoying time with his family, considering expeditions elsewhere—including Mexico and Ecuador.[12] He also wrote to his friend Stuart Hotchkiss about a trip to the Amazon basin.[13]

In late November and early December 1910, however, Bingham began writing letters about his plans regarding Peru. His first was a response to a letter from Albert Giesecke about Giesecke's thwarted attempt to visit Choqquequirau. Bingham sent along photographs from his previous visit, stating that he hoped to revisit the ruins of Choqquequirau soon and spend a couple of months in the vicinity. "Has any archaeologist visited the ruins?" Bingham queried.[14] On December 5, Bingham wrote Adolph Bandelier, the author of *The Islands of Titicaca and Koati*.[15] Bandelier had suggested that Mount Coropuna was the tallest peak in South America. Bingham wrote: "I expect to go to Peru next year, partly to visit Coropuna and partly to see if I can find any remains of the Incas in the valleys North and East of Choqquequirau."[16]

Giesecke was one of Bingham's most significant correspondents.[17] A graduate of the University of Pennsylvania, he went to Cuzco in 1910 to reopen and reorganize the National University of San Antonio Abad of Cuzco (UNSAAC).[18] Although Giesecke was only twenty-six years old, four years younger than the legal age to be rector of a university, Peruvian president Augusto Leguía appointed him rector.[19] Giesecke held the position for fourteen years, influencing the academic community of

Cuzco and becoming involved in census taking, rural education, economic development, and city beautification projects.[20] Giesecke was in many ways a knowledge broker of Cuzco society for Anglo-American scholars. Notable US anthropologists such as John Rowe and Julian Steward, as well as members of the US Department of Agriculture, solicited his assistance.[21] The relationship between Giesecke and Bingham was built on a shared understanding of Peru as a nation "in need," but also a nation "of promise."[22] Like explorers before him, Giesecke considered Peru as a country of past greatness and future potential.[23] Exploration was a vehicle to gain access on both fronts.

Giesecke used his correspondence to apprise Bingham of the current political and intellectual climate in Peru.

> My dear sir:
> I was glad to receive your letter of November 25th, with views of Choq-quequirau. I turned these over to Mr. Juan José Nuñez, as you requested, and in addition read him your letter. He was highly pleased to hear about you, especially about your intention to return shortly. In that case he is ready to go to any measure necessary to insure success in a visit to Choq-quequirau. . . . Professor Max Uhle has not yet been able to visit these ruins, as the government has not voted any money for excavations until present moment. He was in Cuzco several months ago, conducting a party of Americanistas through the place, in his capacity as Director del Museo Nacional de Lima. When I asked him about this affair he said the government would delay appropriations for a cientific [sic] investigation for some time to come. Hence, I think we could do something voluntarily meanwhile.[24]

Six months later, Giesecke followed up by stating that the Peruvian government was going to spend about $2,500 on archaeological work by Max Uhle, but that Uhle would not "receive the money (and hence can do nothing) until the end of the year."[25] Giesecke articulated Bingham's need to act promptly. The language of "we" transformed the scientific work into a national competition, and made the quest to discover ever more urgent.

Bingham sought scholarly advice to help shape the proposal and inform the planning of the expedition through letters. For context, logistical support, and legitimacy in crafting the initial vision of the expedition, he wrote Clements Markham; V. F. Marsters, a geologist who resided in Arequipa and Lima; and Harvard's William Curtis Farabee. Marsters eventually provided information about the most auspicious time of year for climbing Mount Coropuna, the best approach, and the name of a good *arriero* (muleteer). He also recommended where to stay en route (a mining camp in La Victoria).[26] Although Gilbert Grosvenor, director of the National Geographic Society and editor of its magazine, would eventually become one of Bingham's most important interlocutors, for the 1911 expedition Bingham relied on Markham and Farabee for scholarly assurance, authority, and advice. Even with Giesecke's urging, the expeditionary goals remained malleable at first, suggesting that Bingham was strategic and calculating in his planning, the expressed goals of the expedition not quite fixed.

On November 30, 1910, Bingham introduced himself to Markham in a letter. It began with a reference to a previous visit to London and his trip to South America. Bingham had been given a letter of introduction to Markham, but the latter was out of town. After efforts at self-credentialing and a nod to Markham's useful work, Bingham asked for suggestions for good work needing to be done in the coastal range northwest of Arequipa: "Can you tell me whether any one has done any scientific exploring there and where I can find the record of it? Do you know any one who has computed accurately the height of Mount Coropuna? Could you tell me whether Lake Parinacochas has ever been surveyed or sounding taken of it? Anything that you would be so good as to send me regarding this region will be most gratefully received."[27]

Markham replied on December 18 in support of the expedition. Bingham responded on January 4, 1911, thanking Markham for his approval and explaining that the idea of exploring Lake Parinacochas came from Markham's *Desiderata in Exploration* (1907).[28] Bingham, who had lost his copy, asked where might he procure another. Bingham then legitimized himself and the expedition by citing scholarly work—Markham's own, along with efforts such as Antonio Raimondi's map of Lake Parinacochas's contour.[29] He then asked Markham for specific suggestions about scientific work.

On January 18, Markham replied, noting that he had requested a replacement copy of *Desiderata* be sent to Bingham. Markham then proffered advice on the type of boat he should bring, how much sounding line, and which types of scientific instruments: a small theodolite and a good chronometer watch. Markham added that a sextant and artificial horizon were not useful for inland work. He advised on the best route to and from the lake and further expanded Bingham's scholarly frame, noting that a new manuscript had been found at the Copenhagen library.[30]

If you have seen my recent book on the Incas you may have noticed, in the first chapter, an account of the discovery of a very important manuscript in the Copenhagen library, by an Inca noble name Guaman Poma, who was chief of Lucanas; which gives the province a special interest. You might return by Vilcas-Huaman, and make a thorough examination and plan of the ruins. It has only been visited by the Frenchmen Wiener who is not very reliable.

I have not seen any account of your visit to the ruins of Choquequirau, and should be very much obliged if you would kindly send me anything you have published on that subject. Wishing you all possible success I remain Yours Very Truly.[31]

Through the correspondence with Markham, several things occurred. First, a prominent and prolific geographer of South America became aware of Bingham and his work. Second, practical knowledge was exchanged regarding field practices, measurement techniques, and travel routes. Third, Bingham's plans for the expedition were legitimized through Markham's encouraging words and his engagement in epistolary exchange. If Markham had not replied, Bingham could not have drawn on his reputation as authoritative support in his future fund-raising solicitations. Fourth, and perhaps most importantly, the Peruvian interior was solidified as a place in need of scientific exploration.

William Curtis Farabee was the other scholar who was particularly useful for Bingham.[32] He participated in three trips to Peru, including the de Milhau–Harvard Expedition, which he led for Harvard's Peabody Museum from 1906 to 1908.[33] Farabee provided crucial information and support for Bingham, including contacts such as Marsters and important local figures such as Alberto Duque of Cuzco. Duque later took Bingham to several ruin sites and allowed the team to store supplies and equipment at his hacienda.

Farabee's letters further enhanced the idea of Peru as a place in need of exploration. In planning the expedition, Bingham asked Farabee about logistics. How long would it take to get from Cuzco to Santa Ana? Could he purchase supplies in Santa Ana? Would it be possible to follow the Urubamba Valley all the way down from Ollantaytambo? Bingham ended the letter with a display of well-mannered bonhomie, perhaps as a gracious lure or perhaps merely as gratitude for information.

I wish you would come down and spend a weekend with me during the Easter vacation. There are so many things I want to ask you. I have decided to take three men with me and have practically raised all the money for their expenses. If I can get extra money I shall take also a doctor and an assistant topographer. Otherwise I shall be content with a geologist and geographer, a topographer, and a naturalist. Do say you will come and spend a week with me.

Faithfully Yours, Hiram Bingham[34]

Although Farabee did not visit Bingham personally, he responded in detail to Bingham's queries. The distance from Cuzco to Santa Ana was about forty leagues; to Urubamba, eight; four more to Ollantaytambo. There were ruins along the river, as well as places to stop, but he should carry provisions and a tent. The road was good all the way, and they could easily make the trip in two days. They would be treated well by two governmental officials at Santa Ana, and Mr. Duque, who had a large plantation, would be their "best authority and assistant."[35]

Bingham drew on Farabee's experience to plan his route, justify the trip, and eventually facilitate the exploration of the countryside. Farabee had already provided Bingham a map containing information collected from traverses made by traders and rubber gatherers regarding distances and locations in the Peruvian interior. The map included Farabee's own work and astronomical observations. Farabee also shared that the Geographical Society of Lima had a record of all positions in Peru, and the railroad officials in Arequipa knew the positions for southern Peru.[36]

Letters became valuable vectors of information that garnered scientific support. As more letters were exchanged, more people learned of the proposed expedition, securing consensus for its worth. Correspondence with Giesecke, Farabee, and Markham demonstrated Peru's known qualities, but also sustained an imaginary of Peru as a nation where valuable scientific work could be done. What was known and what was unknown worked together to facilitate the need for an expedition.

Bingham went on to solicit information from colleagues such as his friend Ernest Howe, a Yale geographer who provided recommendations for photographic equipment.[37] Through letters, Bingham received maps made by Raimondi and Edward Stanford, geographer to Her Majesty the Queen.[38] Bingham also reciprocated with information, sending his written work to Clements Markham and Carlos A. Romero.[39] The exchange of information continued throughout all the expeditions as Bingham tuned his scholarly sight, promoted the expeditions, and secured both financial and intellectual support.[40] For example, before the 1912 expedition, he again sought guidance from Markham: "In your 'Incas of Peru' on page

291, you say Rodriguez de Figueroa 'wrote an account of the mission' which has been preserved. Will you be so good as to tell me where this account is and whether it has been published? I am trying to unravel the history of Vilcabamba, so far as I can and I am sure this account would be most useful. I do not like to trouble you with this question, but I do not know who else can answer it."[41]

With the initial go-ahead from Giesecke and the intellectual support from Markham, Bingham began fund-raising in early January 1911. Writing first to Huntington Smith,[42] Bingham explained the purpose for the expedition.[43] There would be three members of the expedition: Bingham; Herbert Gregory of Yale, who would do the geological and physiographical work; and a topographer, who would make a map through a section of the country that had not been scientifically explored and only "mapped in the rudest way some fifty years ago." Bingham wrote that a skilled topographer could make an accurate and lasting map that would bolster Yale's research reputation. In this early letter, climbing Mount Coropuna was not mentioned as part of the expedition. Instead, the expedition would study villages, or "human geography," in the mountainous area, which was located in a region of interest for South American history.[44] The team would measure the lake and look for Incan ruins that might be discovered in the "glacier-clad peaks, which separate Choqquequirau from the Urubamba Valley." As Bingham put it: "With this party of three it is my plan to explore a section of Peru, starting from the Sea Coast some fifty miles North of Mollendo and going due North across the Andes into the Amazon Valley as far as practicable." Bingham estimated that the trip would cost about $5,000. He proposed to meet one-third of the total expenses and hoped that Smith might contribute a like amount. All funds would be overseen by Yale's treasurer.

A few things stand out in this initial cast of the expedition. First, enlisting the support of other Euro-American scholars was vital. In none of the correspondence does he mention Marsters or the work of Carlos Romero, whose original *informe* (report) shed light on the whereabouts of the lost city. Instead, he invoked Farabee, who knew the valley and confirmed Bingham's opinion that "the region which I propose to enter is one of the most important unexplored archaeological fields in Peru."[45] He cited Markham's support, saying that he felt the expedition "was one of the most interesting jobs that remain to be done."[46] Bingham's letter suggested that what "remain[ed] to be done" in science was finite.

Bingham felt that much of the world had already been discovered and at least partly explored. The discovery of the North Pole circulated in newspapers in 1909; the South Pole was (controversially) staked by Roald Amundsen for Norway in 1911.[47] The popular feeling about these explorations was that the earth's surfaces had been tracked, mapped, and seen.[48] Not much remained in the realm of earthly frontiers. Scientific exploration was valuable because it could find the last remaining pieces of the jigsaw puzzle, benefiting civilization along the way. In contrast to previous South American scientific expeditions, Bingham's would be specific rather than grandiose. Filling in particular gaps in knowledge contrasted markedly with nineteenth-century expeditionary narratives, in which knowledge of just about everything was viewed as needed. Although Bingham's enterprise of knowledge was significantly expansive, his expedition sought measurable outcomes and useful information for history, business, trade, and government. This frame of commercial and national relevance assisted Bingham in the planning, financing, and execution of his expedition.

Second, the primary goal of the expedition, as expressed in this initial letter to Smith, was cartographical. Though the team would survey and explore the countryside, much of the letter is taken up with explaining mapmaking, its importance, and the value of hiring a topographer. Ed Harkness, an early supporter of the expedition, was not interested in mountain climbing or Incan ruins but rather in conducting a survey along the seventy-third meridian.[49] This perspective was reflected in the plans for the expedition and its fund-raising solicitations. Paying a topographer to make a map was of utmost importance for the scientific value of the expedition. Including an archaeologist wasn't mentioned, and Mount Coropuna would have its height measured, but would not be climbed.

Third and most critically, the hunt for Vilcabamba or Incan ruins generally does not come across as the most vital goal of the expedition. Bracketing the eventual sighting of Machu Picchu, Incan ruins seem to be an afterthought or add-on to an ambitious research plan. Bingham discusses mapmaking, the work of Professor Gregory, Mount Coropuna, and Lake Parinacochas, and then concludes that he is "convinced that there are more Inca ruins to be discovered in that locality."[50] A few sentences discuss archaeological work and ruins north of Choqquequirau. In the end, Huntington Smith did not offer financial support for the 1911 expedition, but the letter, as an initial frame, would be retooled over the subsequent months. Undeterred, Bingham continued his letter-writing campaign, inquiring about personnel, sponsorships, and information from Yale alumni and colleagues.

In late March and early April, a boilerplate solicitation was distributed to several people.[51] The letter cites previous scholars' work to validate

Bingham's claims. But the March letter, although building upon the initial vision in the letter to Smith, shifts the details of the expedition. Bingham begins by outlining the dates for the expedition, which will conduct geographic, archaeological, and historical explorations (anthropological work was dropped). As Bingham outlined it, the expedition would address four central "problems." First and foremost, it would look for more Incan ruins near Choqquequirau and Urubamba, doing "everything we can to visit any ruins that are reported particularly in the Vilcabamba valley." Second, it would conduct a reconnaissance of the seventy-third meridian from the Amazon Valley to the ocean, which was a region of historic significance. Third, members of the expedition would climb Mount Coropuna, determining its height and mapping it, as well as studying the human geography around the mountain. Fourth, they would make a bathymetrical survey of Lake Parinacochas and its shores. All four endeavors would contribute to the ultimate objective of exploring a portion of Peru that was "not yet known to science." Bingham additionally promised to collect and catalogue the flora and fauna of Cuzco. Expeditionary personnel had grown to include a director, a geologist, a skilled topographer and his assistant, a "physiographer" (expert in physical geography), and possibly a surgeon and a naturalist, who would make collections for Yale's museum.[52]

The expedition began to emerge through negotiation and practice.[53] Markham and Farabee continued to be enlisted as legitimizers of Bingham and the scientific expedition. But the plan of the expedition had morphed over the course of three months, suggesting that initial expeditionary desires and goals were inchoate, a product of negotiating the interests of funders and the ideas of scholars as much as of fulfilling personal desires for bagging peaks and locating lost cities. While they would still be measuring the lake, they would also be climbing Mount Coropuna to determine its elevation. The cross-section of the Andes would be made along the seventy-third meridian, the specificity of the measurement lending the expedition an air of scientific authority and clarity. Most significant, however, was the reordering of the expeditionary plan to highlight the search for Incan ruins as the first problem to be solved. The plans for the expedition had been honed. Ruins, whether previously known by Farabee or not, were in need of scientific exploration. The search for a lost city became pressing.[54]

While there is similarity between the letters of January and March 1911, with some of the wording even identical, the discovery of lost cities took root as the expedition's organizing principle. Instead of a small crew of three, the number of personnel expanded to potentially seven. Their work would be extensive, the information and collections to be gathered limited only by the size and ability of the crew. The purpose of the expedition solidified. Through such stabilization, Peru was transformed into a place of scientifically unexplored archaeological fields. Not simply an exercise in reconnaissance or an idealized scientific quest in mapmaking, this expedition was expressly about locating ruins to discover where the last Inca lived after escaping from the Spaniards. The shimmer of science executed through letter writing made that goal both desirable and realizable.

In contrast to January's letter, March's solicitation is more precise in illuminating a plan. The tone is more direct and confident, invoking specificities about reconnaissance, bathymetrical surveys, latitudes, longitudes, summiting Mount Coropuna, and making collections for the Peabody Museum. The March letter gives an unambiguous sense of the expedition's priorities. We see the clarity gained from Giesecke's efforts to push excavation and archaeology, the confidence garnered from Farabee's information about the area, Markham's input on Lake Parinacochas, and even the threat that another explorer might summit Mount Coropuna first.[55] The last solicitation letter showed the culmination of months of collective crafting of the expeditionary vision, resulting in a compelling plan for discovering a lost city.

News about the expedition grew, and people wrote Bingham to see whether they might accompany him. He began writing for specific supplies from Abercrombie and Fitch, Kodak, Winchester Repeating Arms, the Waltham Watch Company, and Smith-Worthington (saddlers), asking for special treatment, since he was outfitting a scientific expedition.[56] Companies donated equipment or gave discounts on goods with the expectation that the items would be tested in the Andean conditions and the results used in promotional literature or future publications. The existence of a company policy, based on the relationship between science and industry, was hinted at in the letters shoring up the notion that what was good for scientific exploration was good for business. The Waltham Watch Company made this explicit in its response: "We are happy to state that it is the policy of this Company to do all within a reasonable limit to assist scientific work, especially of the nature of your proposed expedition, and to that end will be pleased to loan your expedition, and its leaders, the necessary watches for its equipment, with the understanding that you will furnish us with the results of their performance for the period of the expedition, for publication, a matter that we feel you will freely grant."[57]

The pace of letter writing quickened in the months preceding the expedition. Food boxes, which included a set amount of rations for two men for eight days, were purchased in the United States and shipped to Peru.

Bingham wrote to the US treasurer to be spared tariff rates on scientific instruments, and to the Harvard Observatory for assistance in Arequipa. Letters did double duty as they sought sponsorship or resolved last-minute personnel issues while simultaneously promoting the expedition. As the flurry came to a close, one senses Bingham's excitement to finally be en route to Peru.

The practice of letter writing opened up new territories for expeditionary science and thus new territories for visibility.[58] The frame of science in Bingham's letters imagined Peru as a repository of scientific potential. Science, for Bingham, embodied nationalist and antiquarian yearnings to claim success and dominate a geographic and human space through knowledge and discovery. Although Bingham drew on local knowledge and scholarship, these were sublimated in the correspondence. Nowhere in the solicitation letters were Peruvians cited. They were invisible to the quest. Instead, the letters asked people to support Yale for an expedition to an area that had not been scientifically explored. This promise of scientific discovery incubated the expedition and was circulated and inculcated through letter writing. The plasticity of the expedition, with its ability to flexibly morph over the course of several months, along with its reliance on an assortment of technical technologies such as chronometers and astronomical watches, would ultimately add to its allure among North Americans and Peruvian elites. Letters as communicative acts shaped intentions as much as outcomes.

Letter Acts

Interest in the Inca was directed not only from a Yale network onto Peru. Elite Peruvians in search of national modernity facilitated the expedition and its pursuits. Peruvian president Augusto Leguía, along with hacienda owners and merchants, supported the expedition through logistics, know-how, lodging, and comfort. Letters were sent to request assistance but also to curry favor and exert power.

On March 28, 1911, Bingham wrote Leguía. Leguía had worked for the New York Life Insurance Company, traveling to New York and London, before becoming president of Peru in 1908.[59] Leguía encouraged US involvement in all sectors of the Peruvian economy, believing that the "practical" and entrepreneurial spirit of the United States would benefit his country.[60] Consequently, Leguía opened up Peru to foreigners, particularly those who would bring either industrial advancement or new knowledge about Peru's Incan past. Bingham's expeditions were exactly the type of scientific work that interested Leguía, since it coupled the nation's imagined heroic Incan past with commercial possibilities for its modern future.[61] Bingham wrote to Leguía about customs assistance and military accompaniment by J. Caceres.

> I mention these things [details of the expedition] that you may make such arrangements as you see fit in aiding the work of the expedition. I enclose a clipping from the Yale Alumni Weekly, which will tell you of our plans in still further detail. I should like to ask specifically for two favors. The first that the collector of customs of the port of Mollendo be notified of our intention of embarking at that port, and be instructed to pass through the custom house all our outfit without any unnecessary delay, in order that we may begin our field work as soon as possible. All our bags and boxes will be plainly marked Yale Peruvian Expedition, so that he will have no difficulty in identifying them.
>
> The second request, which I have to make of your Excellency, is that you will assign to the party as military aid a bright and intelligent officer who assisted me in my former work at Choqquequirau. His name I believe is J. Caceres. He was so efficient, cheerful, and capable that I am sure his presence with us would be of very great assistance to the cause of science.[62]

In the letter, Bingham informed Leguía of the other men who would be accompanying the expedition, including Kai Hendriksen, who, "owing to the kindness of President Taft," had been released from his appointment to join the expedition as topographer.[63] While this was not precisely accurate, mentioning Taft's name no doubt lent credence to the expedition.[64] Taft's stamp of approval, as seen in the letters, was enough to strengthen future support for the expedition. Bingham closed his letter by thanking Leguía for all his help, appreciation, and interest in the expedition.

Bingham excelled at networking, and the expedition became increasingly appealing to the governments of Peru and the United States and to those facilitating trade between the two countries. Whether to help discover the history of a once-great nation or to improve the current status of that nation, Americans and Peruvians provided Bingham with favors, information, and recommendations. Through letters, each prominent name lent support, enrolling the next. The shipping company W. R. Grace & Co. played an integral role, managing Bingham's freight, shuttling important letters, and transmitting telegrams, as a letter from one of its officers makes clear.[65]

Dear Dr. Bingham

I have just received your letter of August 4th which has delayed some time in reaching me. In the meantime, you will have learned from Mr. Ballén's telegram of the 11th that he arranged that the obstacle to your progressing with your work be removed, and I take it that you will have no further difficulty. I do not know the content of your letter to the President, but suppose that it would now be unnecessary and perhaps inadvisable to make any complaint, and so will not present the letter unless you telegraph to Ballén to do so. I am leaving the letter in his hands, as I expect to be leaving for New York in a week or two. Hoping that you are well, and with kind regards, I am Yours Very Truly.[66]

On both the 1911 and 1912 expeditions, the team negotiated Peruvian customs easily. At the port of entry, the expedition did not have to pay taxes or fees.[67] As requested, the Leguía government supplied Bingham with military accompaniment and also with a letter of support. Being accompanied by an officer of the Peruvian military was one form of power, but to have a letter of support from President Leguía allowed Bingham and the team to explore the countryside without restraint. Leguía's support was critical to the success of the expedition, and Bingham wrote him in 1912, asking for the same privileges as in 1911, namely, the freedom to excavate wherever necessary, with half the artifacts going to Yale and half going to the National Museum in Lima.

With regard to this year's expedition I am delighted that you have been willing to signify to the American Minister your intention to grant us all the privileges that we had last time. If we are to carry out the scientific studies made on the last expedition we should like to secure from [you] the necessary permission to excavate wherever necessary, which you so kindly gave us last time. We should also like to secure for this expedition the privilege of exporting our finds on the principle of sharing them with your National Museum in Lima, on the basis of one half to Yale University and one half to the National Museum. . . . Will you be so kind as to notify the custom-house officials in Callao to facilitate my passage through the custom-house both there and also at Mollendo?[68]

Leguía's letter of support had the desired effect, helping the expeditionary team gain entry at the ports and paving the way for Bingham to excavate and remove archaeological material.[69] While Peruvian law prohibited the removal of antiquities, Bingham was given special dispensation by

Leguía to conduct excavations and remove objects from the countryside.[70] Although the team did not excavate many archaeological ruins during the 1911 expedition, the presence of Yale could have invited conflict and concern if not for the military accompaniment and Leguía's letter communicating his backing.[71] Bingham requested similar letters from President Taft, asking that the secretary of state provide the expedition a "round-robin letter to the American diplomatic and Consular officers and to the Panama Canal Commission."[72] The letter would be useful during the few days the team would be in the isthmus. During the 1912 negotiations, Bingham requested a letter of recommendation from Yale's President Hadley to Leguía, hoping that the direct support of the university would assist him in his negotiations for a concession with the Peruvian president.[73] He again requested a similar letter from President Taft. Bingham went so far as to give three suggestions for the form the letter might take.[74]

Letters of political support acted differently from the scientific and fund-raising correspondence. Besides serving as vehicles for imagining work or as webbing instruments for social networks, letters of recommendation were materializations of power. They showed connection and legitimacy, but also conveyed a subtle threat. Those from Leguía and other Peruvians facilitated Bingham's passage in the country.[75] For example, the expedition would supply its own crates of food, developing tanks for their photographs, and instruments for the topographer, but other items would need to be secured en route. Although the expedition tried to be self-sufficient, interacting with Peruvians was a necessity. Mules, additional food, hotels, taxidermy specialists, local guides and services, and general knowledge of the area could not be shipped from the United States. Consequently, Bingham relied on local elites to aid the expedition. Hacienda owners provided shelter, rest, food, translation, and comforts for the group during its reconnaissance of the Urubamba valley.[76] The government provided general access, and the local elite facilitated the everyday.

Bingham purchased mules and miscellaneous supplies, sent and received telegrams and letters, and received funds through Cesar Lomellini, an Italian merchant who had settled in Cuzco. In addition to providing warehouse space where Bingham could store supplies while doing reconnaissance, the diplomatic Lomellini acted as a bank, providing cash to the team when other banks were unable to honor their bank drafts. According to Bingham, Lomellini provided just prices and negotiated fairly. Working with Lomellini was a welcome relief for Bingham, who often felt that he was being duped.[77] Above all, Lomellini provided advice, information, general sociality, and letters of introduction.

Without Lomellini, the logistical operations of the expeditions would have been significantly more difficult. In a letter to the treasurer of Yale, Bingham requested a memorial be sent to Lomellini as a token of appreciation for assisting the expedition. The letter acknowledged Bingham's reliance on Lomellini's services and his gratitude.[78]

> We have not been very good customers, though he has the best equipped warehouse in Cuzco and we occasionally buy things of him. He has been put to a great deal of trouble by various members of the Expeditions and has never charged us a cent of commission. His advice has frequently been most helpful; his knowledge of the country after thirty years residence is, of course, quite extraordinary, (he is an Italian by birth); frequently he has given us letters of introduction which have opened doors that would have otherwise been closed.[79]

In addition to providing advice and counsel, Lomellini's letters of introduction facilitated the expeditions' movement through the Peruvian countryside. The letters from the wealthy merchant brought favor to Bingham, who was exploring the area as an outsider. Bingham reciprocated via a written memorial for Lomellini from Yale, and by shipping all his materials through Lomellini and expanding Lomellini's connections with other patrons.[80] Bingham also tried to provide Lomellini with a camera and to facilitate his purchases of new merchandise.[81] Privilege and commerce united people transnationally.[82]

Letters became proof of privilege deserved. Although the names of the persons writing the letter provided strength, the actual paper materialized that power. To invoke a name was one thing, but to have the name written on paper transformed that connection into something more potent. The letter tangibly demonstrated the veracity of Bingham's social claims, acting as evidence of Bingham's social membership. The document could be carried and shown at opportune moments, facilitating the production of the expedition's scientific achievements. Directed toward people who might either resist the expedition's requests or have information to share, the letters acted as shibboleth unlocking protected gates of access, allowing for successful navigation and passage through the Peruvian interior.

Reputation Matters

What counts as scientific evidence rests with the observer. That is, the weight or import of the observation is intertwined with the eyes that see. The credibility and skills of the observer are crucial to establishing evidence.[83] Bingham cited work by other scholars in order to draw on their reputations as he built a supportive social network of reputable individuals and organizations. Bingham's position at Yale, his previous experience in South America, and the support of wealthy people and state governments elevated "ways of seeing" to "ways of knowing."[84] Reputations mattered, and the letters of recommendation were materializations of support from a credible community of observers and of the power that community held. The cadre of seers, while allowing Bingham to see, also saw, at some distance. Their visions would come to be refracted through Bingham's subsequent visualizations.

The letter-writing campaign was an extraordinary success. According to the Yale treasurer's office, the 1911 expedition received contributions from a handful of people: Victor Tyler ($500), Mr. Mixter (amount not disclosed and anonymous), Stuart Hotchkiss ($50), Henry Hotchkiss ($50), J. A. Hamilton ($25), J. Louis Schaefer ($250), Minor C. Keith (amount not disclosed), and Otto Banard ($250).[85] Paul B. Lanius's father donated $1,350 for his son's expenses, and Bingham and his wife each gave $1,800. Herbert Scheftel, from the same Yale class as Bingham, agreed to pay $1,800 for a topographer. The 1911 expedition raised $11,905.84 and cost $11,640.88, twice as much as envisioned in the early fund-raising letter.

After the sighting of Machu Picchu, support was more readily forthcoming, and a follow-up expedition in 1912 was quickly organized. Pledges for the second expedition included a $5,000 gift from Edward Harkness,[86] $5,000 from Bingham and his wife, $5,000 from the Yale Corporation, and $10,000 from the National Geographic Society. A former traveling companion and Yale alumnus named Stuart Hotchkiss contributed as well. The financial support of the 1912 expedition was initially figured at $24,373.04, but later corrected to $27,277.51 in gifts, including interest, and expenses were listed as $26,887.64.[87]

For the 1914–1915 expedition, financial support continued to grow. Bingham and his wife donated $10,900; Bingham's mother-in-law, Alfreda Mitchell, $1,000; Edward Harkness $5,000; James Means $2,100; and the National Geographic Society $20,000 ($10,000 per year).[88] Bingham ultimately raised $52,655.87, or over $1.2 million today, and expenses were listed at \$51,851.23.[89] That expedition, which lasted nearly two years, marked the end of Bingham's work in Peru and his career as an explorer.

The network that Bingham cultivated through letter writing generally consisted of wealthy industrialists, many having connections with Yale. Edward Harkness was a noted philanthropist who had inherited money from his father and was an early investor in Standard Oil. Harkness donated millions to Yale for the construction of the Memorial Quadrangle and for faculty salary increases. He and his spouse were patrons of the Metropolitan Museum of Art and collected Egyptian art and antiquities.

Stuart and Henry Hotchkiss were from wealthy families whose fortunes were made from the processing of Brazilian rubber in New Haven.[90] Otto Banard was a financier, and Paul Baxter Lanius, Bingham's assistant, was a student at Yale in the Sheffield Scientific School who joined the expedition to gain experience. Lanius would eventually figure in mining and metallurgy. James Means, contributor to the third expedition, paid for his son Philip Ainsworth Means, a Harvard graduate who later became a respected Andean scholar in his own right.

The coupling of science and industry was perhaps best shown by the discounted shipping rates and contributions offered by both the United Fruit Company and W. R. Grace. Minor C. Keith had helped build a railroad from the interior of Costa Rica to Limón, its port, allowing for the shipping of coffee and other exports to Europe, in the late nineteenth century.[91] Keith was also credited with establishing banana plantations in Central America, eventually becoming vice president of the United Fruit Company.[92] During his tenure, he agreed to allow the Yale team members to travel at half fare from New York to Panama.[93] He also agreed to cover the cost of an archaeological engineer.[94]

W. R. Grace facilitated the members' passages from the Panama Canal to Callao and Mollendo, Peru, as well as the passage of hundreds of cartons that Bingham sent back to Yale from the 1912 and 1914–1915 expeditions.[95] In addition, Grace acted as a liaison with the Peruvian government, ensuring privileges accorded to scientific expeditions such as free customs entry, permission to excavate, and facilities use.[96] J. Louis Schaefer, Bingham's US contact for Grace, personally donated \$250 for the 1911 expedition.

To cover transportation costs while in Peru, Bingham relied on the Peruvian Corporation.[97] W. L. Morkill, its president, became an acquaintance of Bingham during the 1911 expedition. The corporation owned the concession rights to all the railroads in Peru, and Morkill granted all goods and team members free passage on the railroad.[98] Morkill also helped smooth the passage of materials out of the country.

In addition to using the railroads, Bingham capitalized on the foreign-built infrastructure already in place in Peru. The Inca Rubber Co., the Bolivian Boundary Commission, and United Fruit had built trails and roads to bring services to outlying areas of the Peruvian countryside and to more easily extract goods. Bingham used these roads to explore much of the Urubamba Canyon. Twenty years before Bingham's 1911 expedition, the Peruvian government had constructed a mule trail along the banks of the Urubamba River to facilitate shipment of goods through the mountainous terrain. Bingham noted that "this new road enabled us to discover what the Incas—or their predecessors—had left here, in the beautiful vastnesses of Vilcabamba."[99]

Team members used the knowledge gained about Peruvian natural resources and history to secure positions in government or private enterprise. Although some found the system exploitative, others profited from the experience.[100] J. J. Hasbrouck, the engineer for the 1914–1915 expedition, stayed in Peru, securing a position with the Andes Tin Company. Philip Means (1914) became a well-known scholar of Peru. Isaiah Bowman (1911), Harry Foote (1911), Herbert Gregory (1912), and George Eaton (1912) used material gathered in Peru to advance their own academic careers. Paul Bestor (1912) and Osgood Hardy (1912, 1914–1915) returned to the United States to careers in business, using their experiences to demonstrate their ability to work hard and persevere.[101] Although the first topographer, Kai Hendriksen, returned to Denmark after the 1911 expedition and could not participate in the follow-up expedition for personal reasons, the topographer on the 1912 and 1914 expeditions, Albert Bumstead, secured full-time employment with the National Geographic Society and started its first cartography department. Joseph Little (1912) enrolled at Yale to get his master's degree in Latin American import and export economics. Written in consultation with Bingham, Little's thesis was on the Peruvian Corporation. Little stayed in Peru after the expedition to work for DuPont, exploring new nitrate fields in Caravelli. He eventually worked in mining for the Cerro de Pasco Corporation, the largest US investor in Peru in the early twentieth century.[102]

In Bingham's early account of the expedition, the results of the previous correspondence take root: Farabee's suggestion about Duque, Marsters's suggestion about *arrieros* in Arequipa, and the importance of photography.

1911—Tuesday July 4th. Bowman's party leaves this morning. Dr. Erving and Hendriksen have made friends of a young man named Alberto Duque who speaks English and was educated at Notre Dame. His father has a big plantation at Santa Ana. He is interested in photography, and very favorably disposed toward the expedition. To-day he brings in a friend, Jose S. Pancorbo, who tells me that he knows of the presence of some Inca ruins at Rosaspata, opposite Puquiura. He has a sugar plantation and lives in the valley of Vilcabamba at a place called Paltaybamba. He speaks also of the ruins of Choquellusca, opposite Huayrurani, which is between Lucma and Paltaybamba. He has not seen either of these ruins, but has only heard of them. He draws a map of the district, telling us roughly how to get from place to place. He tells us to stop at Urubamba, Torontoy, and Qquillumayu on the way to Paltaybamba. Arrange with Miguel Silva to go as arriero for 80 soles per month and board himself and travel on foot. This is probably too much. The Arequipa arrieros are accustomed to receiving from 60 to 100 a month, but here at Cuzco they are lucky to get 50.[103]

Peruvian national desires for a modern future based on potential discoveries of its imagined Incan past united privilege. Webbed through letters, a cross-cultural elite connected individuals and goods. Insinuating himself into this privileged network, Bingham had access to needed supplies, logistical support, knowledge about the area, social and scientific legitimacy, and recreation, all of which were, at least initially, garnered through letter writing.

Travel and scientific exploration were part of, and were facilitated by, expanding flows of capital and the expansion of corporations across national boundaries.[104] Without these connections, carrying off an expedition would have been more difficult logistically and, more importantly, less imaginable. Bingham had to draw on governmental relationships and corporate sponsors that were interested in the promise of future opportunities between the United States and Peru. Without the support of W. R. Grace, Kodak, and the Peruvian government, the expedition would have been more costly and the outcomes distinct. Bingham's involvement in scientific organizations and his connections with prominent scholars further legitimized the pursuit. Science proved to be a powerful tool. Bingham drew on its ability to connect people from disparate backgrounds, to justify financial support, and to provide a rationale for soliciting government officials to carry out his expedition. The universalized virtue of science and the expansion of markets were a winning combination that Bingham used in his favor.

Ricardo Salvatore has suggested that the search for knowledge played a key role in channeling US capital, expertise, dreams, and power into South America.[105] Library, university, business, and government interests intersected in the quest for scientific knowledge. Philanthropic organizations such as the Rockefeller Foundation[106] played a central role in establishing scientific schools, medical schools, public health campaigns, and agricultural programs in an effort to maintain stable world trade, protect the health of North Americans, and safeguard their investments in Latin America.[107] For its part, archaeology at the time was a "multifaceted project of metropolitan expansion, discovery/recovery, and consumption."[108] This enterprise of knowledge, based on Enlightenment principles and the desire to collect and expand on knowledge about nature and history, was highly nationalistic, and state-sponsored agents aided in the collection of pre-Columbian remains. Transportation networks and large infrastructure projects also facilitated these movements.[109]

Research projects like Bingham's were part of this expansion. If the Yale Peruvian Expeditions could contribute to, correct, or expand on the knowledge recorded by the earlier Spanish chroniclers, then South Americans would recognize the potential of the North.[110] By proving the true origins of the Inca, North America would gain more dominion over South America.[111] Thus, fields like antiquarianism became a key to the expansion of North American cultural influence in South America.[112]

Letter writing was critical to establishing a knowledge network that would help Bingham see. Letters did not simply organize logistics or get people to donate money. Rather, they secured consensus for the expedition by enrolling people to participate imaginatively in it. Besides elucidating and shaping the goals of the expeditions through the exchange of ideas, letters cultivated a network of individuals and corporations interested in discovery and in an industrial future for Peru. This network provided an explanatory framework, camaraderie, ideas, legitimacy, and a belief that the endeavor was worthy. That vision was appealing to those interested in expanding Yale's reach, in pursuing antiquarian interests, in understanding Peru's Incan past, and in securing a future as a modern nation.

Foundational to this enterprise was a trajectory of science that produced Peru as a nation in need—a lack.[113] Science ultimately underscored and helped produce the nationalisms that undergirded the asymmetrical relationship of knower and known, but also built upon, and further solidified, the demarcations of peoples along lines of the civilized. The quest for useful knowledge as it pertained to capitalism and industry made scientific expeditions like Bingham's not only possible but also exciting and desirable for a multitude of actors. One nation had the raw materials, the other the expertise. One nation had the technology, the other the laboratory. One nation had a present, the other a past. Such an outlook necessitated displacement and translation as "conceptual horizons" that had to be first refigured for scientific ordering.[114] The Andes had to become lost in order for important scientific work to be done.

Things We Think With

In the edited collection of essays *Evocative Objects: Things We Think With*, Sherry Turkle draws on Claude Lévi-Strauss to suggest that objects are good (and goods) to think with.[115] A letter is a simple object, made important through the words imprinted on its pages, circulating and captivating the reader's eye. Once a daily practice, letter writing might mistakenly be viewed as innocuous and inconsequential. Letters, however, invite the grounding of broader discussions about imperialism, science, North-South relations, power, and privilege. A letter is a thing that matters.

Examining the correspondence of Bingham's 1911 expedition demonstrates its ad hoc and improvisational composition, but also its calculated strategy. In tracking the names of the correspondents, one begins to see a powerful network take shape. Breaking apart the structure by reading the letters is a way to understand the practice of science and its discoveries. Taxonomy begins to emerge from Bingham's letters. While they generally display the manners and customary scripts of gentlemanly exchange, there are a few specific types. Some letters pose queries about the expedition, the logistics of travel, and the history of the area, and thus encourage a response, building a network through the academic enterprise. Others seek supplies in return for promotional testimony. Still others motivate and offer gratitude, solidifying opportunities for future connection. Others scold and admonish, protecting Bingham's work and his reputation.

All the letters display the importance of this everyday object for connecting people, opening doors, shaping ideas, soliciting information, strategizing, securing consensus, establishing a community of knowing, acting as a repressive strategy, and facilitating movement through geographic and jurisdictional space. Through letters, privilege becomes grounded. Although the letters themselves did not necessarily evoke an emotional response from Bingham, they most likely lent him security during insecure moments. Knowing that as he walked through the countryside, a letter of support was in his pocket and a privileged social scientific network was manifested in his bank account bolstered his cause. United by the same epistemic virtue, a distinctly privileged social network came together to realize the expedition. Letters helped fashion this powerful thought collective that was supportive of important scientific work to be done in Peru.

At the heart of scientific seeing lies the evocation of words bounded in a social network. The words offer hints of visualization in the absence of imagery. Bingham's correspondence demonstrates the assumptions and desires built into seeing Peru and ultimately in finding Machu Picchu. The coupling of commerce and science with the expectation of discovery was foundational to seeing and thus to the making of Machu Picchu. Letter writing established the circle of seeing: what would be seen, and that it would be seen. Without it, a lost city would never have been found.

CHAPTER 2

Huaquero Vision

Grave robbing is at best an unholy venture. The scientific collector of bones doubtless has better intentions than the mere treasure-hunter; but both follow, in part, the same course; and whichever one finds himself last in the race for the prize, probably regards his competitor's work as unwarrantable desecration.
GEORGE EATON, "INDIAN GRAVES AT MACHU PICCHU," 1912

Although popular myth associates Hiram Bingham and his global unveiling of Machu Picchu in 1911 with archaeology, Bingham was trained as a historian and "had little interest in stratigraphy" or other methodologies associated with modern archaeological research.[1] Instead, what was practiced on the three Yale Peruvian Expeditions to Machu Picchu is better characterized as a late antiquarianism-inspired collecting spree—or, less generously, strategic "grave robbing."[2] The teams cleared fields, extracted human remains from caves, and collected things. Collectibles included not only conventional archaeological artifacts excavated from the earth such as bones, pots, jewelry, and household goods, but also exotic animals and species previously unknown to science.[3] The expedition also purchased artifacts, books, and manuscripts in antiquity shops and from private collectors.[4]

The practices and technologies of the expeditions helped mythologize Machu Picchu into a lost city. The expedition team's collecting practices and the frame of science, as well as the types of artifacts collected, helped materialize Machu Picchu, initially imagined by Bingham as the lost Incan city of Vilcabamba, as both a vestige of the Inca race and a scientific discovery. The collecting practices combined prospecting with the notion that science had an unconditional claim on those objects that might contribute to the accumulation of its knowledge. Rather than heed a nation's sovereignty over its territory and history to make its objects collectible, the expedition relied on the universal virtue and supremacy of science.

In the first book-length account of his motivation to explore the Urubamba Canyon, Bingham recalled being inspired by Rudyard Kipling's "The Explorer": "Something hidden. Go and find it. Go and look behind the Ranges— / Something lost behind the Ranges. Lost and waiting for you. Go!"[5] Bingham was motivated by the notion of finding something hidden and revealing it for the world to see.[6] As shown by his collection of skeletal remains, his drive involved more than geographic conquest. Instead, his quest, as demonstrated in practice, centered on intensive exploration embodied in the study of pre-Columbian man. Through the collection of skeletal remains, Bingham could demonstrate that he had gone behind the ranges and found something.

This chapter examines how science as discourse, practice, and technology was used to collect in Peru. Through science, Bingham gained recognition as an explorer who illuminated history, garnered prestige and stature within an elite group of men and women, and was seen as contributing to knowledge universally valued. Such a claim encouraged financial as well as political support from Americans and Peruvians, and legitimized Bingham's imaginings of place.[7] To substantiate the claim of science, however, one had to bring back evidence. In the case of the three Yale expeditions to Peru, scientific knowledge and discovery were materialized through the collection of items related to Peru's Incan past.

The collecting agenda was twofold. First, the expedition focused on Incan remains, which primarily meant anything found in grave sites, including skeletal remains, pottery, metal objects, and textiles. Early colonial manuscripts about the Incas and other antiquities were purchased from private collectors. Second, the expedition focused on natural history, either in the form of plants and animals or through images of Quechua speakers' bodies.[8] Ultimately, skeletal remains and photographs became the focal points of the collecting program. These remains and images were variously conceived of as vestiges of the Inca race, as gross anatomy, as landscapes lying in wait, or as evidence of fantastical cultural practices.[9] In any case, what was useful or collectible for the expeditionary agenda was framed as contributing to the glory and promise of the Incan past for both science and nation. Collecting helped materialize Bingham's racialized vision, providing objects for study and evidence of a lost city scientifically discovered.[10]

Salvage ethnography was in vogue in the nineteenth and early twentieth centuries. Scholars argued that the cultural and racial knowledge

embodied in material objects had to be rescued for science before a particular "culture" or "tribe" "vanished."[11] Such knowledge was considered
valuable evidence of human technical expertise in material culture, such
as basket weaving or textile making, and was also highly prized ethnological evidence for use in debates over human evolution and racial origins.[12]
In Cuzco, objects still in use were collected by elite Peruvians, who relied
on the testimony of indigenous subjects to help determine the meaning,
age, and use of antiquities.[13] This practice relegated living Andeans to the
past, anachronisms whose knowledge had persisted through centuries.[14]

Unlike his Peruvian counterparts, Bingham did not seek out or purchase objects being used by the local indigenous population. Rather, he
was attracted to the remains of the Incan civilization. The expedition was
interested in collecting buried artifacts and purchasing books and antiquities, not in salvaging *tupu* pins from living Quechua speakers. Such an
Inca-collecting bias reflected previous research and ongoing debates in the
study of Peruvian civilization and its antiquities. Racialized understandings of the noble Incan past, juxtaposed with the "fallen" and miserable
indigenous present, inflected the collecting practices of the expedition.[15]
Although the schism between what was considered the glorious Incan past
and the miserable indigenous present had begun to lessen by 1930, Bingham's three expeditions to Peru were based on, and perpetuated, the as-
sumption that what was important for science was the Inca.[16] Traces of
this historical discourse and its racialized implications were materialized in
Bingham's collection of scientific evidence in the form of skeletal remains.

Bingham's scientific imagination focused on understanding the Inca,
mapping archaeological ruins, and studying the origins of man.[17] Other
Anglo scholars of this era, such as Albert Giesecke, taught students in
Cuzco to use direct field observation and statistics, helping turn their
eyes toward their own reality.[18] But the Yale expeditions virtually ignored
Quechua speakers except as useful aids to the expeditions' collecting aims
and as subjects in anthropometry. Keeping with the historical binary of
the noble Incan past and the miserable indigenous present, Bingham's
emphasis remained on the Inca.[19] Although *indigenismo* eventually rose
around Bingham, becoming a source of conflict with Bingham's increasingly antiquated antiquarianism, he focused on conquering a landscape
through physical exertion, photography, surveying, measurements, and
the removal of objects.[20]

The remains of the Inca were not easy to locate at first. The landscape
had to be visualized. Large expanses were cleared, walls were reconstructed,
and the area was mapped. Still, remains proved elusive. Ultimately, the Yale

explorers relied on the knowledge of Peruvian scholars, landowners, and local laborers to assist them in their collecting enterprise. Skeletal remains were located and collected by residents, who were paid, relative to local wages, handsomely for their knowledge of the Andean terrain.

Although studies on archaeology and nationalism have convincingly demonstrated the social and political effects of naming national monuments and the ways in which specific projects have been undertaken and shaped for the goals of nation building, they have been less concerned with the ways in which specific archaeological practices and technologies have participated in the creation and meanings of such heritage.[21] Studies often begin postreconstruction, when the purported scientific understanding and importance of the site has already been established. The status of heritage is assumed. Machu Picchu *is* Peru's heritage. But of course this was not always the case. Even today, Machu Picchu as heritage stays in constant negotiation as what that means is altered through and in practice.

This chapter draws on work in science and technology studies[22] to symmetrically position archaeology and nationalism alongside ideas and instrumentation to make better sense of how the expeditions and their practices and technologies of science produced Machu Picchu and, thus, specific understandings of Peru's Incan heritage. Although many actors came together under the rubric of science and the promise of modernity to bear witness to Machu Picchu as a lost city, this chapter focuses on how science was a first step in making Machu Picchu imaginable and visible — and therefore collectible.

Yale collected in the name of science, and its worldview circulated not only on Yale's campus, but also globally in magazines such as *National Geographic*. Science added a veneer of legitimacy that enabled the expedition to collect materials and remove them from Peru. The Peruvian territory was conceived as a source of useful material and data for Yale University and the scientific community at large, including many Peruvians. Like his European predecessors, Hiram Bingham established scientific knowledge in the contact zone, in this case through the work of *huaqueros* (relic or treasure hunters).[23]

Cave Hunting for Science

No trained archaeologist accompanied the team on any of the three expeditions.[24] This decision was based partly on the difficulty of finding a trained archaeologist willing to assist the expedition without pay, and partly on the fact that archaeology was not a primary goal of Bingham's 1911 expedition. Although excavating became important in the second and third expeditions, a sustained and systematic practice of excavation was neither conducted nor enforced.[25] Despite the lack of an archaeologist, archaeology remained important in name because it provided the explorer and the expedition with a scientific image and legitimized the team's collecting practices.

Several academic peers encouraged Bingham to bring an archaeologist. Writing to him in 1911, the Harvard University professor W. C. Farabee argued that the area to be explored held much promise for science and was the "most important in Peru." Furthermore, archaeological work done without proper training might destroy more than it would unearth.

> Archaeology is different from most subjects in that its material once used is largely worthless for further investigation. If a mistake is made in historical research it matters little because the original sources remain; but in archaeology the evidence is largely destroyed. We know very little about the successive cultures in Peru because in the past all the digging was done by relic hunters. Your archaeological assistant ought to be well acquainted with all the material from Peru so that he may know what to expect to find and what he has found when it appears. Otherwise he may destroy more valuable material than he secures and the world would be none the wiser.[26]

While thanking Farabee for the advice, Bingham explained that the archaeological assistant accompanying the 1911 expedition would be under the personal direction and tutelage of Bingham and would therefore not destroy any valuable material. Moreover, Bingham conceived of the assistant's work not as archaeological excavation but as engineering; the assistant would primarily be constructing roads and bridges, clearing jungle, and assisting in mapmaking.[27]

Collecting objects and shipping them to Yale was not a significant part of the 1911 expedition. Therefore, the lack of an archaeologist did not play as decisive a role in the collecting agenda as it did in the subsequent two expeditions. During the 1912 expedition, the focus on excavating Machu Picchu and its environs made archaeological practice more significant. But finding an archaeologist to accompany the team continued to pose a challenge. Systematic archaeologists were scarce and not interested in working in Peru. Writing to the Harvard professor Roland Dixon, Bingham wondered, "Would it be better to get some young man trained in science who would know how to collect accurately and record carefully what he found and saw, and let somebody in this country study the things we bring out, or would it be better to take even a second or third class archaeologist who could study the things himself after he got back?[28] Bingham vacillated between hiring a "third class archaeologist" and hiring "some young man trained in science" who might carefully collect objects of interest.

On March 15, 1912, Dixon responded to Bingham. Like Farabee in 1911, Dixon was concerned that the Yale expedition would not be able to distinguish the value of the found items: "What you say about a first-class young man of scientific training is perfectly true, but the difficulty lies in the fact that to know what is and what is not of value, to know what is *necessary to observe and what is immaterial*[29] requires some special archaeological training."[30] For both Dixon and Farabee, acquiring a discerning archaeological eye was critical. The expedition did not know which objects were important, which were insignificant, and, most critically, what evidence was necessary to support scientific and historical claims about the found material. In the end, Bingham chose a "young man of scientific training" over a "third class archaeologist," but did take steps to direct and train the expedition members in "archaeology," mainly through packets of information known as circulars.[31] Consisting of loose-leaf paper in binders, the circulars[32] included a variety of useful information for expedition members: details about the packing lists of the food boxes,[33] instructions for daily meals, notes on how to clean a rifle, and rules for hygiene and camp sanitation. The circulars also included information on collecting.[34]

In many ways, the circulars acted as the team's operating instructions and its methods course, and they constituted the only training that the expedition members received in excavating, collecting, recording, and storing archaeological remains. No special group training session occurred before the expedition's departure. Instead, individual meetings were conducted with Bingham, and a notebook of circulars was provided to each member.[35]

Circular number 13, "Collection of Archeological and Osteological Material,"[36] specified where to look, what to collect, how to collect, and what to record. Under "What to Collect," Bingham's only instruction stated: "In general, it will be desirable to bring in not only remains of man, bones, sherds, artifacts, etc. but also the bones of any animals found associated with him." Under "Where to Look," expedition team members were instructed to be on the lookout for osteological and archaeological specimens in gravel banks, "'ash deposits,' kitchen middens, ancient 'camp sites,' and rock shelters as well as in the neighborhood of prehistoric ruins, natural points of lookout, waterholes and ancient cultivated fields." Under "How to Collect," members were told to not be in a hurry, to start note taking before removing materials, and to not allow "loose specimens on the surface to escape you." Bingham emphasized the importance of collecting the skull and jaw of the human skeleton: "Every effort should be made to get these out entire."[37] Under "What to Record," members were instructed to note the geographic location, the general nature of the deposit, and the depth, position, and orientation of all human remains. Additionally, photographs were to be taken before, during, and after excavation, and sketches were to be made showing the extent of the location. Bingham wrote: "Do not be afraid of making notes ample."[38]

The circular for the 1914–1915 expedition, "Special Instruction for the Archaeological Engineer,"[39] though expanded and updated, was similar in content. Bingham provided more information about the possible locations of collectible objects, sharing knowledge of the terrain and grave site conditions obtained on the 1912 expedition.[40] Also included were clearer instructions about the necessity of photographing and diagramming the location of objects in situ before, during, and after excavation. Collectors were not to be rushed, but instead should take time to think about and select the most appropriate method for removing material.[41] Techniques for labeling and packing the excavated artifacts were discussed at greater length, as were instructions on wrapping and storing items for shipment. Most importantly, the circular suggested that items excavated be given a serial number noting the location, grave site, date, and initials of the collector. If several skeletons were located in the same cave, then the bones found should carry the additional labels "skeleton 1," "skeleton 2," and so on. Although the 1914–1915 circular included more details and directions about the packing and labeling of found material, and location of burial sites, the thread throughout the two circulars remained the same. Both emphasized the collection of the "remains of prehistoric or pre-Columbian man."[42]

Photographs were taken of the caves to show how skulls were laid. Drawings showed the floor plans.[43] Whereas other collections emphasized only crania, and thus had serious limitation for advancing research conclusions, the skeletons gathered by the expedition were catalogued by George Eaton as units, something not common among other scientific expeditions of the time.[44] Although Bingham desired contextualization of the collection of material goods at Machu Picchu, the quality of field records for the skeletal material was variable, and detailed information was not always recorded.[45] In addition, there was no systematic survey of the faunal remains, since it wasn't considered a subject worthy of study by the expedition. Bingham never really had an explicit strategy when it came to collecting animal bones, and some of the material collected was not saved.[46] Part of the reason for a breakdown in contextualization was that the people hired to collect did not take notes. And even if they had attempted to organize the collections systematically, the sheer quantity of goods may have overwhelmed them.[47] The exceptions seem to be the maps and Mathewson's work on metallurgy,[48] many of whose noteworthy conclusions are accepted today.[49]

Ultimately, the expedition emphasized "ancient civilizations," the material evidence for which was primarily found in grave sites.[50] The grave sites were typically caves, and once they were located, the removal of materials was remarkably easy. Finding the caves proved difficult, however. Lacking both archaeological expertise and experience in excavating in the Andes, the team found it hard to locate burial sites for excavation. The training of expedition members came via the circulars, but the information outlined in the circulars was quite general. It was difficult to know precisely what one was looking for and what was of critical importance. Team members needed knowledge of the Andean landscape and its history in order to locate caves, middens, and burial sites. To collect remains, one had to acquire a discerning eye that could see specimens for science where others saw only burial sites or lucrative trinkets for gringos. One of the key ways that a trained archaeological eye was acquired was by paying those living in the area to assist the Yale team members. In the end, the Yale expedition was able to see the landscape "scientifically" or "archaeologically" through the experienced eyes of the gravedigger.

Seeing Their Way to Science

After having little luck in finding the objects he sought, Bingham began offering prize money for those who brought finds to the team's attention. The incentive plan, first implemented on the 1911 expedition, became a much more significant part of the 1912 and 1914–1915 expeditions, and a boon to the endeavor.[51] Monetary payments helped overcome workers' reluctance to help the team with its mission, and by accessing the workers' knowledge, the expedition was able to overcome its inability to locate sites worthy of collecting.[52] The Yale expedition paid informants to help locate caves and dig-worthy sites, and a photographic record was taken of the locations. Through their efforts, the paid gravediggers initially determined what was necessary to observe and what was immaterial.

Those hired by the expedition were typically forced or coerced into participating in the collecting spree. The landowner Mariano Ferro, for example, ordered the farmers residing at Machu Picchu to work for the expedition.[53] After finding nothing, Bingham decided to pay a silver dollar to those who reported a cave containing a skull. According to Bingham, those unfamiliar with the area found nothing, but the three who resided at the site found eight burial caves. "At the prevailing rate of wages on the sugar plantations this was more than the three of them could earn in a week," Bingham wrote.[54] Although the collectors worried about the moral repercussions of looting on their livelihood, Bingham wryly noted, "No possible amount of agricultural good luck, however, could compete with the cash bonus such as we had offered."[55] The paid workers found more than fifty caves and earned more in a week than they might have earned in the course of two months. For four months they excavated Machu Picchu. The team maintained the "zeal of the assistants" through a "sliding scale of bounties and gratuities."[56]

Incentives besides monetary payments were used to encourage participation, including intimidation with guns, fear of governmental brutality, and the threat of military conscription.[57] Bingham wrote that those who were unwilling to accompany the expedition were forced to do so by the *gobernador* of the nearby town.[58] Some workers came voluntarily from Cuzco, but the expedition primarily depended on village officials acting under the order of the Peruvian government to supply it with men.

On the 1911 expedition, the geographer Isaiah Bowman resorted to personal threats to help him acquire local assistance. Bowman plied locals with food and drink, brandished his gun, and at one point beat someone into submission.[59] He unapologetically wrote: "I drew my revolver and he quickly obeyed the order to sit down to breakfast, which consisted of soup, meat and army biscuits."[60] On the 1912 expedition, K. C. Heald commented on the dissatisfaction of the workers and the challenge of working in the Andean environment, worrying that they would quit.[61] Frustrated by the resistance of the men, Heald wrote: "Giving the .22 to Tomas I told him to shoot any man who tried to bolt, but to do it carefully around the edges."[62] Although a few laborers might have returned to continue working with the expedition, most were never seen again.[63]

Not everyone employed was successful in locating grave sites. Many of the contracted workers were newcomers unfamiliar with the area. They did not yet know how to see the landscape for science. But Anacleto Alvarez, Torvis Richarte, and Tomás Fuentes, who had moved to the area a few years before Yale's arrival, were highlighted in the field reports as being extraordinarily useful to the expedition.[64] Eaton, who seemed genuinely fond of the laborers, wrote that the team was fortunate to have the services of "such reliable Indians" and that they had won his lasting gratitude, even though they didn't take notes or prepare diagrams.[65] The three men uncovered much of what was eventually collected and shipped back to Yale University.[66]

Bingham was not always present during the excavation of a site, and he offered little specific hands-on direction. In 1912, he was often busy doing reconnaissance in an effort to locate more archaeological sites in the Cuzco area, or he was in Lima, trying to negotiate a concession with the Peruvian government. For the 1914–1915 expedition, Bingham, although considered its director, did not arrive in Peru until 1915, leaving Ellwood Erdis, also a member of the 1912 expedition, in charge of the team for nearly a year. Although the circulars stressed the importance of recording the context of an object, particular attention was not always invested in making detailed measurements or analyzing a few specimens.[67] Instead, the value of Yale's collecting lay in the quantity of material accumulated, accompanied by a general overview.[68] Artifacts themselves became the data.[69]

Erdis was given the titles "archaeological engineer" and "engineer" and was a key figure in the collecting enterprise on the 1912 and 1914–1915 expeditions. Along with Erdis, George Eaton figured prominently in the collection of skeletal remains. A member of the 1912 expedition, Eaton wrote about the schedule of rewards offered to local informants employed by the expedition, noting that "every Indian employed about our camp, was sent out prospecting."[70] Like Bingham, Eaton was often not present at excavations. For example, graves 53 through 107 were excavated after Eaton's departure. According to Eaton, Richarte and Alvarez had acquired "considerable skill, both in hunting for graves and in excavating, under the incentive of the small money prize offered," and they worked through the season, "delivering the booty to the Archaeological Engineer of the Expedition."[71]

The process of collecting began by paying scouts to locate grave sites. The scouts, sometimes unaccompanied by an expedition member, then excavated the tomb.[72] The materials found were delivered to Erdis, who labeled and listed the bones and articles collected. Erdis also recorded the information that the collectors conveyed regarding the location and contents of graves. According to Eaton, Erdis rarely supervised the excavation of grave sites, but managed a team of collectors that doubled the amount taken from Machu Picchu and the surrounding area. Although Eaton relied on Erdis's reports for his analysis of the skeletal remains, Eaton felt that he could not wholly trust what the collectors said, given the level of excitement and their inclination to use hyperbole.[73] Moreover, much of what was found by the scouts consisted of items taken from caves that had previously been looted, and therefore the context of the findings was dubious.[74]

In 1915, vampire bats inhabited a cave where two mummies were found.[75] Before removing the skeletons, the bats had to be cleared. The hired workers, who had located the cave, made a bonfire of the dry mummy wrappings. While they were successful at getting the bats to leave the cave, the specimens were, as Bingham put it, "unfortunately charred."[76] Out of this cave, twenty skulls and a dozen skeletons were collected. In his journal, Bingham lamented the bad shape of the skeletons after the bonfire, but wrote that it was a "fine haul, that would keep [Eaton] busy some time."[77]

Without the efforts and knowledge provided by the hired hands, the expedition would not have been able to pursue such a rapacious collecting practice. The quantity collected would have been significantly smaller, and it would have taken the Yale team longer to see their surroundings "archaeologically" and to identify what was necessary to observe and what was immaterial. In many respects, the Yale members received their true training not from the circulars or an academic course but from people who lived in the area and could provide the details and locations of grave sites and nearby ruins.[78]

A series of abridged excerpts from Erdis's journal entries reflects the mindset and tenor of the expedition's collecting practices generally.[79] For the final expedition, the team, at that point more knowledgeable about the area, was scheduled to spend twenty months in Peru; consequently, the goals of its collecting enterprise expanded, including the collection of animals. Erdis, writing to Bingham in 1912 about an exciting skeleton and the well-preserved skull of a "Quichua," pondered, "I have the feeling that everything we find within four miles of Cuzco is a feather in our Yale cap, don't you?"[80] The 1914–1915 expedition only heightened the quest to add to Yale's repository.

Erdis wrote in 1914 about visiting Don José Marín, who was initially skeptical about the presence of the strangers. After offering several gifts, including money and cigarettes, Erdis asked whether the man had any ollas, idols, or *champes*[81] that he would like to sell.[82] Marín did not, but then the conversation turned to bones:

Aug 9, 1914: . . . Asked him if there were any bones or skulls around. He said "lots," and asked if I wanted any. In six or seven minutes I had four skulls from caves under boulders. Two are regular; one is deformed, and one has been trepanned about 2½ inches in top of forehead. Had no room for more. When I got them packed, he said there was one cave, which had 50 skulls in it. I had already paid him 20 cents a piece on account of the skulls, which pleased him greatly. Told him I would be back maybe in three months and he promised to help me get all the bones I wanted.

Erdis's journal continues to emphasize the team's haul throughout the valley.

August 20, 1914: . . . Cave #11 (open) had two mummies, both lying face downward, one across the other; arms and legs doubled up on chest and abdomen. Underneath were skeletons of three or four others not mummified. On extreme left was skeleton of baby, same level as mummies. Skull was broken, and only got upper half. Several abnormal bones; some diseased; some congenitally deformed, and a collar bone broken and repaired by nature. Got 9½ skulls from this cave, one of which (mummy) was trepanned. Cave #11 is on point 200′ east of adobe houses, and 100′ lower. One mummy skull has about 1½″ diam. of meat on top. Two of the skulls in #11 are slightly deformed. Also got pierced green stone ornament on steep slope 10′ below cave and ½ stone broken ring, animal head, and some sherds. Only took mummies and skulls and odd bones. Cave is about 4′ high × 4′ wide × 3′ deep. In cave #10—open—25′ further uphill than #11, and on left side of point, took two trepanned, and one long deformed skull . . . There's about two sacks of bones in cave #11 yet, but have caves 9, 10, 11 marked for next year.

May 4, 1915—Got 172 skulls in central part of cave. . . . Then got big bronze tupu or pin.

May 8, 1915—After lunch went with Hasbrouck who was cave-hunting all morning. We visited one cave with 15 skulls in sight, one with 18 skulls in sight, one skull of which had five daisy trepans, and the 15 skull one had mummified parts and rope; a number with one or two skulls.[83]

May 16, 1915—Brought down from the cave 2 big sacks of leg bones and pelvises. Tomorrow morning we'll leave for Ollantae with them—17 boxes bones (one big box has [illegible] and is so marked, and 3 boxes sherds—all from Paucarcolla. There are 6 ruins here, viz; Patallacta, Cchuucuchuia, Hollidia (fortress), Qquishuarpata, Holleria, and Llac-

taspatas. The latter is only 7 or 8 boxes but it's the first of the whole 6.
. . . Think I've reported to you that in one cave here we have 26 skulls in
sight, in another 15 and in another 18. One skull is marked by some horrible disease—perhaps syphilis. One skull has 4 very fine trepans, which
will average an inch or more in diameter.[84]

Filling their empty food boxes with specimens to be shipped, offering
money to those finding graves, and constantly discussing their haul con-
firm the image that the expedition was on a mission to collect.[85] But by
the end of 1915, the team members and the local populace had grown tired
of their enterprise. Collecting had to come to a close, but not without
making their object first.

The Science of *Huaqueros*

There has long been a fascination with the interred in the Americas.
Looting of *huacas*[86] was widespread during the Spanish colonial period
and surged during colonization and Christianization.[87] Accounts detail
how the dead were moved to avoid desecration by treasure-seeking conquerors and how colonists trying to understand the Inca sought out mummies.[88] Excavations were conducted by military engineers in the eighteenth century, and by adventurers, gentleman scholars, and *salonniers* in
the nineteenth.[89] By the 1840s, antiquities and bones traveled together.[90]

In Peru, an active commercial network in antiquities was in place by
the early 1900s.[91] Networks consisted of "professional looters (huaqueros)," and antiquities merchants who supplied collectors and museums
in Lima, Europe, and the Americas.[92] Museums and collectors competed
for artifacts, and increased marketization favored collectors who could
discern the existing and potential value of objects.[93] To locate antiquities,
collectors often hired *huaqueros*, and *huaca* companies looted cemeteries.[94]
Crania and bones were seen scattered on fields as hunters discarded items
that they had no interest in.[95] Christina Bueno, writing about early excavations of Teotihuacán, Mexico, suggests the distinction between "scientist
and sacker was quite thin" during this period and that early archaeologists
were looters.[96]

The persistent trend in Peru until the early twentieth century was to
collect for elites and outsiders.[97] Archaeology was about materializing
objects for "the pleasure of discovery or their artistic interest," and objects ultimately were destined for European and US museums.[98] Archaeo-

logical preoccupations in Peru were the province of scientific travelers—with the exception of Mariano Eduardo Rivero, coauthor of *Antigüedades peruanas*—but digging remained in the hands of the *huaqueros*.[99] *Huaqueros* were "pick and shovel" laborers and often worked for scientists and commercial middlemen.[100]

Kimbra Smith, however, argues that not all excavation by nonarchaeologists should be classified as looting or treasure hunting.[101] Traditional *huaqueros*, she suggests, are considered "local experts on the local past and the local landscape."[102] Although their work methods may differ from those of archaeologists, they should not be confused with commercial looters, who work for short periods and "ransack sites thoroughly."[103] The two types are distinct and do not mix, even though they are often conflated in public discourse.

Réna Gündüz likewise argues for a distinction between traditional and nontraditional *huaqueros*. The job of the more traditional *huaquero* is often not considered destructive or even illegal. Rather, it is a job that provides a living and is part of a family tradition and traditional knowledge. *Huaquero*-ing is a way of life as well as a profession.[104] Still, Gündüz notes that traditional *huaqueros* have been pushed by outsiders to conduct their work in nontraditional ways, working only for money.[105]

In this chapter, I invoke the term "*huaquero*" to trouble Bingham's archaeological claims to science and to demonstrate how Yale's scientific vision relied on the vision and bodies of local subjects who were paid to be gravediggers and treasure hunters. As Smith points out, the knowledge of *huaqueros* has been consistently devalued and delegitimized in comparison with archaeological knowledge, even though outsiders often rely on the former's knowledge. What counts as scientific knowledge remains accessible to only a select few.[106] Bingham and his team paid residents in the area for their knowledge of the countryside and coerced others to assist them in accomplishing their goals. The paid laborers acted as nontraditional *huaqueros* for Yale, delivering the bones of the lost city to Bingham.

With their knowledge of the landscape as well as their physical exertion, the conscripted laborers decided what was immaterial and what was necessary to observe. Subsequently recategorized under the reign of science, the lootings became a legitimate and scientific form of collecting. Eaton more or less acknowledged as much when he compared scientific collecting with grave robbing and treasure hunting, noting that it was an unholy venture.[107]

Witnessing the "Lost City" in the Andean Landscape

In their work *Leviathan and the Air-Pump*, Steven Shapin and Simon Schaffer demonstrate that material, literary, and social technologies were necessary to constitute Robert Boyle's seventeenth-century air pump as a matter of fact.[108] These technologies functioned as objectifying resources and worked to "achieve the appearance of matters of fact as *given* terms."[109] Moreover, witnessing, or viewing the display and demonstration of those facts, was critical for the establishment of fact, because it allowed for the unlimited multiplication of witnesses.[110] They could "see and believe," offering collective and public testimony to the true state of affairs in nature.[111] Not everyone counted as a reliable witness, however. Invisibility and conventions of so-called transparency were required to be able to offer accounts that established scientific facts as objective mirrors of reality.

Yale expedition members acted as the first modest witnesses of Machu Picchu as a lost city. Although the team relied on *huaqueros'* vision to see their way through the Andean countryside and collect material evidence of the lost city, the *huaqueros* did not occupy the position of witnesses. To be a modest witness, one had to have science on his or her side.[112] Notably, the presence, prestige, and scientific agenda of the Yale team transformed the grave robbing into scientific collecting. Yale's modest witnessing legitimized the collected objects as scientific evidence.[113]

Deborah Poole has situated Hiram Bingham's gaze at the end of nineteenth-century visual modernity.[114] Like explorers before him, Bingham sought to collect groups of objects that could be measured, and their meanings generalized. Further, Poole suggests that Bingham's source of beauty appeared in the object rather than in the artist's hand. Reading a photograph printed in Bingham's *Inca Land* (1922), Poole demonstrates that Bingham's form of visuality coupled the "mountaineer's (or modernist's) concern with the body and physical discipline, and the imperialist's triumphant sense of geography and conquest."[115] Although physical work, reimagining, and reclassification were required to materialize Bingham's photographs, these interventions were obscured, resulting in so-called objective images.

The expedition's collecting policy paralleled Bingham's photographic gaze. Bingham sought quantities of objects as strong evidence, and the practice of collecting required intensive labor and physical achievement. Collecting required work, intervention, reclassification, and a particular imaginary frame. Although an artifact rendered as evidence of a lost city scientifically discovered necessitated a host of physical achievements, the artifact ultimately remained free from the scientists' hands.

First, the expedition had to ready the landscape for proper scientific witnessing.[116] Only by clearing, collecting, and reconstructing the site could the expedition offer public testimony to the true and natural state of Machu Picchu. One of the primary ways in which caves and monuments were made visible was through burning.[117] Chopping away at the jungle by hand proved slow and ineffective in the eyes of the expedition party. So the countryside was soaked with a flammable substance and set ablaze.[118] Erdis used a carbide lamp to efficiently burn grass on top of walls: It beat using matches, saved time, patience, and cuss words. It also did a good job.[119] Burning the landscape was an expeditious way to make rock walls visible and to facilitate the finding of grave sites and ruins. In his report, K. C. Heald wrote:

> About 4 pm we stopped to rest and again tried the experiment of firing the grass. Again it worked beautifully, the fire taking and in a few minutes roaring up the mountain cutting almost as wide a path as the one which we had first set and of which we could now see the front some two miles off, the dark red flames jumping 40-50 feet in the air and the smoke making it almost twilight. The new fire effectually stopped our progress for the day, so we made camp where we were.[120]

The Andean countryside as an archaeological repository of a lost Incan civilization was initially invisible to the expedition. The landscape had to be cleared, reconfigured, and made into a place where one could witness sites worthy of collecting. Brush was removed, grassy hillsides burned, wildlife culled, and structures rebuilt. Debris that might distract or complicate scientific witnessing had to be removed. The effects of time had to be eliminated so that objects could be collected, wrested from one context, and made into timeless artifacts worthy of science. The discovered artifacts, reclassified as specimens, became evidence that would be used to produce findings and claims about the Incan civilization and the antecedents of an imagined Peruvian national past. The skeletal remains were freed to be reimagined as evidence of the noble inhabitants of the lost city of the Incas, scientifically discovered by Hiram Bingham.[121]

Inherent in their witnessing was the purported transparency of seeing Machu Picchu as it *always was*, a natural fact, a lost city waiting to be found. Subsequently documented by photography and published in magazines such as *Harper's* and *National Geographic*, Machu Picchu as a lost

Incan city became an immutable mobile and traveled globally.[122] Making
things visible was an act of scientific resurrection that made it possible to
witness Machu Picchu as a persistent antiquity, always there, not made but
found. Circulation of the skeletal remains brought forth from its periph-
eries, along with the photographs taken of the site, encouraged a virtual
witnessing of the place as a majestic Incan refuge, hidden from Spanish
conquerors but discovered by science.[123] Becoming discoveries, the objects and the monument could then become the property of science, with
Yale as their custodian.

Collecting a Scientific Discovery

In the conclusion to *Imperial Eyes: Travel Writing and Transculturation*
(1992), Mary Louise Pratt examines the contemporary writings of Joan
Didion and Paul Theroux. Pratt argues that by the late twentieth century,
narratives of science, exemplified by those of La Condamine and Humboldt, had been replaced by a new imperial trope: the civilizing mission.
Characterized by a distant viewing and looking through the windows of
trains, airplanes, or taxis, these late twentieth-century imperial eyes gazed
without engagement. The tenor of these writings is melancholic. In both
Didion's *Salvador* (1983) and Theroux's *The Old Patagonian Express* (1978),
Pratt suggests that the authors lament the presence of poverty and grime,
which foreclose Latin America's quest for greatness.

Bingham's early twentieth-century expeditions bridge Humboldt and
contemporary writers such as Didion and Theroux. Bingham believed in
the promise of scientific discovery and the hope of modernity obtainable
through commerce and trade. Bingham's expeditionary plan, as well as the
relationships he nurtured throughout the expeditions, was framed in the
promise of Peru's future and the grandeur of its Incan past. Like Didion
and Theroux, Bingham wrote as if describing a civilizing mission. Unlike Didion and Theroux, however, Bingham was hopeful. Although the
Quechua present was framed as forgettable and in need of overcoming,
the Incan past was exalted. Peru remained an otherworldly terrain, the
Andes a nature to be conquered, replete with scientific and commercial
promise.

Many people in Cuzco and its environs assisted the expedition. Hired
laborers helped clear the landscape, readying it for witnessing, scouted the
countryside, excavated and collected remains from caves and other grave
sites, and ensured the productivity of other hired workers. They provided

knowledge and physical effort to facilitate and realize the desires of the expedition. Many provided food supplies for the crew from their small farms. Omnipresent was the threat of force from a hacienda owner or a governmental functionary. Without these local actors, the party would not have found Machu Picchu or been able to collect from its grave sites.[124]

Those hired to work for the team were paid relatively handsomely. While some provided help in the hopes of advancing science's quest to learn more about Peru's Incan heritage, others helped in order to help themselves. Still others took part in the expedition because they were forced to at gunpoint. All these relationships were crucial to Bingham and significantly contributed to the production of Machu Picchu. The insights and efforts of the local laboring population helped make the site collectible and visible, readying the place and its contents for scientific witnessing.

For things and ideas to be fashioned into collectible objects, a new way of witnessing the landscape at Machu Picchu was necessary. The clearing of the landscape and the collection of skeletal remains not only helped transform Bingham from a little-known professor of South American history to a world-class explorer but also facilitated a new signification for Machu Picchu. Decontextualized bones drew on previous racialized exploratory narratives, reclassifying Machu Picchu as a lost city, the last or the first capital of the Inca, a place hidden behind the ranges. Once resurrected by science, the site further exaggerated and highlighted the loss. As part of Yale's scientific collection, the objects manifested the regnant imaginary of a noble Incan past and an absent or miserable indigenous present.

The aura of the benign sovereignty of scientific knowledge dissolved national borders and involved a multinational populace that was implicated in the collecting enterprise.[125] Coercion and monetary incentives made the excavations possible. Clearing, construction, collecting, and photography were expeditionary techniques and technologies that eventually joined to produce Machu Picchu as lost city. Under the authority of science and backed by the state, Bingham claimed the by-products of *huaquero* vision as his privileged domain, inspiring others along the way to join him in the cause.

CIRCULATION

CHAPTER 3

Latin America as Laboratory

*Would anyone believe what I had found? Fortunately . . . I had a good camera
and the sun was shining.*
HIRAM BINGHAM, *LOST CITY OF THE INCAS* (1952)

Through our lens today, Machu Picchu is remembered for its beauty, its
energy, its mystery, its iconicity as national heritage, and its commercial
possibilities as a new modern wonder of the world and premier tourist destination. Quickly in tow is a photograph buttressing such claims. The fact
that the 1911 Yale Peruvian Expedition, which first photographed Machu
Picchu, was initially rooted within a scientific frame has become a forgettable backdrop to the current discourse. Nonetheless, a failure to read
Bingham's pursuits as scientific would be to miss a critical aspect of the
three Yale expeditions to Peru and the ways in which so-called discoveries were made and publicized. The expeditions were not the superficial
adventures of an Indiana Jones, nor did they happen by chance, destiny,
or luck. Nor were they simply conspiratorial deceits of agents of empire.
Bingham hoped that the expeditions would contribute to knowledge universally known. The frame of science facilitated his expeditions, validated
his practices, and legitimized his findings. Bingham's most powerful scientific expeditionary tool, the camera, materialized and made factual the
imagined discovery of a lost city in the clouds. In many ways, Bingham's
most significant and most lasting contribution was, and remains, a photograph of Machu Picchu (fig. 3.1).

In this chapter, I focus on Bingham's use of the camera to examine the
relationship between expeditions and the formation of scientific knowledge about Peru and Machu Picchu. I argue that photography, like collecting, was considered a primary scientific practice conducted on the ex-

Figure 3.1. Hiram Bingham with his camera, 1912. Courtesy of National Geographic Society.

peditions, since it allowed the team to bring back material evidence of its explorations and findings.[1] Through the camera, landscapes were negotiated and scenes framed, creating compelling and popular narratives about Bingham, Yale's discovery, Peru, its Incan past, and its indigenous present.

Although conceived of as a laboratory to test Kodak's latest technology, Machu Picchu and the Andean landscape were not docile subjects of Bingham's objectification. Nor did Bingham share his cameras with Peruvians.[2] Although a camera was stolen from Bingham's saddlebag during the 1911 expedition, and photographs were taken of Peruvians for scholarly and social purposes, the cameras were operated only by Bingham and a few select team members.[3] Although some locals were perhaps awed by the technology and its power to produce a photograph, the camera remained the sole purview of expedition members.[4] This does not mean, however, that Kodak's camera technology "flowed"[5] to Peru or that images were not negotiated, translated, and transformed in practice. Kodak's cameras were not simply taken out of their cases and used. Instead, there was friction in the technology's diffusion in the contact zone, because of the cameras' users, the technology itself, and the Andean climate.[6] A variety of actors, human and nonhuman, had to be considered in order to obtain a photograph. Here I examine the work exerted through the camera—a negotiated practice—to manifest a specific, scientific imagining of Machu Picchu as a lost city discovered by Yale.

Science and the Camera

By the early twentieth century, a camera was considered indispensable for scientific and anthropological fieldwork. Images were critical evidence for legitimizing the anthropological discipline as a whole as well as the findings of scientific explorations.[7] Professional photographers were hired to accompany scientific expeditions, and guidelines outlining what constituted a scientifically valuable photograph were widely distributed to travelers and amateur explorers.[8] Photography was considered invaluable because it was thought to capture what words could not, offering a form of mechanical objectivity.[9] Moreover, photography's imaging technology could record cultural practices and physiognomic features as a way of documenting those peoples thought to be fast disappearing.[10] Photography acted as a documentary technology and evidentiary object, and it was used to bring faraway places home for future study.[11] As a mechanism for collecting and materializing evidence on the Yale Peruvian Expeditions, photography was a powerful tool for stabilizing facts about Peru, since it elided cultural making and claimed to produce an objective reality.

Indeed, one of Bingham's primary scientific instruments on the three expeditions was the camera. Bingham and the other expedition members used photography and topographic drawings to document expedition sites, mapping the area geographically, geologically, and ethnographically. The camera assisted the topographer in mapping sight lines and reference points, recorded rock formations that could not be removed and brought to Yale, and acted as a medical technology documenting maladies and body formations. Although Bingham undoubtedly wanted to make a name for himself, the three expeditions to Peru were meant to be more than a traveler's delight, and the camera was one technology for manifesting and materializing that goal.

Considering the photograph as a collected object or scientific evidence obtained through a specific type of laboratory technology is often obscured when thinking about the power of photography's imaginings.[12] Scholarship on photography has emphasized the visualized referent, the image itself, and the power of the photograph's reproducibility. Photography has been examined for its importance as a technology of seeing;[13] for the types of gazes exhibited in its frame;[14] for the creation, expression, and perpetuation of racialist understandings of the Other;[15] for its role in state formation;[16] and for the ways in which it creates and consolidates powerful conceptualizations of nations.[17] Photographs are powerful producers of knowledge, indexical imaginaries that are, themselves, material objects—a "melding of image and form, both of which are direct products of intention."[18]

In her work on the Torres Strait expedition (1898), Elizabeth Edwards demonstrates that photography acted, much like Boyle's literary technology, as a witness allowing a seemingly unlimited number of people to verify the truths of A. C. Haddon's expedition.[19] Photographs offered both British and Torres Strait publics an opportunity for witnessing, which, when combined with rhetorical effect and display, convinced the viewing public of the reality of the Torres Strait society. This technological shift in the philosophy of vision influenced the way in which expeditions were executed, and they came to rely on the camera to both observe and create documentary evidence that could circulate beyond the darkroom.

Lorraine Daston and Peter Galison build upon Shapin and Schaffer's research on virtual witnessing to argue that while display had been crucial for establishing scientific fact, photography, invented in 1826, offered a new form of mechanical objectivity whereby raw and contingent experience could be transformed into an experience that was easily digestible.[20] The machine, free from the taint of human will, was considered authentic and able to produce a more accurate observation than a human report. Jennifer Tucker adds that photography was used in late-Victorian science as a way to image truths that could not be seen by the naked eye.[21] Coupled with a microscope, the camera could yield "fresh and truthful observations."[22] Photography became the preferred mechanism for visualizing nature, since it was considered more faithful than an artist's rendering.[23] Coupled with new technology such as the microscope, photography could visualize hidden truths, unlocking them for scientific inquiry and human understanding. Photography became an extremely powerful mechanism for stabilizing facts because of its instant obscuring of cultural making and its claim to produce an objective reality.[24]

Within the burgeoning field of archaeology, photography became a fundamental tool.[25] Artists relied on drawings and photographs for creative inspiration, but also to build and perpetuate interest in pre-Hispanic pasts.[26] In his analysis of the photographs of Claude-Joseph Désiré Charnay, a French explorer and archaeologist who traveled to Mexico, Adam Sellen argues that the camera created a visual register that was used for both commerce and study.[27] Expanding his analysis to encompass a variety of collectors in the late nineteenth and early twentieth centuries, Sellen writes, "Photographs were an extension of the classificatory process carried out by the original collectors and came to be important components in the analysis of archaeological materials."[28] Photography and other so-called objective visualizations like mapmaking were instrumental in shaping scientific claims and social relationships because images could be exchanged, manipulated, and used as independent tools of verification, the socio-technical relationships involved in an object's making neatly obscured.[29]

The camera was a potent technology of extraction, an inscription device materializing scientific desires.[30] Although Yale Peruvian Expedition images were published worldwide and used in a variety of lectures,[31] here I focus on the use of the camera on the expeditions. I argue that it is critical to figure camera technology and its deployment into a discussion of expeditionary photography in order to further explicate how intention and imaginaries were initially married into facts and to understand how this visualizing technology was deployed in the Andes.

The photograph as a by-product of intention did not begin with its insertion into text. The images Bingham produced appeared to be divorced from his rendering,[32] and they circulated widely in *National Geographic*, museum exhibitions, illustrated lectures, and newspapers. Further, the specific camera equipment and its use initiated the technological framing of the site as an exotic find, a native utopia, and a national treasure. Camera technology and its negotiated practice in the laboratory of Latin America was a necessary step toward translating and manifesting the discovery of a lost city for a global public.

Visualizing Science: Kodak and the Panoram Camera

Bingham and his team were avid and conscientious photographers, taking over twelve thousand photographs on their three expeditions. Many of the images were landscape views that highlighted the spatial organization of the monument. Other photographs documented the location of material objects within the remaining structures of Machu Picchu and other archaeological ruins.[33] The few photographs of the Andean people who inhabited the site and its environs served either to reinforce anthropometric conclusions and typologize the customs and dress of Quechua speakers or to highlight medical ailments such as massive goiters and skin diseases.[34]

Kodak was a significant corporate sponsor of the expeditions, contributing more than any other organization except the National Geographic Society.[35] Bingham wrote Kodak on March 25, 1911, asking whether the company would like to provide camera equipment "for a scientific expedition in the tropics."[36] Kodak agreed to provide the expedition with an entire photographic outfit on the condition that Bingham and the other members use the equipment properly, report on their work, and test out the equipment in various conditions.[37] A month before departing for Peru, Bingham confirmed the agreement with George Eastman, stating that he would do all in his power to abide by the agreement, including making reports and developing the pictures as soon as possible after exposure. In exchange for outfitting the expedition with cameras, tank developers with solution, and film at no charge, Kodak was "to secure the benefit of our experiments with this material in damp tropical valleys and . . . have the benefit of this experience for advertising purposes."[38] The 1911 photographic outfit provided by Kodak included four cameras with lens attachments, tripods, three tank developers with chemicals, and 284 film cartridges containing 2,608 exposures.[39] Although it had been suggested to Bingham that he bring a Panoram camera so that inclusive pictures showing the relationship of topography to ruins to terraces might be taken,[40] he disagreed. Panoramic pictures were "misleading though fine to look at," and Bingham preferred to use a tripod, camera, and compass to determine the exact direction of the picture.[41] Although Bingham changed his mind about the Panoram camera for the second expedition, Kodak's camera contribution brought home noteworthy results.

Returning from the 1911 expedition, Bingham wrote George Eastman that the camera outfit supplied by Kodak had worked "splendidly" and "the results certainly justified our efforts."[42] Bingham added: "I don't know how high your Kodaks have been carried before but we took two to the top of Mount Coropuna, which is probably about 22,500 feet above sea-level." In general, the Yale team followed the agreement with Kodak, developing the film a few days after the pictures were taken. When water was lacking, the expedition sealed the tins with the film and developed it two to three weeks later.

Kodak also supplied film and cameras for the 1912 expedition. Although the second expedition conducted additional survey work and mapmaking, Bingham emphasized collecting as a primary goal. Bingham brought along more men, wanted to take more photographs, and, most of all, wanted images of the Urubamba Canyon. Their primary sponsor, the National Geographic Society, wanted photographs. While George Eastman initially offered Bingham a speed Kodak, Bingham said that Kodak's Panoram camera would be more useful. Bingham's revised choice reflected the subjects and views he privileged. Having witnessed the area, he was able to articulate the specific needs of the expedition for panoramic vistas, anthropometric measurements, and collecting. What Bingham had previously considered a misleading technology ultimately produced one of his most important photographs. Bingham wrote Eastman:

> I am almost convinced that it would be extremely advisable to have one Panoram Kodak in the outfit. I do not feel so sure about the Speed Kodak. We do not have to take pictures of the fastest moving objects. There are no automobiles, and athletes and race horses are equally scarce. I have understood, however, that the lens is better than that in the 3A Special, and will give finer details. Can you give me some advice on this? . . . In many of the deep canyons where we are expecting to work it needs a Panoram Kodak to show the opposite side of the mountain up to the top. . . . If you can give us three new 3A Specials, and one No. 4 Panoram we shall have nine Kodaks in the outfit and ought to be well equipped for the scientific work that lies ahead of us.[43]

Visualizing geographic landscapes as panoramas was not an innocent choice. In her work on the German archaeologist Heinrich Schliemann, Kathrin Maurer suggests that the reliance on visual techniques such as panoramic painting commodified history through the collective gaze of modern tourism.[44] No longer revealed in a descriptive narrative through time, places were simply depicted spatially, transforming ruins into spectacles.[45] Writing of the view of New York City from the top of the former World Trade Center, Michel de Certeau suggests that the pleasure of "seeing the whole" acted to totalize the view. Separated from traffic and the "rumble of so many differences," the elevation of a panoramic view transformed the spectator into a voyeur. Distance became critical to the possession of space by making it "readable." Thus, he writes, "the fiction of knowledge is related to this lust to be a viewpoint and nothing more."[46]

Panoramic photography positioned Bingham as both knower and finder. The panoramic gaze expended on the landscape functioned through a totalizing frame, subsuming difference and change through space and distance. People and practices were no longer highlighted or of interest as the landscape became a viewpoint. Unlike Schliemann's paintings, however, Bingham's photographic panoramas had an ocular power that was magnified, since they were easily reproduced and circulated.[47] Photographs were not simply what Bingham saw but were part of a "developing argument."[48]

Bingham's aesthetic of discovery sought to visualize the mysterious and hidden beyond. Nonetheless, instruments were important adjuncts to human senses because they imposed both a correction and a discipline.[49] Specific camera technology was needed to manifest Bingham's scientific vision. Kodak's camera technology—such as the 3A Special fitted with a wide-angle lens, which was useful for highlighting details at shorter focal lengths (for example, the rocky walls of the monument)—facilitated Bingham's collection of views, ultimately materializing his imagining of Machu Picchu.[50]

Bingham's reliance on the panoramic camera shaped how knowledge about Machu Picchu and its history was fashioned. Only the Kodak Panoram camera could help Bingham "show the opposite side of the mountain up to the top."[51] Kodak's Panoram camera allowed Bingham to conjure a specific framing of Machu Picchu as "lost and hidden behind the ranges," discovered by the resolute Yale historian. The Kodak 3A was useful for capturing the details of archaeological remains. Without the 3A and Panoram cameras, Bingham's gaze would never have materialized and circulated. The scientific evidence of the Andes, with their wistful panoramas, detailed rock formations, and expansive landscapes devoid of inhabitants, was made possible because of Kodak technology.[52] The next step was to make pictures.

Photographing a Lost City

Although understood as a primary scientific practice on the expeditions, making pictures involved skill, time, and careful translation. The photographs were not intended to be a traveler's snapshots but to serve the scientific goals of the expedition: documenting and surveying the landscape and its remains. In this section, I discuss how Kodak's camera technology was deployed to communicate a specific vision of Peru to the expeditionary team and to document the work involved in translating that vision into scientific evidence. The camera was an unstable tool, and Bingham expended much effort to obtain "accurate" images.[53]

Circulars were distributed to team members about taking photographs and using the cameras. The 1912 and 1914 circulars on photography provide a sense of how the camera technology was understood as a tool for obtaining scientific evidence, but was also suspect and unstable.[54] The *Wellcome Photographic Exposure Record and Diary* was also given to team members, who were encouraged to fill in the date, time of day, aperture, shutter speed, and light.[55]

The instructions on the 1912 circulars suggest that visual documentation was not sufficient on its own as evidence.[56] While the collection of views provided a visual record of the activities of the expedition, additional work was needed to fashion those views into useful data. The combination of labeling, color scheme notations, and connections between photographs and more detailed drawings formed a minable database indexing itineraries, geographies, practices, and people. The 1912 circulars primarily contained instructions on the use of photography as an aid in documenting collected materials.

Bingham instructed team members that photographs, considered supplements to sketches, should be taken before, during, and after excavations.[57] The images needed to record the geographic locality, geological formation, and the position and orientation of all human remains.[58] Specific instructions for labeling the photographs were included in an attempt to enable the collector to link specimens with locations. A random assortment of images would not be useful for future study. Instead, the photographs had to be tethered to other information.[59] Consequently, photographs were to be marked with the serial numbers given to them by the quartermaster on the lower right-hand corner of the glossy side of the negative print on the margin of the film so as not to show on the image. On the left side, the photographer needed to write in the month, day, and his initials.[60] This contextualization was done with other expeditionary practices, too. Luther Nelson, the physician on the 1912 expedition, was contractually obligated to keep a comprehensive record of his entire time with the expedition. Photography and meteorological notations were crucial. For his images, he needed to include "date, time of day, weather condition, exposure of the place, direction of the camera, and position of the camera, whether level or slanting. Also a full agreement of the subject of the picture, describing in clear, concise, exact terms, with native names, and all available data."[61]

Like others of his era, Bingham was concerned about the role that personal subjectivity played in science, and he enlisted technologies that might mitigate the perils of personal bias and suppress the self. He hired topographers and geologists who could measure and assess findings, and he brought along cameras to document expeditionary feats. In *Across South America*, for example, Bingham lamented the camera's deficiency in duplicating the grandeur that the eye sees: "Photographs absolutely fail to do it justice, for at best they show only a few boulders, a small part of one of the walls. If taken far enough away to show the whole fort, the eye loses all sense of the great size of the stone units owing to the fact that they are so much larger than any stones to which it is accustomed."[62] The camera did not translate intention accurately by reproducing what Bingham had seen. Despite the technology's deficiency in capturing Bingham's eye, it

Figure 3.2. An untitled lantern slide, hand-tinted by W. C. Ives in Mystic, Connecticut, for use in Bingham's illustrated lectures, 1911. Yale Peruvian Expedition Papers (MS 664), Manuscripts and Archives, Yale University library.

was still better than "mere sketches or drawings." In writing about his visit to Tiahuanaco, Bingham cited the work of Squier, only to lament that his drawings gave "an erroneous impression of the size of many of the mountains which are not so large as he has represented them."[63] Attempting to represent Bingham's eye faithfully was the burden of scientific observation and calculation.

Instructions for coloring the slides were included in the 1912 circular. Anticipating the images' future use as evidence and illustrations for public lectures, Bingham told expedition members to use the Golsch reference color chart and number the film accordingly.[64] For example, the foreground could be numbered 41; foliage, 17; poncho, stripes alternation 8 and 1; small stripes 24, and so forth (see fig. 3.2).[65] Bingham assured team members that while marking the image for future coloring took a great deal of time, it was not wasted if accurately and carefully done. Bingham's instructions attempted to stabilize the technology, reducing not only the noise inherent in the capturing of one's intention, but also the black-and-white photograph's fleeting, slippery, shifting, and lost meaning.

The photographic circulars for the 1914 expedition expanded upon the instructions from the 1912 expedition. Perhaps in part because of Bingham's absence during the first year of the expedition, the 1914 circulars offered greater detail and direction on expeditionary photography. The instructions for the 1912 expedition provided careful detail for labeling the images and using photography as a complement to sketches when collecting archaeological remains. In contrast, the 1914 circulars contained specific direction on the making of pictures. They thus provide insight into the evolving needs of the expedition and the ways in which making pictures became the expeditions' most valued scientific practice.

Photographic negatives were assigned to each member based on the kind of work he was doing, the number of photographs taken by other members of the expedition, and the person's skill in taking photographs.[66] So, for example, Erdis was given negatives 6,000–6,200, and the surgeon, Ford, was given 8,201–8,400. The most negatives were given to the naturalist, Edmund Heller (6,401–6,800) and to the topographer (7,505–7,999). Negatives 8,580–9,004 were left open for later assignment.

For the 1914 expedition, Bingham sought to further direct and discipline the gaze of the expedition photographers. He offered explicit guidelines on which subjects were desired and how to obtain accurate views. The city of Cuzco, for example, was not of interest. Rather, Bingham wanted all film reserved for use in the field. Moreover, landscapes or objects connected with other departments of the expedition were to be taken only on request of the director or if it was likely that nobody else had already taken the picture.[67]

Simply snapping pictures was not enough. Taking pictures that would become valuable evidence required a considerable amount of know-how. Accuracy was required. For Bingham, accuracy meant materializing his original intention. Bingham urged the members of the expedition to understand the camera and to spend time making good pictures.

> The more painstaking the process of setting up the tripod, leveling the camera, using a small diaphragm, and accurate time exposure, and exact records of the time, place and subject, the better the results of the Expedition will be. No time is better spent than in studying your negatives after they have been developed and dried, with the record book in hand, seeing whether you got what you desired, whether the exposure was too much or too little, and whether the camera is working according to your expectations. Careless and hasty work in photography means waste of time, loss of opportunities, and poor results.[68]

Team members were instructed to go slow at first, becoming familiar not only with the camera, but also with the atmospheric conditions, the exposure meter, and the level.[69] Members were encouraged to learn to estimate the distances and focus of the camera, taking test images to ensure the reliability of the camera and its operator.[70] Snapshots were not desired. If it was not worth the effort of setting up the tripod, leveling it, and getting the exposure correct, "the photograph was not worth taking."[71] Above all, members needed to make records immediately after taking the image.[72] Without contextualizing the photograph and marking it according to weather conditions, the image was of little use as an accurate record.

Anyone who has taken photographs can sympathize with Bingham's frustration. After a period of time, one forgets the initial meaning of the view. Where was it taken? When was it taken? Why did I take it? The photograph is slippery as a record. Separated from contextualizing clues, the framed image becomes useless as scientific evidence. The expedition members took thousands of photographs. In the absence of contextualizing information and some level of skill in production, the images could not function as Bingham intended: as data and records for future study or as evidence of discovery. To mobilize photographs as facts, Bingham had to fix intention, disciplining observation through a lens. But Kodak's technology was not enough. The camera was only as scientifically useful as the hands of its operator.

During the second year of the third expedition, Bingham circulated detailed instructions on how to develop the negatives, including fixing solutions and baths, tank developing, and printing photographs.[73] The considerable number of steps, coupled with the conditions in which members developed the film, offers a sense of the vulnerability of photographic evidence and, by association, of the outcome of the expedition and Bingham's reputation.

First, expedition photographers were told how to prepare the developing solutions. They were provided with two powders to be mixed and dissolved in hot water in the developing tanks. The mixed solution was good for only one roll of film.[74] After developing, the tanks had to be washed with at least three changes of water before establishing the fixing bath. The film was fixed with an acidifier consisting of acidic acid, powdered aluminum, and sulfide of soda; that solution could fix fifteen to twenty-five rolls of film. The film had to be developed in a tank in which one had to wind the film in a darkened box. The cylinder was then removed, kept tightly closed, and placed in a developing solution. Prints had to be left in the hypo bath for at least twenty minutes and then washed for about twenty minutes or longer.[75]

Taking pictures was a challenge.[76] It was difficult to differentiate the "find" because of flat light, lack of color variation, and overgrown surroundings,[77] and the technologies themselves were often problematic.[78] After returning from the third expedition, Bingham wrote George Eastman about the significant challenges of the Cirkut (panorama) camera. He complained about the poor quality of the mechanism: "carelessly made" film spindles that did not turn easily, and a tripod head that was bent. But Bingham's main frustration focused on not getting satisfactory results: "I did not entrust the Cirkut camera at first to anyone else, as I was very anxious to get as good results as possible, and I realized that the percentage of loss was going to be high."[79] Bingham went on to explain that even though he cared for the cameras, keeping them oiled and cleaned, he lost more than half the exposures, a higher percentage than on the previous expeditions. He blamed the machine: "Even so I was repeatedly disappointed and chagrined to find that, after climbing at great expenditure of time and energy to . . . a high mountain, with a half dozen films in my pocket, I could not get the machine to give me one single perfect exposure." Bingham eventually gave up on the machine, which was meant to be used by the topographers: "For heaven's sake don't ever send an explorer away again with a lot of carelessly made Cirkut films! I never have cursed so much in my life as I did when up on the top of cold and frequently snow-clad mountains, to have the Cirkut cameras . . . refuse to turn, stick and turn irregularly!"

The amount of time and effort expended by members on taking images, hauling and heating water, processing the negatives, and labeling and systematizing their records affirms that photography was a critical, though suspect, expeditionary practice. The camera did not necessarily capture intention, and the photograph, as fact, was unstable.[80] At times, the machine seemed to be at odds with, even a direct adversary of, manifesting expeditionary desires. To produce the reality of Bingham's lost city, team members, the landscape, and the camera were negotiated to realize the shot into scientific evidence. The collecting of views passed through trials of strength, necessitating a keen sense of work, effort, dedication, diligence, and negotiation on the part of the photographer to quiet the silent actors of time, memory, atmosphere, and the camera.[81] The photographic extraction from Kodak's cameras of team members' intention was anything but a reflection.

Circulating Evidence, Mobilizing Facts

Returning after the 1911 expedition, Bingham remarked that while he was not permitted to bring a wall of Machu Picchu back to the United States, he did have excellent photographs.[82] Bingham sent the collection of negatives to Eastman Kodak in Rochester, New York, where they were printed in their entirety for a special price.[83] Bingham selected the specific tone, treatment, and paper for printing the negatives based on the effect that they would lend to the photographs as scientific documents.[84] Kodak assembled the photographs, mounting them in chronological order in albums.[85] Bingham and his secretary then pasted typed descriptions beneath the photographs to provide contextual details. Often, the images cross-referenced one another to help provide a sense of completion (see fig. 3.3). The donated films and camera equipment provided Bingham and the National Geographic Society with ample evidence for unveiling Machu Picchu to a global public.[86]

The accumulation of thousands of images affirmed the privileged position held by photography as a scientific expeditionary practice. Certain members were provided with a camera and film and given a set of instructions on how to take pictures, where to take pictures, which subjects were appropriate for pictures, and how to properly develop the negatives in the field. They were asked to make test images to ensure that they could capture and inscribe intent. Finally, they were asked to label and contextualize the images for future research and to provide color matches for hand tinting. Photographs were then catalogued and organized for future study.[87]

Using the expeditions' most important scientific tool required a significant amount of time and attention on the part of the team. Paul Bestor, Bingham's assistant on the 1912 expedition, spent much of his time developing and assisting in the taking of photographs. In two journal entries about Bingham's visit to Machu Picchu, he wrote that after he left camp at seven a.m. on July 25, he took dictation and assisted Bingham in photographing the ruins. On the following day, Bestor developed six films and typed orders.[88] Bestor's time was centered on crafting photographic evidence.

And yet the photograph, once it was visualized as scientific evidence, eclipsed the work, relationships, and technology involved. The camera technology, climate, and labor involved were elided in the reproduction of prints in a variety of media. Although obtaining an image required the thoughtful negotiation of Kodak's camera technology, Bingham's instruc-

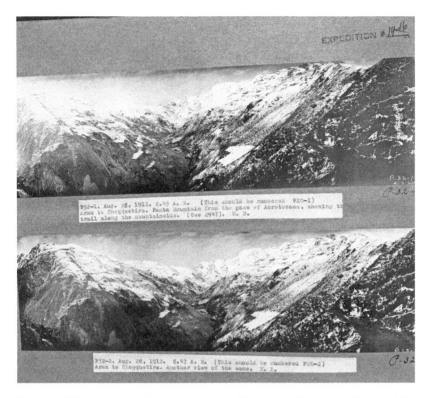

Figure 3.3. Two panoramic photographs in expedition photo album, 1912. Photograph by the author.

tions, and the damp and changing Andean climate, the images were considered direct imprints of reality, even though Bingham publicly discussed how challenging it had been to obtain a photograph.[89] The successful coupling of displacement and representation allowed for the photographic translation of Andean landscapes to constitute the facts of the expedition, and of Machu Picchu as a lost city discovered in the clouds.[90]

In April 1913, *National Geographic* published "In the Wonderland of Peru," an issue entirely dedicated to Bingham and the Yale Peruvian Expedition.[91] In it was a specially printed, hand-folded panorama photograph (fig. 3.4).[92] The panorama not only sat in the hands of the magazine's readers, but was also picked up as illustration for newspaper copy. On June 15, 1913, "Lost City in the Clouds Found after Centuries" was published in the *Boston Morning Herald*, along with the panorama photograph of Machu Picchu.[93]

Photographs became critical actors as evidence of the last (or perhaps

Figure 3.4. "The Ruins of the Ancient Inca Capital, Machu Picchu," Hiram Bingham, 1912. The photograph was made possible by Kodak's panoramic camera technology. Courtesy National Geographic Society.

first) place of the Incas, and as a flexible technology. Photography tested in the tropics allowed the expedition to bring back evidence of its explorations, producing compelling narratives about scientific expeditions generally, but also about Incan discoveries, lost cities, Andean landscapes, and native subjects. Obtaining images necessitated figuring the camera and expedition members to work toward that end. The expeditions' most powerful scientific evidence relied on a disciplining practice that sought to stem the tide of both suspicion and unruliness.

Making pictures in the laboratory of Latin America produced and therefore claimed the Andes as a dedicated space for US scientists. This was not a scientific expedition by patriots to help marshal a nation into modernity.[94] Rather, this was an expedition reminiscent of those of an earlier era, when outsiders removed evidentiary objects and local knowledge for reflection and production at home.[95] Although Peruvians such as Martín Chambi eventually used camera technology to frame their own imaginings of Machu Picchu,[96] Yale's laboriously produced images brought Machu Picchu and indigenous subjects into a field of visibility, enabling a powerful gaze that quickly circulated into a variety of spatial and textual fields throughout the United States, in Peru, and abroad. The panoramic view in particular acted to obscure difference and history through its totalizing frame. Through the panorama, Bingham claimed the Andean space, fetishizing it into the lost city. Peruvians helped guide Bingham to Machu Picchu, but making its picture was the exclusive privilege of Yale.

Ultimately, the team's photographs became collected objects, evidencing and indexing a monumental find for scholars, aficionados, and a global public. Circulating beyond their initial intent as an extracted record of and for scientific inquiry, the photographs became potent fixers and fixations of people and history. Yet the vulnerability of the camera's capacity as a scientific technology of extraction marks Machu Picchu and the Yale Peruvian Expeditions, promulgating a multiplicity of competing desires around the site that continues today. As the images resulting from the expeditionary lab work circulated, their meaning and informational content shifted, based on their insertion within diverse narrative frames. The camera was full of promise as an inscriber of scientific knowledge, but its products remained elusive and ultimately impossible to stabilize.

The panoramic image continues to circulate today. For the celebration of the centennial of Hiram Bingham's initial visit to Machu Picchu, an enlargement of the panoramic photo was included in the exhibition *Machu Picchu 100 Years: A Glimpse of the Expedition That Astonished the World*. The exhibition was displayed on the fourth floor of the Sumaq Machu Picchu Hotel, with images on loan from the National Geographic Society. The panoramic photograph was also included in National Geographic's exhibition *Machu Picchu: A Lost City Uncovered; Photographs from the Hiram Bingham Expeditions, 1911–1915*, which ran from July 24, 2011, through September 11, 2011. Most recently, National Geographic and Yale celebrated the centennial of the "In the Wonderland of Peru" issue by comparing the photographs of the expeditions with current photographs of Machu Picchu. The panoramic comparison was highlighted on National Geographic's website as evidence of the remarkable unchanging sameness between now and then.

In contrast to the perception of indexical persistence, this chapter demonstrates the role and importance of camera technology on the three tours that Bingham made to Peru. The camera was not simply a tool that easily or automatically reproduced Bingham's scientific intentions. Rather, both the technology and its product were suspect. Much work and effort were expended to shore up such instability.

The photographs produced through the expeditionary lens continue to be used as evidence of historical discovery, locating the site within a specific time and gaze. The life of these photographs, while continuing to offer up the lost city, has been both unstable and remarkably malleable. Paradoxically, such flexibility is the photographs' strength, marking them as potent and persistent meaning makers for both Bingham and Machu Picchu.

CHAPTER 4

Discovery Aesthetics

The Indians are very fond of having their pictures taken. One Indian, when he found he could have his picture taken free, dressed in his Sunday clothes. The next day he returned to see the photograph. When he was shown the negative he refused to believe that it was his picture because he couldn't see the colors and the spangles that decorate that Sunday coat he wore.
LUTHER T. NELSON, 1912

After Bingham returned from the 1911 expedition, he attracted the attention of the director and editor of *National Geographic Magazine*,[1] Gilbert Grosvenor.[2] Grosvenor wrote Bingham that he believed Machu Picchu was by far the most important geographic discovery made in South America, and he wanted to find out more about the lost city and its inhabitants.[3] The National Geographic Society became a major sponsor of the 1912 and 1914–1915 expeditions to Peru, granting Bingham $30,000 for them. The 1912 expedition was the sixteenth that the society supported, but only the seventh with funding.[4] Bingham published four articles about the expeditions in the magazine: "Exploration in Peru," "In the Wonderland of Peru," "The Story of Machu Picchu," and "Further Explorations in the Land of the Incas."[5] In 1930, *Machu Picchu: A Citadel of the Incas* was published by Yale University Press for the society.[6] The April 1913 issue of *National Geographic Magazine* consisted of 244 illustrations and was entirely dedicated to Bingham's expeditions in Peru.[7] The issue circulated worldwide, its images and text being reprinted and translated in a number of publications, including the Peruvian periodicals *Ilustración Peruana*, *Peru To-Day*, and *La Crónica*.

The documentary, framing, and reproducible nature of photography were critical for the science of Bingham's Yale Peruvian Expeditions and the subsequent invention of Machu Picchu as national patrimony. Here I address how the framing of the initial photographic images of Machu Picchu was shaped by scientific, commercial, and national desires and designs. Through a reading of the images and text of the April 1913 edition of *National Geographic* and those of *Ilustración Peruana* that appeared shortly thereafter, I extend the analysis of representation to situate the photographs not simply as depositories of form or gaze, but rather as circulating imagined materials that shaped, and continue to shape, enduring global images of the archaeological site and a nation.

Photographs became one of the primary and most powerful forms of evidence of the expeditions' research and findings. Newspaper and magazine articles, often accompanied by photographs, recounted the incredible find and positioned Bingham and the expeditionary team as noble adventurers sacrificing themselves for the global good of science. In US publications, the ruins were said to be overgrown with vegetation, virtually deserted, and mysterious.[8] Much of the site, however, had been cleared by local inhabitants by the time the Yale expedition arrived, and several haciendas, or estates, producing wood and tea claimed the area.[9] Machu Picchu was regionally known before Bingham's discovery, and thinly inhabited. Some of Bingham's initial photographs from the 1911 expedition show those inhabitants.[10] Nonetheless, the US media image of Machu Picchu as a discovered lost city circulated globally through newspaper articles, museum exhibitions, illustrated magazines, and lectures, in time becoming the iconic image we know today.

Uniquely, photography acted as the technology for both the collection of scientific evidence and the collected object. In the printing and reproduction of photographic images, the expeditions' view was materialized or commoditized. Ideas were registered in the frame of the photograph. Like maps, Yale's photographs relied on their insertion in texts to establish meaning, denying the objects' makers and their history.[11] But as the imagining of scientific authority about Peru was differentially materialized and inserted into new texts and contexts, its initial meaning, itself unstable, could be modified. As Elizabeth Edwards and Janice Hart have suggested, the visualized referent and the photograph as object are inseparable.[12] Instead, we might think of photographs as "material performances that enact a complex range of historiographical desires."[13] Nativist sentiments of Peruvian patrimony were espoused alongside claims of universal scientific discovery. The photograph as scientific object was, like all texts, unstable as it circulated and was translated, rematerialized anew.

"In the Wonderland of Peru": Bingham and *National Geographic*

The National Geographic Society began in 1888 as an amateur scientific organization that targeted gentleman scholars.[14] Focused on geographic and commercial possibilities abroad, the society sought to bring home to its members "the world and all that is in it."[15] Grosvenor, along with Alexander Graham Bell,[16] sought to expand the society's presence and the magazine's readership by focusing on popular rather than technical articles.[17] Photographs became a primary avenue toward this end, and images quickly became an integral part of the magazine.

In 1905, Grosvenor, desperate to fill the pages of the magazine's January edition, included eleven pages of photographs. The issue was so successful that he apparently said that the word "photograph" became as musical to his ear as the jingle of a cash register to a businessman.[18] As the cost of photoengraving came down, it became cheaper to include images in the magazine. Additionally, travelers, diplomats, and amateur photographers submitted most of the photographs printed in the magazine—and did not charge the society for their use.[19] By 1908, pictures filled more than half of the magazine's pages.[20]

The photographs included in the magazine were considered straightforward. That is, because travelers supplied the images, the photographs did not rely on artistic or pictorial treatments, but rather were somewhat naïve prints from amateurs.[21] Consequently, the society adopted a "realist code" for images that implied a direct transcription of reality, one that could be read and understood by any reader without deep study.[22] Bingham's images of landscapes, cultural types, and rock formations were characteristic of such realism; they sought to show the wonderland of Peru through a scientific and naturalistic eye.

Sponsoring the second two expeditions and their archaeological goals was not initially an obvious move for the society.[23] Archaeology was not part of the society's geographic mission, and Grosvenor had difficulty in encouraging board members to sponsor Bingham's 1912 expedition. Bingham wrote that the plans he had developed for the 1912 expedition specifically emphasized "the archaeological side of things," in keeping with Grosvenor's interest in "ruins, the lost cities, and the bones."[24] Eventually, the society agreed to sponsor two expeditions, but declined to sponsor one in 1917.[25] The arrangement for the 1912 sponsorship included $10,000, along with any instruments needed by the topographer, in exchange for publication rights to any reports and articles emanating from the expedition.[26] National Geographic also helped Bingham find a topographer.[27] After seeing the photographic results from the 1912 expedition, Grosvenor believed there was much more to know. Bingham was the best person for the job and needed to continue his work. As Grosvenor put it: "Somebody is going to solve the mystery connected with these ancient peoples. Let us get there first."[28]

The agreement between Bingham and the society was clear.[29] In return for significant monetary sponsorship, Bingham would grant *National Geographic* rights of first refusal on any popular articles emanating from the expedition, including the preliminary report, "*illustrated by the best photographs taken by the expedition.*"[30] A month after the publication of the preliminary report in *National Geographic*, Bingham could publish technical and scientific articles in scientific periodicals. The Memorandum of Agreement also stipulated that Yale University would use "every means in its power to prevent any article or photograph from being given to any other magazine."[31] Bingham agreed to perform a scientific expedition that would include a geologist, an archaeologist, a surgeon, a civil engineer, and suitable assistants.[32]

The Memorandum of Agreement for the 1914–1915 expeditions differed only slightly.[33] It included a commitment to receive a popular article of 6,000–7,000 words written by Bingham, with an option for a second article covering material not highlighted in the first article. The magazine was given first rights of refusal on all publications derived from the expedition. No other magazine or scientific journal could publish articles until after *National Geographic* published its first article. Lastly, the society had the option of collecting and publishing a technical memoir consisting of all the papers and technical results of the expedition. The society continued to have first rights to use photographs and maps made by the members of the expedition. If the magazine recouped the publication expenses for an issue devoted to the expedition, Bingham would receive a 15 percent commission on all copies sold thereafter.

By the time the "Wonderland" issue was published in April 1913, *Harper's Magazine*, the *Bulletin of the American Geographical Society*, the *Proceedings of the American Antiquarian Society*, and the *American Journal of Science* had published several stories about the expeditions.[34] US newspapers had documented the discovery, too: "Explorers Find a City That Was 'Snuggled under Corn Fields,'" *New York Herald*, December 22, 1911; "Bingham's Climbing of Mt. Coropuna," *Boston Transcript*, December 16, 1911; "Taxi Ride His Most Thrilling Experience."[35] Still, Grosvenor believed that not enough people were aware of the discovery of Machu Picchu and its importance.³⁶ Many of the publications were aimed at smaller scientific audiences, and the stories in *Harper's* were published with practically no illustrations. Because of that lack of imagery, Grosvenor believed that the importance of the discovery of Machu Picchu was "grasped by very few people," and that the general geographic public, whom the society represented, knew nothing of it.³⁷

In many ways, Grosvenor was Machu Picchu's first publicist, and he was instrumental in making the image of Machu Picchu familiar around the world. In addition to encouraging the National Geographic Society to fund the expeditions, he oversaw the 1913 "Wonderland" issue, advising Bingham on what to include in the story. Although Grosvenor believed that Bingham's first draft was the "most extraordinary narrative of discovery in South America" that he had read, he requested several changes and additions for the article.³⁸

On December 31, 1912, Grosvenor wrote that what the society really wanted was "'meat,' facts and information rather than personal movements of various members of the party." It wanted information on ancient peoples and new cities—not so much mapping as human interest, including the "manners, life and civilization of the ancient people who built this remarkable city."³⁹ For a meeting on January 11, Grosvenor hoped that Bingham could bring "a large number" of photographs and that they might talk over the article then.⁴⁰

Ultimately, Grosvenor requested a brief review of the 1911 expedition and a number of images showing "the extraordinary beauty of the route to Machu Picchu."⁴¹ He wanted to give the complete story of Machu Picchu and its discovery by Yale. He asked Bingham to bring readers up to date about how Machu Picchu was found by the expedition, accompanied by "two natives."⁴² He requested several paragraphs about why Machu Picchu was superior to previously discovered Incan ruins and why the discovery of Machu Picchu, "the cradle of the Inca race," was especially important.⁴³ He asked Bingham questions: "How many people do you suppose lived at Machu Picchu?" "Is the soil on the terraces fertile?" "Would it not be well to add to the article a paragraph describing Machu Picchu in reference to the panorama?" "Would it perhaps be well to refer to the special monograph planned on Machu Picchu?" "Add some more about Vitcos?" Grosvenor wanted Bingham to speculate about whether any of the buildings at Machu Picchu resembled ancient ruins in Egypt or Asia.⁴⁴ He wrote that Bingham shouldn't omit anything he had written, but simply add.

Grosvenor selected the illustrations to accompany the text and had the final say on the arrangement of the magazine's layout. References to the panorama insert and place-names used in connection with the description of pictures were considered helpful. Grosvenor wrote Bingham: "In your Geographic article you give a fine description of how the bridge was made, but a picture of the wild country is also needful."[45] It was also difficult to choose the best photographs to use because they weren't titled. Bingham needed to provide the general subjects of the photos and explanations of which ruins they referred to.[46] Grosvenor directed Bingham to arrange all the proofs in sequence and to use the "titles and descriptive text for the pictures to form a more or less consecutive story or description."[47] He also needed names inserted on an outline map, including all places mentioned in the text.[48]

Bingham dutifully responded to Grosvenor and attempted to create a cohesive narrative around the images.

> I have tried to plan the titles and descriptive text for the pictures to form a more or less consecutive story, or description as you requested. It has been harder to make the titles than the descriptive text. I have included pictures of the ruins of Pacaritampu, but regret that we have none of the ruins of top of Huayna Picchu. I have also advised you regarding the best pictures of the monolith at Vitcos.
>
> I am now going to try to add to the article a few paragraphs telling how we found the city in 1911, and some other paragraphs regarding the extraordinary beauty of the route to Machu Picchu, and I will try and follow your other suggestions as far as I can.[49]

As publicist, Grosvenor had control over the story. Besides directing the narrative of the story in the "Wonderland" issue, he managed the story's rollout.[50] When Grosvenor learned that the *New York Times* was about to publish an article accompanied by photographs from the 1912 expedition before the "Wonderland" issue went to press, he sent an urgent telegram to Bingham, asking how the paper had gotten the story and accompanying images.[51] The National Geographic Society had exclusive rights to the 1912 Yale Peruvian Expedition story, and Grosvenor did not want even the *Yale Alumni Newsletter* to see an advance copy or pictures of the edition.[52] As the society's contract with Bingham stated, it had exclusive rights to the first popular story of the expedition, illustrated by the best photographs taken by the expedition. Premature newspaper coverage threatened to spoil the powerful unveiling of Machu Picchu, and Grosvenor admonished Bingham: "I do not think even you realize the sensation that the article will make as produced in our Magazine."[53]

The editorial team at *National Geographic* consisted of Grosvenor and John Oliver La Gorce. The two men were committed to bringing the article out in a "most striking and emphatic form."[54] This meant an issue heavily illustrated with artistic, beautiful, yet instructive photographs— the "best" the expedition had taken. The editorial philosophy of the magazine was to organize and structure the magazine along photographic lines, with the text being shaped to support the images.[55] Grosvenor insisted that without photographs, the public would know nothing of the discovery and would not be able to understand or imagine the place. Photographs were essential: it was through the images of Machu Picchu that Bingham's work came to life. The discovery was the photographs. The society had exclusive rights to the first article with the "best photographs taken by the expedition" and consequently to the story of Machu Picchu's discovery. Wonder and the "intense pleasure of looking" were part of a strategy to claim possession that was realized not simply through words but also by images.[56]

Grosvenor selected the illustrations for the "Wonderland" issue out of albums provided by Bingham. The albums assembled by Kodak were used as a reference tool for requesting reproductions.[57] Engravings, too, were made from the albums.[58] The photographic imaginings of Machu Picchu contained evidence that, although indexical, could be manipulated, enhanced, shuttled, and exchanged.

From the albums, Grosvenor crafted a compelling and sellable narrative about Machu Picchu. He selected 202 photographs and 16 panoramas from the 1912 albums.[59] He tailored the issue to be more popular than technical, telling Bingham that he should publish the scientific articles one at a time in several journals to gain more publicity for the expedition.[60] Although Grosvenor said that the society eventually wanted to publish the articles in a separate volume, publicity and prestige would be better achieved by the publication of a series of articles, eventually culminating in a monograph.[61] Grosvenor was excited about the "Wonderland" issue, telling Bingham in February 1913, "We are going to astound the public when we get this article out in our March number."[62]

The "Wonderland" issue privileged the photographic frame as the primary means of conveying Machu Picchu to *National Geographic*'s readership. As a result, maps were marginalized, even though their creation had played a prominent role in the work of the expeditions. Mapmaking in Peru was the full-time employment of several men, and the drafting of the map required the full-time dedication of the topographer, Albert Bumstead, after he returned from the field in 1912. Mapmaking had been a primary scientific goal of the first expedition, too, and the work of the topographer, Kai Hendriksen, was so valued that he was the only paid expedition member. Since mapmaking offered tangible proof of scientific work, Bingham urged Grosvenor to include the map in the "Wonderland" issue.[63] For Bingham, the map, quite costly to make, had artistic value and was also of great scientific interest.[64] Grosvenor, however, was not interested in including the map in the "Wonderland" issue. He insisted that the map be printed separately because it was of interest to select readers and would be too costly to print in the issue.[65] Although the society acquired prestige from its reputation as a scientific organization, it did not tailor the magazine to the science-minded public.[66] Expeditionary feats coupled with beautiful imagery made for better copy than maps did.[67]

At the time of the "Wonderland" issue, the magazine's print run exceeded 210,000 copies.[68] Grosvenor informed Bingham that each copy would be examined and read by (at least) five people on average.[69] Altogether, nearly one million people or more, Grosvenor said, would read the edition on Machu Picchu.[70] Grosvenor was intent on expanding the readership of the magazine, and the impressive "Wonderland" issue was an effort in that direction.

> My dear Bingham:
> The next time you are in Washington I am going to take you down to see the printing shop. You will then appreciate what a tremendous job getting out the National Geographic Magazine is. Six big and most modern presses working night and day, week in and week out, are not able to take care of the job, and therefore the printer is building a large new plant, which will afford room for the installation of additional machines.
> Yours Faithfully,
> Gilbert Grosvenor
> P.S. Our circulation today is double that of Century, and I believe at least 100,000 more than Harper's.[71]

Dedicating an entire expanded issue to one story was a significant statement for the society, and no expense was spared. The issue included the specially printed, hand-folded panorama photograph. The expensive insert was thought to be not only visually arresting, but also exciting for the reader, as Grosvenor told Bingham: "As I have previously written you, your work in Peru is by far the most important geographical discovery made in South America, to my knowledge. For this reason our Society is sparing no expense to bring your article out in a most striking and emphatic form. The panorama is going to cost about $2,000, and we are, furthermore, devoting not only an entire magazine to the subject, but are making the month's issue considerably larger than usual in order to contain the complete series of pictures."[72] Although the "Wonderland" issue came out nearly two years after the initial sighting of Machu Picchu, Bingham later admitted that he did not realize the magnitude of his findings until he saw his photographs published there.[73] In October 1913, Bingham wrote Grosvenor: "Your prediction about our articles in the National Geographic Magazine was more than justified by the results. I was astonished to see how many people knew about it and what a large percentage had read it. Of course, presenting it in the attractive form that you did, giving us not only the whole magazine, but making the magazine practically a double number, aroused an unusual amount of interest."[74]

The *National Geographic* issue did reach millions of people.[75] The photographs and text were translated into a number of global publications. The *Illustrated London News* and the French version of the illustrated news carried the images.[76] In Peru, two prominent magazines, *Peru To-Day* and *Ilustración Peruana*, mimicked the *National Geographic* issue. The expeditions' photographs were also made into hand-painted lantern slides to be used in lectures like those given to the American Geographical Society in New York on November 25, 1913.[77] The photographs were displayed in several exhibitions, including one by Kodak that toured the United States for two seasons. The display consisted of bromide enlargements accompanied by lantern slides used to illustrate lectures.[78] In 1914, Kodak sponsored an exhibition of expedition photographs at the Panama-Pacific International Exposition in San Francisco.[79] The National Geographic Society developed an exhibition of 200 photographs that were displayed in connection with the second Pan-American Congress, and the society exhibited Yale Peruvian Expedition photographs in its offices in January 1916.[80] A similar exhibition was displayed at Yale in 1916. By 1917, Yale University had opened a Peruvian exhibition room featuring artifacts and photographs from the expeditions to Peru.[81] The images have been, and continue to be, published in a variety of contexts, reinforcing the naturalness, timelessness, and obviousness of a lost city discovered in the clouds, today an icon of Peru.[82]

Visualizing Discovery

The images in "In the Wonderland of Peru" tend to be landscapes or detailed close-ups of the granite walls of Machu Picchu. Breathtaking distant vistas are included, along with examples of the ruins before and after clearing. The photographs highlight the remoteness of the place by emptying the landscape of work and of people. Very few images of the expedition team, workers, or work being done are included. Of 244 illustrations, six show workers or work being done (or about to be done). In other images, people act as indicators of scale, as evidence of racial types, or as adornments adding interest to an image. The photographic narrative is predominantly scenic: picturesque country, lush vegetation, rocky outcrops, terraced hillsides, impressive stone masonry, and the occasional "Indian."

The issue begins with a small reference map of the region explored by the expedition, which serves to orient the reader for the photographic journey ahead. As the article opens, we join Bingham at the seaports through two images: one photograph of the team members in front of a fisherman's hut with reed boats, and another with a fisherman and his catch of the day—two manta rays. Before heading off to Cuzco via Juliaca on the train, the team members visit Lima, where they witness a Corpus Christi procession. From there, we journey across the Andean countryside, through several photographs of llamas taken near various railroad stations and town plazas. In the countryside, we see the local people in photographs labeled "Group of Mountain Indians," "A Typical Mountaineers' Hut," "A Typical Peruvian Indian Woman," "A Scene at Sicuani Station, Southern Peru."[83] The Peruvian scene set, we cross the Apurímac River and begin our exploration of the Andean mountains.

The "Wonderland" issue is a photographic narrative of travel. As the reader turns the heavily illustrated pages, we accompany Bingham as he experiences the wonderland of Peru. We witness and perform our own scientific discovery as we read the copy and view the photographs. As we wait in Lima to catch the train that will take us into the Andes, we view Quechua speakers in their different styles of dress, spinning yarn—visual objects of the countryside. We see dozens of llamas. In the Andes, we must build a bridge to cross the river and join a mule train up the mountain trail. After making the arduous journey, we turn the page, and arrive at the sumptuous visual feast of the sanctuary of Machu Picchu. The reader performs discovery with each turn of the page, virtually witnessing, and thus concretizing, claims of the Yale Peruvian Expeditions' feats.

Figure 4.1. "Bird's-Eye View of Machu Picchu (During Clearing) and the Urubamba Canon," Hiram Bingham, 1912. Courtesy National Geographic Society.

In *National Geographic*, Bingham's aesthetic is physical achievement and conquest. After being shown the team's difficulty in crossing the Apurímac, the reader is presented with the photo "Bird's-Eye View of Machu Picchu (During Clearing) and the Urubamba Canon" (fig. 4.1). Shot from a distanced and elevated position the image captivates the viewer, its mysteries beckoning. As the river winds around the mountains, we see faint, tantalizing views of the ruins. Additional images of the Urubamba Valley depict mule trails winding up the mountainside. Finally, detailed photographs of the monument are shown. Intermingled with the numerous photographs of terraces, rock walls, niches, and stairwells are depictions of precipitous heights and long and lean cloudy-skied panoramas.

The aesthetic of discovery beckons the reader to travel with the scientific expedition on its journey. Photographs highlighting team members building a bridge, crossing the Urubamba River, and following mule trails are included to carry the viewer along on the expedition, and also to act as visual evidence of the expedition's physical achievements and scientific exploration. The "Wonderland" issue is the tale of an arduous physical journey and the discovery of the once hidden. Bingham's success, as framed in *National Geographic*, is to unveil what had been there the entire time. With this narrative of travel couched in an aesthetic of discovery, the readers of the magazine journey on an expedition to discover for themselves the wonderland that is Peru (see fig. 4.2).

Images of human subjects in the "Wonderland" issue are limited. Except for the half dozen images of typical "Quechua Indians" presented in the initial pages of the story, representations of human subjects are sparse. The hired laborers are sometimes included in the detailed photographs of the monument's stairwells, walls, and niches to indicate scale or perhaps to add interest to an otherwise mundane image. The workers, however, are not the subjects of the image. Rather, they are incidental to the impressive stone construction of the ancient city (see fig. 4.3). In addition to these images of workers as human yardsticks, the "Wonderland" issue includes a photograph of men working to clear the sites, three images of men with the team members in caves, and close-up portraits of two workers.[84]

The portraits of the two workers are displayed midway through the issue. The first, titled "A Cheerful Workman From Cuzco," is of Alegría, "Mr. Happiness." The caption conveys that while he was one of the most consistent employees of the expedition, many of the other contracted workers were less reliable. As Bingham put it: "Most of the workmen were content with what wages they could earn in two weeks, and kept us continually busy trying to replace them."[85] Alegría is the presentation of anomaly, and he stares curiously into the camera. The second portrait, of Enrique Porres, is included to document the Andean practice of chewing coca. Titled "The Best type of Indian Workman: Southern Peru," the photograph shows Porres with a slight bulge in the cheek (fig. 4.4). The caption reads:

> Portrait of Enrique Porres, one of the most intelligent workmen that we had to assist in excavating Machu Picchu. In his cheek may be observed a swelling showing the presence of a quid of coca, the leaves of the plant from which cocaine is extracted. Nearly all the Mountain Indians chew the coca leaf. A quid is carefully made up at the beginning of the day's work, during the middle of the morning, at the commencement of the afternoon's work, and in the middle of the afternoon.[86]

The tight, decontextualized frames of the images, coupled with *National Geographic*'s titles and captions, essentialize and dehumanize Porres and Alegría. The two men, framed as Quechua types, are spectacles and objects one might see when traveling in the Peruvian wonderland. While Bingham seems to be quite fond of the two gentlemen, showing personal familiarity and an appreciation for their work in the article, the workers

Figure 4.2. "A Good Mule Road in Southern Peru," Hiram Bingham, 1912. Courtesy National Geographic Society.

Figure 4.3. "The Altar of the Chief Temple of Machu Picchu," Hiram Bingham, 1912. Courtesy National Geographic Society.

are displayed impersonally and without betraying details. As presented in the "Wonderland" issue, the two read not as helpful assistants participating in the expedition and its discoveries, but as curiosities that one might encounter, or employ, en route to discovering Machu Picchu. Even with Bingham's nod to their efforts, albeit one rooted in a racist comparative exceptionalism, the workers were not equivalent subjects to US expedition members.

The three subsequent photographs showing contracted laborers are titled "Excavating at Machu Picchu (Lt. Sotomayor, at the Right, in Charge of the Gang of Indians)," "Collecting the Skeletal Remains of the Ancient Inhabitants: Machu Picchu," and "A Large Burial Cave: Machu Picchu." The images and captions highlight expeditionary science in action, but seem inconsequential compared with the dozens of photographs highlighting the majesty of the views, stone walls, stairwells, niches, and rocky outcroppings of Machu Picchu. Instead, the workers fade into posed decorations of the monument and of discovery itself. Even though the team relied on local laborers for their knowledge and their fortitude, only expedition members are shown as the holders and makers of scientific knowledge. These few photographs serve to strengthen Bingham's and the team's subject position as makers and doers of science. The preparatory letter writing, fund-raising, and planning; the reconnaissance; and the clearing, excavating, and reconstructing of Machu Picchu

Figure 4.4. "The Best type of Indian Workman: Southern Peru," Hiram Bingham, 1912. Courtesy National Geographic Society.

are masked in the magazine, and the reader simply becomes a witness to the remarkable unveiling of a discovery.

The "Wonderland" issue closes with six images of Quechua "types" taken by the expedition's surgeon, Luther T. Nelson. Printed three to a page across the fold, the types are presented in a frame commonly used for expeditionary and early anthropological photographs.[87] Pictured in their unique dress, the subjects are shown in profile or facing the camera. The layout of the photographs, the images themselves, and the titles frame the individuals as types: "A Typical Cuzco Girl," "Another Quichua Woman: Cuzco," "Types of Indian Women in The Marketplace," "The Father of his Country," "Quichua Girl: Cuzco," and "A Typical Old Indian Woman in Cuzco" (fig. 4.5). Like the final photographs, an arranged still life of ceramic vessels, and a photograph titled "Sheep and a Little Mountain Shepherd near Chincheros," the portraits appear as curiosities collected on the scientific expedition—mere specimens. The "type" photographs reinforce the representation of scientific explorers discovering a lost but wonderful land.

Throughout the "Wonderland" issue, Machu Picchu is depicted as hidden, lost, or unknown. Bingham's scopic regime organizes Peru's territory through depopulation of the countryside, framed in a trope of tropicality. The aerial and long-distance panoramic views replace detail with the fantasy of conquering the unknown. Overgrown brush connotes heroic sacrifice and hidden lands. The site becomes devoid of people, and local knowledge is stripped from the images of Machu Picchu. Instead, the imaginative geography as printed in *National Geographic* demonstrates the physical achievement of the expedition through breathtaking vistas and bridge crossings. The aesthetic of discovery translated in *National Geographic* made Machu Picchu safe and consumable, serving up difference in the form of the distant and spectacular, inviting exploration. Readers of the photographic travel narrative could participate in the expedition from the comforts of their homes, discovering and conquering the place anew with each turn of the page.[88] *National Geographic Magazine* placed Machu Picchu in the laps of readers around the world, who could then perform their own imaginative travels to, and discovery of, the lost city, even enlisting a few exotic laborers in their cause.[89] Such virtual witnessing of Bingham's experiment helped solidify Machu Picchu as a discovered lost city in certain readers' minds. Cleaved from the social practices that brought it into sight, the circulation of photographs helped establish discovery as fact through its unlimited multiplication of witnesses.

Figure 4.5. "A Typical Cuzco Indian Mother and Baby," Luther T. Nelson, 1912. The caption reads: "She is patiently holding the surgeon's yardstick and wondering why she was having her picture taken." Although this is not from the last page of six, it is identical in style. Courtesy National Geographic Society.

Peruvian Translations

Since the publication of Benedict Anderson's *Imagined Communities* (1991), a significant body of scholarship has centered on nations and their representations.[90] Much of this work has focused on the rise and use of particular representational forms, whether in texts, images, or architecture, to reflect on how the state or populace negotiates and participates in the creation of nationhood. Scholars often conceive of texts and images as ideological imprints of domination and apparatuses of state and global power.[91] Others analyze texts and images as vehicles for popular expression and resistance to hegemony.[92] More recent scholarship extends this work to suggest that far from being fixed, national images are contingent and contested sites of identity and alterity, in constant reproduction and reassembly.[93] Mauricio Tenorio-Trillo suggests that we need to tell a story of how people define, consume, reject, and transform national images: "All in all the destinies of the various identities within a nation are constantly changing, challenging, and utilizing the nation according to specific circumstances."[94] National images, which are used across factions and classes, form a complex arena in which nations define one another through affirmation or negation.[95]

With respect to photography and science in Latin America, Deborah Poole has focused on how photography shapes identities and nations.[96] At the root of her research is an examination of how visual images and practices structured and reproduced particular scientific projects, cultural sentiments, and aesthetic dispositions characterizing the Peruvian nation in the late nineteenth and early twentieth centuries. In *Vision, Race, and Modernity* (1997), Poole provides a methodological framework in which the visual is part of an economy consisting of a network of exchange relationships that produce social relationships and knowledge about nations and their subjects.

Tracing the movement, exchange, and contextualization of photographs, Poole argues that they were critical to cultural and intellectual formations of Peru from European and Peruvian perspectives. She suggests that scientific understandings about race were made and challenged through photographs.[97] Poole's work highlights that the materiality and movement of the image is as important as its celluloid content.

I suggest that while images are not uniformly totalizing, an emphasis on translation and exchange might help illuminate the web in which national representations are suspended, and thereby help us understand how national logos are framed, felt, and embodied.[98] Such a reliance on translation and exchange necessitates the framing of the photographic image not only as an indexical referent or a visual representation, but also as material moving and circulating through space and time, the content of its imaging shifting along the way. In his posthumous text on visual forms, Alfred Gell rejects claims of semiotics that position art as simply a system of meanings for communication.[99] Instead, Gell argues that art is about doing and that it is generative. Drawing on Marilyn Strathern's notion of partible subjects, Gell suggests that objects become invested with personhood upon exchange and therefore should be conceptualized as parts of people circulating through and influencing social networks from a distance. Art is meant not simply to encode the world but to change it, and its study should begin with an inquiry into an object's effect in maintaining specific types of social relations. Representation is agential.

Photographs remain unique objects even as the image and its meaning are reproduced and reshaped in a constellation of contexts. The circulating photograph shapes actors and knowledge in distinct ways, but is also shaped by its actors. Thus, in the translational and relational process of its photographic wanderings, expeditionary photography operates distinctly as a practice of collecting and as an object for collection that, once in circulation, contributes to the formation of specific understandings. I follow one thread of photographic circulation to examine how the images published in *National Geographic* were received and reframed in a Peruvian national magazine. The intent is to demonstrate how the shifting aesthetics of discovery subsequently helped fashion social relationships and national identities. As Nicholas Mirzoeff has suggested, while visuality can be a medium of authority, it can also be an opportunity to mediate that authority.[100]

Ilustración Peruana was an illustrated biweekly magazine published in Lima.[101] Inspired by magazines such as *Prisma*, *Ilustración Peruana* included portraits of national figures and articles on fashion, art, and international affairs.[102] Most issues included graphic displays of the republic, including cities such as Cuzco, as well as articles about Peru's history by intellectuals such as Horacio Urteaga. Although news of Hiram Bingham's discovery of Machu Picchu was covered in Lima's and Cuzco's daily periodicals in 1911 and 1912, the editor of *Ilustración Peruana* wrote Bingham in 1913 after seeing the "Wonderland" issue:

> Peru recognizes the worth of your beautiful work published in National Geographic Magazine; the press of this capital noticed the beautiful description of Machu Picchu that was inserted in the columns of the

magazines, producing for you just and deserved praise. The Director of Ilustración Peruana, an illustrated biweekly magazine edited in this city has begun a month ago, to translate your valiant work with the reproduction of some of the more curious photogravure that illustrate it; in this way a grand service is lent to the culture of this country, that once in a Castilian version, one will taste the animated and erudite description of the explorer of the Urubamba. I wish you a thousand congratulations on your work, and thanks, as a Peruvian, for your propaganda in favor of my patria.[103]

The story in *Ilustración Peruana*, translated into Spanish by Julio Hernandez, covered bits and pieces of the *National Geographic* text. The Peruvian magazine managed to reprint 142 images from the "Wonderland" issue and about a quarter of the text.[104] The translated version spanned nine issues, each one carrying five to six pages of translated "Wonderland" text and photographs.[105]

In the July 10, 1912, issue, the editors of *Ilustración Peruana* wrote to the readers about the newly focused mission of the magazine: "Leaving aside the information of today and the literature of political order, Ilustración Peruana, in this new stage of its existence, wants to present itself, corresponding with its name, as a magazine displaying our culture, in which alongside the artful and historically evocative photograph and drawing, we broadly study our most interesting problems and publish a selection of stories and poetry by national authors." Besides presenting itself as an exponent of culture, *Ilustración Peruana* sought to promote Peru's modernity and promise as a nation through favorable visual propaganda. Through images of Peru's capital, ports, and monuments, *Ilustración Peruana* sought to expound a "general graphic knowledge of our vast territorial extension, not only in the country, but also especially internationally, where as it is well known there is a large group of people who still do not forget the feathers of the savages of our jungles nor do they imagine a city more or less habitable or comfortable in the majority of American republics" (June 7, 1911, 1097). Testing these suppositions was the magazine's "constant object." The translated pages of the "Wonderland" issue sought to demonstrate Peru's territorial extent and to promote the country's modernity through its beautifully imagined past.

Ilustración Peruana did not produce a facsimile of the "Wonderland" issue. Photographs were printed in a different order, though not wildly out of step with the original edition. The captions were translated directly, but the narrative of the article was edited to fit around a different layout. The

Peruvian version had a higher image-to-text ratio, and much of Bingham's narrative was therefore not included. Most significantly, however, were the editorial changes made to the photographs. The illustrations chosen for reproduction were primarily those that detailed the archaeological monument of Machu Picchu.

The first page of the Peruvian version featured a reduced reproduction of the panoramic image of Machu Picchu, with the title "Ancient Ruins of the Incan City Machu Picchu." The caption read:

> This marvelous city, constructed by the Incas probably 2,000 years ago, was discovered in 1911 by Hiram Bingham of the University of Yale and revealed in 1912 under his direction and the auspices of the National Geographic Society of Washington and University of Yale and is considered the most important group of ruins discovered in South America since the conquest of Peru. The city is situated on a summit surrounded by cliffs, 2,000 feet above river level and 7,000 feet above sea level, in the grand canyon of the Urubamba, one of the regions least accessible of the Andes, 60 miles north of Cuzco. It is formed of nearly 2,000 structures of white granite that includes palaces, temples, sanctuaries, baths, fountains and many steps. Accordingly, it seems the city was not known by the Spanish during their dominion. (July 16, 1913, 171)

Below the panorama and caption, the route map of 1912 was included, along with the title "En la Maravillosa Tierra del Perú."

The Peruvian version of the "Wonderland" issue began with translations of the first pages of Bingham's article. The magazine outlined the general plan and route of the expedition, the personnel accompanying the expedition, the overall health of the explorers, and indigenous beliefs about vaccinations. The photographs reproduced were taken from the first pages of the "Wonderland" issue and, together with the narrative, helped explicate the arrival scene. The photograph of reed boats, a photograph of the procession at Corpus Christi, the photograph of a fisherman at Salaverry, six photographs of llamas and other animals, five images of Quechua-speaking subjects, and the two images of the river crossing were included in the first installment.

The remaining eight installments, subtitled "The City of Machu Picchu, Cradle of the Incan Empire," focused on the monument itself.[106] Most of the images detail the rocks, niches, stairs, areas, and caves of Machu Picchu. The two photographs of laborers digging a trench and the group excavating in the cave were reproduced. Noticeably missing were the panoramic vistas that intrigued and captivated readers of the *National Geographic* version. Instead, the Peruvian version highlighted Peru's past as it was embodied in the rock formations, and emphasized detailed depictions of Machu Picchu itself.

Each of the nine issues in *Ilustración Peruana* had a special section titled "Charlas Quincenales" ("biweekly chats"). The introductory page discussed notable books, events, and other items of interest to readers. Preceding the magazine's first translation of the "Wonderland" issue was a *charla* that framed the work of Bingham. The editors explained the importance of the *National Geographic* story by situating the discovery of Machu Picchu in the broader context of investigating Peru's ancient history:

> Today more than ever, history is documented in field investigations. Antiquarians and geologists, historiographers, osteologists and the learned of all branches of human knowledge organize repeat field trips alone or in groups to extract of those ruins the secrets of the millenarian life. They explore and profane tombs and palaces to expose in high relief some wall, or in a temple half crumbling, the key to some allegory, the mystery of their primitive rites; to determine comparatively the age of a race; to reconstitute perhaps some fossilized fragments, the characteristics of a species disappeared. (July 16, 1913, 170)

The *charla* posited that investigative work was important because it allowed Peru to relive its past, to imagine the ancient habits and work of its people. By visiting the ruins, one could let one's imagination drift across the ages to "relive the laborious life and think of the beings that breathed, worked and loved" there. Archaeological ruins were valued because the "ample and evocative silence should intensify the charm for the thinker, the dreamer and the poet."[107] Rock walls, fossilized fragments, skeletal remains, and terraces gave body to a nostalgic imagined historical community.[108]

A year before the translation of Bingham's text, the magazine printed an illustrated story about Machu Picchu by José Gabriel Cosio. Cosio, a colleague of Albert Giesecke and a professor in Cuzco, had met Bingham during the 1911 expedition. After Bingham sighted Machu Picchu, Cosio visited the sanctuary and wrote about his experience in *Revista Universitaria*.[109] Cosio had been contracted by the Peruvian state to accompany Bingham's 1912 expedition and to verify the excavations and shipments of artifacts. As a Cuzqueño intellectual, Cosio imagined the importance of Machu Picchu differently than did Bingham and the National Geographic

Figure 4.6. Untitled, *Ilustración Peruana*, 1912.

Society. In his article, Cosio did not highlight the adventure or the personal and physical achievement of the expedition to Machu Picchu. Instead, his patrimonial account frames Machu Picchu as a part of Peru's national legacy. Tellingly, the article closes with the sentence, "Now it is up to the Government to take measures for its preservation and defense."[110]

The article describes the "perfection and symmetry" of Machu Picchu and details "the noble edifice" in the Andean landscape. The article includes five pages of photographs and text describing the location and size of its impressive features. For example, Cosio provides measurements of each lateral stone in a wall and gives the distances between each edifice, literally mapping the place out in text. Cosio's text reverently describes in minute detail the dimensions of stone walls and the distances between locations. Unlike Grosvenor, who wanted to demonstrate and even excite the fantasy of discovering a lost city, Cosio's romantic imaginings fetishized the archaeological object into a national homecoming.

Cosio's illustrations provide a striking contrast with Bingham's images. Rather than framing the archaeological monument through expansive panoramic landscapes, Cosio's images depict Peruvians in three-piece suits and hats climbing the walls of Machu Picchu (fig. 4.6).[111] In Cosio's photographs, Machu Picchu becomes a backdrop for group photographs; the exoticism and the hidden, vast expanses are excised from his images. The inclusion of people posing for portraits radically shifts the meaning of Machu Picchu, and the result is a narrative not of travel or physical achievement, but of belonging. Through Cosio's eye, Machu Picchu, though persisting as a lost city, is refigured as a place of national heritage. Machu Picchu is occupied, the lost city finally home.

The insertion of Cosio's text and photographs, along with the significant edits made to Bingham's article and photographs, dramatically alters the reading of Bingham's vision as initially framed in *National Geographic*. Although Bingham's edited text still narrated the expedition's discovery of Machu Picchu, without the photographs of captivating landscapes and Quechua types, or much of Bingham's article, the "Wonderland" account no longer reads as the unveiling of a depopulated and hidden city, or even as an arduous adventure. Instead, the story becomes a voyage of self-discovery conducted in favor of the Peruvian nation (fig. 4.7). When refashioned around detailed photographs of the sanctuary and Cosio's images of group visits to the sanctuary, the "Wonderland" story became translated into an instructive national history lesson. Even the inclusion of the two images of workers at Machu Picchu read not as curiosities but as Peruvians working in service to the nation. Like the much earlier use of Humboldt's rhetoric for Creole desires of self-rule and independence,

Figure 4.7. Untitled, *Ilustración Peruana*, 1912.

early twentieth-century Peruvian intellectuals appropriated the work of Bingham for their own desires and designs while claiming the glorious past as their own.

In *Ilustración Peruana*, Machu Picchu continued to be heralded as an astounding discovery. Though it and *National Geographic* framed Machu Picchu as a lost city, what this meant depended entirely on the magazine. In *Ilustración Peruana*, the images and text of the "Wonderland" issue were translated as evidence of the ancient harmonies of the Peruvian nation—an Andean utopia. Machu Picchu was the ruin of Peru's glorious past, and "her" sophisticated technologies and masonry could now "surprise the world." The earlier inclusion of Cosio's text and his images of group portraits reflected this sense of ownership and belonging. The photographic selections from *National Geographic* continued the narrative of getting to know the nation's ancestors through the detailed images of the monument. In *Ilustración Peruana*, an imagined historical community with Machu Picchu at its center was made possible through the circulation and translation of Bingham's photographic evidence as discovery in "In the Wonderland of Peru."

Lost Cities

In a letter dated January 14, 1913, Gilbert Grosvenor complimented Bingham on his 1912 expedition:

> I want to tell you that I think you have brought back to the National Geographic Society full value for the subscription we made to your last expedition. You were very wise to confine your efforts so largely to the wonderful city of Macchu Pichu [*sic*], and I hope that the plans for a special monograph profusely and handsomely illustrated, such as we discussed, may be realized. It will be a very fine thing for you and a credit to the Society as well.[112]

At the end of the letter, Grosvenor added a handwritten note:

> I don't think you yet appreciate the splendid work of your last half year in Peru. From your private references to it, I expected that you would not have much to show for your last trip to Peru and was agreeably surprised at the great results. Your photos of Machu Picchu are wonderful. You underestimate your work.

Machu Picchu has been imagined as the nostalgic loss of ancient wisdom, the final site of Incan resistance to the Spanish conquerors, a spiritual landscape lying in wait for its mysteries to be unveiled, a heritage lesson for the future of a nation, and an awe-inspiring location worthy of a tourist snapshot. The photographs of Machu Picchu and its subsequent visualizations in *National Geographic*, *Ilustración Peruana*, museum exhibitions, and newspaper articles were powerful means of defining, organizing, and controlling a geographic area and its subjects. *National Geographic* helped cull and crystallize Machu Picchu into shape, training our eyes where to look and how to see Peru. But the mechanical reproduction of Bingham's evidence produced instabilities.

Many scholars have argued that expeditionary photography assumed an imperialist gaze that was materialized in landscape and anthropometric views.[113] Dean Worcester's photographs printed in *National Geographic* between 1898 and 1913, for example, framed how North Americans imagined the Philippines, but also worked as evidence that the Philippines still needed US intervention.[114] The photographs acted as proof that there was civilizing yet to be done.[115] The continuities between Bingham's teams' expeditionary photographs as presented in *National Geographic* and the work of other expeditionary photographers are difficult to ignore. The camera sought to bring light to darkness, classified landscapes and people according to types, and focused on the geographic. The few depictions of people were meant to function as illustrative types or aesthetic accompaniments to the landscape. Bingham's vision as presented in *National Geographic* depopulated Cuzco and its environs, and in so doing sought to conquer and possess the landscape for Yale, for science, and for the National Geographic Society.

But the initial meaning of Machu Picchu was not stable. Expedition photographs traveled, and the imperial gaze that was thought to be embedded in the celluloid frame changed with this movement. The "Wonderland" issue initially crafted a vision of Machu Picchu as a lost city discovered by Bingham. The aesthetic of discovery was framed as a photographic narrative of travel wherein the reader journeyed with the expeditionary team. A specific way of seeing Machu Picchu, namely, as exotic and depopulated, was framed. The translation of the "Wonderland" account in *Ilustración Peruana*, however, demonstrated that the vision produced by Bingham and Grosvenor in the pages of *National Geographic* lent itself to other readings. Framed in *Ilustración Peruana*, the imagined material of Machu Picchu shifted to become a lost city found for the nation's glory, couched in an imagined Creole national narrative of belonging forged in earlier centuries, in which the Inca were domesticated as ancient Peruvians. The sheer power of the images stemmed from their refusal to be contained. Machu Picchu as a lost city discovered by science thus began its second career as Peruvian patrimony.

Bingham was interested in a pictorial census of the Peruvian landscape as a way of scientifically documenting the expedition and its findings. Bingham's perspective and way of seeing and thinking about Peru were subsequently framed in an aesthetic of discovery in *National Geographic*. His photographs relied on a discursive framework of science that enabled the images to circulate unquestioned, their contents purportedly exemplifying universal truths. Nonetheless, the materialized photographic imaginings of Machu Picchu resisted such totalizing and uniform categorizations. In Peru, the expeditions' photographs of Machu Picchu became inspiring evidence of a nation's past. Images of the archaeological ruins' rock walls, stairways, and niches, the specific details of the place, became evidence of the technical sophistication of a proud nation's ancestors. As James Ryan has suggested, photography does not so "much record the real as signify and construct it."[116] Even this, however, was slippery, since it was circulated in different contexts with different aims, desires, and audiences.

Collecting Machu Picchu through photographs was instrumental in shaping not only scientific claims but also notions of national heritage. Visualization connected the United States and Peru, making Peru known and safe for US consumption while simultaneously promoting the mystery of an Incan past. Being able to participate in the exotic journey vis-à-vis a magazine, newspaper, or public lecture helped elevate Machu Picchu as a known destination. The contrasting implications of the images of Machu Picchu, and their insertion into differing narratives of discovery, nationalism, and heritage, foregrounded the conflict between science and nation. The motif of a lost city traveled well.

The images taken by Hiram Bingham continue to circulate today. Upon publication in *National Geographic*, they became part of the global domain of knowledge and thus part of our collective imagining and musings about Machu Picchu. Consequently, they have been called up in a number of political moments and events involving Peru. The 1913 edition is now part of a boxed set of compact discs containing past issues of *National Geographic*. One can read the entire issue, experiencing Machu Picchu not only as it looked in 1913, but also as it was before it became Peru's iconic tourist destination and a UNESCO World Heritage Site.[117] Global sharing of the site's images created and create novel understandings of the meaning of Machu Picchu and its role in Peru's and the world's history.

Perhaps more impactful is Bingham's image of Huayna Picchu. Subsequently photographed and made into a motif of indigeneity by Martín Chambi, it continues to circulate on T-shirts, souvenirs, websites, and promotional materials — and of course in the mind's eye of those who see their own discoveries in and around Machu Picchu. Bingham and the other expedition photographers sought to collect views and types and document the landscape through their photographs. Generally lacking people, the photographs inscribed a specific way of seeing Peru as a territory lying in wait for discovery, a lost city. This image, consistently circulated, perpetually encourages us to fantasize its rediscovery, albeit for new aims: New Age spirituality, Incan identity, *indigenismo*, reconquest, national heritage, personal adventure, advertising, and, of course, a twenty-first-century vision of an Andean utopia.

CHAPTER 5

Picturing the Miserable Indian for Science

I have my saddle bags all packed and loaded for my pack mule. Would it interest you to hear just what? In my left forward bag is a 3A Special Folding Pocket Kodak. In the right a .32-20 Colt (pistol), letters for the camp down river, a map and gun cleaner. Under my right bag will be a rifle. In the left rear bag (usually filled with medical supplies) snow glasses, neck handkerchief, two rolls of films, exposure book, pocket tool kit, matches, folding lantern, candle. In the right—drinking cup, notebook, cotton gloves, cartridges, lunch. On the back of the saddle is my poncho. I carry or wear gloves, quilt, binoculars, knife, compass, whistle, alarm watch, etc. On my pack mule will be blankets, bag with extra clothes & sweater and valuable little things—these in a long bag. On the other side a fiber case with large medical case, measuring instruments, books, boots, photo developing outfit, etc. Then there will be my folding bed and tripod.
DAVID FORD TO HIS MOTHER, APRIL 29, 1915

Heritage and the past are not synonymous concepts. Some places or practices never make the grade of heritage. While the Yale Peruvian Expeditions were seminal in shaping the meaning of Machu Picchu, many aspects of them have been forgotten, made invisible, or obscured, then and now. As Bingham often pointed out, work other than excavating was conducted on the expeditions. Mapmaking, for example, never entered the public lexicon for Machu Picchu and the Yale Peruvian Expeditions in the way that the iconic image of Huayna Picchu has. Although *National Geographic* helped picture Machu Picchu for the world, most of the expeditions' photographic images never made it into the public arena.

This chapter examines some of the photographs taken by the physician David Ford in 1915, to further explicate how Machu Picchu and Peru were seen.[1] These photographs, taken as part of the expedition's desire to document Peru's indigenous population through anthropometry, were not widely circulated. Ford's findings and accompanying images were originally intended for Aleš Hrdlička, a well-known physical anthropologist based at the National Museum (Smithsonian).[2] Hrdlička was a prolific collector, amassing nearly twenty thousand skulls over his four-decade career.[3] In the end, the museum did not want the information, since Hrdlička was too busy with his own studies. Eventually, Harry Burr (H. B.) Ferris, a Yale professor of anatomy, analyzed and published Ford's work in 1921 under the title "Anthropological Studies on the Quichua and Machiganga Indians."[4] Ferris also published the anthropometric data collected in 1912 by the physician Luther T. Nelson in *Memoirs of American Anthropological Association* in 1916.[5] A few images of Quechua speakers taken on the 1912 expedition were included in *National Geographic* to demonstrate the ethnic "types" found in "In the Wonderland of Peru."

Anthropometric photographs were never included in the popular narrative of Bingham's heralded discovery of Machu Picchu, precisely because they did not celebrate the glorious Incan past. This is not to say, however, that the images did not support this imaginary. The anthropometric photographs of Quechua speakers as primitive oddities sustained the imaginary of the glorious Incan past by documenting its opposite: the miserable indigenous present. Thus, the same race-inflected categorization of the past that sustained practices such as the collection of antiquities made possible the collection of native bodies through photography. There could be no glorious Incan past, with its accompanying vision for the future, without the degenerative or primitive indigenous race to overcome. In an effort to usher in modernity, scientists treated native subjects as something to study (but otherwise avoid), starkly juxtaposing them with the glories of the Incan empire. On the faces of the marginalized indigenous population lay the aspirations of both science and nation.

Anthropometric Photography

During the nineteenth and early twentieth centuries, race was the primary concern in anthropological study. In his study of the formation of the Anthropological Institute of Great Britain and Ireland, George Stocking traces the organizations that eventually came together as the institute—along with their attendant philosophies of race.[6] Whether racial difference was the result of evolution (monogenism) or a matter of separate species (polygenism), and what to do about racial difference morally and scientifically, was foundational to the anthropological discipline.[7] The Ethnological Society of London, a precursor to the institute, for example, focused on ethnological research to understand whether "mankind was of 'one blood' and [whether] the 'distinguishing characteristics' of different groups were simply modifications of one original type or whether they represented differences in the original hereditary make-up."[8] In 1863, a separate organization, the Anthropological Society of London, was established. It sought not only to study the "history or science of races" but also to understand man's broader relation to nature, the physical universe, and the laws that allowed some nations to develop.[9] Both societies came together in 1871 to form the Anthropological Institute, where racial difference persisted as fact but how to study and think about it remained contested.

A similar dichotomy occurred in the United States. In the first half of the nineteenth century, polygenism and the study of races as separate biological species were prevalent.[10] Samuel Morton, whose disciples included George Gliddon and Louis Agassiz, believed that race was correlated with geographic region. He sought to demonstrate that races represented different species of humanity by comparing crania size.[11] Morton's significant contribution was in measuring internal skull capacity, not facial angle or length, as an indicator of group differentiation. This new methodology allowed exchange and comparison with others interested in understanding racial difference.[12] Such measurements helped establish the racial differences that the collectors themselves had invented.[13]

Although Ann Fabian suggests that by the 1890s scholars had begun to sort humans by language and not skull shape,[14] the anthropometry performed on the Quechua-speaking population by Bingham's expeditionary physicians still relied on comparing cranial sizes.[15] In an effort to understand the relationships among types of people, as well as their geographic distribution, groups were categorized by skull shape and then compared with Hrdlička's collections as well as those established by others such as Julio Tello and Adolph Bandelier.[16] Oblong skulls were indicative of those from the mountains, and rounded, or "brachycephalic," people were coastal types.[17]

Although polygenist thought persisted as racial groups were mapped onto taxonomic categories and depicted as "branches of an evolutionary tree," by the early twentieth century scientific inquiry had shifted toward evolutionism.[18] Groups were conceptualized as discrete entities exhibiting differing and independent evolutionary advancement, and they were ordered based on their location within this hierarchy.[19] As in British anthropology, scientific racism persisted in the United States as an organizing principle and foundational explanation for the differences in cultural practices and beliefs.[20]

Deborah Poole has suggested that the conceptualization of race as a marker of the visible came about around 1800. Drawing on the theory of molecular organisms proposed by Georges-Louis LeClerc, comte du Buffon, and on the "interior mold" (a somewhat mysterious force that helped ensure species similarity from one generation to the next), eighteenth-century science did not conceive of races as fixed types.[21] Instead race was contingent on nature and was thus changeable. Invisible bonds, rather than visual ones, bound people into groups.[22] Poole suggests, however, that the work of Alexander von Humboldt ushered in a new economy of vision in which Buffon's ideas were replaced by an emphasis on typological or physiognomic experience.[23] Photography, with its ability to image, became a primary tool and technology of a "visual economy of modernity," and images could be used as evidence in statistical comparisons of the body.[24] Knowledge was to be garnered through comparison, visually enunciated.

Anthropometry sought to address debates on racial origins through the collection and comparison of body measurements and categories such as age and sex. The emphasis on ordering and typologizing all humankind made anthropometry a mainstay on colonial expeditions.[25] Measurements were taken to rank human beings on a hierarchical scale of development that positioned Caucasian at the top.[26] In particular, the study of skulls was privileged, since head shape and size were thought to be evidence of both physical and moral traits.[27] Physical attributes were thought to betray one's cognitive development and one's moral behavior.[28]

Taking measurements of indigenous bodies became popularized as an attempt to enable the traveler or amateur scientist to collect information free from the prejudice that might arise from individual bias. Pamphlets such as *Notes and Queries on Anthropology* offered information on how to take useful, objective anthropometric measurements.[29] Charts included in the pocket-sized booklets allowed one to match noses, lips, eyes, hair, and skin color. Those in foreign lands were encouraged to record descriptive characteristics, to measure height and skull circumference, and to observe types of social behaviors. Professional scientists and scholars would later mine this data for patterns and generalizations.[30] Photography was a critical tool of anthropometry, since it was through the "type" photographs of individuals that specific characteristics could be shown to exemplify the group generally.[31] Although the scope of anthropological photography had broadened somewhat by the early 1900s, the Yale Peruvian Expedition images, which sought to situate Quechua and other non-Spanish speakers within a hierarchical racial spectrum, reflected the use of photographic types common in mid-nineteenth-century visual anthropology.

David Ford and Luther T. Nelson were US physicians who accompanied the expeditions, primarily to provide health care for the team members.[32] Bingham felt that with a little training, they could also be useful to the scientific agenda of the expedition by conducting research on the "native population." Some of the expressed goals of the 1914–1915 expedition were to understand the origin of man in South America, the distribution and migration of ancient tribes, and the formation of the Incan Empire. It was felt that anthropometry could help answer these questions.[33] Citing a talk by Aleš Hrdlička, Ferris (the Yale professor of anatomy) suggested that the impetus to collect body measurements was to help solve the problem of the racial genesis and affinities of the Peruvians.[34] Spurring the expedition to conduct anthropometry was the fear that the Indian was vanishing because of miscegenation. In a brief report, Ferris wrote that "the importance of an early study of so-called pure races is admitted by anthropologists, as it is simply a question of a comparatively short time when there will be no race that has not suffered recent admixture."[35] The team wanted to measure and capture data from "pure" Peruvians before the inevitability of "admixture" diminished their ability to solve the problem of racial origins.[36] Racial purity was an observable characteristic based on skin, iris color, and features such as the sparseness of the beard, the straightness of the hair, and the individual's physiognomy in general.[37] Photography was the ideal technology for documenting the observable characteristics of race embodied in the native subject.

Hrdlička offered Luther Nelson a two-week training session as well as advice on what he felt were the most important questions to study.[38] He also shared tips on how to persuade the "Indians" to be measured.[39] In contrast to the seemingly docile subjects depicted in the photographs, Quechua speakers were not keen on having their pictures taken. As Nelson wrote in his journal: "At Huadquina [hacienda] the Indians were ordered to a room to be measured. One subject objected strenuously and made it as difficult as he could for any measurements to be taken. He would not stand straight nor sit straight, nor assume any position correctly. Finally, when the measurements were all taken he was offered the usual medio for his trouble. This he promptly refused and wouldn't have a bit of it."[40] Nelson took measurements of the workmen at Machu Picchu as well as the laborers on nearby haciendas, whose managers forced them to participate.

In the city of Cuzco, as Bingham noted, it was necessary to employ force: "The method followed was to have the officer or soldier who was assigned to us go out on the streets and arrest any Indians that seemed to be of pure blood and who proclaimed by their costumes and general appearance that they were typical Mountain Indians."[41] They were brought to the doctor's room at the Hotel Central, where forty-one measurements were taken, along with photographs, fingerprints, and other information about deformations, developmental anomalies, peculiarities, characteristic features, and eye and hair color.[42] Some feared they were being recruited for service into the army, "and not a few shed tears at the thought."[43] For their trouble, they were given a five-cent piece to buy a glass of *chicha*.[44]

Ford articulated similar challenges in photographing Cuzco's people. He found them "very difficult to handle," with "an instinctive fear of the camera and a deep suspicion of the foreigner."[45] Much to his chagrin, they could not be bribed, since they cared little about money and believed that the camera saw through their clothing. In Arequipa, Ford was simply not allowed to take photographs.[46] Instead, Ford measured those who had come to consult with him about their health and ailments. Desperation enabled him to subject the population to the "'white man's medicine' and measuring-tape, calipers and camera."[47] He measured ninety men and sixty-three women, and photographed nearly as many.[48] Ultimately, indigenous subjects were forced into being measured by police officers, the lieutenant accompanying the expeditions, or hacienda managers, or else they relented because they needed medical treatment in exchange.[49]

Enunciating Bodies

For the 1912 expedition, Nelson used a chart prepared by Hrdlička. Titled "The Anthropological Measurements for Field Use," the chart included blank spaces alongside categories such as name, tribe, locality, age, hair, and the date of the examination. Also included were measurements for eyes, ears, nose, teeth, and skin. Lips could be thick, medium, thin, or everted. Information could be obtained through direct observation (for example, straight hair, brown eyes) or by using special tools.

Instruments included a craniometer for measuring the face and head; small sliding calipers for the nose, mouth, ear, and hand; a steel tape for height and span; and a dynamometer for testing handgrip strength.[50] On the 1912 expedition, researchers took Bertillon measurements;[51] instruments included long and short folding rods, along with ink and a roller

Figure 5.1. Untitled photographs, labeled "F," taken by David Ford, c. 1915. Yale Peruvian Expedition Papers (MS 664), Manuscripts and Archives, Yale University Library.

pad for fingerprints. In addition to all the measurements, 433 photographs were taken. The subjects were 144 men and 1 woman, representing sixteen provinces and sixty towns (see the examples in fig. 5.1).[52]

Dionysius Rios, from Ollantaytambo, Urubamba, was one of the men measured. With the exception of his age and number of offspring, what we know about him is gleaned entirely from the surface of his body as seen through the clinical eye of the physician. He was approximately forty-two years old with abundant black hair. His nose was straight, marked as 73.33,[53] its length .045, and breadth .033. His nostrils diverged slightly. He had thirty teeth (including two molars) and two cavities; his incisors were vertical. He had a thin build with medium lips. Rios's ears were marked 50.00, the length .064, and the breadth .032, with a large auriculo-temporal angle. His skin was light brown, not oily, with no tattoo marks, freckles, naevi (birthmarks), and scant pilosity (hair). His eyes seemed to be light brown.[54]

On the back of the form were categories that sought to document deformations as well as body and head calculations. The entire body was articulated through quantifying measurements: height to chin, to presternal notch (the top of the sternum), to knee, to umbilicus—sitting and kneeling. The length of the arm, forearm, hand, and foot were measured, as was the face. Toward the bottom of the chart, the note taker wrote that Rios had four children in his family, was of Spanish blood, and had a ventral hernia in the upper-left quadrant. Rios's picture was recorded on images numbered 3,750 and 3,751.

Researchers on the 1912 expedition measured people in a variety of provinces throughout the Department of Cuzco. By contrast, the 1915 expedition mostly confined anthropometric measurements to inhabitants of Urubamba and Convención. The altitude in the regions was also measured. Anthropometric data were collected through "measurements, inspection, physiological, and photography."[55] Full-face and profile photographs were taken of each subject to document the person measured and to provide future visual evidence for statistical comparisons.

Conclusions about the Quechua-speaking population were assembled by situating them within previously collected data sets. Ferris compared measurements from the 1912 and 1915 expeditions with work by Arthur Chervin and Alcide d'Orbigny. D'Orbigny, author of *L'homme americain* (1839), studied and observed Quechua and Aymara speakers. Chervin, author of *Anthropologie bolivienne* (1908), examined the skeletal remains gathered at Tiawanaku, along with living persons, for his study of the "racial physiology" of Bolivia.[56] Through the statistical analysis of photographs taken by travelers and his assistant, Chervin drew conclusions about Bolivia, its population, and its future.[57]

Like Chervin, Ferris worked with the material provided to him, making statistical comparisons that were then used to situate Quechua speakers among other races. To make the mass of measurements meaningful, he compared his conclusions with those arrived at for other groups. In addition, he made further mathematical calculations, such as "relation of width of mouth to breadth and height of face, breadth of nose and to age"; those calculations were summarized in a table.[58] Ferris also drew on other scholars' work, such as the anthropologist Franz Boas's research on the Alaskan Eskimo. Average height, both standing and sitting, for example, put the Quechua-speaking male above the Labrador Eskimo but significantly below the English male. For Ferris, the so-called Quechua were similar to the Shoshone and Eskimo.[59] Measurements such as facial height and breadth were extrapolated and compared with other racial data. In some instances, these comparisons led to the Quechua speaker being placed somewhere between the Jews and the Tibetans.[60]

The measurements of living Quechua speakers' bodies were compared with those of the skeletal remains collected and studied by George Eaton, which included twenty-one measurements of the bodies and extremities.[61] After comparing the cranial index of three skulls found at Machu Picchu, Ferris concluded that there was no material difference between the ancient skulls and the "living Quechua."[62]

Other observations noted that the grip of Quechua speakers was weak when compared with the average grip strength of white males, suggesting a poorly developed forearm muscle. Quechua speakers had fewer caries than their civilized counterparts (except those who worked on sugar plantations).[63] The ear index of the "Quechua" was intermediate among the races. They were of low stature, with broad shoulders. They had straight black hair and sparse beards; graying and alopecia were rare.[64] Ferris's conclusions were comparative visual descriptions of so-called race groups mathematically imparted.

The language of Ferris's two reports relied on the use of scientific nomenclature to substantiate the claims of anthropometry. Rather than write that a subject had a long torso, Ferris wrote, "In relation to stature the upper extremity was long, especially the forearm, and the lower extremity short, especially the thigh, and the *triceps surae* muscle greatly developed."[65] Ferris used scientific terms when characterizing the Quechua speakers—for example, referring to subcutaneous fatty tissue as the "panniculus adiposus"—and noted that certain Quechua speakers were mesticephalic and hypsicephalic (had heads of medium proportion with a high forehead). As to the face, Ferris wrote: "They are euryprosopic [short or broad face] with prominent malar [cheek] region, lips somewhat thick and procheilous, ear mesotic, nose with straight or slightly sinuous dorsum and divergent nostrils and mesorrhine [moderate width] in proportions."[66] Their estimated brain weight averaged 1,265 grams, placing them in the mesocephalic group.[67]

Observations of pathology included information such as whether subjects were pockmarked or scarred, or had any congenital malformations. A few of those measured had oriental sores, or Leishman-Donovan, today referred to as cutaneous leishmaniasis. Goiters were found in 12.9 percent of the males measured and 16.1 percent of the females.[68] Pulse rate, temperature, rate of respiration, average age, number of children (average: 2.8), and the sex of the children, as well as the shape of the breasts, were recorded. Mandible angle and "alveolar prognathism," or dental protrusion, were measured, perhaps in an effort to correlate a relationship to Neanderthals.[69] The Quechua speaker's body was further fragmented and dissected into measurable parts, including chin prominence, eye color, lip thickness, forehead height, supraorbital ridges, mouth, sitting height, hand and foot measurements, leg circumference, thorax, and ears. The table of contents to the 1921 report fragmented the entire body into components for comparative cross-referencing.

Numerous charts and figures—more ways of visualizing the fragments—accompanied the reports. Streams of tables dividing each measurement by male and female were included in the 1921 publication, along with four foldout charts providing indices and inspection records of all the subjects. In the 1916 publication, measurements were first subdivided by provinces, then further sorted into three groups: all subjects, those of pure blood, and those of mixed blood (white).[70] The dizzying array of numbers added to the objectification of the subjects as composite types, and simultaneously conveyed the idea that the expedition did productive scientific work.[71] Like the anthropometric photographs, the tables were meant to visually show racial difference. And as with the photographs, the intended meaning was indecipherable without explanation and contextualization. The caliper and the meter stick affirmed that the bodies that labored for Bingham's scientific enterprise were also the raw material upon which to craft its knowledge.

Unstable Evidence

Anthropometry was not a fixed science. There were neither agreed-upon best practices nor a universal and systematized way of rendering bodies legible. While anthropometry sought to remove subjectivity through measurement and statistics, thus ordering people into distinct and fixed types, anthropometry was anything but stable. Ferris lamented as much in his report when he wrote that the challenge for physicians, and thus for science, was the lack of consensus on which measurements were needed, the methods to use, and how to use them comparatively: "The consequent lack of uniformity as to measurements, technique and the method of estimating the indices many times renders it difficult to impossible to make comparisons."[72]

For example, when analyzing Ford's data about eye color of the subjects sampled in 1915, Ferris noted this information was relatively useless, because the results, which had been recorded as dark brown, medium brown, light brown, or black, could not be compared with data from the previous expedition, which used the Bertillon system to classify eye color. Likewise, Nelson's team had made thirty-six measurements of each subject: eighteen of the body, six of the cranium, and twelve of the face, including observations on eyes, teeth, skin, deformities, and anomalies. The information was compiled into a table composed of averages and extreme body measurements among pure races and mixed. In contrast, the 1915 expedition made only eighteen measurements of each subject. Ferris regretted the omissions from the 1915 expedition, since "some interesting facts relating to the proportions of the segments and extremities were ascertained by the Expedition of 1912 and it was desirable to check these results by further observations."[73]

Because of the lack of uniformity in collecting measurements, not all data was considered accurate. Often the results were considered suspect. For example, nose measurements differed dramatically on both expeditions, causing Ferris to write: "A comparison of these measurements with those obtained by the Expedition of 1912 shows them so regularly larger, especially the height, that one must believe that a different technique was employed."[74] Special attention was paid to the face, including measuring the "palpebral fissures" (the opening between the eyelids) and the "Mongolian fold," or epicanthus. Ferris questioned how face heights were measured on the 1915 expedition, since they averaged 135 millimeters for males and 127 for females, but the racial variation was 103–127 in males and 107–117 in females. This discrepancy led Ferris to believe that Ford had inaccurately measured from the glabella, the area between the eyebrows.[75]

Even when practices for obtaining accurate measurements were followed, conclusive results did not always occur. The expedition teams based their measuring of the cranium on Hrdlička's system of measuring skulls.[76] But after seeing the results of the 1915 expedition, Ferris concluded they were "distinctly greater than Chervin's results or those of the Expedition of 1912."[77] Such a statistical anomaly caused consternation over the accuracy of data collection. In contrast, Ferris suggested that the head heights recorded by the 1915 expedition were in line with Chervin's data, but not with the findings of the 1912 expedition.

The relevance of the measurements was also questioned. The foot length of the Quechua speaker, for example, was similar to that of the Chinese, the Colorado Indian, and the Brazilian Indian. Ferris, however, felt the measurement had "little value as a racial character."[78] He questioned why some measurements were used rather than others. He wondered why anthropologists did not use the bizygomatic breadth (facial width between the cheekbones) as the base for determining both the physiognomic and morphologic facial index.[79] Anthropometry was challenging not simply because obtaining consistent and accurate measurements across populations was difficult but also because its correlation with race was open to dissent.

For the general public, anthropometric information was generally uninteresting. The use of scientific names, coupled with impenetrable numerical charts and admittedly suspect comparisons, made publishing the material challenging. Neither expeditionary physician worked up his own material. Instead, the National Geographic Society encouraged Ferris to write up a report.[80] In addition to the narrative and the numerical tables, photographs were included in an appendix. The images were visual proof of the conclusions therein. All one had to do was to look at the quantity of numbers and photographs to see the truth of the racial order visible in the Quechua speakers' bodies.

Photographing the Indian for Science

In his work on photography and the British Empire, James Ryan argues that the camera was one instrument in an armament of strategies to produce and document physical characteristics of imperial subjects.[81] Images taken on British colonial expeditions did not reflect the use of anthropometry to the letter, but instead exhibited an "ethnographic picturesque." The picturesque reflected a stylistic composition reminiscent of profiles framed by meter sticks, but also a romanticized depiction of the Other.[82] Annie Maxwell suggests that photographs of people being measured with calipers and meter sticks against gridded backgrounds were generally uninteresting and not readily accessible to a public unfamiliar with anthropometry.[83] In contrast, humanistic and ethnographic representations were popular, and thus ethnographic depictions were encouraged.

Ford's images published in the 1921 report do not reflect anthropometric photography to the letter, nor do they exhibit a humanistic or ethnographic picturesque. Instead, the photographs were thought to visually

Figure 5.2. Plate 2 from H. B. Ferris, *Anthropological Studies on the Quichua and Machiganga Indians.*

attest to and document the racial data gleaned through the painstaking charting of the indigenous body. Ford's published images exhibit a clinical gaze that reflected an interest in the gross medical conditions of Andean peoples. In these portraits, race and culture come to be observed or seen only through the face and neck: deformities, exotic paint markings, and profiles of foreheads and jawlines. Most photographs were of men, but a few women were included.[84] Photographed with an unflattering gaze, subjects were scoped before being visualized. Their deformities, their less-than-ideal bodies, and their atypical attributes were displayed with a distancing medical gaze as they were translated into visual proof of racial difference. In keeping with anthropometric practice, Ferris emphasized the subjects as types. Photographs exemplified the varieties of mouths, lips, and ears found in the Quechua-speaking population. Massive goiters, scars, and malformations were printed uniformly and in classifiable rows (see fig. 5.2). Individuality was replaced by the group.[85] "He" or "she" became the comparative "they." As printed in the report, the photos appeared as trading cards of specimen lots.

Although the profile frames and the massive goiters dehumanize the individuals, the communication of anthropometric meaning through the image is not readily or easily ascertained. For the photographs to have scientific value, they must be viewed with the measurements in mind. Ferris included an explanation of the plates to direct the proper viewing of the images. Foreheads, for example, were divided into retreating, vertical, narrow, broad, and low. Lips and mouths, head forms, noses, ears, and faces also had accompanying specifications. The reader could find out that image 119, for example, showed a sinuous dorsum. In addition to Quechua types, photographs included examples of a Negroid, enlarged thyroids, and an osteoma (benign bone tumor).[86]

The effect of such typologizing was to generalize about the entire population through the representation of a few individuals. The most misleading example of this is the presence of goiters. While only 12–16 percent of the population was found to have thyroid enlargements, the organization of the images into types made these individual attributes representative of the Quechua population generally. Thirty-nine plates of Quechua speakers showed types of foreheads, lips, mouths, and head form, among others. Eight of those images included people with goiters. Since there are three frames to a page, three of the thirteen pages feature a subject with some type of thyroid growth. If separated from Ferris's explanation, the photographs become further decontextualized. No longer do viewers witness the intent of showing a specific type of nose, but instead see a generalized ethnocentric view of the Quechua-speaking population as degraded primitive oddities, replete with physical grotesqueries.

Unlike Ryan's ethnographic picturesque, these images do not encourage the idea of a lost nobility to be salvaged. These subjects were not considered heroic examples or vestiges of the great Incan civilization, nor were they felt to represent the noble heritage of the Peruvian nation. They were not paraded around and printed in globally distributed magazines. Instead, these subjects represented the miserable native present, which lamentably prevented the Peruvian nation from recapturing its glorious past. They were evidence of Peru's lack.

While the profile frame was an ethnographic photographic trope, the depiction of these individuals seemed designed not just to typologize but also to shock and awe. Witnessing the massive goiters and scars further degraded the degraded. The individuality of the person faded from the photograph as sickness and deformity were highlighted. These images were graven, and the subjects' accusing stares highlighted the death of the indigenous as equivalent subjects. Although their disappearance through exogamy spurred scientific study, the subjects themselves do not nostalgically lament the vanishing past or conjure a romantic notion, à la Martín Chambi, of "el indio."[87] Instead, the series of images showed racial inferiors and medical problems to be analyzed and resolved. They are haunting reminders of human suffering and physical and emotional pain wrought through expeditionary photography.

Slips in the veneer of anthropometric calculation did not occur often. But in his report on the Machiganga, Ford is broadly descriptive: "The village consists of one large building and four small shelters including a very neat hen-coop. Everything is of Saga palm. . . . The huts are very cool and clean inside. Mats of woven palm leaves gave comfortable seats. To the roof were hung baskets, nuts and gourd bottles with corks of corn cobs. Bunches of arrows of various sizes and design were stuck in behind the rafters."[88] Ford measured eighteen males and fifteen females of the Machiganga population. Although the women were "indifferent to the exposure of their breasts," Ford wrote that they did not smell and did not object to having their calves measured as long as the dress did not go above the knee. According to Ford, they enjoyed posing, and one lady was "peeved" because Ford did not include her in a group photograph. While he documented other pathologies such as smallpox scars (about 80 percent of the population) and overo, a parasitic skin disease, Ford went on to describe marriage and feast rites, cultural practices, music, pets, play, specific illnesses, language, and foodways. He treated malnutrition, ant bites, oriental sore,[89] malaria, conjunctivitis, and heart lesions. Such practices and descriptions hint at a more complicated and interactive relationship that belies anthropometric conclusions.

Nonetheless, the descriptive information was lost in the highlighting of physiognomy and its attendant images. Information that might have exemplified Ford's descriptions became testimony to the physical body. The cords, for example, hanging around the necks of the Machiganga were used as extra bowstrings and to climb trees. When published in Ferris's report, that information was reframed to constitute and reflect the visual facticity of the Othered body. Through anthropometric science, cultural subjects became numbered specimens.

The anthropometric images and the people featured in the photographs are left out of the grand narrative and origin story of Bingham and Machu Picchu. Although these images are not stereotypical anthropometric photographs replete with calipers or meter sticks, the images reflect the same visual trope of profile and type common in anthropometric photography from the nineteenth and early twentieth centuries. With the aid of the camera, the scientific lens that the expedition pursued showed the miserable Indian population as perhaps a fallen or degenerated race of the Incas.[90] This evidence, couched in scientific discourse and the technology of measuring, shored up the trope of the lost city. The present population was raced, and a logic of primitiveness imposed upon them.[91]

Talking Skulls

Ford's brief foray into cultural description makes one wonder about other personal interactions that may have existed with the local population.[92] Writings about the Peruvian population are not as frequent in the expeditions' papers as one might expect. While there is some information about Augusto Leguía, Carmen Vargas, and other privileged persons who assisted Bingham, information on those employed by the team is rare. Nonetheless, the moments captured on paper mingle curiosity with contempt.

> While my peons did not do a quarter of the work that white laborers would have done, they did very well for natives. I found that an occasional mild kick and a reward to the best worker at the end of the day did far better and pleased them much more than talking to them. Everyone except the kickee enjoyed the physical remonstrance against laziness, and he mostly took it with a grin. Also with an accession of energy which was very gratifying. Their habit of stopping three times a day to renew their cuds of coca is a nuisance, but one for which there is no remedy.[93]

The report on Machu Picchu by K. C. Heald, assistant topographer on the 1912 expedition, quoted above, confirms the physical violence that the team inflicted upon the hired laborers and the frustration felt at their refusal to be willing participants in the expeditions' agenda.

While it is not clear whether all members took the same physical approach with the laborers, the writings suggest that the Quechua-speaking population was generally considered inferior.[94] Hiram Bingham notes in a journal entry dated May 5–6, 1915:

> The Indian of Peru would be a pretty good kind of raw material. They are not so bad as I used to think, and some of them are really good citizens—according to their lights. I think enforced service in the army is good for them, as it gives them a certain amount of education and a new viewpoint. At all events they are patient, steady plodders—when not drunk or nearly so. They made good material for the Incas to work with. One can understand the wonderful old stone work when one realizes how patient and plodding the Indian of to-day is.[95]

In an article in *Popular Science Monthly* in 1910, Bingham describes the "race [that was] rising in South America."[96] South America was becoming a hybrid, evolving from the mix of different peoples. Bingham attributes table manners and social conventions of courtesy to race. Habits such as making comments to women as they pass by were considered a Latin habit and therefore a racial right.[97] Even if Bingham came to tolerate the expeditions' laborers, his frustration often overcame him. Although there were exceptions, he thought of Quechua speakers as members of a weaker race that often tried his patience and led him to treat them poorly.[98]

The racialized viewing of Quechua speakers as primitive subjects caused the team members to fear for their own moral contamination. Worried that their work ethic and standards might worsen, Bingham instructed the expedition members to not become particularly friendly or close with those unlike them. While it was fine to associate with hacienda owners and businessmen, fraternizing with Quechua speakers was not encouraged. In a letter to Joseph Little, Bingham warned: "There is only one word of caution that I feel disposed to inflict upon you. Don't ever let your surroundings in Latin America affect your ideals of work and faithfulness to duty. I have noticed over and over again in South America a spirit of carelessness towards one's employers and lack of loyalty. It is extremely difficult to maintain one's New England sense of conscientious attention to details and everlasting hustle when one is surrounded by such laziness and easy going ways as are prevalent in many parts of South America."[99] Isaiah Bowman, the geographer of the 1912 expedition, ascribed to the belief that all peoples or races had a place or region to which they were best suited. Society and climate were mapped together and were "intimately related."[100] In *The Andes of Southern Peru*, Bowman's account of his work on the 1912 expedition, he wrote: "No one can imagine the poverty and ignorance of these mountain shepherds. They are filthier than beasts. I have to watch them constantly or they would sell parts of the flocks, which do not belong to them, or try to exchange the valuable alpaca wool for coca leaves in distant towns. They are frequently drunk."[101] Although he criticized Peru's labor system for its treatment of the native population, Bowman remained steadfast in his belief that the Indians still lived as primitively as they did at the time of discovery.[102]

Osgood Hardy, a member on the 1914–1915 expedition was the only member specifically commissioned to learn Quechua. He was to learn the challenging language so that he would be able to document native folklore and beliefs. He was to describe native feasts and ascertain their dates, causes, and potential linkages to "agricultural husbandry or herdsmanship."[103] Bingham suggested that it might be worthwhile to employ a "Quichua" as a servant, training him to "cook in a clean manner, so as to save your own time." Bingham wrote from experience: "At Machu Picchu we had two or three . . . who would be perfectly satisfactory for the purpose I have in mind."[104]

Bingham wanted Hardy to learn Quechua as a way to learn "vestiges of early custom."[105] The expedition members viewed the indigenous as something for their use, a source of information, supplies, labor, and sometimes shelter. They were viewed almost always as obstacles to the greater task at hand, even though without their assistance the goals of the expedition would not have been achieved.[106] More than that, their beings contained within them raw data to be unlocked and transformed by foreigners for the good of science. Their cultural practices were of interest only because of what they might say about the Inca.

On very few occasions did the team members experience theft or have their lives threatened.[107] The relative lack of conflict noted in the reports and writings of the expedition might lead one to assume that the local population was relatively sanguine about having Yale rummage through its backyard.[108] Yet dispersed through the papers are observations about the "illogical superstitions" of the indigenous population. While the superstitions were noted in journals and reports as evidence of the backwardness of the Cuzco population, they might be better considered responses and reactions to the violent reordering being unleashed on the landscape and their bodies. The collecting of skeletal remains in particular was a source of moral conflict.

Eaton wrote about Alvarez, who had a "strong superstitious dread of incurring trouble through his sacrilegious labors as my fellow grave-robber."[109] Eaton noted that this fear was so marked that any type of ailment was blamed on the practice of collecting skeletons. Eaton refers to one persistent malady that affected Alvarez. Although Eaton thought it was due to an excess of "vino et venere" (wine and sex), Alvarez insisted the rash he had acquired was "retaliation by the malevolent spirits whose sepulchers he had desecrated."[110] Eaton wryly notes that "lavish rewards" brought Alvarez back to the "unholy but profitable quest."[111] He continued to assist the team.[112]

In her work in Melanesia, Holly Wardlow suggests that we should not view such superstitions as an iteration of a folk belief system. Instead, they might be better understood as a vehicle for producing a new form of consciousness.[113] The reordering required of the landscape and native bodies to produce scientific knowledge was not a benign reshuffling of meaning. Rather, making the place and people legible in an expeditionary scientific register relied on violent acts of both obfuscation and visualization. The population's rendering as anthropometric specimens only aided in their disappearance.

The Noblest Sense

Though not widely publicized, the portraits of medical ailments were still part of the history and making of Machu Picchu in the twentieth century. Built on the marginalization and exploitation of the Quechua speaker's body, these subjects were not part of the noble Incan past that Bingham and the other expedition members sought to collect. Instead, the indigenous bodies were captured as the potentially inferior vestige of Peru's racialized past or as a separate race altogether. Although the skulls and skeletons collected in the countryside were conceptualized as the remains of Quechua speakers' distant ancestors, the present indigenous subjects had no rights to them or to their own bodies. Instead, the photographs as collectibles offered evidence of primitiveness of the Andean countryside, the difference being medicalized and pathologized. Like their skeletal counterparts, the photographed bodies furthered the portrayal of Machu Picchu as a lost city by emphasizing the historical chasm between the noble Incan past and the indigenous as "epigones incapable of contributing to Incan greatness."

Time has occluded this documentation and these individuals. It is doubtful that Cuzqueños have ever heard of Ford. In my interviews in Peru, nobody was aware of the anthropometric component to Bingham's work in Peru. Instead, these photographs are hidden. They are not glorious. They do not enunciate a great find. They are not hand-painted and neatly placed between panes of glass for magnification in darkened lecture halls.[114] They do not grace the pages of illustrated magazines or exhibition walls.[115] These photographs do not make heroes, but they do give testimony regarding the unpublicized formation of the native medical specimen, and the ways in which race and science in the twentieth century fashioned heritage out of historical rock.

Although Ford's photographs were not used in *National Geographic* or on the pages of newspapers, they were situated in the same understanding of Machu Picchu as a lost city. The exotica of deformed Quechua speakers' bodies surrounding the treasured archaeological monument were rooted in the suspicion that the contemporary Quechua were either unrelated to, or at best the degraded remnants of, the glorious Incan race. Unlike the subjects of other expeditionary or colonial photographs, these

Quechua speakers were not framed in an ethnographic picturesque, but instead were captured as unfortunately persistent. While the lost city was shrouded in clouds and brush, the Quechua speakers were considered racialized medical curiosities and the inferior laborers of science.

In his article "Invisible Empire," Nicholas Mirzoeff discusses the apparent paradox of photographs of torture and sodomy at Abu Ghraib, whereby images circulated widely within the prison but were not popularized by the world as indicative of current events in Iraq.[116] Tactics of humiliation, particularly through the transgression of sexual and cultural norms, were documented through the photographs. The photographs displaying victims of torture on screen savers, and video footage of guards having sex with female inmates, were shared and displayed among military personnel within the confines of the prison. Mirzoeff concludes that the acts of sodomy, a means of disciplining the body into a hierarchy, were subjugated to vision. One has to wonder, however, was the camera sodomizing them as well?

Just as soldiers at Abu Ghraib subjugated prisoners, the expeditions' physicians subjugated the Quechua-speaking population to vision. The right to gaze and photograph, particularly by those invested with the authority of science, subjugated its victims into a certain optic of logic. They were not human beings but abstractions of medical maladies, rationalized and standardized to prefigured measurements—breadth of nose, cranial circumference, handgrip strength. Like the photographs of Abu Ghraib, these images exhibited the sensibility of incarceration; the borders of the photographic frame keep the natives in place while making them legible in a specific and specified order.[117]

The anthropometric photographs are powerful reminders and traces of the privilege that science exerted in the Andean countryside. Collecting skeletal remains from grave sites has become so commonplace that describing it may feel quaint—so too perhaps with anthropometric images. We seem numb to the power differential reflected in these deeds. And yet the images are stark reminders of the camera as a tool and technology of power, and of the way that racialized understandings of Peru and its imagined past, present, and future indelibly marked a now-iconic piece of national patrimony.

This chapter rides an ethical line. In circulating these images, does it work violence anew? They were taken not that long ago—whose family members might these be? Does some imperative for discussion about science and discovery in the early twentieth century make their further objectification tolerable? Now digitized online by Yale University and accessible for the world to see, can these images be somehow transformed into acts of heroism? Is discussing what took place better than ignoring it, or is it another act of science's privileged sight?

Undoubtedly, publishing these images is an attempt to instill a different vantage or memory about lost cities. While there are images here that I find particularly evocative or to have a particular presence—a "punctum" or resonance—it would be ahistorical to assume that my feelings are the subjects' feelings.[118] As has often been pointed out, it is impossible to comprehend everything about a photograph.[119] But this is not what this chapter aspires to detail. Instead, this chapter attempts to demonstrate how native subjects were conceptualized and subsequently imaged; how they were "stipulated" through the camera's lens for science.[120] While the meaning of photographs is inherently unstable and cannot be fixed, it is possible to document at least partially the circumstances and context in which the act of anthropometric photography occurred on the expeditions. In this sense, photography, rather than being considered only a technology *of* memory,[121] might also be considered a technology *for* memory, actively constituting personal and collective memories, made not in the past but in the present. The photograph escapes containment even with the technology of the capture and its subsequent reproduction.

Anthropometry was an aspect of scientific practice to be completed on the expedition. What the photographs show is the preexisting notion of a miserable present, and its persistence. While the aesthetics and meanings of the image are open to interpretation, the situation in which the photographs were taken is not. Considered subjects of science, these human beings became unfortunately persistent remnants, degradations of a glorious past. To see the lost city required a certain blindness.

CONTESTS

CHAPTER 6

The Politics of Seeing

The President of the United States attended a Meeting of the Yale University when the matter was discussed and expressed a great deal of interest in the subject. It was therefore suggested that it would be advisable to ask the Government of Peru to give a concession to Professor Bingham and his associates giving them the right to excavate and explore ancient sights [sic] and the ruins of Cities and Temples for a period of years. The concession is to be for educational purposes only, with no idea whatever of making it a commercial project. The question is, do you think that the Government of Peru will grant such a privilege?
LOUIS SCHAEFER TO MR. BALLEN, FEBRUARY 15, 1912

The most high moral and patriotic value has the attitude and work of don Eugenio Larrabure: to discover the secret of the past to anticipate the glory of the future.
J. MATÍAS LEÓN, INTRODUCTION TO EUGENIO LARRABURE Y UNANUE, *MANUSCRITOS Y PUBLICACIONES*

Although the exploitation and subjugation of rural Quechua speakers did not significantly affect or alter the expeditions' agendas or practices, the removal of objects from Machu Picchu and other archaeological sites became more problematic with each subsequent expedition. The removal of Peru's perceived ancient past by robbing its ancestral grave sites became highly controversial, culminating in an injunction to halt excavations in 1915. This chapter focuses on two significant conflicts between the Yale Peruvian Expeditions and the Peruvian government, to examine how Machu Picchu acted as a boundary object between Bingham and Peruvian nationalists.[1] The first significant conflict ensued after Yale attempted to

win an exclusive concession to remove artifacts in 1912. The second occurred toward the end of the 1915 expedition, when Yale attempted to ship
collected antiquities back to New Haven.

Ricardo Salvatore argues that these tensions were part of an effort on
the part of cultural nationalists to resist disciplinary conquest.[2] I deepen
his argument to more fully explicate the context and history in which
Machu Picchu became meaningful as patrimony for the Peruvian nation
in the first part of the twentieth century. Cultural nationalism around
artifacts didn't surface with Yale's presence. Rather, beginning with independence, Peruvians had a long-standing conversation about the relationship between nation, modernity, Incan objects, and their removal.
The Yale expeditions inflamed the discourse, sparking a public discussion,
led by the Creole elite and Cuzqueño intellectuals, about the commercial, scientific, and public treatment of monuments on Peruvian soil. The
controversy, rooted in a civilizing and modernizing discourse about the
future of the Peruvian nation, helped transform a lost city discovered by
foreign scientists into a national emblem of Peru. Science per se wasn't
the enemy—just its use by foreigners.

In 1912, Yale University, under Bingham's guidance, sought a concession from the Peruvian government to explore and conduct archaeological
work. The concession would allow Yale to excavate and remove antiquities
from Peru for a specified number of years. Although the Peruvian Congress never approved the concession, the request for it was controversial
in both Peru and the United States, and placed Bingham in the midst of
Peruvian political wrangling, presidential factions, and scholarly jockey-
ing. In the end, Yale was not granted a special concession, but was granted
permission to ship artifacts to the United States that had been excavated
during the 1912 expedition. The team was to cease excavations on December 1, 1912, and to leave duplicates and one-of-a-kind objects at Lima's
National Museum.[3] José Gabriel Cosio was charged with making an inventory of the objects, with the agreement that the artifacts were to be
returned when Peru asked for them.[4]

In 1914, the third Yale expedition team returned to Peru and remained
there until the end of 1915. Bingham had been successful at networking
and negotiating with important Peruvian stakeholders for the 1911 and
1912 expeditions, but he was largely absent from the 1914–1915 expedition.
Instead, he sent Ellwood Erdis to direct operations until he arrived, which
happened a year into the operation. Unfortunately, Erdis did not secure
the correct permits for excavation. Coupled with a significantly heightened collecting enterprise, the lack of permits caused the team bureau-

cratic difficulties in shipping the collected materials back to Yale. Bingham
left Peru in 1915 frustrated and unsure when the excavated materials would
be shipped to Yale for study. Erdis stayed in Lima to negotiate an agreement with the Peruvian government and the National Museum. Eventually, seventy-four boxes of materials were shipped in 1916 to Yale, with the
stipulation that their contents be returned in eighteen months.[5]

Both the 1912 concession and the 1915 injunction served as catalysts for
a public discussion about the role, care, and meaning of Machu Picchu and
archaeological remains more generally. In these contests, Peruvian intellectuals drew on established patriotic discourses to frame Machu Picchu
as national patrimony. This chapter traces how the critique of the expedition and its removal of artifacts from Machu Picchu and its environs relied
on a patriotic epistemology that privileged knowledge embodied in antiquities over the assertions and claims made by foreigners.[6] This patriotic
epistemological stance attempted to provide an alternative to the present
through an understanding of the past while seeking to map a novel future.[7]
The protectors of Peru's archaeological objects, particularly Machu Picchu, from outside interlopers like Bingham fashioned antiquity as the em-
bodiment of national patrimony and the key to national development.[8]

In his work on translation, Michel Callon suggests that enrolling actors
in the making of scientific fact involves trials of strengths and processes
of stabilization. "Controversy," Callon writes, "is all the manifestations
by which the representativity of the spokesman is questioned, discussed,
negotiated, rejected, and so forth."[9] In *Science in Action*, Bruno Latour
argues that science is a collective process through which facts and machines are constructed and translated.[10] As a result, it is critical to study
science as a process, to witness the trials of strength and negotiations, to
see how controversy is settled and, ultimately, how a dispute ends. Susan
Leigh Star and James Griesemer add that negotiations take place among
a host of potential actors and can go in a number of directions.[11] Creoles,
intellectuals, and the broader Peruvian public questioned Bingham's integrity, his scientific bona fides, and his claims' veracity on the second and
third Yale Peruvian Expeditions. These contests demonstrated not only
the shakiness of Machu Picchu's translation, but also the national interest at stake: Peru as a modern nation, one with the ability to chart its own
future through its remains.

Previous scholarship on these conflicts has tended to focus on the law
and the legality of Bingham and the Yale team's actions. Mariana Mould de
Pease writes that one of the first laws to designate antiquities as property
of the Peruvian nation was established in 1822.[12] In 1893, a law was passed

to protect artifacts. Mould de Pease draws on these laws as well as international agreements to question the legality and ethics of Bingham's expeditionary practices and to rally for the return of cultural goods.[13] Christopher Heaney discusses the law around the expeditions to suggest that the law of August 19, 1911, which sought to strengthen the 1893 law regarding Peruvian antiquities, was directly shaped by Bingham's expeditions.[14]

Rather than focus on the specifics of the laws and the expeditions' legality, this chapter examines the conflict as a series of discursive trials of strength that articulated ideas of archaeological objects as treasures of both Peru's past *and* future. Through an examination of the conflicts over artifacts between Yale and Peru, the struggles to fix Machu Picchu—whether as an object of universal science or as national patrimony—are illuminated. The historical discourse of the noble Inca acted with Peruvian patriotic epistemologies to subvert Machu Picchu as Yale's scientific discovery, in effect repositioning Machu Picchu as a part of national patrimony rather than only a lost city discovered by science.[15]

In his analysis of the archaeological site Vilcas in Peru, Jon Beasley-Murray writes: "There is no such thing as an ancient ruin, for the ruin is always a modern concept. Ruination and modernity go hand in hand: the modern displaces the ancient and marks it as irredeemably part of the past precisely by construing it as ruined."[16] Beasley-Murray suggests that the concept of ruins should be historicized and that the "stories ruins are made to tell are almost always stories of power."[17] Not all cultural artifacts are considered patrimony. Those that are must be relevant to national narratives.[18] As Stefanie Gänger rightly points out, "Antiquities are categories, not objects of collecting."[19]

Power over the ability to define and thus control national futures is displayed throughout the struggles over Machu Picchu's translation and attempts at fixity. Unlike Mexican scientific projects of the same period that were rooted in its present-day indigenous population,[20] the Peruvian scientific project was mainly rooted in antiquity.[21] In halting Yale's concession and regulating expeditionary collecting practices, actors speaking on behalf of the Peruvian nation began to set limits on Machu Picchu as Yale's universal scientific discovery. They began instead to situate Machu Picchu as the heritage of the nation, positioning its artifacts as critical evidence not simply of a Peruvian past but also of a Peruvian future.[22]

The Ruins of Heritage

Bingham was not the first explorer or archaeologist to rely on the virtue of science to extract remains and take them out of the country. During the nineteenth century, archaeology was used to fashion a national identity by Peruvians and foreign explorers alike, and questions about objects and their ownership had been present since the establishment of the first law.[23] Max Uhle, for example, conducted fieldwork in Peru in 1896-1987, 1899-1901, and 1903-1905. During his last exploration, Uhle was hired by the Peruvian government to develop and lead a national museum of archaeology, which opened in 1906.[24] He worked there until 1912. Uhle relied on *huaqueros* for objects to buttress the collections for the National Museum in Peru, but differentiated between "'scientific' archaeology and 'amateur' antiquarianism."[25] Although the noted *huaquero* Felipe Morales supplied Lima's private collections as well as the National Museum, Uhle dismissed private collections as lacking in scientific rigor.[26] Uhle's contract was terminated when he was accused of sending objects outside the country.[27] Initially desired because he was European, Uhle was later dismissed for the same reason.[28]

Peruvian scholars, too, drew on science and the quest for knowledge, albeit for nationalist aims. Julio C. Tello, who had a storied career in Peruvian archaeology, was a native Quechua speaker from the highland town of Huarochirí.[29] In 1905, he began excavations in and around his hometown, developing a collection of skulls that later served as the basis for his university thesis on the antiquity of syphilis.[30] Tello received his master's degree in anthropology from Harvard University, where he studied with the scholars Roland Dixon and William Farabee, the same men who had consulted with Bingham.[31]

Tello emphasized the national benefit of archaeological science, understood as universal. Science would "revalorize the genius of his ancestors" and would help "overturn inaccurate and prejudicial preconceptions."[32] He pursued archaeology in service to the nation, unlike those who pursued nonscientific collecting.[33] He consulted and collaborated with foreign scholars such as Aleš Hrdlička and found favor with Leguía and other members of the Lima elite.[34] Tello was later criticized for these associations, and like Bingham, he was accused of illegality and excavating without a permit.[35] Although Tello disagreed with Uhle's theories about Peruvian archaeology,[36] he sold collected materials to Harvard, sought to export excavated materials for study, and purchased antiquities in Peru and sold them abroad.[37] Tello considered a museum a "living organism" and the mechanism through which to share knowledge and increase the moral and intellectual ground of society.[38] Scientific institutions should unite to create, develop, strengthen, and guard the national spirit.[39]

Creoles fashioned themselves as inheritors of a pre-Hispanic past, and sought a common homogeneity for the Peruvian people by appropriating indigenous aristocratic discourses, as Cecilia Méndez has shown, as well as Incan symbols.[40] Lima elites in particular sought new forms of visibility through scientific knowledge and pursuits such as mapmaking, geography, botany, and mineralogy.[41] Archaeology was important for nation building, and a variety of actors drew on ancient history for territorial and political claims, all of which contributed to shaping collective identities and erasing the distance between past and present.[42] As Sara Castro-Klarén points out, "The task of linking the glorious but ruined past to the rising nation fell not to history (documentary and archival) but rather to archaeology (visible, tactile, and measurable, and nonalphabetic)."[43] Thus, archaeological science became deeply imbricated with patriotism and Creole nationalism.

In 1825, Simón Bolívar decreed the protection of Incan monuments as relics of a glorious past, and that same year the Friends of Cuzco antiquarian society was founded.[44] Science was not simply or only an imperialist project conducted by outsiders, but also a tool of former colonies seeking to advance independence and nation building.[45] By the early twentieth century, pre-Columbian material and imagery, along with public discussion of that material, had an increasing presence in Lima.[46] A modern nation needed a national science, and archaeologists helped provide that identity.[47] Expeditionary and archaeological sciences were tools for foreign explorers and scientific nationalists alike in the early twentieth century. The conflicts over the removal of artifacts by Yale demonstrated both the entanglement of science and nation, and the efforts to manifest Machu Picchu as Peruvian patrimony.

Yale Excavating in Peru

Two months after returning from the first expedition to Peru, Bingham began to consider the need for a special concession that would allow Yale University to excavate Peruvian archaeological sites and ship the collected materials back to the university for study. He broached the idea with President William Howard Taft in February: "We have discovered a large number of clues, including not only the so-called glacial bones, but also the ruins of half a dozen ancient cities, which make it extremely desirable to undertake the work of archaeological exploration and excavation."[48] The only difficulty, Bingham wrote, was the Peruvian bureaucracy.

A 1911 Peruvian law decreed that all ruins and ancient cities were the property of the Peruvian state. Private persons, the law stipulated, could not excavate such property. Bingham believed that the law was mainly directed at local treasure hunters; it nonetheless forbade the exportation of Peruvian antiquities. From Bingham's perspective, the law impeded the completion of investigative scientific work. A special concession negotiated between the Peruvian government and Yale University could circumvent the problem. The agreement would allow Yale to "freely excavate and explore the remains of ancient cities" for fifteen to twenty years.[49] Additionally, the concession would allow found materials to be shipped to the United States. What lay beneath Peru's soil was of scientific importance and universal value. Bingham's connection with Leguía gave him hope that winning such a concession might be feasible.

On February 13, 1912, Bingham wrote his trusted contact at W. R. Grace & Co., Louis Schaefer, to inform him of the plan for a concession.[50] Bingham requested information about the political climate in Peru and the most appropriate time to seek a concession. After contacting people in New York and Lima, Schaefer assured Bingham that the upcoming 1912 expedition would not interfere with the proposed concession. If anything, Schaefer wrote, Bingham's presence in Peru "should materially assist [him] in getting the concession."[51] Schaefer wrote his counterpart in Lima, Mr. Ballen, who agreed to inform Bingham of the most auspicious time to formally present the request for a concession.[52] A code was set up so that Ballen could discreetly tell Bingham when the timing was right.[53]

President Taft asked that an informal query be made of the Peruvian minister of foreign affairs about the possibility of excavating and exporting Peruvian antiquities under Peruvian law, and about the possibility of receiving a multiyear concession.[54] It was decided that it would be unwise for Taft to directly intervene to assist "American enterprise," and that the desire for a concession should be administered by proxy through State Department channels.[55] Taft requested that all proper support be given to Bingham and his expedition.[56]

The State Department wrote the US legation in Peru on February 26, 1912, alerting it to the fact that Bingham wanted a concession.[57] By early April 1912, plans were under way in Peru to secure the concession for Yale. Both the State Department and the US embassy in Peru wrote Bingham letters of support for the concession.[58] The acting secretary of state,

Huntington Wilson, wrote Bingham on April 8 that President Leguía had agreed to submit to Congress a bill granting Yale exclusive rights for archaeological explorations for twenty years, even with the prohibitions imposed by existing laws.[59] An extra session of Congress was planned for June, and Wilson urged Bingham to approve the concession while Leguía, a longtime ally of the United States, was still in office.[60] Meanwhile, through the State Department, Bingham requested that the US ambassador in Lima secure the same privileges for Yale's 1912 expedition as the 1911 expedition had received, namely, the right to excavate and remove antiquities from Peru.[61] By April 13, 1912, President Leguía had granted Yale and Bingham those privileges and had agreed to the negotiation of a concession.

The correspondence over the concession eventually took on a sense of urgency. H. Clay Howard of the US legation in Peru wrote to President Taft about Yale's plan for exhaustive archaeological explorations in Peru. Having secured the cooperation of President Leguía and Peru's minister of foreign affairs, Howard requested from Taft the exact details of the bill to be submitted to the Peruvian Congress. According to Howard, Leguía supported an exclusive concession to Yale for twenty years because it would allow for the conservation of Peruvian antiquities. Peru's existing law, with its haphazard enforcement, inhibited scientific exploration and encouraged treasure hunting. According to Howard, Leguía was in favor of granting the concession to a US institution. A prestigious university such as Yale would be "even better." Furthermore, Leguía would "rather have such rights placed in the United States than in Europe; and granted to such a university as Yale, than be the subject of indiscriminate concessions of conflicting rights, and perhaps to irresponsible concessionaires."[62] Leguía suggested that the concession be secured while he was in office, because in Peru "nothing [was] certain but uncertainty."[63]

Yale's attorneys were asked to draft a proposal that would be submitted during the special session of the Peruvian Congress. The first draft, given to Bingham on April 17, 1912, was written by John Bristol of the firm Bristol, Stoddard, Beach and Fisher. Bingham responded to the draft with a few suggestions, including a request to research how concessions had been granted in Egypt. Bingham and Bristol agreed that some of the more specific terms would need to be changed when translated into Spanish. But as Bristol informed Bingham, it was best to throw as much as possible into the proposed concession in hopes that some things "may stick."[64]

Although Bingham felt that his presence in Lima would assist in the passage of the concession, he was concerned about asking for exclusive rights. Exclusivity might cause firm opposition in the Peruvian Congress and grief in the United States.[65] Nonetheless, the concession's exclusivity clause remained. On April 24, Bingham wrote to Arthur Hadley, the president of Yale, regarding the details of the concession.

> I am advised by W. R. Grace and Company that they have heard from their confidential agent that this is a favorable time for securing the concession in Peru, and that they will telegraph later when I ought to go. The State Department advises me that they have received another cable from our Minister in Lima assuring us that the President will grant all necessary privileges for this year's expedition, according us the same favors granted us last time. It seems to me we are now in a position to go ahead without any further difficulties except those that can easily be overcome as they arise.[66]

Hadley did not make any changes to the concession, and a final draft copy named Bingham as the agent to secure the concession for the Yale Corporation.[67] As the petitioner, Bingham could make any changes necessary while in Lima. Yale was poised to propose the concession to the Peruvian Congress.

Before the concession was submitted, the details of its passage began to worry Bingham. Talk of a special treaty, rather than a concession, between the United States and Peru had surfaced.[68] Bingham wanted a concession, which would not involve the difficulties surrounding a treaty. A treaty would require approval by the US Senate, and Bingham felt that the Senate was unlikely to pass a treaty granting exclusivity to one university. Although Peru seemed uninterested in granting rights to more than one concessionaire, the exclusivity clause continued to disquiet Bingham.

As details of the concession began to be debated, legal questions over the ability to carry out archaeological excavations on public or vacant lands rather than private lands surfaced. Bingham's lack of knowledge of Peru's laws and legal system began to press on him as he questioned whether asking for a concession would really have any effect and whether it was advisable to ask for exclusive rights.[69] During the first week of May 1912, Bingham sent letters to Schaefer, Wilson, and Taft, among others, inquiring about the necessity of a treaty, its urgency, and the timing with which the concession needed to be made (since the current president's term was coming to an end). He also asked about the best way to proceed.[70] Simultaneously, Bingham continued to make plans for his upcoming expedition, writing to his trusted contacts for discounted rates, special favors, and financing.[71] On May 11, the request for a concession, without the need for a special treaty, was sent from the White House to the State Department and communicated to the legation in Peru.[72] The State Department translated the petition into Spanish, and Yale gave Bingham power of attorney.[73]

Negotiating the 1912 Concession

By July 1912, the expedition party had arrived in Peru.[74] Bingham, however, was reluctant to leave Cuzco for Lima and work for passage of the concession. Instead, he spent four months in Cuzco surveying and excavating, traveling to Lima only as necessary. Bingham asked Morkill of the Peruvian Corporation to continue to support the concession while he remained in Cuzco.[75] Bingham was confident that the concession would pass easily: "I should feel very badly indeed to have to return to Lima on account of the concession. As there is little if any opposition to the project I believe that the only thing necessary is to see that it does not die a natural death from neglect or oversight."[76] A similar letter was sent to Mr. Ballen of W. R. Grace. Bingham later came to regret his decision to stay in Cuzco.[77]

Not only were the president and Congress in favor of the concession, but the press in Cuzco had also been extremely supportive of Bingham's return to conduct another expedition. For his part, Bingham saw no need to return to Lima, because he did not anticipate any difficulty with the approval of the concession. Meanwhile, Bingham kept President Hadley of Yale abreast of the expedition and of the general political climate in Cuzco. Hadley, in turn, congratulated Bingham on his ability to maintain such good connections with both sides.[78]

In retrospect, remaining in Cuzco proved unwise for Bingham. Without his constant presence and pressure, the request for the concession languished. Heeding the advice of President Leguía, Bingham entrusted a Peruvian lawyer to review the document in Lima, making a few necessary changes.[79] On August 19, 1912, a contract was drafted by the minister of justice, education, worship, and public benevolence and signed by the president. The contract gave an exclusive concession to Yale for ten years.[80] Bingham couldn't sign the contract, since he was still in Cuzco. Instead, the US minister in Lima, H. Clay Howard, signed it.[81] At that point, it lacked only congressional approval. Leguía was surprised that for something so important, Bingham did not give it his personal attention.[82]

Of greater concern was the fact that Bingham was working in Peru under verbal permission and that once Leguía's term expired, so would that permission.[83] Howard expressed his concerns to the State Department about having the legation "log-roll" to influence legislation.[84] In October 1912, the bill still had not been submitted to Congress.

The bill had been passed to the Committee on Education, where, Bingham ruefully noted, it was "peacefully sleeping."[85] Bingham arrived in Lima in late September to urge passage of the delayed bill. It was finally reviewed and passed on to the Instituto Histórico.[86] Bingham attempted to meet with the high-ranking members of the institute.[87] The concession was not seen as being of preeminent importance, especially because Bingham had not been present to advocate for it. Bingham felt that Yale's concession was not being prioritized over the last-minute favors and acts of nepotism that filled Leguía's final months in office.[88] Other US institutions, such as Harvard's Peabody Museum and the Smithsonian, wrote the US State Department and their contacts in Peru in protest of Yale securing a concession.[89]

By October 7, it had become clear to Bingham that the concession's chances of passing had taken a turn for the worse. Bingham met with the president of the Instituto Histórico, Eugenio Larrabure y Unanue, who was also Leguía's vice president and had requested that Carlos Romero write the *informe* that Bingham read in 1910.[90] Larrabure y Unanue informed Bingham that he had personally, and recently, introduced a bill prohibiting the exploration and removal of objects of archaeological or antiquarian interest. Consequently, there was no way he could support the concession without compromising his own integrity.[91] President Leguía recommended that Bingham withdraw the request for a concession until a more auspicious time.[92]

In 1905, Larrabure y Unanue had become the first president of the Instituto Histórico. During his installation, he stated that there was nothing more interesting than the history of Peru.[93] He wanted to attract Americanists to Peru to investigate and study the origins of the indigenous populations of the Americas. He noted that just as Peru was a place rich with minerals and a variety of climates, it was equally rich in archaeological monuments and historical sources.[94] Considered one of Lima's "most salient antiquaries," he believed that the collections and the rich history found in objects never stayed in the country, in contrast to the practice in Europe.[95] Any traveler "could take a gang of peons and disinter mummies and objects without anybody's permission, as if they were in their own home," he wrote.[96] The minister of justice and instruction,

Jorge Polar, believed that through the institute, art and science, truth and beauty, would flourish. Strengthening nationalism was the institute's highest mission, and through the study of Peru's past, it would acquire a clear awareness of the country's destiny, maintaining the road to "our generous historic ideal."[97]

Many in Peru had begun to protest the special privileges granted Yale on the 1911 and 1912 expeditions.[98] The press, formerly supportive, excoriated Leguía for granting Yale privileges to excavate and remove artifacts.[99] Leguía's departure from office drew attention to the Yale expeditions and their special treatment, and many questioned the North Americans' motives. Bingham had closely aligned himself with Leguía, requested special favors, and relied on persons appointed by Leguía to assist him in carrying out his expeditionary goals. Although this alliance produced favorable results initially, when the political tide turned against Leguía, Bingham was swept up in its wake.

Guillermo Billinghurst, the mayor of Lima since 1909, came to power as a populist champion of Peru's working class, even though he was a wealthy politician.[100] As Leguía's pro-American, capitalist stance fell under scrutiny, Bingham and the expedition came to signify all that was corrupt in Peruvian politics.[101] A frustrated Bingham wrote Hadley on October 21, 1912, just days before withdrawing the concession request: "Peru is like all the rest. The only difference was that the former president smiled on our scientific work—and so all the government officials smiled. The present President yawns (or would if he dared) and the Peruvians copy his manners."[102] Although Bingham withdrew the request, he "hoped to have more than a hundred boxes of stuff for the Museum."[103]

The controversy and the negative press did not sit well with Bingham, nor did it quickly dissipate. He continued to be the subject of editorials criticizing Yale's presumed right to ship goods, which was based on a false sense of "international etiquette."[104] Letters of support for Bingham from Giesecke, Ballen, and the Geographic Society of Cuzco were published in Lima's papers in response to the public criticism. On February 28, 1913, a letter to the Instituto Histórico from the future Peruvian ambassador to the United States, Federico Alfonso Pezet, was printed in Lima's *El Comercio*. He criticized the US treatment of Peru and wanted respect for the intellectual property of Americans as well as Peruvians.[105] Two months after returning to the United States, Bingham learned of the editorial. Feeling that Pezet had painted Yale in a poor light, Bingham responded by stating that he had never wanted a monopoly and had acted in the general interest of science.[106]

After the concession failed, other ideas circulated about how to work productively in Peru and abide by its laws regarding the removal of antiquities. The idea for a museum and school of archaeology in Cuzco was actively promoted by Albert Giesecke. He felt that such an institution would "minimize the antagonism" of individuals and institutions in Lima and go a long way toward achieving the goals of science.[107] Bingham was interested enough to write both the Archaeological Institute of America and the Carnegie Institution of Washington. He proposed that a farm be purchased in the Cuzco area, where suitable residences could be built for two archeologists, their families, and four or five research assistants. A farm appealed to Bingham because it would allow the archaeologists to produce their own vegetables and other supplies that were either difficult to procure in Cuzco or not to Bingham's liking. Using the farm as a base, researchers could carry out excursions and expeditions in the surrounding area—an area that, according to Bingham, contained enough ruins for forty, perhaps eighty, years of work.[108] While a Peruvian government concession would probably be necessary, an institution that could undertake firsthand work, provided that it left all materials in Peru, was an idea that Peru might favor. The farm never materialized, though a collaborative partnership and museum became a reality in 2011.[109]

Trials of Strength, or How the Concession Failed

Bingham's request for a special concession and the presence of foreign scientific expeditions in Peru received significant coverage in the country's press. In addition to *El Comercio*, periodicals such as *La Crónica* and *La Nación* published news of the conflict.[110] In an effort to tell his side of the story, Bingham responded to the editorials through letters to the editor.

Peru To-Day had covered Bingham's expeditions favorably since 1911. The magazine highlighted the biographies of expedition members and applauded Yale's efforts to explore the interior of Peru. Printed in English and published in Lima, *Peru To-Day* was aimed at English-speaking foreigners in Peru. It was more favorable than Lima's dailies to Bingham's concession request and to the presence of foreign expeditions in Peru. In "Valuable Scientific Expedition" (October 1912), *Peru To-Day* commented on Bingham's work:

The exceedingly important explorations being conducted under the direction of Dr. Hiram Bingham of Yale University are looked upon all over the world with greater interest than the people of Peru appreciate. And no people will derive greater benefit from the knowledge acquired by these means than the Peruvians themselves. . . . Quite aside from the scientific value which attaches to such work, and descending to the question of profit and loss, Peru is offered the chance of having the ruins explored without cost by competent men and the findings will be written up, not only for their fellow-scientists, but in the magazines and newspapers and many tourists will come here to see for themselves, as they have done to equally ancient, but no more interesting Greece, Italy and Egypt.[111]

Peru To-Day published follow-up stories about the expeditions in December 1912, January 1913, March 1913, and July 1913. In the January issue, the magazine tackled the reasons why the concession did not pass. The editors argued that opposition came from two sources: those who were concerned about their own commercial interests, and Larrabure y Unanue. The story noted that Peru didn't lack appreciation for the expeditions, but did "reserve the right to discuss matters which affect its possessions and take time about any decisions affecting the same." The editors felt that Bingham should have stayed in Lima to secure passage of the bill rather than returning to Cuzco, and that Billinghurst had made noteworthy efforts at compromise.[112] The editors went on to quote a passage from an editorial that Larrabure y Unanue had written in the *West Coast Leader*: "We regret that he [Bingham] should have been so hurt at having the big motives of Yale University brought into question that he considered a dignified withdrawal of the project his only course, and should thereby have taken away the splendid chance that was offered and have given his opposers an opening to appear as patriotic deliverers from purely imaginary dangers."[113]

In letters to *Peru To-Day* and *El Comercio*, Bingham argued that he never wanted an exclusive concession. Upset at accusations that the Yale expeditions had harmed artifacts and monuments, Bingham took it as a personal slight when the team was granted a temporary privilege allowing excavations to continue only until December 1, 1912. Bingham felt that his work was both noble and beneficial to Peru. The Yale Peruvian Expeditions sought to bring light to monuments, and they made topographical maps that were universally useful. Bingham relied on the good of science to justify the expedition's actions: "If the government of Peru can elaborate a more favorable contract for the science of the world, regulating the method that should dominate in all excavations for the truthful advancement of archaeology, the university will have great pleasure because we only pursue admirable scientific ends and the ability to amplify some knowledge about anthropology, geology, geography, osteology, ethnology and general (knowledge) about history."[114] Bingham said that Yale had no commercial interest in the work and was motivated only by the love of science.[115] He concluded that scientific knowledge would ultimately benefit Peru by attracting tourists and travelers seeking to admire the marvels of the Incan Empire. While Bingham was not interested in commercializing antiquities, perhaps Peru might be.

Opposition to the proposed concession served as a rallying point for Lima's intellectuals. Emilio Gutiérrez de Quintanilla, who succeeded Uhle as director of the National Museum in Lima, became a vocal opponent of foreign scientific expeditions and was especially critical of Bingham and Yale.[116] Gutiérrez was an elite Limeño who sometimes advocated for the Europeanization of Peru.[117] The question that vexed so many elites was how to modernize when much of the population was indigenous.[118] Gutiérrez believed that Peru's problems stemmed from a lack of integration into modern society.[119] Consequently, he advocated for the need to bring the Indian into the nation.[120] A prodigious writer, Gutiérrez wrote "for the moths [and] for the mice."[121]

In a lengthy editorial in *La Nación*, Gutiérrez equated the sacking of Peru's subterranean treasures with the depredations of the Spanish conquistadores: "The modern culture invokes scientific and historic interest, but forgets that in their supreme norms figure justice, rights, the law, solidarity and fraternity of the human races. To destroy an indigenous sepulcher in order to take advantage of its contents as a treasure or as a document is to exercise an established right by law as above the title that the consciousness of the *raza* has as more legitimate."[122] Gutiérrez questioned: "What legitimate cause incorporates them today in the public domain, putting an end to the religious idea that explains its existence and suffocating the most revered sentiments of the defeated race, shackled, debased, but alive still?" He asked whether the Peruvian would "judge this same event tomorrow if it were the cemeteries of our fathers that were destroyed?" Science should not be elevated above other types of reasoning, other practices, and other beliefs. The benefit of such equality, Gutiérrez expounded, would be not simply human rights, but also the possibility for "national unity, military power and economic force, all critical for global commerce and industry."[123]

Published in September 1913, nearly a year after the Yale concession was withdrawn from Congress, Gutiérrez's editorial questioned how Bingham saw Peru. Rather than being seen as treasures fit for a museum, the Incan remains should be conceived of and valued on their own terms and in their own right, even if the present Quechua population was defeated, shackled, and debased, but alive still. Targeting laws that permitted excavations, Gutiérrez felt that symmetry was needed for national unity. Scientific reasoning and rationales ought to be placed on par with other humanistic and universalist logics. Without such equality, the country would continue to be fragmented, unable to fulfill the ultimate goal of participating in and partaking of the benefits of global commerce.

Gutiérrez does not connect objects of the past with the current indigenous population. Rather, he questions the translation of objects from the sacred to the secular.[124] In attempting to persuade the republic, he asked how Peruvians would feel if their recent ancestors were unearthed and placed on public display or used in scientific study. Peru, he suggested, would never have a role on the world stage if it placed the rights of some of its peoples over those of others. Buried objects were evidence of a storied and heroic national trajectory. Peru's soil and its contents were critical for nation building. Artifacts provided material evidence of a potentially cohesive narrative of belonging and national identity.[125] Shifting the location of the objects threatened that narrative and, thus, the nation's future. Controlling the context and meaning of the objects became a lesson for nation building. The key to Peruvian modernity was the artifact of its imagined indigenous ancestors.

Indigenismo and Utopia

In Latin America, race went hand in hand with questions about modernity and civilizing. As Marisol de la Cadena and others have shown, race was central to nation building in the late eighteenth and early nineteenth centuries.[126] After independence, Creole elites pondered what to do about their "Indian problem." Colombia and Argentina sought to civilize and modernize through a process of whitening and miscegenation with European immigrants.[127] Although whitening through immigration was also part of Peruvian ideas about promoting modernity, Peru, like Bolivia, remained largely indigenous.[128] Consequently, elite Peruvians faced a conundrum: they sought a national identity that was rooted in Indian ancestors but didn't contaminate the nation by incorporating its inferior, present indigenous population.[129]

Indigenismo flourished in Peru in the early twentieth century. Because of Cuzco's history as the capital of the Incan Empire, *indigenismo* was par-

ticularly strong there between 1910 and 1930, when Andean intellectuals sought to be taken seriously by their Limeño counterparts.[130] Rather
than emphasize phenotypes, Cuzqueño intellectuals, largely urban and
mestizo, emphasized cultural ideas of morality and decency, along with
what they understood as native cultural forms.[131] This allowed indigenous
intellectuals to thrive and gain social capital, even if doing so meant reproducing a social hierarchy that classified rural Indians as ignorant.[132] Ultimately, this culturalist notion resulted in a form of paternalism whereby
indigenista intellectuals spoke for indigenous populations. Rather than
support Indian struggles or uprisings, local intellectuals protected the
status quo of hacendados and saw Indian literacy as a means of rational-
ization and full political participation.[133]

The turn toward regional Andean self-discovery through *indigenismo*
coalesced around the interests and research of foreign ethnologists.[134]
Through ethnological investigation and its conclusions, the indigenous
population was transformed into a valuable and important, albeit essen-
tialized, object of study.[135] In *Tempestad en los Andes* (1927), Luis Valcárcel,
who studied under Albert Giesecke and was initially a critic of Bingham,
wrote about Peru's indigenous population as the soul of the nation and the
true Peru.[136] He advocated for the need to return to the authentic purity
of pre-Conquest Incan society, seeing *mestizaje* as degenerative.[137] Cuzco's
surrounding Quechua-speaking population began to be reframed as descendants of the noble race of the Incas.

Jorge Coronado suggests that "foreign theoretical models stoked new
perspectives on what role the indigenous population should play in modern Latin America."[138] Although seemingly opposed to dominant frameworks, *indigenismo* was taken up by Peruvian politics, informing laws and
becoming part of "establishment practices."[139] As a response to increasing
technology, democratization, and the importation of foreign ideological apparatuses, *indigenismo* was at its core a conversation about modernity and a specific attempt to wrestle with the conditions of colonialism.[140] Unlike alternative nationalisms or the creative engagement of rural
peoples, *indigenismo* was a clarion call to create an educated populace seeking modernity. *Indigenismo* became part of the country's official Creole
tradition.[141]

Gutiérrez's justification for the protection of archaeological remains
was not new. In 1851, Mariano Eduardo de Rivero, the first director of
Peru's National Museum, cowrote *Antigüedades peruanas* with Johann
Jakob von Tschudi, a Swiss naturalist.[142] In it, de Rivero argued that past
civilizations, including Peruvian antiquity, could serve as nourishment

and instruction for national progress.[143] Many other historical texts were dedicated to Spanish royalty, but *Antigüedades* was dedicated to the Congress of Peru and the "cause of National Sovereignty," or the cause of memory against ruin. Antiquity and ancient history had become reliable sources of self-knowledge, replacing the history of the Spanish monarch with a history of the people.[144] Gutiérrez drew on de Rivero's patriotic epistemological stance. But instead of replacing the history of the king, Gutiérrez's goal was to replace the history provided by foreign scientists. Excavation and removal of antiquities by outsiders was increasingly seen as contrary to the best interests of the nation.[145]

During this period in Peru, the vandalizing and looting of archaeological sites was not uncommon. Editorials and news stories discussed the protection and conservation of antiquities and ruins. An article in *Peru To-Day* positioned the unearthing and selling of objects as being detrimental to national imaginings and hopes for the future: "If we deserve the title of civilized, we should pledge ourselves to conserving them [the monuments], so that we will be able to liberate ourselves from the anathema of the new generations."[146] Objects were needed for a national imagining of a future great nation. To go forward, Peru needed to look back, toward its buried objects.

The *Boletín de la Sociedad Geográfica de Lima* (Bulletin of the Geographic Society of Lima) published several articles on Yale's work in Peru.[147] The bulletin also published articles by José Gabriel Cosio on ruins in the Cuzco area. In the conclusion of a thirteen-page article detailing the ruins of Machu Picchu, Cosio wrote about criminal actions that were rapidly destroying "the monuments that are the glory of our past and source of our history in all places in which they exist, whether it is in towns, separate villages, cities and in private collections."[148] Cosio referred to the looters of Sacsayhuaman and expressed concern about less well-known monuments in the Cuzco area such as Ollantaytambo, Písac, Torontoy, and Kkenco (Quenco).

In Cosio's eyes, the remodeling of houses in Cuzco and the mutilation of a stone collar of faces that had once adorned the base of the Intihuatana at Machu Picchu served as evidence of the degeneration of the public's respect for historic artifacts. Although the article was written on December 31, 1912, no mention was made of Bingham, the concession, or the commercial demand for artifacts. Rather, Cosio directed his critique at the Peruvian public. Such degeneration threatened the nation's future prospects.[149] Thus, the fortification of the nation was an internal battle waged against scientific researchers and those who looted indiscriminately. The treatment of objects was moralized, and Cosio demanded governmental support to help stop the destruction of the monuments.

The criticism of excavation at the hands of foreigners and looters seeking commercial gain emphasized the need to protect Peruvian soil and its contents. Framing Peruvian earth as bountiful drew on historical understandings of Peru's climate having uniquely contributed to the brilliance of Peruvian civilization.[150] Creole naturalists such as José Hipólito Unanue (1755–1833) argued that Peru's abundant and representative altitudinal climates had fostered "genius" and that genius "had created sagacious and beneficent social laws of indigenous origin."[151] Like the claims of Unanue and de Rivero, Gutiérrez's and Cosio's arguments were rooted in the notion that Peru contained everything it needed for greatness. Protecting antiquities and the soil that housed such antiquities was a national responsibility.

Gutiérrez, Cosio, Larrabure y Unanue, and Bingham all relied on tangible objects to manifest their specific discourses of modernity. For Bingham, collected skeletal remains were evidence of expeditionary success. Artifacts materialized science. They were the objects out of which study, universally valued, could be performed. For the three Peruvians, disinterred artifacts represented the key to the Peruvian nation's future. Without the objects, the nation would be lost, never materialized. Antiquities were critical to imagining and manifesting a national future, and possession was critical to realizing progress. In response to foreign scientists and indiscriminate collectors, Gutiérrez, Cosio, and Larrabure y Unanue suggested a national ideal that was located in the subterranean.[152] Thus, the objects removed from historical sites by Hiram Bingham and the Yale Peruvian Expeditions became animating objects for imagining a future.[153] The once-interred objects were viewed as repositories of the past and the future; they motivated various publics. This future past informed the fractious discourse around national patrimony.

Although a long-term concession from the Peruvian government was never revisited, Yale returned to Peru in 1914 and was granted the same privileges to explore and excavate as it had enjoyed on the 1911 and 1912 expeditions. The publication of "In the Wonderland of Peru" ameliorated tensions in Peru over the 1912 concession for a time. News of the "Wonderland" issue was heralded in Peruvian media and in private circles.[154] By 1915, however, the conflict over shipping antiquities out of Peru, and thus over the well-being of the nation, had once again become a matter of public discussion and controversy.

Artifacts of the Nation: The 1915 Injunction

While still in the field, Bingham updated Gilbert Grosvenor on the work being carried out in 1915.[155] Although the government had not interfered with their work, Bingham wrote that rumors and malicious lies were being circulated about the team in the Peruvian press. As in 1912, Bingham dedicated a significant portion of his time to diplomacy rather than exploration. He met with officials in Cuzco, including members of the Instituto Histórico del Cusco (IHC), to explain and to verify the nature of the expedition's work and to deny charges of illegally removing antiquities.[156] By June 1915, Bingham had written a response and official statement in the local paper.[157]

Among other things, the team was accused of bringing a steam shovel from Panama to get the treasures out of the mountains more quickly for transport.[158] Stories circulated that the expedition had secured anywhere from $500,000 to $5 million worth of Incan gold, shipping it out of the country via Bolivia. People claimed to have seen a dozen mules packed with objects of gold and silver and pottery.[159] Others thought the team had used eighty mules to carry out the mountain's riches.[160] In Osgood Hardy's journal, he noted that the prefect of Cuzco ordered the expedition to stop excavating, exploring, and exporting because someone had accused it of shipping antiquities by night via Arica, a Chilean border town.[161] Since no duplicate objects were found in the museums, people wanted to know where they were.[162]

The team had planned to stay for almost two years in the Cuzco region. Consequently, it set up headquarters in Ollantaytambo and rented a building that served as both lodging and a warehouse.[163] There, the expedition members could regroup and organize their materials before deciding what to ship to Yale. One evening, a group from Cuzco visited the team. The visitors included officials from the municipality, a Jesuit priest, the president of the Society of Artisans, and members of the IHC, including its president, Luis Valcárcel. The group asked to examine the materials stored at the "*yanquihuasi*" (Yankee house), and all of the boxes were opened.[164] According to Hardy's journal, the men departed at nine p.m., saying they were quite satisfied that the team was not doing anything harmful. Apparently, the confusion came about because Ellwood Erdis had initially requested permits from only four cabinet officials, overlooking one person.[165] Technically, the expedition had been breaking the law for the entirety of the expedition.[166]

The debate over the presence of Yale was carried out publicly in newspapers. On June 21, 1915, the editor of *La Crónica* wrote about Victor Guevara, a member of the "Antiquarian Society of Cuzco," and Eduardo Caceres, a former railroad engineer. The article details how Caceres saw Bingham's mules laden with objects. The mules were carrying not only pre-Hispanic materials but also colonial objects, including paintings and beautiful statues. After Bingham responded to Caceres that he was collecting objects to form a national museum, Caceres asked him, where are these objects that are going to be exhibited in our museum? There was no reply.

José Gabriel Cosio was not necessarily Bingham's biggest ally. In 1911, he had written in *Revista Universitaria* an article hinting that the expedition had damaged the Intihuatana stone during clearing and excavation.[167] Still, in 1915, Cosio defended Bingham against mounting public criticism in a letter to the editor of *La Crónica* on July 20, 1915.[168] Responding to the earlier letter recounting the story of Guevara and Caceres, Cosio discussed his work for the 1912 expedition. As a government delegate, he had received the artifacts and made a careful inventory of the materials that the team shipped to Yale.[169] The Ministry of Instruction (and Cosio) possessed a copy of the inventory of objects from Machu Picchu, Choqquequirau, Ayusbamba, Cuzco, and other locales.[170] Furthermore, an agreement between the expedition and Peru had been drafted and signed. In the agreement, the government of Peru reserved the right to demand the return of the objects that it deemed important. He closed with an emphasis on the valuable scientific outcomes of the expedition. In the effort to assure the public that the expedition was not hauling mountains of gold out of Peru, Cosio seemed a trustworthy witness.

On July 5, 1915, Bingham responded to the accusations.[171] He reminded the Peruvian public that he worked transparently, allowing all boxes and objects to be viewed by the Instituto Histórico del Cusco. Only one piece made of silver—and nothing of gold—was found. Moreover, he pointed out that in 1915 the Yale team did not conduct excavations in Machu Picchu. Contrary to the rumors, the team had employed only two archaeologists at the time. Working with them were six men, not the dozens of people fantastically imagined in the newspapers. Furthermore, Bingham wrote that the expedition team consisted of scientists—topographers, a naturalist, agronomists, and a physician—who were conducting valuable scientific work, searching for ancient roads and populations. The expedition took many pictures for *National Geographic*, which had more than

400,000 members. Bingham argued that the team's scientific work should be important to Peru because it brought attention to the area and highlighted its fame.[172] He concluded by saying that he was open to more discussion, but that he was incapable of breaking the law. He was an honorary member of the University of Cuzco, the Geographic Society of Lima, and the IHC.[173]

In the same newspaper, Enrique Palomino wrote that the rumors about Yale were fantastical.[174] He claimed to have been a secretary to Bingham, working with him in 1909 on his first visit to Cuzco. Palomino hoped that the public would not judge too quickly; there was an important difference between shipping goods for sale to individual collectors and sending them to those who were working in the name of universal science.

> The very jealous defenders of our national antiquities, have too late sounded the alarm in Cuzco; they should recognize the public notoriety that this department has, that some of the foreign houses have made a monopoly of the commerce of cloth, *huacos* and ancient and colonial utensils, exporting in large quantity and for the benefit of individuals; enriching many national merchants that have their special business with these objects, whose worth for them is in the 20 to 30 pounds that the tourists give them. . . . And this business is so extensive, reaching to the capital, patiently seen by the government and all the scientific institutes; that, in this occasion has lamentably confused, the high scientific ends of the universities of the US. . . . [The criticism] serves to block explorations that have only high interests, not only for America, but also for Universal Science . . . men of science can guarantee quality in contrast to merchants who ship goods.[175]

Even with Peruvian intellectuals' support, the fracas continued to escalate. In the summer of 1915, Bingham felt support for the expedition diminish. As the cases of skulls, bones, and potsherds were prepared for shipment in the fall of 1915, measures were taken to prevent the team from removing them. An agreement was finally reached on January 27, 1916.[176] Paperwork and the need to obtain official permission delayed shipment, but on June 20 the cases were shipped, arriving on or about July 20–25 in New York.[177]

Bingham had described the shipment from the 1915 expedition as consisting of about twenty-four cases of sherds of very small value.[178] The other boxes contained mostly bones and skulls, including some with interesting trepanations, and "a number of archaeological objects of no great value."[179] Bingham felt that the decree of the Peruvian government requiring return of the objects was superficial, since the majority of the materials shipped to Yale were duplicates. They would be useless in Peru and therefore discarded in the museum basement or sold on the street. Bingham felt the actions of Peru's bureaucrats amounted to political lip service to demonstrate to the public how concerned the politicians were about the nation's archaeological treasures. That Peru would benefit from Bingham's scientific investigation wasn't obvious to Peruvians. Nationalism, in contrast to the so-called neutrality and objectivity of science, was deemed irrational.

Gutiérrez presided over the inventorying and shipment of the Yale materials in 1915. In an article published in *La Prensa* on January 8, 1916, he argued that the arrangement with the Yale Peruvian Expedition revealed how unsatisfactory the Peruvian laws were.[180] He urged the government to take its time and stop the shipment of goods. Making such a decision was within the rights of Peru under the antiquity laws of 1893 and 1911. Gutiérrez published the inventory of the seventy-four boxes, listing the bones, the wrappings, rocks, pots, and potsherds that they contained. The list was translated from the inventory initially provided by Ellwood Erdis. After listing the contents of the boxes, Gutiérrez wrote in frustration:

> It seems well that the expedition organized by the University of Yale traveled the Department of Cuzco in demand of Peruvian antiquities, ignoring national sovereignty in the same fashion as those expeditions of Cortes and Pizarro examined the states of Montezuma and Atahualpa, in the name of religion and treasury of Carlos V. No acceptable end justifies, nor reconciles the means, if Peru is not today much more crude than in the time of the Inca, abandoned at the enthusiasm of the first occupant. In protection of the respectability of this land, always so mistreated by its own or strangers, and fulfilling a need imposed by the position I hold, I point out the irregular manner in which the expedition members of Yale University carried out their operations; a manner that injures the patrimonial sentiment.[181]

This section was also printed in his official report, which contained his inventory.[182] The report continued, "Is it time to match the zeal of the American scientific expedition, with the current provisions, and with the principles adopted by the Americanist Congresses attended by delegates of Peru?" Seemingly at wit's end, Gutiérrez concluded his editorial and his report by highlighting the absurdity of being asked to review 74 boxes, contemplate 626 objects, and write 99 pages of notes in a few short weeks.

The conservation and preservation of Peru's antiquities became Gutiérrez's passion. He made two further reports to the director general of instruction in 1916 about Yale, the abuse of laws, and the exportation of artifacts.[183] In 1921, Gutiérrez wrote a memoir.[184] Perhaps best described as a frustrated longing for national greatness, it contains many pages recounting the scandal and the fact that at the time of the memoir's printing, the artifacts still had not been returned.[185] He argued that the ability of Bingham to remove objects in 1912 in the name of international etiquette and in the face of the 1911 law demonstrated that scientific "corporations" could easily test the weakness of Peruvian laws. Gutiérrez referred to the rumors that had circulated around Bingham and the expedition, noting that numerous mules were used to transport cargo clandestinely via Arica and through Bolivia by river.[186] He complained about the inaccuracy of Ellwood Erdis's testimony in describing the interment of objects as occurring "a few to thirty inches" below the surface. For Gutiérrez, this was clearly a fabrication, and any knowledge of the sedimentation and geologic constitution of the medium in which the objects were excavated was worthless. He wrote that anything other than a general opinion about the ancient civilizations could not be supported, "nor would new light penetrate those prehistoric periods that preceded the current terrestrial geography."[187] He asked incredulously whether all the diverse objects of interest to science were to be found "smiling at the sun."[188]

For Gutiérrez, the past was still alive, and its objects would guide Peru to a prosperous future.[189] An ancestral criterion continued to be the key to resolving the complicated problems of Peru. The nation could not be born through outsiders' knowledge. Rather, only through the ancient history of Peru as embodied in its antiquities could Peru take shape as a prosperous nation. Nationalism, coupled with an object-oriented patriotic epistemological stance, obligated Peruvians to be concerned with, and to take care of, their ancient history located in objects. Science in the hands of outsiders threatened modernity: "Tradition, history and national soul are not another thing. The resurrection of the past in a symbol or a monument is an integral part of the present life, and its influence is exercised in the future. To relinquish ourselves of that past is to tear out the primary entrails. To consent to it, would be suicidal."[190] At the end of his memoir, Gutiérrez demanded that Yale return the materials shipped from the 1912 and 1915 expeditions. Furthermore, he suggested that the university be required to send an authentic copy of the studies and related reports of the explorations of 1912 and 1914–1915.[191]

Archaeological ruins had come to form part of the spirit and future of the nation. Since independence, the scientific and patriotic care of ruins translated into the pride and brilliant future of the Peruvian nation. Yale's excavating of the ruins and profiting from them threatened to damage not only the spirit of the nation but also the possibility of Peru again achieving glory. Intellectuals called for the enforcement of laws and the establishment of a museum in which the local historic institute and the national government could conserve the nation's antiquities.

Failure to Translate: The Denouement of Bingham the Explorer

Upon returning to Yale after the 1912 expedition, Bingham wrote to his friend and colleague at the Smithsonian, William Henry Holmes, regarding future scientific work to be conducted in Peru:

> Dr. Hrdlička called on me last Friday, and I was very glad indeed to see him. He is going to have, I am afraid, considerable difficulty in getting permission to investigate graves and export bones. . . . Accordingly, I venture to suggest, in the interests of science, that you urge upon the State Department the necessity for cabling the American Minister in Lima to secure the necessary decree before Dr. Hrdlička arrives. . . . Although the material which he is after is of no particular value to the Peruvians, and although they would not know what to do with it if they had it, the very fact that he is willing to come such a long distance and spend money in securing it, is sufficient proof to them that the material that he is after is material that they ought to keep in the country.[192]

By 1915, Bingham's frustration with Peruvian laws and the conditions placed on the excavated objects had intensified. Bingham wrote Gilbert Grosvenor that he was tempted to let the Peruvians "whistle for" the objects.[193] Grosvenor offered more sober advice: "I feel that we ought to abide by the letter of our agreement with the Peruvian Government and return all the material that we contracted to return, and I am glad you share this view with me. Why don't you have plaster casts made of the more remarkable skulls?"[194]

Grosvenor admonished Bingham for making the fight public: "I realize all the facts are on your side, but you can't make the public realize the justice of your statements. The smoke that you would raise would dim the brilliance of your work in Peru. . . . Don't do anything that will detract from the brilliance of the Machu Pichu [*sic*] discovery. This discovery will loom larger every successive year."[195] Both Bingham and Grosvenor felt that the treatment the expedition received was unfair and unjust.

In January 1916, *National Geographic* offered to do a story on the controversy. Bingham declined, feeling that it would "rake up the matter again" and cloud work that had been successfully completed.[196] Both Bingham and Grosvenor finally agreed that it would be detrimental to tangle with the Peruvian government over the matter. Bingham's career as an explorer ended with the 1915 expedition.[197]

Machu Picchu came to be defined as Peruvian heritage in response to foreign expeditions, the goals of science, and the needs of nation building. The excavation and removal of Peruvian antiquities by Yale drew on what Jorge Cañizares-Esguerra, in his work on eighteenth-century Spanish and Spanish American debates about the precolonial American past, has called patriotic epistemology. Such an epistemological stance highlighted the shortcomings of Europeans, privileging eyewitness accounts of native noblemen and the material cultural remains of indigenous civilizations.[198] Mark Thurner has demonstrated that a patriotic epistemological stance contesting European narratives of Peru was consistently deployed by Peruvian intellectuals throughout the nineteenth century and into the twentieth.[199]

The excavation and removal of objects in the name of science became the locus for two epic battles. For Bingham, the artifacts were important for science, universally valued. Science could benefit Cuzco and the nation of Peru by bringing fame and renown to the area, and thus help develop the tourism industry. Within Peru, the artifacts were imagined by elites as a heritage road map directing the nation toward a prosperous future; the less tangible object was a desired modernity. Such "monumental ambivalence"[200] relied on a positioning of objects as invested with a type of ancestral knowledge that was useful to all factions, encouraging them to see themselves and their future in archaeological objects and in the sepulchers of Peru's imagined ancestors.

Those claiming the objects of archaeological ruins weren't doing so based on biological descent and inheritance. Rather, the conflict over Machu Picchu and its artifacts was an elite Creole project that drew on strains of *indigenismo* to position the Inca as national ancestors. Gutiérrez, Cosio, and Larrabure y Unanue thought of interred objects as the way toward modernity and a glorious future. Bingham claimed science as a universal and noble pursuit, but intellectuals and elite Peruvians rebuffed such universality in the hands of outsiders, nurturing instead a patriotism with ruins managed by elite Peruvians at its center.

The Yale Peruvian Expedition proved to be a valuable instigator. Around the boundary object of Machu Picchu, actors negotiated its translation as either a universally valued scientific discovery or an emblem of national heritage, and also sought to standardize the treatment of archaeological objects. Notably, this tacking back and forth persisted through the return of Machu Picchu's artifacts in 2011. Remains needed to be excavated by trained archaeologists and cared for in specific ways in museums and noteworthy collections. Foreign scientists might at times be welcomed, but at other times the translation of the remains into a neutral scientific universality was questioned. Creoles and intellectuals used Machu Picchu to tailor and eventually normalize themselves as inheritors of a glorious pre-Hispanic past, something that they helped manufacture and that ultimately became a potent national truth. The separation between the noble past and the miserable indigenous present persisted as a patriotic epistemology framed objects of the past into Creole ancestry alone, effectively articulating, "Machu Picchu sí, indios no."[201]

Artifact

There is no getting beyond pictures, much less world pictures, to a more authentic relationship with Being, with the Real, or with the World.
W. J. T. MITCHELL, *WHAT DO PICTURES WANT?* (2005)

In 1921, the *Guía General del Sur del Peru* was printed to celebrate the centenary of Peru's independence. It was dedicated to President Leguía.[1] The book began with a comment from the "untiring boss of the commission of Yale University, Hiram Bingham," about the importance of Cuzco.[2] After a brief history of the Inca, the book listed steamship companies, their schedules and rates, and details about Peru's imports, exports, commercial houses, souvenir options, and monuments of interest to tourists. The guidebook then discussed a visit to Machu Picchu. After describing the best approach to take and the best place to find supplies and rest one's animals (at Melchor Arteaga's, in fact), the guidebook advised: "The tourist should take something to eat and drink for all of the companions and in no way forget to bring along their Kodak."[3] The section was repeated nearly verbatim in a subsequent guidebook, *La Meca de la America del Sur*, in 1924.

Since then, Machu Picchu has been promoted and developed as a world-class tourist destination.[4] In 1948, a zigzag road named the Hiram Bingham Highway was built to improve access to the ruins.[5] In 1936, talk began of constructing a hotel near Machu Picchu and cleaning up the site further;[6] in 1951, architects estimated the cost of the hotel to be approximately $379,000.[7] Albert Giesecke, as head of the Peruvian Tourism Corporation, was still working on building the hotel in the mid-1960s.[8] By 1964, nearly 40,000 tourists were visiting Machu Picchu annually.[9] Today that number is closer to one million, and plans were announced in 2016 to build a space at the ruins' entrance that would offer an enhanced ex-

Figure 7.1. *Grupo en Machupichu*, Cabrera Brothers, 1940. Courtesy Fototeca Andina, Centro Bartolomé de las Casas, Cuzco, Peru.

planation and contextualization of the site.[10] Tourists continue to follow the early guidebook's advice, packing snacks and something to drink, and never forgetting to take along their cameras.

Shortly after Bingham's visualizations, professional photographers began making Machu Picchu a backdrop for their work. Martín Chambi's iconic image of a vacated Machu Picchu was taken in 1925. Others, like the Cabrera brothers, took group portraits of people on tour, dressed in their finest attire, from the 1920s to the 1940s (fig. 7.1).[11] In the 1950s, David Salas made compelling images of tourists visiting the site by rail (fig. 7.2).[12] Filmmakers increasingly imagined the area as a setting for their productions. Dorothea Knox Martin wrote Luis Valcárcel in 1932 about the possibility of filming the story of Yucay, a "Peruvian princess," in the area. Her novel *Yucay: A Romance in Early Peru* was published in 1941, and on February 2 of that year she followed up with Valcárcel regarding a screen adaptation of the book, asking whether he wanted to act as technical director on the film.[13] *The Secret of the Incas*, starring Charlton Heston, came out in 1954 and was filmed on location at Machu Picchu. In 1958, *The Incas*, an instructional film, considered using Machu Picchu as the site for one

Figure 7.2. *Turista en Aguas Calientes,* David Salas, 1955. Courtesy Fototeca Andina, Centro Bartolomé de las Casas, Cuzco, Peru.

of its scenes.[14] Enrico Gras, an Italian filmmaker, made a documentary entitled *Machu Picchu* in 1953; it was lauded as part of the birth of Peruvian cinema in magazines such as *Caretas.*[15] The picturesque persisted as Machu Picchu's and Peru's most enduring asset.

The fame of Machu Picchu has meant significant growth and change for the towns that surround it. Aguas Calientes, the town at the base of Machu Picchu, has developed haphazardly while trying to keep up with increasing tourist traffic.[16] Cuzco, now a major tourist hub for the area, is increasingly oriented toward visitors. Café Ayllu, a longstanding favorite among tourists and locals alike, was once located in the central plaza, but has been displaced by rent increases. A Kentucky Fried Chicken outlet now stands in its place. Starbucks has also arrived, replacing a smoky but brightly lit bar that once overlooked the plaza. McDonald's competes with the national chain Bembos for hamburgers fried on the quick. Signage has been kept modest, and unless you are looking for them, these outposts of global homogeneity fade into the plaza's background chaos. Cuzco is now home to luxury boutique hotels, upscale restaurants (Gastón Acurio has two),[17] and cooking classes for tourists. Still, people continue to walk the streets, vending their wares and asking whether tourists want to take their picture. Parents and grandparents wait outside elementary schools to pick up their gleeful, uniformed children. Dogs jog through the streets. Women line up along Sacsayhuaman to sell corn and cheese. Tourists and locals soak up sun on the plaza benches.

Throughout the past century of commercial and touristic development, Peruvians did not forget about the objects that became part of Yale's collections. In 1918, a minister of the Peruvian government wrote the National Geographic Society about the return of seventy-four cases of materials shipped in 1915. Grosvenor replied that Hiram Bingham had been in the US Army "almost continuously" since making the agreement and hadn't been able to study the remains. He thought that at the end of the war, Yale might resume study.[18] In 1920, Peru cabled again to request the return of materials.[19] Bingham wrote Grosvenor to discuss the matter, lamenting that he would have to raise more funds to return the material, which he considered valueless and of little interest to a museum.[20] Grosvenor replied to Peru that Bingham still hadn't been able to study the artifacts and needed more time.[21]

   The quest continued. In the 1960s, Albert Giesecke communicated with Bingham's son, asking when the objects might be returned from Yale. Hiram Bingham Jr. responded that he had viewed the materials at Yale, noting that each piece of pottery had been numbered and catalogued for easy reference. He believed that an archaeologist was soon to be assigned to the collection for further study.[22] Six months later, he responded to another inquiry from Giesecke, saying that the Bingham family didn't have much material for the new museum at Machu Picchu, because all of it was stored at Yale. "It seems to me," Bingham Jr. continued, "that much of the collection of Inca pottery that is now carefully listed and stored at Yale could be returned to Peru. Much will depend on the attitude of the Department of State, the Yale authorities and the confidence placed in the measures and security to be provided at the new museum."[23]

   By 2000, Peru still hadn't received all the materials.[24] In 2001, the Belgian anthropologist Eliane Karp, who was also Peru's First Lady, urged her husband, Alejandro Toledo, the first Peruvian president of indigenous ancestry, to hold his presidential inauguration not in Lima's congressional palace but on the soil of Machu Picchu. Toledo, although of Quechua-speaking parents, was born and raised in the coastal town of Chimbote, far from the Andean highlands of Cuzco. Nonetheless, at Machu Picchu millenarian conceptions of birth, death, and the promise of a new Peruvian era would be welcomed majestically and spiritually through dialogue with the Inca. After negotiating a multiplicity of desires, a small ceremony was held in Machu Picchu after the official inauguration in Lima. Machu Picchu had become the official nationalism of the state, and as national patrimony, it was embodied in the Peruvian national imaginary.

The following year, Karp met with Yale University's attorneys regarding the repatriation of objects.[25] It was not until May 2005, however, that negotiations on an agreement began in earnest.[26] At the time, Peru viewed legal action as premature and hoped for an amicable resolution through dialogue. But by July 2005, it had become clear to the Peruvian parties that a more aggressive strategy was needed. The new strategy involved moral, political, and legal avenues.[27] Additionally, the Peruvian team began to research the legal documentation surrounding the removal of artifacts by Bingham, from the perspective of both Peruvian law and international rights. Peru also secured the services of an American law firm to assist with its case and represent it in negotiations. The Peruvians inquired about the cost of a lawsuit, but opted for continued negotiations.[28] An ad hoc committee with Yale was formed to negotiate and devise a plan for the return of objects.[29] As negotiations began in earnest in early 2006, Peru was highly aware of the cost it would incur in legal and personnel fees if it opted to pursue a more litigious course of action.[30]

On September 14, 2007, Peru and Yale University released a joint statement. They had signed a Memorandum of Understanding (MOU) agreeing to the return of various artifacts.[31] Both Peru and Yale acknowledged that Machu Picchu was rightfully recognized by UNESCO as cultural patrimony of the world and treasured by humanity. The MOU stated that Yale had acted as a good steward of the materials and that Peru honored the achievements and memory of Hiram Bingham, whose "discoveries and contributions to archaeology and geography are respected worldwide."[32] Peru expressed its gratitude for the "stewardship, conservation and intellectual contribution of Yale in connection with those Materials for over nine decades, and for the groundbreaking scholarship and exhibition of the Materials that has occurred under Yale's sponsorship."[33] In return, Yale expressed its gratitude to the Peruvian people, "whose ancestors created the historical Materials that scientists and curators at Yale have conserved, displayed and studied in those nine decades."[34]

As part of the MOU's proposed collaborative framework, the parties would cosponsor a museum exhibit that would travel internationally and feature objects from the historic Yale Peruvian Expeditions as well as dioramas and other multimedia materials developed at Yale for its 2005 museum exhibition *Unveiling the Mystery of the Incas.* The government of Peru would lend objects to the traveling exhibition that would complement those from Yale. The exhibition was intended to promote understanding of Incan life and culture and to nurture tourism to Inca sites in Peru. More critically, income from ticket sales would go toward subsidizing the building of the "Machu Picchu Museum and Research Center" in Cuzco.[35]

Although both sides initially hailed the agreement as a "new model of international cooperation providing for the collaborative stewardship of cultural and natural treasures," it was only a short time before Peruvians began to protest provisions of the MOU. Peruvians were concerned about the return of only "museum quality"[36] pieces and the requirement that a new museum be constructed to house the artifacts.[37] What was meant by museum quality? Who decided? What were the non-museum-quality pieces, and how many were there? Why weren't all the objects being returned? Anything short of the total return of objects, without conditions, was unacceptable to many Peruvians, including Peru's cultural and intellectual elites.

Some wondered how Peru would come up with the funds to build and care for the center. The location of the new museum also created a flurry of speculation. Some felt that the new museum should be near Machu Picchu. Although there is a small site museum at the base of the mountain of Machu Picchu, many in Cuzco expressed the desire to nationalize the expensive hotel nestled next to the entry to Machu Picchu and convert it into a museum and research center. Others felt that the museum should be built in Cuzco on what was then part of the university's soccer fields. A new, contemporary, state-of-the-art facility could be built in Cuzco as a showpiece for the repatriated objects.[38] Still others believed that an existing high-quality museum in Cuzco could be renovated to house the center. Regardless, to many it felt as if Yale was dictating Peru's form of care as a condition for Yale's return of Peruvian patrimony, when Peru should be receiving the objects without conditions.

On February 23, 2008, Eliane Karp published an op-ed in the *New York Times*, stating that "Yale continues to deny Peru the right to its cultural patrimony, something Peru has demanded since 1920."[39] Karp's editorial was translated and republished two days later in the newspaper *El Diario del Cusco*.[40] Above the fold on the first page, Karp, wearing an emblematic Tawantinsuyo scarf, was featured to the right of the caption "Eliane Karp de Toledo Shows That the Agreement Was a Trick." In a larger font, the headline read: "Yale Will Not Return the Treasures of Machu Picchu." That was the final straw.

Karp's editorial marked the beginning of an onslaught of vocal and public criticism of the MOU. As a way of exhibiting due diligence, the director of the National Institute of Culture (subsequently renamed the Ministry of Culture), Cecilia Bakula, visited Yale on March 3, 2008, to witness the pieces for herself. Richard Burger, a professor of anthropology and curator at Yale's Peabody Museum of Natural History, had been charged with creating an inventory and determining the quality of the pieces.[41] Many in Peru became suspicious of his inventory and wondered how Peru would know it was getting everything that Yale had in its possession.[42] Bakula visited Yale to verify the collection, make her own inventory, and assure the nation that Peru had not been tricked into signing the MOU.[43] Public criticism of the MOU continued in Peru with what seemed like weekly updates.[44]

Increasingly unsatisfied with the MOU, in late 2008 the legal representatives of the Republic of Peru declared that they would sue Yale University. On December 5, 2008, Peru filed a general civil suit against Yale University in the US District Court for the District of Columbia. The cause of action was for the return of property "wrongfully, improperly, and fraudulently" retained by the defendant.[45] Yale moved to dismiss the case, saying that Peru had filed in the wrong court and that its claims were "stale and meritless."[46] On July 30, 2009, a federal district judge ruled that he did not have jurisdiction over the case and moved the case to a federal district court in Connecticut.

In the end, a court battle was avoided. The former rector of UNSAAC, Victor Raúl Aguilar, helped direct talks between the two universities to work toward a collaborative solution.[47] According to Lucy Salazar and Richard Burger, all parties were motivated to do something before the centennial of Bingham's 1911 expedition.[48] Ernesto Zedillo, a former president of Mexico and director of Yale's Center for the Study of Globalization, helped iron out the details.[49] On November 23, 2010, a new memorandum was signed. Yale University and the government of Peru agreed to establish a foundation for collaborative education and research. The agreement recognized both the importance of the Machu Picchu materials to Peru's national identity and Yale's good stewardship of them. In a catalogue published by the US embassy in Lima celebrating the Machu Picchu collection, the former Yale University president Richard Levin suggested that "in many respects Bingham's work helped to pioneer the entire field of Inca archaeology."[50] The objects would be returned at Yale's expense in three installments. The first delivery arrived in Peru on March 30, 2011.

Peru celebrated the centennial of Machu Picchu's scientific discovery with a week of activities in Cuzco, including local dances, orchestral performances, a photography exhibition, and the much-anticipated opening of an exhibition displaying the return of artifacts collected during the Yale Peruvian Expeditions.[51] Machu Picchu was host to a light and sound show, with performances by actors dressed as Incas reenacting the creation of the Incan city, its abandonment, and its rediscovery by Hiram Bingham. According to President Alan García, 2011 was the "Year of Machu Picchu's Centennial to the World."

Today, La Casa Concha in Cuzco houses the artifacts and is designated the UNSAAC-Yale International Center for the Study of Machu Picchu and Inca Culture. The center is meant to foster cooperation, study, conservation, conferences, and educational exchanges.[52] Located just off Cuzco's central plaza, La Casa Concha was a former palace of Túpac Inka Yupanki, son of Pachakuteq, builder of Machu Picchu. According to the marker that adorns the building, the Spanish occupied the house for several centuries and hosted important events and celebrations there. In 1840, the Peruvian state took possession of the house, and it subsequently became a prison and barracks. In the mid-twentieth century, the building became headquarters of the Police Special Services unit. In 2001, UNSAAC took over the building and began a long process of restoration.

Like many colonial buildings, the edifice's facade belies the elegance inside. At the entrance, an expansive open-air courtyard is surrounded by a balcony that frames the second-floor breezeway. A ticket counter and a small theater are off to the side. Twelve themed rooms that display the artifacts open onto the courtyard: Discovery Cave, Historical Photographs, Casa Concha Excavations, Machu Picchu Model, Archaeo-astronomy, Chicha Production,[53] Inca House, House Explorations, Everyday Life, Lab/Ongoing Investigations, Metallurgy, and Interactive Exploration. The tour begins at the first room on the left and circles around the first floor before continuing to the second floor. A small gift shop and a temporary exhibit are also included.

The museum's display essentially consists of Yale's 2005 *Unveiling the*

Mystery of the Incas exhibition. Included is the scene of the House of the Sapa Inca with the same mannequin of an Inca wearing gold sandals and a special headdress being served by two men holding gold drinking vessels. On an audio recording in Quechua, speakers discuss the protection of gold mines and the need to bring double the amount of coca leaves to Machu Picchu. There are sections on everyday life and metallurgy, along with a diorama of Bingham and a vitrine of his memorabilia. The exhibition in Cuzco does not include the section highlighting the lives of living Quechua speakers; perhaps it seemed irrelevant in Cuzco. There are also items on loan from Cuzco's Inca Museum and a brief explanation of some of the excavations at La Casa Concha.

The 2005 exhibition at the Peabody Museum began with visitors walking into a small anteroom to watch a short video narrated by Edward James Olmos.[54] After views of the breathtaking scenery, the film ended with an invitation to "see yourself at Machu Picchu . . . an ancient ruin in the clouds ready to reveal itself, a journey of discovery." The sound of a camera shutter clacked away as the film screen disappeared into the ceiling slowly and tantalizingly. At La Casa Concha, the same film was shown, translated into Spanish with English subtitles. The camera shutter still clacked away at the close of the film, and the idea of discovery was reiterated throughout the film. Bingham was shown "about to make a spectacular discovery," and the viewer was invited to think of that first moment in the "forbidding cloud forest." Visitors were encouraged to see themselves at Machu Picchu, a site ready to divulge its secrets. As the film darkened, visitors could begin their own journey of discovery.

An abundance of photographic imagery fills the exhibits. Reproductions of the Yale Peruvian Expeditions' photographs are sprinkled throughout the La Casa Concha exhibits, alongside more contemporary images. Large-scale reproductions of photographs of Machu Picchu paper the walls where the video is screened.[55] Enlarged prints of the hand-painted lantern slides hang on the walls of the Historic Photographs section. In the room with a large model of Machu Picchu is a video of the Yale scholars Richard Burger and Lucy Salazar explaining Machu Picchu's significance, accompanied by breathtaking images of the site. The model of the site has small lights that illuminate when Burger or Salazar discuss a certain location. Aerial photographs supplied by the American Museum of National History add to the photogenic appeal of Machu Picchu.

The last room in the exhibition houses several interactive computer stations. There a visitor can navigate the center's website, clicking on icons such as "Scholar Insight" to listen and see expert explanations of the architecture of the site. Visitors can learn about the materials uncovered in the area and the clues they might hold about the original inhabitants of Machu Picchu. An archaeoastronomer discusses the Intihuatana stone, refuting lore that the stone had something to do with ritual astronomy. Instead, he suggests that it was probably a seat or a throne. The scholar Amy Oakland Rodman holds a *winchuno* found at Machu Picchu and explains its use in weaving. Discussing the Incan custom of burying individuals with objects, Rodman explains how researchers can make assertions about what was important about a person's life based on their funerary objects. Because chisels and knives have been found, scholars speculate that perhaps a metallurgical workshop existed at Machu Picchu. Jean-Pierre Protzen discusses architecture and the Temple of Jagged Rocks. In talking about the reconstruction of buildings at Machu Picchu, he notes that there is not necessarily evidence for certain buildings to be so high. But, he says, after a few rainy seasons, one can't tell the difference. If there is no evidence for a particular reconstruction, what, he asks, is its justification?[56]

Sprinkled throughout the virtual world of Machu Picchu are clickable icons with Yale Peruvian Expedition photographs. Opening one of these links leads to a slide show of several photographic reproductions. The photographs automatically scroll, accompanied by narration. An actor impersonating Bingham describes what the images mean and what he was thinking about when photographing or excavating a certain part of Machu Picchu.[57]

Throughout the exhibition, photography is an omnipresent feature in the visualization of Machu Picchu. The images are meant to be apolitical illustrations, proof of the reality of the wonder of Machu Picchu. Their intention, however, did not necessarily mean that everyone was willing to let them be mere window dressing for the artifacts on display. The first time I visited, I was reading the text accompanying some expeditionary artifacts when a Peruvian tour guide entered. In the room was a diorama of Bingham with his tripod. The guide explained to his group that the photographs demonstrated what Bingham was looking for and how Bingham saw Machu Picchu. Pointing to the picture of Bingham with the lieutenant and a little boy (referred to as Pablito), the guide stated that these were the first tourists. The group laughed and the guide grimaced. I couldn't tell whether the guide was disappointed in their lack of critical self-reflection or simply tired of making the same joke to pleasure the tourists.

In an article published in Cuzco's daily *El Sol*, Bertha Bermudez Zamalloa suggests that the return of objects has not followed the agreement and that the exhibition itself acts as a eulogy for Bingham.[58] Highlighting factual errors such as those in the *chicha* room that portray making *chicha* as singular and universal, she criticizes the language of hacienda or estate used to explain the function of Machu Picchu. The concept of hacienda is applicable to fourteenth- and sixteenth-century Spain, she says, and should not be applied to Machu Picchu. She also feels that there is a haphazard treatment of the interpretative contexts of the objects in the museum, and she suggests that the museum should be focused on Machu Picchu instead of being a monument to Hiram Bingham. What is currently presented, she states, is a distorted truth. Highlighting the letter of agreement between Yale and UNSAAC, she argues that the museum is supposed to deepen understanding of Incan culture so that visitors will understand Machu Picchu better. As it stands, the exhibition at La Casa Concha is a fallacy, and she urges university authorities to do more, remembering that Machu Picchu is part of the cultural and natural patrimony of humanity.

Viewed in the context of Cuzco, the presence of Yale and Bingham in this exhibition of repatriated artifacts can feel jarring. The exhibition refers to Bingham without mention of other explorers or the assistance that Bingham received. There is no in-depth look at how the expedition happened. Also missing is any mention of the conflict over the return of artifacts and the attempts over the last century to have the materials returned. Instead, the story is told from Yale's perspective, and I left wondering how a Cuzqueño curatorial board might tell this story differently.[59] Would it situate Machu Picchu and the role of the Yale Peruvian Expeditions within a larger context of Spanish American exploration? Would it highlight the extensive work of Peruvian scholars who have also excavated and worked in and around Machu Picchu for the last century? Would it tell the story of repatriation? How might it display and communicate the ways in which local identity has been linked to its Incan past? Curating and installing exhibitions are time consuming and costly, and using Yale's *Unveiling the Mystery of the Incas* no doubt resolved an immediate need. Still, I wonder whether and how the exhibition will evolve, and how Yale's interpretation will be repositioned.

Victor Raúl Aguilar, the rector of UNSAAC, has suggested that the return of artifacts and the presentation of Machu Picchu to the world made a "landmark in Peru's history" and that Machu Picchu was "the most emblematic symbol of our identity."[60] Still, as Bermudez pointed out, the exhibition extols the virtue and myth of discovery, in effect celebrating Bingham and Yale. The lost city persists, with Yale at the helm once again in Peru; the materials were repatriated, but not quite the vision. In this

Figure 7.3. *Los Turistas*, Marcel Velaochaga, 2007. Acrylic on canvas. Image courtesy of the artist.

sense, one might ask whether all the artifacts of Machu Picchu were returned or whether they ever could be.

In a series of paintings by the Peruvian pop artist Marcel Velaochaga, narratives of history are juxtaposed with an ephemeral Peruvian present. The series entitled "Machu Pictures" features the iconic image of Huayna Picchu with the terraces and sections of the Machu Picchu sanctuary neatly laid at its feet. In all the paintings, Huayna Picchu is painted in neat fluorescent swatches of acrylic pinks, yellows, greens, and blues. Against the pop depiction of Machu Picchu, Velaochaga juxtaposes another moment in Peru's imaged history, creating a playful and probing dynamic about the myths of Peru's past and future.

In *Los Turistas*, the Homer Simpson family gazes at the viewer (fig. 7.3). Are they visiting Machu Picchu? Or is it a commentary on the pop com-

Figure 7.4. *Los Prisioneros*, Marcel Velaochaga, 2007. Acrylic on canvas. Image courtesy of the artist.

mercialism of the sanctuary? Or both? In *Los Prisioneros*, four black-and-white-striped llamas stare bewildered, yet accusingly and inquisitively, at the viewer (fig. 7.4). Are the llamas a metonym for the Andean peoples, or are they a commentary on the ubiquitous tourists at Machu Picchu, led around like pack animals? In another poignant depiction, ex-president Alberto Fujimori climbs a set of stairs with downcast eyes, a nod to an image from the Japanese ambassador's residence in Lima during a hostage crisis in 1996. Is he commenting on the violence of Peru's past and present? What images of Peru are at play in its global portrayal? Another painting features Lenin and Stalin, a pairing that came about after Velaochaga viewed the 2006 film *The Motorcycle Diaries*.[61] In an obvious reference to Hiram Bingham, one painting casts Indiana Jones playfully gazing at the viewer. The slippage between 1911 and 2007 is easy—the global myth of the adventure-seeking archaeologist alongside Machu Picchu's discovery and exploitation.

Influenced by Andy Warhol, Velaochaga says that he uses iconic images to explore the seemingly constant story in Peru. The same history, he says, is always at play in Peru.[62] Inspired by a tourist snapshot displayed at one of Lima's many photocopy and print shops, Velaochaga uses the theme of tourism to examine the connection between consumption and culture in a society that has become all spectacle. Velaochaga hopes that the paintings help us see the "spectacle-ization of reality that can become a daily nightmare, constant, one of which there is no waking."[63] Velaochaga was perhaps prescient, or maybe he was just paying attention to the fact that Machu Picchu was everywhere in the visual landscape of Peru. In the same year of his exhibition, Superman went to Machu Picchu in the famous comic book series.[64] Homer Simpson indeed took his family to the famed ruin during one of its episodes. And, in late 2008, *South Park* staged an episode at what is fast becoming a profitable Hollywood Machu Picchu studio.[65]

In Lima's *El Comercio*, Enrique Planas reviewed Velaochaga's exhibition. Planas describes Machu Picchu as a "symbol of a lost nation, ideological frame of indigenismo, terra incognita for gum-chewing tourists, space of the most delirious pseudo-archaeological theories and, of course, icon of fast-food tourism, today more popular than ever after having been recognized as one of the seven modern wonders."[66] By the end of 2008, nearly all the paintings in the series had sold, and Velaochaga was working on more paintings for the series, one to include an image of US forces invading Iraq.[67] The striking aspect of each painting is how a new commentary is easily created when juxtaposed with the stable, vacated icon of Machu Picchu. Machu Picchu is meant to represent Peru, if only in the most stereotypical way. The psychedelic hues, juxtaposition of images, and mixture of references encourage a viewer to reevaluate many of society's most dearly held myths. Presidential power, political figures, and the act of conquering are Velaochaga's chosen subjects.

Tourism is of course one of the most prominent themes, and Velaochaga's critique seemed both humorous and scathing to me. The images of the llamas held captive at Machu Picchu or of the silly face of Homer Simpson quickly convey the absurdity of what Machu Picchu has become. Velaochaga admitted that he had not been to Machu Picchu in ten years when he painted "Machu Pictures." "I don't know how it is now, but what I paint in the series is the idea that I have of Machu Picchu, full of tourists.

Families that go without knowing where they are or where they step."[68] Implicit in Velaochaga's paintings is a critique not simply of tourism, but also of a history of mistrust and mistreatment of the Peruvian nation by those in power. "Machu Pictures" is Velaochaga's set of imagined postcards, his own form of prospecting.

Not everyone in Peru worships Machu Picchu. Many are cynical about its exploitation and its constant commercial presence. Today, Machu Picchu symbolizes the struggle for postcolonial justice in the world arena as much as for economic opportunity. While most agree that it has become the logo or icon of the nation, many do not feel they are represented in this national image. Velaochaga is not alone in his critique of how the site has been managed and what it has become. In passing conversations and in some of the formal interviews I conducted with tour guides, people confessed a reluctance to champion Peru's rights to the artifacts excavated by Yale. Secretly, they admitted that they did not trust the National Institute of Culture and that the objects of Machu Picchu would probably be better cared for in Yale's Peabody Museum. Prominent state actors were criticized as crypto-indigenists.[69] Postcolonial ambivalences about the nation and state surfaced under Machu Picchu's watchful eyes.

Throughout this book, I have argued that Machu Picchu started its twentieth-century career as an effect born of a specific way of seeing. Ivy League connections, lettered men, wealthy persons, and commercial desires came together under the rubric of science and the promise of modernity to bear witness to Machu Picchu as a discovery. The potential of the expedition to gather knowledge about Peru's Incan past acted as a point of contact uniting multiple actors across national lines. Corporate sponsorships, financial donations, transnational social networks, governmental support, special privileges, and "good" families ultimately aligned to facilitate the successful expedition. Letters helped network this powerful circle of seeing, acting as an instrument of imagination and power.

In search of a lost city, the team excavated the countryside, relying on coerced local labor and knowledge to bring home tangible scientific proof of its monumental find. Armed with Kodak technology, the team made thousands of photographs depicting landscapes, caves, rock faces, and cloudy skylines. Discovery aesthetics in *National Geographic* subsequently promoted Machu Picchu as a faraway place, an exotic wonderland to visit and explore. Audiences could journey with Bingham and his team on a photographic narrative of travel, conquering the Peruvian landscape and discovering the lost city for themselves with each turn of the page. Many of these powerful materializations circulated worldwide, popularizing and making fact not simply Yale's science but also the very idea of a discovered lost city high in the cloud forest. Anthropometric photographs were also taken of indigenous subjects. Although they weren't popularized, they lent credence to the notion of a glorious Incan past and a miserable indigenous present, reinforcing the idea of the superiority of the US explorers and the validity of their enterprise.

Lost cities were scientific discoveries for some and patrimony for others. The presence of the Yale team and its removal of artifacts were criticized by Peruvian intellectuals and elites who positioned Incan objects as national ancestors and the key to a modern Peru. Rooted in a long-standing patriotic epistemology, the public negotiations in effect disrupted Yale's privileged sight. Machu Picchu, as exemplar of a glorious past, was welcomed home. Throughout, ideas about race undergirded how Bingham and his team conceptualized Peru and its people, informing their treatment of the population as well as shaping their expeditionary goals.

By focusing on the practices, technologies, and materializations of Hiram Bingham's three expeditions to Peru, this book argues that while Bingham's expeditions relied on the labor, knowledge, and support of local actors, including elites, intellectuals, and peasants, their efforts and know-how were transformed through scientific witnessing to become Bingham's and Yale's alone. In addition to letter writing and collecting, photography was a particularly potent scientific technology, both evidencing the find and circulating it, inviting audiences to participate not simply in Bingham's imaginary, but also in their own fantasies of discovery and conquering. Such visualization reiterated a lost city in the clouds discovered by Bingham and Yale to global audiences. Myths of discovery have persisted to the present without recognition of the racial underpinnings and imperial shadows of such narrative fictions.

Bingham's iconic imagery of Machu Picchu circulates widely today, marking Peru with its own visual referent. The same image of Huayna Picchu used in Velaochaga's paintings is ubiquitous in Peru. Machu Picchu is plastered on bus stops and vending carts; embroidered on handbags; used as art in magazines, newspapers, calendars, and corporate logos; and used to sell nearly every imaginable product, including Kotex (fig. 7.5). In 2008, at the entrance to the Lima airport was a large billboard with an enormously encompassing image of Machu Picchu, welcoming visitors to Peru and urging them to buy Merrill sneakers. That Machu Picchu and its artifacts are a national treasure of intrinsic and important cultural significance is at odds with its commoditization by nearly everyone. Instead, Machu Picchu seems a scrim on which to project one's commentaries

Figure 7.5. Advertisement at a Cuzco bus stop, 2008. Photograph by the author.

and desires. Nations, institutions, and individuals are free to drift toward the scientifically vacated site's mythical magnetism, spinning virtual gold through sovereign claims.

Such commercial images are not innocent replications or indexical one-offs. Instead, the photographs of Machu Picchu do something. Whether reproduced on a handbag or included as illustrations in a museum exhi-

bition, the images motivate. With their ability to be exchanged and manipulated while still serving as independent, and therefore objective, tools
of verification, the photographs first rendered by Bingham in 1911 have
helped brand the Peruvian nation. As shown by Yale's museum exhibition in New Haven and Cuzco, photography continues to be inextricably
linked with Machu Picchu. Divesting Machu Picchu of its image is impossible; doing so would diminish its power and its ability to conjure histories
and dreams. There is no getting beyond its picture to a more authentic
relationship.[70] Machu Picchu *is* the photograph. It has become its most
powerful artifact. Vision and image continue to be what matter most: the
wallpaper reproducing our myths, conjuring our fantasies, provoking our
politics, and inspiring our desire to claim and consume. Machu Picchu remains the lost city that never was, one always on the move.

Notes

Abbreviations

AAG   Albert Giesecke Archive at Instituto Riva-Agüero, Lima, Peru
AGN   Archivo General de la Nación, Lima, Peru
BFP   Bingham Family Papers, Yale University, New Haven, CT
BN   Biblioteca Nacional, Lima, Peru
CBC   Fototeca Andina, Centro Bartolomé de las Casas, Cuzco, Peru
IRA   Instituto Riva-Agüero, Biblioteca, Lima, Peru
LEV   Archivo de Luis E. Valcárcel, Instituto Nacional de Cultura, Lima, Peru
MRE   Ministerio de Relaciones Exteriores, Lima, Peru
NA   National Archives, College Park, MD
NGS   National Geographic Society, Washington, DC
YPEP   Yale Peruvian Expedition Papers, Yale University, New Haven, CT

Introduction: Seeing Science

The epigraph is taken from Bingham to his wife, July 26, 1911, YPEP, box 5, folder 26.

1. Andean Air 2011. According to Peru's Instituto Nacional de la Cultura, the total number of visitors (national and international) to Machu Picchu in 2007 was 439,122. In 1986, the number of visitors was 146,000 (Flores Ochoa 1996).

2. Throughout this book I use "patrimony" and "heritage" interchangeably. In Spanish, "heritage" is translated as "*herencia*," but more typically Peruvians refer to Machu Picchu as "*nuestro patrimonio*" or "*el patrimonio de la nación*." The word "patrimony" is not common in the United States, but there is significant heft to the word in Peru, implying ownership from a physical, personal, spiritual, and historical standpoint.

3. Salvatore 2003.

4. Spivak 1988; see also Coronil 2004.

5. Said 1978.

6. This literature is vast, but some prominent works include Hulme 1983; Haraway 1989; Wolf 1989; Greenblatt 1991; Shumway 1991; Sommer 1991; Asad 1995.

7. T. Kuhn 1962; Biagioli 1993; Golinski 1998; Salvatore 1998; Cañizares-Esguerra 2002; Daston and Galison 2007.

8. Haraway 1989.

9. Latour 1987; Dumit 1997, 2004.

10. Daston and Lunbeck 2011, 1.

11. Foucault (1972) suggests that modalities of seeing are rooted in materialities and techniques.

12. In June 2013, *Social Studies of Science* published a special issue titled "A Turn to Ontology in STS?" Like John Law and Marianne Elisabeth Lien (2013), I believe that empirical studies in ontology have existed for some time in STS, even if not referred to as such.

13. Traweek 1988; D. Miller and P. Reill 1996; Dumit 1997, 2004; Rapp 1997.

14. Mol 2003; Brives 2013.

15. Thomson 2002a.

16. Some of the places included the Quinnipac Club, History Club, Lampson Lyceum, Seaside Club in Bridgeport, Patria Club of New York, and American Alpine Club (W. Bingham 1989); see also BFP, box 101, folder 69, and box 103, folder 80. The naturalist on the 1915–1916 expedition, Edmund Heller, gave a lecture titled "Hunting Experiences in the Peruvian Andes" to the Explorers Club in New York. After the talk there was a smoker.

17. BFP, box 100, folder 58.

18. A magazine at the time referred to Bingham as an industrial scout (see R. Miller 1976, 144). Char Miller believes that Theodore Roosevelt's *A Strenuous Life* (1900) influenced Bingham. The text posited that men of means should not work at a desk (C. Miller 1982, 135).

19. Salvatore 1998, 81.

20. For example, see Mauricio Tenorio-Trillo's (1994) work on Mexico, the world's fair, and the desire for modernity.

21. Knauft 2002.

22. "Modern" not only is a descriptive and periodizing term in the development of capitalism, but also indicates the desires and imagining of what modern looked like in the form of behavior, dress, and attitudes (Ivy 1995).

23. Benjamin (1955) 1969; D. Poole 1997; López Lenci 2004.

24. Thomson 2002b, 2. Lawrence Clayton suggests that the articles and images published in *National Geographic Magazine* were crucial to opening up the American reading public to a world previously known only by industrialists, diplomats, and occasional tourists (1999, 95). Ricardo Salvatore refers to the expedition as a "machine producing mass images of Peru" (2016, 81).

25. H. Bingham 1930, 20.

26. Mitchell 2005.

27. Jordanova 1989, 2000; Pratt 1992; Chambers and Gillsepie 2000; Majluf and Wuffarden 2001; Pimental 2001; Podgorny and Lopes 2008; Podgorny 2009. Although not typically associated with scientific expeditions, Spanish chronicles of the sixteenth century prefigured ethnological sciences of the nineteenth and twentieth centuries, seeking to order difference through observation and descrip-

tive text (Salomon 1985; Greenblatt 1991, 1993). Works by Father Cristobal de Molina, such as *Account of the Fables and Rites of the Incas* (1573), and by de Molina and Father José de Acosta, such as *Natural and Moral History of the Indies* (1590), provided detailed accounts of pre-Hispanic religion as well as a scientific description of Andean agriculture. Pedro Cieza de Leon's *The Discovery and Conquest of Peru* ([1553] 1999) included minutely detailed descriptions of Incan administration, local organizations, and the relationship between the state and agriculture, placing events in historical time frames. Two centuries later, the naval officers Jorge Juan and Antonia de Ulloa described the marriage rites and social mores of Quechua subjects in *A Voyage to South America* ([1748] 1964). The duo later wrote a clandestine book about the colonial oppression and abuses of the Spanish Empire in 1826.

28. Pratt 1992, 15.

29. Pimental 2007. Andean peoples who assisted in the social and material outcomes of expeditions often remained invisible in European accounts, their contributions underplayed (Safier 2008).

30. Pratt 1992, 120; see also Padgen 1993. Scientific expeditions that served as instruments of expansion for European nations relied on contact and an exchange of ideas with the local populations (Pratt 1992; Cañizares-Esguerra 2006). Alexander von Humboldt's interpretations and conceptualizations of the Andes as a microcosm of all climates, and thus as containing all the flora and fauna of the world, were based on the contacts made with Spanish American intellectuals (Cañizares-Esguerra 2006). Humboldt's representations of the Americas, formed in a contact zone, were as much a product of European desire as Spanish American science (Pratt 1992).

31. Wulf 2015, 51; Trigo 2005. At the time of his death, Humboldt was the second most popular person in Europe, behind Napoleon Bonaparte. He was a wealthy Prussian aristocrat who "discarded a life of privilege to discover for himself how the world worked" (Wulf 2015, 3). Humboldt's books were published in a dozen languages, and his explorations of Latin America with the French botanist Aimé Bonpland from 1799 to 1804 were memorialized in the multivolume set *Le Voyage aux Régions Equinoxiales du Nouveau Continent* (1814–1820). Numerous smaller editions were also published. Included in these volumes were color prints and engravings.

32. Wulf 2015.

33. *Vues des Cordilleres* contained sixty-nine engravings of South America (Wulf 2015, 135).

34. Humboldt inspired many naturalists and artists, including Frederic Edwin Church. Church took two trips to South America. His *Heart of the Andes* (1859) was acclaimed for its detail and naturalism.

35. Salomon 1985; Edwards 1990; Podgorny and Lopes 2008; Riviale 2000.

36. Castro-Klarén 2003, 189.

37. Ibid.

38. Until the work of William Hickling Prescott, North American ethnologists' field of vision did not encompass the modern Andes.

39. Sir Clements Markham and George Ephraim Squier are perhaps the best known, but others such as Adolph Bandelier, Percy Fawcett, Lardner Gibbons,

and Richard Spruce contributed to the US imagining of the Andes and Amazonia. Fawcett is best known for his disappearance in the Amazon on his quest to find "Z," an ancient lost city. Gibbons was a lieutenant in the US Navy whose exploration was captured in William Herndon's *Exploration of the Valley of the Amazon* for the US Navy. Markham has been referred to as an imperial botanist and biopirate (Hecht 2013). Prescott, though not an explorer, is credited with writing one of the most influential histories of Peru, *The Conquest of Peru* (1862). For a discussion of the impact of these explorers on, for example, cocaine, see the study by Gootenberg (2008).

40. Poole 1998; Barnhart 2005; Ravines 1970.

41. Poole 1998, 121. Ethnology for Squier was a race-based pursuit for studying humanity scientifically through antiquities. Working during a period of great debate between monogenism and polygenism, Squier pressed for a focus on science rather than on biblical doctrine for the origins of humankind.

42. Pillsbury 2012, 51; see also McElroy 1985. Sara Castro-Klarén notes that it is impossible to "separate the history of archaeology in Peru during the first half of the nineteenth century from the history of scientific travel and exploration" (2003, 184); see also Pillsbury 2014.

43. Salomon 1985. Photography was central to the depiction of antiquities after the work of Frederick Catherwood in Mexico (Pillsbury 2012).

44. Hiram Bingham refers to this text in his book *Across South America* (1911).

45. Blanchard 1991.

46. López-Ocón 1995.

47. Bonfil Batalla has suggested that Squier's expeditions were also based on exoticism rooted in capitalist expansion, since he sought investment opportunities in trade routes and collected antiquities (Batalla 1996, 108).

48. In the late nineteenth century, Britain dominated trade in southern Peru.

49. Markham 1892, 503.

50. Ibid., 505.

51. Bernasconi 2001; Salomon 1985; Tamayo Herrera 1980; Riviale 2000; Thurner 2003.

52. Feldman 2016; Gänger, Kohl, and Podgorny 2014.

53. Salomon 1985, 86; see also de la Cadena 2000.

54. Thurner 2003.

55. Appelbaum, Macpherson, and Rosemblatt 2003.

56. Gänger 2014, 9.

57. Ibid., 252.

58. Ibid., 45.

59. H. Bingham 1909.

60. Ibid., 49.

61. At one point he makes observations about the worker ants in Venezuela.

62. One notable exception is the photograph titled "The Mistress of Cana Flores." Unlike the myriad other views, this image captures a connection between Bingham and the subject. She smiles wistfully, her body half turned, arms crossed, and hand resting on her face.

63. Race imbues the story not only in his treatment of "Negroes" and "Indi-

ans," but also in revealing slips such as his approval of an innkeeper who was of "good stock with blue eyes."

64. H. Bingham 1909, 116.

65. At one point in the text, Bingham is aghast at the differences in gender roles and refers to himself as an "Anglo-Saxon observing."

66. Salvatore (2016) argues that congress was foundational in expanding US research interests and exploration in South America.

67. H. Bingham 1911; see also H. Bingham 1910a and 1910b.

68. H. Bingham 1911, 378.

69. Ibid., 388.

70. Salvatore 2003, 2016.

71. Cotler 1978a, 1978b.

72. Neil Smith argues that Isaiah Bowman, the geographer who accompanied the 1911 expedition, was included in the expedition because his presence evidenced a scholarly purpose. Bowman's 1911 research dealt with topographic reconnaissance and mapping. He wrote about the shock of modernity in Peru and the effect of the railroad in rural areas. He was also a scientist-entrepreneur whose research was intended to extend US business interests and open up the region for commerce (2004, 79).

73. Only those who were literate could vote.

74. Julio Cotler argues that the War of the Pacific (1879–1883) destroyed Peru's promising economy and political organization; beginning in 1895 with the Pierola government, forty to fifty families whose interests were aligned with exports directed the government (Cotler 1978a, 128). Historians, however, have questioned the strength and reach of such an oligarchic system for political power. Instead, they argue that clientelism and specific interests linked coastal families with regional hacendados from the sierra (Jacobsen 1988).

75. Jacobsen 1993; see also D. Poole 1994.

76. Klarén 2000, 208; Jacobsen 1993, 195. Nils Jacobsen notes that exploitation was not accepted "fatalistically," since wealthier peasants tried to consolidate their inheritances in order to compete (Jacobsen 1993, 195). Paul Gootenberg (1988) also argues that there was a dual process of resistance and accommodation.

77. Tamayo Herrera 1981, 134. Disputes often erupted over the use of indigenous labor by hacendados and more "modern" industrialists.

78. D. Poole 1994, 102.

79. Klarén 1973; Jacobson 1993.

80. Cotler 1978a; Jacobsen 1993.

81. Orlove 1994.

82. Klarén 2000, 210; Jacobsen 1993.

83. Cotler 1978a; Klarén 2000, 206.

84. Deborah Poole demonstrates that in Chumbivilcas, a province in the Department of Cuzco, *pandillas*, which were "groups of between 5 and 60 armed and mounted men who worked under a patrón," waged terror across the countryside, stealing livestock from Indians and mestizos and often evicting people from their homes and pastures (D. Poole 1994, 107).

85. Klarén 2000, 233; Jacobsen 1993, 330.

86. On January 21, 1914, Bingham delivered an address to the American Manufacturers' Export Association at the Whitehall Club in New York. He emphasized Peru's mineral wealth and the possibilities of its deposits of copper, nitrates, and tin. Extracting these goods would require more railroads. Besides the lack of infrastructure, race was also a problem. Bingham felt that the entire economic system was built on vice—cocaine (that is, coca leaf) and alcohol—the chief consumers of which were Indian laborers (H. Bingham 1914; see also *Bulletin of the Pan American Union* 1914).

87. Burger and Salazar 2004, 23.

88. Stephen Greenblatt suggests that Columbus's possession was made possible through language and facilitated by the imaginary of wonder and the marvelous (Greenblatt 1991). The pre-Conquest population of Machu Picchu has been estimated at about 750 inhabitants (Burger and Salazar 2004, 24).

89. Choqquequirau is around seventeen miles on foot from the town of Cachora, which is about a hundred miles west of Cuzco.

90. H. Bingham 1911, 319–323.

91. Ibid., 322.

92. In *Crónica Moralizada del Orden de San Augustín en el Perú, Libro III* (1630s), Calancha discusses the whereabouts of Vilcabamba based on observations by the Augustinian friar Marcos García.

93. H. Bingham 1911, 323.

94. In a prescient remark, Hiram Bingham writes: "The Quichua Indian carriers and workmen watched our operations with interest, but they became positively frightened when we began the careful measurement and examination of the bones. They had been in doubt as to the object of our expedition up to that point, but all doubts then vanished and they decided we had come there to commune with the spirits of the departed Incas" (H. Bingham 1911).

95. When Nuñez met Bingham, he had already organized a group to unearth Choqquequirau's treasures.

96. Mould de Pease 2005, 206.

97. C. Romero 1909; see also A. Bingham 1996, 171. Bingham remarked that while the work gave a good overview of the written accounts of Choqquequirau, "it does not add to our actual knowledge of the early history of the ruins" (H. Bingham 1911, 323).

98. March 17, 1911, YPEP, box 5, folder 6.

99. Bingham's rationale for a large expedition was that it was "worthwhile from a point of economy to have as many branches of sciences as possible." He gives the example of a naturalist looking for several weeks to find the location of a spectacled bear but coming up short, while the director found one doing reconnaissance (H. Bingham 1916, 435–437).

100. Flores Galindo 2010, 27.

101. Ibid.

102. Ibid., 49.

103. Burger and Salazar 2004, 23. Carrasco's full name is believed to be Fabián Carrasco Escalante. For more on both Carrasco and Arteaga, see the study by Vilela and de la Puente (2014).

104. What Bingham felt when he first sighted Machu Picchu has been a source

of debate. His son Alfred believes he did not think it an exceptional find (A. Bingham 1989). In letters Bingham wrote to his wife, however, it seems that the place made quite an impression on him. Also, in Bingham's *Citadel of the Incas*, he writes: "It did not take more than a glance . . . to convince the most skeptical that Machu Picchu was worthy of the most careful and thorough investigation" (H. Bingham 1930, 1).

105. H. Bingham 1913a, 719, emphasis in the original.

106. Vilela and de la Puente (2014) believe Lizárraga was a tax collector who lived in the area.

107. H. Bingham 1913a, 709.

108. Ibid., 712.

109. Bingham field journal, YPEP, box 18, folder 1, emphasis in the original.

110. H. Bingham 1930, 115.

111. H. Bingham 1952, 186; see also A. Bingham 1989, 26.

112. Mould de Pease 2000, 134. Cosio's name is spelled differently in various publications. I have written it without accent to conform to how his name was printed in the articles he wrote for *Revista Universitaria* and other publications. Marisol de la Cadena (2000) and Ricardo Salvatore (2016) also use this spelling, as does Parker (1919).

113. Mould de Pease 2001, 2003.

114. Cosio 1912, 20; Cosio 1913, 1915.

115. Mould de Pease 2003, 56.

116. Mould de Pease 2001, 270.

117. Mould de Pease 2005, 203.

118. Keys 2008.

119. Mariana Mould de Pease, presentation at the Universidad Nacional San Antonio Abad del Cusco, April 2008. In 1916, Bingham was accused by Carl Haenel of plagiarizing from von Hassel's 1900 work titled *Evias de la Montaña*; a news clipping is in the National Geographic Society archives. Bingham responded that he had never heard of those men nor used their materials. The society looked into the allegations and found no connection (WJS to La Gorce, September 9, 1916, NGS, 11-15, 73F6).

120. AAG, file AG-D-035.

121. S. Romero 2008.

122. Owens 1991.

123. Pratt 1992; Cañizares-Esguerra 2006. Gene Savoy, inspired by Bingham to search for the lost city, published his findings in *Antisuyo: The Search for the Lost Cities of the Amazon* (1970), which is written and illustrated much like Bingham's discovery narratives.

124. Throughout the book, I work under the theory that Machu Picchu is a discourse object that has an archaeology of its own, with its own particular rules of formation and systems of dispersion (Foucault 1972, 37–38). The term "discourse" is often used as a synonym for "dialogue" and is bandied about as an intellectual replacement for "speech." In Peru, the Spanish term for discourse, "*discurso*," is commonly used in everyday parlance as a way to denote an entire conversation or conversational style. In the chapters that follow, discourses of science and patrimony refer not simply to words as conversation or speech. Instead, the term is

meant to encompass something broader—the relationships between statements (31). In this way, discourse is a package consisting not only of words, but also of values, myths, materiality, and people connected. Discourse is a language use articulated with forms of power that also demarcates hierarchical forms of representation (Foucault 1974; Certeau 1984; Ivy 1995).

125. In the biography of his father, Alfred Bingham suggests that competition with Annie Peck, a female mountain climber and explorer, motivated his climb (A. Bingham 1989, 108–109; 116).

126. C. Miller 1982; Heaney 2010; A. Bingham 1989, 1996; Gade 2016.

127. As with "lost city," the quotation marks around "discoverer" and "discovery" are meant to indicate the construction of this term and its invention and deployment in conquest and imperialist narratives. I insert quotations around "discovery" to demonstrate that the term has a political history in South America that perpetuates the myth of lost cities, primitive peoples, and all-knowing Anglo-European outsiders. I typically do not place quotation marks around these terms in the rest of the text.

128. Axel 2002, 3.

129. Murphy et al. 2011.

130. Haraway 1991.

Chapter 1: Epistolary Science

The letter quoted in the epigraph is in YPEP, box 5, folder 2.

1. Yale's archivists have organized the correspondence of the Peruvian Expedition Papers into two categories: general and select. General correspondence is located in cartons 5–12, and select correspondence to and from Kodak, National Geographic, and the Treasurer's Office, in cartons 14–17. Each piece of paper is neatly stored in a numbered folder that is in turn stored in a numbered carton or box.

2. Bingham's father and grandfather were Christian missionaries to the Hawaiian Islands. Bingham's first wife, Alfreda Mitchell, was the granddaughter of Charles Tiffany (C. Miller 1982).

3. Latour and Woolgar 1986.

4. Hayden 2003.

5. Goldgar 1995.

6. Barad 1998.

7. This network is now being mapped digitally; see Stanford University's Mapping the Republic of Letters project, republicofletters.stanford.edu.

8. Goldgar 1995.

9. Shapin 1984.

10. Discussed in Bingham to Tello, March 27, 1914, YPEP, box 10, folder 128; see also Mould de Pease 2001. I thank Christopher Heaney for alerting me to this correspondence.

11. Romero worked at the National Library in Lima and was Ricardo Palma's assistant. He was one of the founding members of the Instituto Histórico del Peru and the sole editor of *Revista Histórica* (Parker 1919). Christopher Heaney believes

that Romero wrote the article because he "wanted to see these symbols of the Incas' anticolonial rebellion found" (2010, 78).

12. Heaney 2010.

13. W. Bingham 1989, 107. Alfred Bingham notes that in April 1909, Bingham sketched his life's program with goals. No mention was made of further exploration. Instead, he became focused on teaching (A. Bingham 1989, 103).

14. Bingham to Giesecke, November 25, 1910, AAG, file AG-0140. Giesecke's first letter is not in the archives and has not been found. Thank you to Christopher Heaney for communicating with me the precise contents of Bingham's response.

15. According to Bingham's sons, Alfred and Woodbridge, this book motivated the organization of an expedition; see also the account by Neil Smith (2004).

16. Quoted in W. Bingham 1989, 141.

17. Giesecke formally welcomed the members of the 1911 expedition upon their arrival to the city, and soon invited them to lunches, dinners, and conferences. Giesecke became an important moderating figure, negotiating conflicts between Bingham and the Historical Institute of Cuzco, as well as those between the expedition team and Cuzco society at large. While Giesecke served as president of the Cuzco Geographical Society, Bingham consulted with him to determine the correct spelling of the native place-names on the maps of the Cuzco valley (Bingham to Giesecke, March 6, 1913, AAG, file AG-0140). Bingham's writings about the expeditions and their findings, as well as expedition updates, were published in the National University of San Antonio Abad of Cuzco's journal *Revista Universitaria*, which Giesecke founded. Bingham was named an honorary professor of UNSAAC's Faculty of Letters in 1911 (H. Bingham 1912a, 23). During the ceremony, Bingham read a paper and gave a shield of Yale University to UNSAAC in honor of their scientific brotherhood. For more on their relationship, see the article by Mould de Pease (2000).

18. Giesecke was chosen by Manuel Vicente Villarán, the minister of education. Villarán had been searching for a specialist in economic sciences and administration to help UNSAAC implement reforms (Giesecke memoir, AAG, file AG-D-055).

19. Giesecke memoir, AAG, file AG-D-055.

20. Bingham to Giesecke, March 6, 1913, AAG, file AG-0140. After his tenure as rector, Giesecke moved to Lima with his Cuzqueña wife, where he worked in the US embassy as a liaison. Giesecke eventually became involved in developing Peru's tourism. He served as a consultant for films made at Machu Picchu, including the 1954 Hollywood film production *Secret of the Incas* (AAG, file AG-1226).

21. Giesecke correspondence, AAG, files AG-0648, 1013, 1302, 1441. Following the Yale Peruvian Expeditions, Giesecke continued to provide references and translations for maps and photographs to Bingham and the National Geographic Society (see, for example, Kip Ross to Giesecke, February 10, 1950, AAG, file AG-1296). In 1951, Giesecke was named a Jane M. Smith life member of the society in recognition of his many years of cooperation with its expeditions (Grosvenor to Giesecke, February 6, 1951, AAG, file AG-0141).

22. In 1916, Ernest Patterson asked Giesecke to write an article about Peru for the American Academy of Political and Social Science. On July 20, 1916, Giesecke wrote an extensive reply, which began: "It is not an easy problem to give

an opinion of the future needs of foreign capital in the governmental and industrial fields of Peru without making mention to the underlying conditions that affect the inversion of foreign capital." Still, he was guardedly optimistic: "Peru is essentially a country of abundant raw materials, including almost all minerals (although little iron and coal are produced at present owing to transportation difficulties) and a large variety of agricultural products. . . . Capital and modern business organization are perhaps the chief elements that are lacking. Suitable highways (for commercial and military purposes) are still needed" (July 20, 1916, AAG, file AG-1169).

23. Giesecke encouraged his students to understand the contemporary social realities of Peru, notably influencing intellectuals such as Luis Valcárcel, who would become prominent in the *indigenismo* movement (Tamayo Herrera 1980, 177).

24. Giesecke to Bingham, December 26, 1910, YPEP, box 5, folder 1.

25. Giesecke to Bingham, May 2, 1911, YPEP, box 5, folder 17.

26. Marsters to Bingham, March 27, 1911, YPEP, box 5, folder 8.

27. Bingham to Markham, November 30, 1910, YPEP, box 5, folder 1.

28. In 1893, Markham gave a talk to the Royal Geographical Society titled "Geographical Desiderata, or Exploring Work to Be Done and Geographical Problems to Be Solved." In 1907, George Earl Church, a colleague of Markham's, wrote *Desiderata in Exploration*. It is unclear from Bingham's letters to which he is referring.

29. Raimondi was an Italian-born Peruvian geographer. Isaiah Bowman relied on maps made by Raimondi during the expedition.

30. According to the Royal Library in Denmark, the work is addressed to the Spanish King Felipe III. Most likely, the manuscript first went to Spain, where it was subsequently acquired by a Danish diplomat and brought to Denmark. A digitized version is available on the library's website. The work has been the subject of much scholarship; see, for example, the study by Rolena Adorno (2000).

31. Markham to Bingham, January 18, 1911, YPEP, box 5, folder 2.

32. Farabee had a doctorate in physical anthropology from Harvard.

33. His findings were published in 1922 under the title *Indian Tribes of Eastern Peru*. The collection of images and artifacts is available online for viewing.

34. Bingham to Farabee, March 25, 1911, YPEP, box 5, folder 8.

35. Farabee to Bingham, April 2, 1911, YPEP, box 5, folder 11.

36. Farabee later had much to say about the collection of archaeological remains. He recommended reading Markham's *Incas of Peru* (1910) and Squier's *Peru: Incidents of Travel and Exploration* (1877).

37. Howe's papers, at Yale, consist of nineteen boxes of material related to the North Star Mining Co. For making photographs, he suggested using plates instead of negatives.

38. Specifically, he received sheets 25, 27, and 28 of Raimondi's maps (sheet 26 was out of print). Stanfords is still in the business of selling maps.

39. Christopher Heaney notes that Bingham sought out Romero on his first day in Lima (2010, 111).

40. A few months after returning from the 1911 expedition, Bingham received an encouraging letter from Waldo Lincoln of the American Antiquarian Society:

"This Society is much interested in your projected endeavor of making archaeological and geological explorations in Peru, and sincerely hopes that the funds for such a purpose will be raised and the concession from the Peruvian government obtained. We realize, as you do, that the history of the Incas and the earlier races, which preceded them, cannot be written until more thorough excavations and explorations have been made. As President of this Society, which is interested in the history and ethnology of the two Americas, I desire to express my heartiest recommendation of your plan, and to extend our cooperation in such an important undertaking" (Lincoln to Bingham, February 27, 1912, YPEP, box 6, folder 36).

41. Bingham to Markham, March 22, 1912, YPEP, box 6, folder 40.

42. After graduation in 1909, Huntington Smith Jr. became vice president of the Huntington Realty Company, managers of Griswold Farms, St. Louis, Missouri. He was a generous contributor to Yale's library, particularly its section on South America.

43. Bingham to Huntington Smith, January 11, 1911, YPEP, box 5, folder 2.

44. General Sucre campaigned in the area before the Battle of Ayacucho.

45. Bingham to Huntington Smith, January 11, 1911, YPEP, box 5, folder 2.

46. Ibid.

47. The conflict over whether Frederick A. Cook or Robert E. Peary was the first explorer to arrive at the North Pole persists today.

48. Neil Smith suggests that Bingham's romantic discovery narrative was also an expression of angst at the closing of global frontiers (2004, 77).

49. He had made his fortune in oil and agreed to support the expenses of a geologist (A. Bingham 1989, 116). Herbert Scheftel paid $1,800 for a topographer.

50. Bingham to Huntington Smith, January 11, 1911, YPEP, box 5, folder 2.

51. From the archive, it is not entirely clear who was sent the letter, although multiple copies are in the file.

52. March 17, 1911, YPEP, box 5, folder 6. Although expenses were covered through the YPE funds, most of the 1911 expedition members were not given salaries or compensated for their time. Harry Foote and Isaiah Bowman were paid no salary, although they were granted a leave of absence from Yale and their expenses were covered (Bingham to Smith, January 11, 1911, YPEP, box 5, folder 2). The remaining expedition members went as volunteers whose expedition expenses were paid. Often assigned titles like assistant topographer or assistant to the director, many of the team members did not have prior experience on scientific expeditions and were asked to do a variety of tasks that involved more cooking and clearing brush than exploring or surveying. After the success of the 1911 expedition, sponsorship grew and compensation became more customary, though not abundant, for the personnel on the 1912 and 1914-1915 expeditions. Some members quit the 1914-1915 expedition, citing unfair pay. The 1911 expedition team consisted of Hiram Bingham, director; Isaiah Bowman, geographer and geologist; William G. Erving, surgeon; Harry Ward Foote, naturalist; Kai Hendriksen, topographer; Paul B. Lanius, assistant; Herman L. Tucker, archeological engineer; and Casimir Watkins, collector naturalist. Watkins was added at the last minute to help Foote (A. Bingham 1989). Erving was a Yale classmate of Bingham's in practice in Washington, DC. Foote was a friend and professor of chemistry who was interested in the collection of flora and fauna.

53. Pickering 1999.

54. In a letter asking for the free entry of goods for the proposed scientific expedition, Bingham highlighted that he wanted to explore the region of Vilcabamba, where he believed the last Inca had made his home. He hoped to "make a good report of the interesting region which shall include not only its physiographic and topographic features but also its geologic resources, in addition to increasing our knowledge of that fascinating subject the early history of Peru" (Bingham to Felipe Pardo, February 28, 1911, MRE, Embassy Correspondence).

55. Annie Peck wrote Bingham on April 3, 1911, saying that she was determined to climb Mount Coropuna and hoped to "cooperate on one or two points to our mutual advantage" (Peck to Bingham, April 3, 1911, YPEP, box 5, folder 11; see also W. Bingham 1989).

56. From Abercrombie and Fitch, Bingham received the standard 10–20 percent discount for explorers; he purchased tents and camping equipment as well as the entire outfit for the YPE (Abercrombie and Fitch to Bingham, March 3, 1911, YPEP, box 5, folder 4). Guns and ammunition were purchased from Winchester Repeating Arms, and saddles were purchased from Smith-Worthington. The saddles were so popular in Peru that additional catalogues were sent to several interested Peruvian buyers (Bingham to Curry of Smith-Worthington, August 4, 1911, YPEP, box 5, folder 27). With the exception of the watches, cameras, topographical equipment, and rifles, all goods were sold in Peru before returning to the United States, in order to offset shipping costs and recoup some of the expedition's initial expenses.

57. Waltham Watch to Bingham, March 6, 1911, YPEP, box 5, folder 4.

58. Dirks 1992.

59. Clayton 1999, 99. Leguía is best known for his *oncenio*, or his eleven-year presidential term, which began in 1919. He also helped start the British Sugar Company (1896), organized and led the Sud América Insurance Company, and was president of Banco Nacional del Peru. He was minister of finance in 1903. In 1912 he lived in the United States and London, returning to Peru in 1918.

60. Callirgos 2007; Clayton 1999.

61. For a discussion of the way pre-Hispanic ruins became part of the effort to attract foreign investment in Mexico during a similar time period, see the studies by D. Berger and A. Wood (2010) and Boardman (2010).

62. Bingham to Leguía, March 28, 1911, YPEP, box 5, folder 9.

63. Throughout the months leading up to the expedition, Bingham became increasingly concerned about his inability to find a qualified topographer who was interested in accompanying the expedition. The topographer was a key component of the endeavor: he would lend scientific legitimacy through measurements and the possibility of materializing the expedition's work in a map. The map would provide proof of having done scientific work. Without it, the science of the expedition would be jeopardized, along with its financial support. Panicked, Bingham wrote President Taft, a Yale alumnus, for suggestions. Ultimately, a letter from the president's office helped find Kai Hendriksen. Hendriksen, the only member of the 1911 expedition to be financially compensated, was paid a small honorarium of $50–$75 a month, approximately $250 in total (Bingham to Smith, January 11, 1911, YPEP, box 5, folder 2). Bingham also received scientific instruments duty-free

from England. Early on, he discussed plans for the expedition with Taft (Bingham to Taft, March 10, 1911, YPEP, box 5, folder 4). In 1912, he communicated with Taft to negotiate a concession with Yale and Peru.

64. In a letter from Charles D. Norton, secretary to the president, Hendriksen was said to be willing to give up doing boundary work for the US Coast and Geodetic Survey to accompany the expedition.

65. W. R. Grace & Co. was started by William Russell Grace (1832–1904) in 1872. Grace emigrated from Ireland to Peru with his family in 1851. He returned to Ireland and in 1866 moved to Brooklyn, New York, where he began developing a shipping business with his brother and John Bryce, both located in Peru. Their first contract was to provide supplies to help build the railroad in Peru. Their business expanded to include banking, imports and exports, sugar plantations, nitrate production, paper manufacturing, and passenger steamship operations, among others. Grace also became mayor of New York City in 1881 and sought to build a canal across Nicaragua (see Clayton 1985; R. Miller 1976).

66. Inglehart of W. R. Grace to Bingham, August 28, 1911, YPEP, box 5, folder 27. In 1912, Bingham wrote Louis Schaefer, also of W. R. Grace, about his proposed concession for removing materials from Peru to Yale: "Your interest in our work of scientific investigation is very greatly appreciated by all of us and I cannot tell you how grateful I am to you for being willing to further this present plan." Enclosed with the letter was a copy of a letter Bingham wrote President Taft requesting government assistance and outlining the particulars of the plan (Bingham to Schaefer, February 13, 1912, YPEP, box 6, folder 34).

67. This practice was not uncommon for scientific expeditions. In the MRE archive are many letters requesting free duty. For example, personal effects for those on the Harvard College Observatory expedition received the same privilege, as did Frank Chapman, curator of ornithology at the American Museum of Natural History; Dr. Richard Pearson, professor of tropical medicine at Harvard; and Captain J. C. Beasley (see letters dated September 22, 1911; January 23, 1913; June 12, 1913; August 12, 1913, MRE, Embassy Correspondence). This special treatment was extended to the two subsequent Yale expeditions, including free entry on 770 tins of meat and boxes of arms (letters dated May 18, 1912; April 13, 1912; April 24, 1914, MRE, Embassy Correspondence).

68. Bingham to Leguía, May 3, 1912, YPEP, box 7, folder 56.

69. Christopher Heaney refers to Leguía's letter as a "magic talisman" (2010, 100).

70. Magazines such as *Peru To-Day*, which catered to English-speaking and foreign businessmen, applauded Leguía's actions as benefiting the country and contributing to the world's scientific knowledge. The magazine was a source of travel information, country updates, book reviews, and advertisements for products available in Peru.

71. Undoubtedly, the connection with the United States was not lost on Leguía. In a letter dated November 30, 1912, he asked Bingham to act as legal guardian for his son while he attended a preparatory school in the United States.

72. Bingham to Taft, May 29, 1911, YPEP, box 5, folder 21. For the 1912 expedition, President Taft wrote a lengthy letter to H. Clay Howard, asking that he "render all proper support to Doctor Bingham and the other representa-

tives of Yale University in their undertaking which, it is assumed, will result in making better known to the world the great historic past of Peru" (Taft to H. Clay Howard, March 2, 1912, MRE, Embassy Correspondence).

73. Bingham to Hadley, May 6, 1912, YPEP, box 7, folder 58. Bingham also requested that memorials be given to the president of Peru and the prefect of Cuzco.

74. Bingham to Secretary Charles Hilles, February 22, 1912, NA, 823.927/2.

75. Heald, for example, in his report on Machu Picchu, wrote about when he and his team (pack mules, two *arrieros* named Mariano Pantigosa and Santos Garcia, a boy named Marcelino Huamán, and a soldier named Tomás Cobines) stopped at the subprefect's house to deliver a letter. The subprefect in turn provided Heald with a letter directing the *gobernador* of Ollantaytambo to supply Heald with men for the journey to Machu Picchu. Heald goes on to write about the payment negotiations for the laborers, who ultimately had been "collected" at the local jail. They numbered eleven at first, but three had to be returned to haciendas from where they had been sneakily removed by the *gobernador* (Heald report, YPEP, box 25, folder 24).

76. Carmen Vargas and the Finca Huadquiña served as a safe place for the expedition to meet and regroup. The finca provided comforts that the team was accustomed to—electricity, dances, prepared meals, and hired help. In many of the members' reports, the finca was described as a place where one found relief and a sense of sameness and home, a similar way of being in the world (see, for example, Heald report, YPEP, box 25, folder 23). The Lopez hacienda, owned by a wealthy man who divided his time between Abancay, London, and Paris, likewise assisted the expedition. He had a piano, which struck the expedition as incongruous, given the location of the hacienda.

77. Bingham to George Parmly Day, October 20, 1914, YPEP, box 16, folder 281.

78. "As I said in the preliminary report of the Expedition of 1912, his firm (which means Don Cesar himself) have acted as our agents and placed at our disposal their excellent facilities for handling the difficult situations which arise in connection with the organization and administration of an exploring expedition, and all without charging us any commission or rent, although we occupied large room in their warehouses as our headquarters for many months" (Bingham to George Parmly Day, October 20, 1914, YPEP, box 16, folder 281).

79. Ibid.

80. There is some indication that Lomellini was given a diploma as well.

81. Writing to Smith-Worthington from Santa Ana, Peru, during the first expedition, Bingham suggested that the firm send its catalogues to Lomellini & Co. because several people admired the expedition members' saddles. Bingham wrote: "Dear Mr. Curry: The saddles which you made for the Yale Peruvian Expedition are the admiration of everyone who has seen them. We opened the outfit in Cuzco, a month ago, and have been the envied ones ever since. Nothing we pass has received so much favorable comment and have been coveted so much as our saddles. Everybody wants us to sell them when we leave Peru! . . . I think you would have some orders (Bingham to Curry of Smith-Worthington, August 4, 1911, YPEP, box 5, folder 27).

82. There is a wonderful photograph of the Lomellini family taken in 1928

by Martín Chambi at Colcampata, Cuzco. It can be viewed on the website of the Museum of Modern Art, New York.

83. Daston and Lunbeck 2011.

84. Daston and Galison 2007, 368; see also Daston and Lunbeck 2011.

85. Yale treasurer's report, April 29, 1912, YPEP, box 16, folder 271; August 8, 1912, YPEP, box 16, folder 272. Ed Harkness, class of 1897, had offered to pay for the expenses of a Yale professor of geology to accompany the expedition.

86. Harkness also helped with the acquisition of books.

87. H. J. Ostrander of the Yale Treasurer's Office to Bingham, December 27, 1912, YPEP, box 16, folder 272; December 31, 1913, YPEP, box 16, folder 277.

88. Bingham to George Parmly Day, October 27, 1914, YPEP, box 16, folder 281.

89. H. J. Ostrander to Bingham, expedition account balances, January 25, 1917, YPEP, box 16, folder 289.

90. A. Bingham 1989, 107; Finlay 2009.

91. Keith was the nephew of Henry Meiggs, the first and primary client of W. R. Grace. Meiggs was contracted by the Peruvian government from 1869 to 1871 to begin building railroads in Peru. Meiggs built the Southern Railway, which began in Mollendo and headed south to Arequipa and then to Lake Titicaca. Grace also became the supplier for the railroads in Costa Rica (Clayton 1985).

92. Evidence suggests Bingham owned stock in United Fruit Co. (BFP, box 100, folder 71).

93. United Fruit Co. to Bingham, May 22, 1911, YPEP, box 5, folder 20.

94. According to Alfred Bingham, Keith donated $1,800 for an archaeological engineer (1989, 13). However, in Yale's treasury correspondence, the precise amount was not disclosed.

95. March 2, 1911, YPEP, box 5, folder 4. Men were enlisted from the United States to go to Peru, and men from Peru were sought to help with the follow-up research at Yale. Julio Corazao, a Peruvian, was asked to return with the expedition to study at Yale and to assist in the processing of the Peruvian collection. In the agreement, Corazao would be given free tuition at Yale, but had to cover nearly all his expenses the first year and was expected to spend a lot of time in the classroom and laboratory learning English and working on the collection. In the end, Corazao did not spend the year at Yale, but the reason for this is unclear from the documents. According to Bingham's son Woodbridge (1989), the Bingham family brought a Quechua speaker named Ricardo to Connecticut. He worked for them in New Haven and Salem.

96. March 10, 1914, YPEP, box 10, folder 124.

97. For more, see Moreyra 1997.

98. YPEP, box 8, folder 86.

99. H. Bingham 1913a, 715.

100. For the 1911 expedition, Yale connections were critical in securing qualified specialists to accompany the expedition. The geologist, Isaiah Bowman, educated at Yale, was also a professor there. The naturalist, Harry Foote, whose training was primarily in chemistry, was a professor at the Sheffield Scientific School at Yale. William G. Erving, also a Yale graduate, was contracted as the expedition's surgeon. Perhaps the only person without Yale connections was Herman Tucker,

who was contracted at the last minute to serve as the archaeological engineer, despite having no training in archaeology. He later became a thorn in Bingham's side when he wished to lecture about the expedition, because he needed money. Tucker wrote Bingham several letters complaining about not being from a wealthy family and not being able to provide for himself (March 4, 1912, YPEP, box 6, folder 37; April 14, 1912, YPEP, box 6, folder 45; April 30, 1912, YPEP, box 6, folder 53). Additional members of the expedition were not required to be college graduates, but had to be bright young men from respectable and wealthy families. The final requirement was a matter not just of snobbery, but also of practicality, since the members' work was unpaid.

101. Hardy also wrote about the commercial potential for Peru (Hardy 1914).

102. Clayton 1996; see also the Little report, YPEP, box 26, folder 26. They searched for crude oil, rubber, and vanadium.

103. Bingham's preliminary account, June through September 1911, YPEP, box 18, folder 3.

104. Salvatore 2016, 1998.

105. Ibid., see also Taussig 1993.

106. Bingham gave an address to the Rockefeller Foundation in 1916, saying, "I have come to believe, as the result of sixteen years of study of South America history and institutions and of five expeditions to that country, that the one thing South America needs more than anything else is comprised within the word 'education'. I believe that what is meant by thorough fundamental education is so little understood in most South American countries that the establishment of a number of institutions in a few strategically important centers,—institutions manned by well trained American teachers, using the best American educational methods,—might reasonably by expected to accomplish the following highly desirable results." He then went on to list things such as raising the intellectual level of the people so that they could handle the difficult problems facing them, cultivating leaders, and generally improving mankind, because of the "enormous ignorance" and "moral degeneration" among a large portion of the population (BFP, box 100, folder 64).

107. Cueto 1994, 3.

108. Batalla 1996, 110; see also Reid 2002.

109. Salvatore 2006, 665.

110. Salvatore 2003.

111. Ibid., 72.

112. Ibid.

113. Bhaba 1994; Chakrabarty 2000; García Canclini 2002.

114. Flores Galindo 2010, 71.

115. Turkle 2007, 5; Lévi-Strauss 1966, 89.

Chapter 2: *Huaquero* Vision

The source of the epigraph is found in YPEP, box 24, folder 10.

1. Wall text from *Unveiling the Mystery of the Incas*, a Yale University exhibition, Peabody Museum, 2005.

2. George Eaton report, 1912, YPEP, box 24, folder 10.

3. Edmund Heller, a member of the 1914–1915 expedition, collected material at several altitudes, including Puno and the Amazonian forests. Heller brought back nine hundred specimens of mammals, seven hundred specimens of birds, two hundred specimens of reptiles, and one hundred specimens of fishes.

4. One of Hiram Bingham's most significant library purchases was from Mr. F. Perez de Velasco. Bingham paid £2,500 for his books, pamphlets, and papers dealing with America; in all, thirty-one cases were shipped (letter on W. R. Grace stationery signed by both Bingham and Perez de Velasco, dated October 25, 1912, YPEP, box 7, folder 71). Bingham also purchased maps, illustrations, and a collection of antiquities, including textiles, representing the civilization of the southern Peruvian coast (Bingham to George Parmly Day, January 28, 1916, YPEP, box 16, folder 285).

5. Quoted in H. Bingham 1922, 2.

6. D. Poole 1998; A. Bingham 1989.

7. The analysis of science in Latin America has evolved from studies of scientific diffusion from the center to the periphery, to an emphasis on postcolonialism and the ways in which local agents reordered the center, to examining both these dimensions in tandem (Rodriguez 2013). Julia Rodriguez argues that the "centers" cannot simply be ignored in discussions of how Latin American science has been framed. Instead, she suggests that scholars ask how knowledge moves from "one particular location into general circulation" (Rodriguez 2013, 808). She hopes to move beyond the global-local dichotomy into a complex, multimodal analysis of science in which the state is not the only actor (814).

8. The expeditions' physicians captured or "collected" the bodies of living Quechua speakers through anthropometric photography on the 1912 and 1914–1915 expeditions; see chapter 5.

9. Trepanned skulls were of particular interest.

10. Miruna Achim (2014) suggests that the study of bones and antiquities reinforced a gulf between the glorious Incan past and the degraded indigenous present, since questions about human origins gained importance and bones were used to document differences between human groups.

11. Urry 1972, 1991; Hinsley 1985; Banta and Hinsley 1986; Stocking 1987; Cannizzo 1989, 1998; Hooper-Greenhill 1992, 2000; Barringer and Flynn 1998; Conn 1998; Maxwell 1999; Gosden and Knowles 2001; Penny 2002; Gosden 2004.

12. Edwards 1990; Wallis 1995; Riviale 2000.

13. Gänger 2014, 79.

14. Ibid., 137.

15. At the time, there was little consensus on the "racial" origins of the Incas.

16. The lessening of this historical schism is attributed in part to the *indigenismo* movement, particularly by intellectuals in Cuzco, including Luis Valcárcel, who questioned Bingham's motives in 1915 but later praised his efforts.

17. At one point Bingham suggested some bones might be Paleolithic. This conjecture, however, resulted in embarrassment when they turned out to be of bovine origin.

18. Salomon 1985, 88.

19. For more on the history of this binary in Peru, see Méndez (1995).

20. D. Poole 1998.

21. See, for example, Arnold 1990; Kohl and Fawcett 1994; Schmidt and Patterson 1995; Kohl 1998. See Silverman (2002) for discussions of heritage, human rights, and the politics of tourism in Cuzco. See Breglia (2006) and Castañeda (1996) for compelling ethnographies of the politics and history of archaeological heritage in Mexico.

22. Barnes and Bloor 1982; Latour and Woolgar 1986; Latour 1987; Traweek 1988; Law 1992, 1999.

23. The team did not use the term *huaquero*. Instead, they mostly referred to their laborers as peons or gravediggers.

24. The "archaeological engineers" Herman Tucker (1911) and Ellwood Erdis (1912, 1914–1915) were members of the expedition. Philip Ainsworth Means, an "archeological assistant," accompanied the 1914–1915 expedition, but quit after a few months in the field. Julio C. Tello also sought to be included on the first expedition as an archaeologist (Heaney 2012).

25. Although archaeology was still in its nascent stages, the German-born Max Uhle had conducted important work in Peru—in fact, he is considered the father of Peruvian archaeology, although he earned his doctorate in linguistics. The results of his research at Pachacamac, conducted for the University of Pennsylvania in 1896 and 1897, were published in 1903 as *Pachacamac Report*. The groundbreaking, influential work continues to be used in courses on South American archaeology. Uhle worked at the University of California, Berkeley, from 1899 to 1905. Bingham, who received his master's degree in history from Berkeley in 1900, actively sought all current publications related to Peru before his departure in 1911 and met with Uhle in 1911 (Rowe 1954).

26. Farabee to Bingham, April 7, 1911, YPEP, box 5, folder 13.

27. Bingham to Farabee, April 26, 1911, YPEP, box 5, folder 16. Originally, Lincoln Ellsworth was hired as the assistant. In the end, he could not go and Herman Tucker took his place.

28. Bingham to Dixon, March 11, 1912, YPEP, box 6, folder 38.

29. Emphasis added.

30. Dixon to Bingham, March 15, 1912, YPEP, box 6, folder 38.

31. Dixon wrote to Bingham a week after his initial correspondence, offering to train Bingham's men. While the men might not get firsthand experience in excavating, Dixon believed that a semester-long course in the methods of archaeology, including taking measurements, recording observations, and understanding the main features of the region, would be better than no training at all (Dixon to Bingham, March 24, 1912, YPEP, box 6, folder 40.) It appears that at least one man received a few weeks of training from Dixon. Circulars continued to be used as instruction and training on expeditions well into the 1950s (see Pupio 2005; McCray 2006).

32. Each member of the 1912 expedition was given a copy of *Hints for Travellers*, vol. 2, a small booklet published by the Royal Geographical Society. Members were expected to read the booklet on the trip from New York to Peru (circular no. 16, YPEP, box 19, folder 17).

33. Bingham felt that food was important for "efficiency and enthusiasm" (H. Bingham 1915b, 437). The boxes contained things such as "biscuits, rolled

oats, salt, sugar, tinned butter, cheese, corned beef, chipped beef, bacon, pickles, jams, sweet chocolate, prunes, apricots, tinned milk, George Washington coffee and dehydrated vegetables" (Ford Manuscript, n.d., NGS, 11-15, 73F5).

34. Other circulars included important addresses, itineraries, and blank contracts, and dealt with such topics as personal equipment, drinking water, dentistry, food preparation, passports, snakebite, and the care and selection of mules. General orders about ship times and packing instructions were also included. Throughout the expedition, additional circulars were distributed to party members as a way of communicating new information such as shipping schedules and travel arrangements (see, for example, General Orders for 1915, nos. 1 and 3, YPEP, box 23).

35. Bingham also held meetings on the ships en route to Peru.

36. Circular no. 13, Alfred Bumstead journal, 1912, YPEP, box 19, folder 17.

37. Care was also to be taken to save teeth and keep body parts together. Trinkets found with human remains were to be collected, noting individual associations. If the skeletal remains were damp, they were to be dried out slowly.

38. Circular no. 13, Alfred Bumstead journal, 1912, YPEP, box 19, folder 17.

39. Circular no. 17, J. J. Hasbrouck notebook, YPEP, box 23, folder 55.

40. For example, the circular explained how bodies were buried in the area, noting that although several types of graves were found in the area, most skeletal remains were found in natural and artificial caves.

41. Pottery, implements, and ornaments were likely to be found with human remains and were to be collected. Clothing and mummy wrappings were also to be saved.

42. J. J. Hasbrouck notebook, circular no. 17, YPEP, box 23.

43. In his 1916 account, Eaton describes each cave, with accompanying images and drawings.

44. G. Miller 2003, 66.

45. Ibid. Richard Burger and Lucy Salazar believe that Bingham's most scientific book, *Machu Picchu: Citadel of the Incas*, "gives an excellent overview but does not offer a comprehensive cataloging of the collection" (2003, xiii).

46. G. Miller 2003, 1; Burger and Salazar 2003, xiv.

47. Foote, for example, collected a vast number of insects (A. Bingham 1989, 161).

48. Mathewson 1915. In 1912, a local farmer's son showed Mathewson several sites, where he collected nearly two hundred metal objects; see Burger and Salazar 2012, xiii).

49. Burger and Salazar 2012, xi.

50. This is not to say that other items were not collected. Ceramic pieces and metal objects were collected, along with agricultural products. Photographs of the environs and map measurements were collected and recorded. For those items received from the local population, the team often traded coins, sticks of chocolate, cans of sardines, beads, or cheap pocketknives (Orator Fuller Cook to Bingham, February 4, 1915, YPEP, box 11, folder 152).

51. Officials of several towns also offered to assist the team in their collecting spree (see Heller report, YPEP, box 27, folder 46).

52. Eaton report, YPEP, box 24, folder 10.

53. H. Bingham 1930, 14. Heaney argues that Ferro made a deal with Bingham to receive a third of the "riches" found at Machu Picchu (Heaney 2010, 134). Ricardo Salvatore suspects that Bingham did not accept the proposition (Salvatore 2016, 98). In the Yale archives there is a signed contract detailing the agreement between Bingham and Ferro. In exchange for permission to excavate on the property, Bingham would give Ferro a third of the treasures or riches found there, after giving half to the government, as required by law. The agreement was signed on July 9, 1912; it can be found in YPEP, box 1, folder 11 (not box 2, as detailed in Heaney 2010). Whether Bingham kept up his end of the bargain is difficult to know.

54. H. Bingham 1930, 14.

55. Ibid., 15.

56. Ibid., 16.

57. Erdis journal, April 26, 1915, YPEP, box 19, folder 20; Kenneth Heald report, YPEP, box 25, folder 23; Joseph Little report, YPEP, box 26, folder 26; Bingham to Colt's Firearms, general correspondence, March 20, 1914, YPEP, box 10, folder 126.

58. H. Bingham 1930, 5. Bingham felt that the "Quichua Indians" were discouraged and unwilling laborers (37).

59. Bowman 1916, 100; see N. Smith 2004 for an extended discussion.

60. Bowman 1916, 99. In 1911, local "Machiguenga" (Machiganga) guides didn't want to accompany Bowman downstream because of the violent plantation owners and slave traders (Bowman 1916, 63). On that particular trip, Bowman went with five replacements and one boy interpreter, who tragically ended up accidentally firing a gun, blowing off some of his fingers and wounding the chief (64). A boy also accidentally died, apparently swept downriver as he tried to cross while carrying expedition instruments. Other accidents included people slipping, cracking their heads, falling, and puncturing their feet on sticks (H. Bingham 1913b, 559).

61. YPEP, box 19, folder 24.

62. Heald report, YPEP, box 25, folder 23. In his writings, Heald speaks of shooting wildlife such as condors and bears.

63. H. Bingham 1930, 10.

64. MacQuarrie 2007.

65. Eaton 1916, 55.

66. In 1912, the work of collecting was performed principally by Richarte and Alvarez, who, after spending a month with Eaton, continued to work for the expedition throughout the season. Tomás is also named in members' reports as being a useful assistant; see Kenneth C. Heald, "Choqquequirau," n.d., YPEP, box 25, folder 23.

67. As with the collection of skeletal material, the problem with the collections brought back by Heller was their lack of context. Frank M. Chapman from the American Museum of Natural History wrote Gilbert Grosvenor, editor of *National Geographic*, requesting to visit the area where the collecting took place, because he would "then be in a position to gain much information at first hand, and to prepare a paper which would be of far greater value than one based merely on a study of so many bird-skins" (May 3, 1916, YPEP, box 16, folder 263).

68. This lack of documentation is in stark contrast with the detailed measurements and drawings the topographers made on all three expeditions.

69. Gänger 2014, 9.

70. Eaton report, YPEP, box 24, folder 10.

71. Eaton 1916, 55.

72. Most skeletons were found in cramped locations in caves, sheltered from sunlight, moisture, and wind. Where there was sufficient headroom, the mummies were placed upright. Often the mummies were buried a few inches deep, presumably to keep them from falling over. Such placement meant that remains could be collected quickly. George Eaton, "Indian Graves at Machu Picchu," 1912, YPEP, box 24, folder 10.

73. Eaton report, YPEP, box 24, folder 10.

74. General correspondence, n.d., YPEP, box 7, folder 71. There was often speculation about whether the tombs had been raided by previous "treasure hunters" (Eaton 1916, 15). Bowman speculated that Arteaga's ancestors had already pillaged Machu Picchu (Bowman 1916).

75. Hiram Bingham journal, May 4, 1915, YPEP, box 20, folder 33. This cave was not at Machu Picchu.

76. Ibid.

77. Ibid.

78. In Heald's field report, he remarks: "If one of the peons had not been over the trail [on the way to Choqquequirau] before and remembered it with the tenacity of memory of these mountain Indians, we would soon have been hopelessly lost" (YPEP, box 25, folder 23).

79. Not all the excerpts are specifically about collecting at Machu Picchu, but I use them here to convey both the sense of finding things and Yale's mindset about collecting in the Cuzco region.

80. Erdis, n.d., YPEP, box 7, folder 71.

81. It is unclear what the word "*champes*" refers to. "*Champa*" is a Quechua word meaning either a piece of kindling or a brick of earth mixed with dried straw.

82. Ollas are ceramic jars or vessels that are most often left unglazed.

83. Erdis journal, April 18, 1914–February 1916, YPEP, box 21, folder 38.

84. Erdis to Bingham, May 16, 1915, YPEP, box 11, folder 161. Erdis was not the only person to record cave-hunting exploits. Bingham wrote in his field journal: "May 3rd . . . We went because we thought we ought to. A stiff climb of about 600 feet followed by a hard scramble up another 40 feet and there in truth was a pair of mummies! And nearby a couple of deformed skulls. The best mummy had a trephined [*sic*] skull! We filled four cases that afternoon, and while Hardy struck the camp and got already for our return, I went into the inner cave the next morning (May 4) and excavated more bones and parts of mummies enough to fill all of our boxes! We just had boxes enough" (Hiram Bingham journal, May 3, 1915, YPEP, box 20, folder 33).

85. Gilbert Grosvenor had written Bingham on May 2, 1912: "We all hope that you will be able to excavate and bring back a shipload of antiquities for your museum at Yale" (National Geographic Special Correspondence, YPEP, box 15, folder 238).

86. According to Réna Gündüz, the modern usage of *waka*, or *huaca*, is best understood as a sacred house, sanctuary, or sacred geographic space (2001, 72). The *huaca* was the primary means of organizing religious, spiritual, political, and economic life, and the tomb was "visualized as if it were a body" (82). Great efforts were taken to conserve and dress the dead as they were when alive, and bones were not moved, to keep them together for resurrection (87).

87. Tantalean 2014; Gündüz 2001, 105. See the study by Jorge Zevallos Quiñones for a fascinating discussion of *huacas* and *huaqueros* from 1535 to 1835 in Trujillo. Colonists and their descendants searched for gold and other treasures in tombs. Their consciences were untroubled because the *huacas* were considered non-Christian and therefore not sacred (1994, 11). Local Indians were hired to help in the raiding. Contracts, licenses, and companies were established to deal with the materials.

88. Bonavio and Ravines 1970.

89. Kohl, Podgorny, and Gänger 2014, 9.

90. Achim 2014, 39.

91. Gänger 2014, 84.

92. Ibid., 152.

93. Penny 2002. In addition, Stefanie Gänger (2014) notes how collectors had to navigate the increasing number of forgeries. Ricardo Roque (2010) says such forgeries played an important role in the increasing desire for the contextualization of objects.

94. This was not unique to Peru. Mexico's Law on Archaeological Monuments of 1897 nationalized monuments and allowed for the expropriation of ruins. Leopold Batres used "dig and haul" techniques to excavate Teotihuacán (Bueno 2010).

95. Gänger 2014, 152. Aleš Hrdlička notes something similar: "peons" disturbing graves at Pachacamac and selling the materials for profit. They abandoned things they could not sell, and materials were often damaged in the process of digging (Hrdlička 1911, 4, 18).

96. Bueno 2010, 60.

97. Ravines 1982.

98. Ibid., 41.

99. Castro-Klarén 2003.

100. Batalla 1996, 272. In referring to those who dug for profit, Anglo scholars used the term "treasure hunters," which roughly translates as *huaquero* (see Hrdlička 1914, 51).

101. She draws on the work of the Peruvian archaeologist Victor Pimental.

102. K. Smith 2005, 151.

103. Ibid.

104. Gündüz 2001, 127–128.

105. Ibid., 115.

106. Ibid., 159.

107. Eaton report, 1912, YPEP, box 24, folder 10; Eaton 1916, 15. Both Bingham and Eaton refer to looters as treasure hunters.

108. Shapin and Schaffer 1985.

109. Ibid., 77.

110. Ibid., 60.

111. See also Edwards 1988; Daston and Galison 1992; Tucker 1997; Daston 2000.

112. Haraway 1997; Callon 1999; Latour 1987.

113. In his study of La Condamine, Neil Safier suggests that knowledge in colonial science "emerged from a broad narrative interaction involving multiple sites of collection and codification" (2008, 15). Scientific knowledge thus depended on locations both north and south and relied on particular tactics of suppression and abridgement.

114. D. Poole 1998.

115. Ibid., 124.

116. Latour and Woolgar 1986; Latour 1987; Callon 1999.

117. Heald tells of setting fire to the cane in order to cut a trail to Choqquequirau (Heald report, YPEP, box 25, folder 23). In his report on Machu Picchu, Heald notes that some of the workmen "fired the cane," and the blaze unexpectedly roared toward them. They ran down the hill to get away from the fire, and in the process Heald fell down an "eight foot jump-off" and got "beautifully bumped." Once the trail was completed, they started "to clear the city of Machu Picchu" (Heald report, 8–9, YPEP, box 25, folder 24).

118. Both Heald and Erdis comment on this practice in their journal entries. On the use of a carbide lamp for burning, see Erdis journal, April 26, 1915, YPEP, box 21, folder 38. Bingham, too, writes about setting fire to cane to clear the brush (H. Bingham 1913b).

119. Erdis journal, April 26, 1915, YPEP, box 21, folder 38.

120. Heald report, YPEP, box 25, folder 23.

121. Initially, most skeletal remains were thought to be those of women. The inference from this so-called osteological fact was that Machu Picchu was a safe haven or harem for *acllacuna*, or Inca virgins. This claim has been disproved.

122. Latour 1987.

123. Bingham acknowledged that Ferro owned the area and that people farmed the terraces, but he continued to consider the buried skeletal remains part of the sovereignty of science.

124. Alfred Bingham ruefully wrote that his father's research methodology consisted mostly of "pumping natives" on the whereabouts of ruins (A. Bingham 1989). Bingham carried an index of the places referred to in *Spanish Chronicles* and questioned locals about those places (H. Bingham 1913b, 520). In his 1916 article, Cook wrote that the team finally secured a native who knew the trails "across the unexplored area to Huadquiña in the direction of Machu Picchu" (450).

125. For the reliance of scientific knowledge on collectivity, see Latour 1987, 1993; Callon 1999. For more on the circulation of objects as knowledge production, see Gosden and Knowles 2001; Edwards and Hart 2004; Edwards, Gosden, and Philips 2006.

Chapter 3: Latin America as Laboratory

1. There is limited public access to most of the expeditions' photographs, which are catalogued in albums assembled by Kodak and stored at Yale's Peabody Mu-

seum and the National Geographic Society. A handful of images and a smattering of lantern slides are found in the Sterling Library's Manuscripts and Archives.

2. See the volume edited by Medina, da Costa Marques, and Holmes (2014) for a larger discussion of how technology has been imported and reconfigured in Latin America.

3. Heald humorously refers to the absurdity of having Alberto Duque, a "true son of Cuzco," carry a "load." Heald gave him a camera to carry, but Duque gave up after about a mile and "turned it over to a peon who would not mind the small addition having already 75 pounds on his back" (Heald report, YPEP, box 25, folder 23).

4. Luis Valcárcel eventually obtained a camera from the 1914–1915 expedition. It is unclear from archival evidence when that occurred. After returning from the third expedition, Bingham wrote Kodak an extensive letter complaining about the cameras' poor functioning on the expedition. Kodak asked that all the cameras be returned for testing. Kodak tested the cameras and found nothing wrong with their ability to focus (Bingham to George Eastman, September 28, 1915, YPEP, box 14, folder 229; Folmer to Bingham, November 19, 1915, YPEP, box 14, folder 230). In the correspondence there is no mention of a missing camera or of a camera being given to someone in Peru. Photography eventually became important to Valcárcel, who founded the Department of Photography and Cinematography at the National Archaeology Museum in the 1920s. In 1933, he asked Bingham for a list of indispensable instruments for a proposed scientific investigation of archaeological material in the Cuzco region. Valcárcel, then director of the National Museum in Lima, anticipated having approximately $5,000 to spend on scientific instruments and wanted to acquire proper technologies for the inauguration of the Archaeological Institute. He also wanted a catalogue with prices (Valcárcel to Bingham, October 12, 1933, LEV). Bingham responded in 1933 that the most important scientific instrument was photographic equipment, followed by drawing equipment, camping equipment, tools for excavation and topography, and medicine for expedition members (LEV, Correspondencia Terceros, 1933). In the 1950s, George Kubler from the Department of the History of Art at Yale purchased a camera for Valcárcel (LEV). For a discussion on the photographs found in Luis Valcárcel's collection and their attribution to the artist Manuel Figueroa Aznar, see Ranney 2000.

5. Appadurai 1996.

6. Tsing 2005; Pratt 1992.

7. Edwards 1988, 1990, 1992, 2001b; Ryan 1997; Majluf and Wuffarden 2001.

8. Garson and Read 1892; Freire-Marreco and Myres 1912.

9. Daston and Galison 1992.

10. Edwards 1992. In Peru, photography was used to document not only indigenous types but also national monuments and archaeological sites (McElroy 1977, 1985).

11. This practice of photographing faraway places was conducted not only between the North and the South, but also within Peru to reconstruct the nation after the disastrous effects of the War of the Pacific (1879–1884). The Peruvian photographer Fernando Garreaud was supported by President Nicolás de Piérola to photograph the Peruvian republic for display at the Universal Exposition in

Paris in 1900 (Majluf 2000; Majluf and Wuffarden 2001; McElroy 1977). Garreaud's *República Peruana 1900* was a testament to the relevance of the photograph in fashioning national imaginaries, and the Peruvian state used photographic technology to project nationalist desires to the Peruvian public.

12. Scholarship on collecting in the early twentieth century has tended to privilege and examine the collection of more traditional ethnographic objects (Gosden and Knowles 2001; Edwards, Gosden, and Phillips 2006; Barringer and Flynn 1998). This emphasis is perhaps due in part to the fact that until quite recently, photographs in museum collections were not registered as part of formal collections and were stored in multiple spaces within the museum (Crimp 1993). This is changing, and more scholars are interested in photographs as historical artifacts (Pillsbury 2012).

13. Crary 1990; Dumit 1997; Tucker 2006.

14. J. Berger 1972; Barthes 1981; A. Kuhn 1985; Lutz and Collins 1993.

15. Alloula 1986; Chavez 2000; Poole 2004.

16. Sekula 1983, 1986; Tagg 1988.

17. Anderson 1991; Ryan 1997; D. Poole 1998.

18. Edwards and Hart 2004, 2. The authors go on to write that photographs were critical for scholars, and that images were used to share ideas and information. Philip Means wrote Valcárcel in July 1934, thanking him for sending photographs; on September 14, he asked for additional photographs for a human-interest story for *National Geographic* (Means to Valcárcel, July 7, 1934; September 14, 1934, LEV).

19. Edwards 1988.

20. Daston and Galison 1992, 85. Crary remarks that the nineteenth century marked a turning point for the modernization of vision: a "new set of relations between the body on the one hand and forms of institutional and discursive power on the other redefined the status of an observing subject" (1990, 3).

21. Tucker 2006.

22. Ibid., 187.

23. Tucker 2006; see also Ginzburg 1986.

24. Donna Haraway (1997) has examined the social effects of scientific practices and visual technologies arising from the mapping of the human genome. She asserts that the gene is not a thing or a master code, but is a signification of a node where many actors meet. The gene obscures and disavows the very socio-technical relationships that generate both objects and value (142–147).

25. Pillsbury 2012, 4. Excavations accompanied by illustrations begin appearing in the late eighteenth century, with the best known being products of military surveys (14). Tomb illustrations were also early manifestations of archaeological investigation (Trever 2012).

26. Pillsbury 2012, 23.

27. Sellen 2012, 215.

28. Ibid., 221.

29. Haraway 1997. This did not mean that great efforts were not taken to circumvent personal subjectivity and suppress the self (Daston and Lunbeck 2011, 36).

30. Latour and Woolgar 1986.

31. For example, in a talk that Bingham gave to the National Geographic So-

ciety, he used about a hundred colored lantern slides (Bingham to Grosvenor, January 5, 1912, NGS, 11-1, 73F1).

32. D. Poole 1998.

33. D. Poole 1998; López Lenci 2004.

34. Some of Bingham's initial pictures captured locals and their livelihoods at the site, but these were few and not circulated (Thomson 2002b).

35. Salvatore 2003.

36. Bingham to Kodak, March 25, 1911, YPEP, box 14, folder 210.

37. Bingham recaps the conversation he had with Eastman in a letter (Bingham to Kodak, May 16, 1911, YPEP, box 14, folder 210).

38. Bingham to Kodak, May 16, 1911, YPEP, box 14, folder 210. Eastman sent Bingham specific instructions about developing photographs in the field. In particular, he preferred that scientific expeditions use a tank developer. He cautioned about expecting the film to keep as if it were a canned good, and sent a notebook on developing film in the tropics.

39. Specifically, Kodak provided a No. 3A Special Kodak with a leather case, portrait attachment, color screen, wide-angle lens, and a Kodak metal tripod No. 2; a Bull's-eye tripod; two No. 3A Folding Pocket Kodaks with portrait attachments, wide-angle lenses, tripods, and leather cases for packing on saddles; 200 film cartridges of 10 exposures each, $3\frac{1}{2}'' \times 5\frac{1}{2}''$, specially packed in tin boxes; 24 cartridges of 12 exposures each and 40 cartridges of 6 exposures each for a No. 4 Screen Focus Kodak, Model A; 20 cartridges of film, 6 exposures per cartridge in a tin box for a No. 3 Folding Pocket Kodak; and three complete tank developers with the necessary chemicals (Bingham to Kodak, May 16, 1911, YPEP, box 14, folder 210). For a useful compendium listing all of Kodak's cameras, along with illustrations and details, see the history by Coe (1988).

40. Tucker to Bingham, June 2, 1911, YPEP, box 5, folder 22.

41. Bingham to Tucker, June 3, 1911, YPEP, box 5, folder 23.

42. December 27, 1911, YPEP, box 14, folder 210.

43. Bingham to Eastman, April 15, 1912, YPEP, box 14, folder 11.

44. Maurer 2009, 315. In his history of tourism, Orvar Löfgren argues that "the panoramic gaze was part of a new technique of vision: looking in, from an outside position. A sweeping glance set the landscape in motion in front of you, at a pace you controlled" (1999, 45). Technological changes facilitated the capturing of such views, and the panoramic gaze ultimately was critical to facilitating tourism.

45. In 1804, the first permanent rotunda housing an enormous panorama landscape painting was built (Huhtamo 2013). Erkki Huhtamo suggests that the panoramic view, besides answering a romantic yearning to "peek beyond the horizon," offered a mastery of the scenery not unlike that enjoyed by the guard in Jeremy Bentham's Panopticon (2013, 5). Although the moving panorama was popular in London in the 1850s, public interest had faded by the early twentieth century. Lantern slides were used in an attempt to make the panoramas more relevant, but they became viewed as static. For more on the use of panorama with archaeology, see Villela 2012.

46. Certeau 1984, 92; see also Urry 1991 and Foucault 1977.

47. Benjamin (1955) 1969.

48. Thomson 2002b, 11.

49. Shapin and Schaffer 1985.

50. Bingham asked Eastman for information on how to take a good photograph. Eastman promptly provided Bingham with copies of the pamphlet *How to Make a Good Picture*. The choice of words is interesting: "making" implies human involvement and manipulation, whereas "taking" connotes a direct replication without intervention.

51. Bingham to Eastman, April 15, 1912, YPEP, box 14, folder 11.

52. Ibid. Although documents suggest that the team reported minimally on how the cameras performed in the tropics, Kodak used the images for advertising purposes. Several photographs were used in a traveling Kodak exhibition and for display in the Panama-Pacific International Exposition in 1915 in San Francisco.

53. For a discussion of the camera and "accurate" images, see the study by Daston and Galison (2007).

54. See the article by Deborah Poole (2005) for a discussion of how suspicion has been part of the photographic process since its inception.

55. Thomson 2002b.

56. Derrida 2002.

57. This was consistent on both the 1912 and 1914–1915 expeditions (circular no. 17, YPEP, box 23).

58. Alfred Bumstead journal and notebook, June–September 1912, YPEP, box 19, folder 17.

59. Hugh Thomson points out that Bingham was detailed and thorough in his photographing of the site and used a reference map to provide locations for the photographs (2002b, 11). From the 1914–1915 expedition there is a list of pictures taken of the Panama Canal, with a numbered column of negatives corresponding to a column of descriptions. There are also handwritten paper indexes, which have the negative number coupled with a description (for example, 6004 — Tarahuasi Ruins — North Side). The indexes give a sense of the enormous photographic survey of Peru that the expedition was intent on making.

60. Circular no. 14, 1912, YPEP, box 19, folder 17. Ricardo Roque suggests the early value of skulls as scientific objects for museum collections depended on an attachment to histories and texts (2010, 121).

61. Surgeon's contract, NGS, 11-15, 73F5.

62. H. Bingham 1911, 275.

63. Ibid., 251.

64. Circular no. 19, 1912, YPEP, box 19, folder 17.

65. Lantern slides are gelatin-silver positive images on glass plates (Mulligan and Wooters 1999, 746). Hand-tinted lantern slides were made of several of the images in Mystic, Connecticut, by W. C. Ives. Several in the YPEP archive demonstrate the art of enlivening a black-and-white photograph through color.

66. Circular no. 20, YPEP, J. J. Hasbrouck notebook, box 23.

67. Ibid.

68. Ibid. Bumstead is later quoted as saying: "Then I would take a series of photographs around the horizon, with the camera set on the leveled plane-table. In my photographic record I noted the direction of the camera by measuring the angle with a protractor between it and a true meridian drawn on the plane-table sheet. From these photographs I hope to be able to fill in much of the detail that

it was impossible to sketch in the limited time before everything was obscured by fog" (quoted in H. Bingham 1915b, 209).

69. Bingham instructed members to use the exposure index found in the back of the red Burroughs Wellcome photographic record book.

70. Circular no. 20, J. J. Hasbrouck notebook, YPEP, box 23. In the circular, Bingham suggested taking approximately six test images.

71. Ibid.

72. Developing was to occur "definitely before 3 weeks time."

73. It is unclear from the archive whether this was the only circular providing detailed instructions on developing the negatives. The circulars cited are from expedition members' notebooks and may be incomplete.

74. See notes on developing in the J. J. Hasbrouck notebook, February 16, 1915, YPEP, box 23, folder 55.

75. Two types of paper for printing were used in the field: "E hard" was for soft effects, and "E hard X" was for contrast. The hypo bath cleared away the silver bromide.

76. The clipping from the *Washington Star*, dated January 1, 1916, gives a lengthy description of the expeditions and the 1916 National Geographic exhibition, which displayed 200 photographs out of the 12,000. Part of the story is subtitled "Difficulty is getting pictures." Bingham is quoted as saying that taking photographs in the Andes was "often accompanied by unexpected impediments." Some of the challenges were "topographical," such as finding the correct place to balance on boulders in order to get the desired image. "Human obstacles," the other sort, "were the most difficult to overcome." For example, spontaneous snapshots were not as good as pictures taken on a tripod. He goes on to discuss the usefulness of having soldiers on hand when trying to obtain pictures of the local population (BFP, box 97).

77. Thomson 2002b.

78. Sometimes it was difficult to get the right angle. Eaton, for example, writes that he couldn't secure a good photograph of cave 14 because of the steep mountain slope (1916, 19).

79. Bingham to Eastman, September 28, 1915, YPEP, box 14, folder 229.

80. D. Poole 2005.

81. Latour 1987; Callon 1999.

82. *New York Herald* 1911.

83. Craig to Bingham, January 28, 1913, YPEP, box 14, folder 214. Bingham made research albums for all the photographs. Long typed lists contained the negative numbers with descriptions of the images.

84. From a series of letters written in January 1913 to Mr. Craig at Kodak (Kodak special correspondence, YPEP, box 14, folder 214). Bingham wanted the pictures mounted on black and slate or dark gray paper (at the request of the National Geographic Society) and printed as "Glossy Velox prints." The glossy was to be burnished to prevent hindrances for reproduction. Printing-paper options included Eastman Royal Bromide Smooth, Brilliant Velvet, Velvet, and Enameled.

85. Bingham kept these albums as research references and made copies of them, donating a set to the National Geographic Society. Evidence suggests he made

an album for the Hispanic Society of the Americas, but the archive currently has only loose images.

86. March 14, 1912, YPEP, box 14, folder 211. Students in Bingham's classes wanted to know how to get enlargements of certain images (Miss H. E. Williams on behalf of Bingham to Mr. Craig, April 22, 1916, YPEP, box 15, folder 233).

87. Sometimes images were pasted onto the notebook paper in an effort to classify rock structures.

88. Paul Bestor journal, June–November 1912, YPEP, box 19, folder 14.

89. Bingham seemed to be aware of this slippage. After detailing how difficult it was to obtain a picture on the expedition, he stated: "As a matter of fact, the professionals who risk their lives in getting exciting moving picture films have led us to look upon this sort of danger as a part of the day's work for any one who is striving to make first-class picture records of explorations" (quoted in the *Washington Star*, January 1, 1916, BFP, box 97).

90. For a discussion of the ways in which early anthropological photographs came to be "facts in themselves," see an edited volume and an article by Edwards (1992, 2001a).

91. H. Bingham 1913b.

92. Hugh Thomson refers to this image as a "pack shot," an "instantly recognizable symbol of all that ancient American civilization stands for" (2002b, 14).

93. The panoramic photograph is also displayed on *National Geographic*'s website under the tab "Rediscovering Machu Picchu."

94. Cukierman 2014.

95. Pratt 1992.

96. Scorer 2014.

Chapter 4: Discovery Aesthetics

The chapter epigraph is taken from Luther T. Nelson, report regarding photographs #3555–3556, YPEP, box 26, folder 27.

1. The magazine was officially titled *The National Geographic Magazine*. For ease, I refer to it simply as *National Geographic*.

2. While Grosvenor did not attend Yale (he went to Amherst College), President Taft was his cousin by marriage. Grosvenor's father-in-law was Alexander Graham Bell, who helped found the National Geographic Society.

3. This was not the first time the two had communicated with each other. In 1908, Bingham sent an unsolicited article to the National Geographic Society, which was rejected. Eight months later, Grosvenor wrote Bingham, saying that Thomas Barbour of Harvard had suggested that Bingham might submit something to the magazine. Grosvenor asked for a 4,500-word article on the "least known section which you traversed," along with a large selection of photographs. Bingham curtly responded that his original article had been refused—the "very cream of my first trip." More correspondence ensued as they negotiated an article on Choqquequirau. See correspondence dated October 17, 1908, through July 20, 1910, NGS, 11-15, 73F1).

4. The first was Peary's 1907 expedition to the North Pole.

5. H. Bingham 1912b, 1913b, 1915b, 1916. In 1918, Bingham published the article "Building America's Air Army" in the magazine.

6. Grosvenor thought that the illustrative features of the book were very important. He gave Bingham a list of images that he thought should be included (Grosvenor to Bingham, April 19, 1916, NGS, 11-15, 73F6). Although Grosvenor was keen to publish the book, it did not appear until 1930. Bingham asked Philip Means, who had quit the third expedition, to collaborate with him on a scientific book about Machu Picchu. In 1924, Means sent Bingham a book-length manuscript entitled "Machu Picchu: A Citadel of the Incas," by Hiram Bingham and Philip Ainsworth Means. According to Bingham's son Alfred, Bingham kept the title, chapter headings, and organization, but omitted the lengthy historical introduction. He revised Means's draft and published it in 1930 under his own name (A. Bingham 1989, 324–325).

7. The May 1916 edition was also entirely dedicated to the expeditions, although with one article by Bingham and the other by Cook. Bingham published his findings in other scientific journals such as *American Anthropologist* (H. Bingham 1915c).

8. Thomson 2002b.

9. Muniz n.d.; Thomson 2002b.

10. Thomson 2002a.

11. Craib 2004.

12. Edwards and Hart 2004.

13. Edwards 2009, 130. Edwards has also noted that photographs produce "a fracture, which makes us intensely aware of what lies beyond" (2001a, 17).

14. Lutz and Collins 1993, 16.

15. The National Geographic Society, modeled on Britain's Royal Geographical Society, sought to create an organization where members could meet regularly, exchanging and sharing ideas in an effort to increase and diffuse geographic knowledge, broadly defined (R. Poole 2004, 27). To become a member of the society, one had to be nominated or sponsored by an existing member. See the institutional history by Robert Poole (2004) for details on the birth and rise of the society.

16. Bell controlled the financial side of the magazine, and took over after the death of the society's founder.

17. Lutz and Collins 1993, 21. Lutz and Collins conclude that the National Geographic Society became a maker and broker of scientific knowledge, but was not constrained by the scientific community. The society's magazine was a mix of science and entertainment packaged for at-home consumption.

18. R. Poole 2004, 66.

19. The Lhasa photographs used in the 1905 edition were given to the society free of charge.

20. In his year-end report for 1914, Grosvenor codified the editorial philosophy of the magazine. The first principle was to strive for "absolute accuracy," and the second was to provide an "abundance of beautiful, instructive, and artistic illustrations." The remaining points were as follows: everything in the magazine

had to have "permanent value"; "all personalities and notes of a trivial character" were to be omitted; "nothing of a partisan or controversial character" was to be included; only material of a "kindly nature" was to be published about "any country or people, everything unpleasant or unduly critical being avoided"; and the "contents of each number" were to be planned with a goal of timeliness. Grosvenor expanded on the final point: "Whenever any part of the world becomes prominent in public interest, . . . the members of the National Geographic Society have come to know that . . . they will obtain the latest geographic, historical, and economic information about that region, presented in an interesting and absolutely nonpartisan manner, and accompanied by photographs which in number and excellence can be equaled by no other publication" (quoted in R. Poole 2004, 115–116).

21. Lutz and Collins 1993, 26.

22. Ibid.

23. Eventually, archaeology became important for the society, which sponsored archaeological investigations in the southwestern United States and in Mesoamerica.

24. Bingham to Grosvenor, March 18, 1912, YPEP, box 15, folder 237.

25. Bingham requested $8,000 from the society to return to Peru in 1917 (Grosvenor to Bingham, January 8, 1917, YPEP, box 16, folder 266).

26. National Geographic began sponsoring scientific and exploratory expeditions when it gave a $1,000 grant to Robert E. Peary for his quest to reach the North Pole (R. Poole 2004, 85).

27. For the 1915 expedition, the society hired Frederick Westerberg, who was paid $25 a month (Bingham to Grosvenor, April 7, 1915, NGS, 11-15, 73F4). Grosvenor wanted the expedition to have the "right sort of man," who could see "something in their work besides angles and contours." He thought the person should have a scholar's point of view and be able to do more than "mere mapmaking" (Grosvenor to Bingham, April 9, 1914, NGS, 11-15, 73F4).

28. Grosvenor to Bingham, January 16, 1914, NGS, 11-15, 73F4; copy in YPEP, box 15, folder 247.

29. The agreement is remarkably similar to the one used today for grant recipients.

30. Emphasis added. In addition, Grosvenor asked Bingham to purchase professional photographs taken by Peruvians that showed ruins and native types. The photographs were to be added to the society's library collection (Grosvenor to Bingham, May 16, 1912, NGS, 11-15, 73F2). It appears that 8″ × 10″ photographs from Arequipa were purchased.

31. Memorandum, enclosed in Grosvenor to Bingham, April 24, 1912, YPEP, box 15, folder 237.

32. Memorandum of Agreement, NGS, 11-15, 73F3.

33. For the 1914–1915 expedition, Grosvenor wanted to have monthly reports sent to the society in order to maintain press interest in the story. A similar agreement regarding rights to photographs was agreed upon for the final expedition.

34. See H. Bingham 1912b, 1912c, 1912d, 1912e, 1913a.

35. Bingham scrapbook, BFP, box 97, folder 13, newspaper and date unknown. In the newspaper article "Taxi Ride His Most Thrilling Adventure" (newspaper

unknown), the subhead is "Prof. Bingham Home after Planting College Flag at Top of 22,500 Foot Peak; Refers to South American Adventure Modestly; Discovered Old City."

36. *Harper's* had agreed to pay $250 apiece for four articles (general correspondence, March 14, 1911, YPEP, box 5, folder 15). The initial article focused on the expedition's adventurous accomplishments and the discovery of a partial skull and bones near Cuzco (H. Bingham 1912d). Although eight photographs were included in the article, only two were of Machu Picchu. The photographs were printed side by side, and the caption read: "The Ruins of Machu Pichu [*sic*], A city probably built by the megalithic race, who preceded the Incas: discovered by Hiram Bingham on his 1911 Expedition to Peru."

37. Grosvenor to Bingham, April 7, 1913, YPEP, box 15, folder 242; copy in NGS, 11-15, 73F3.

38. Grosvenor to Bingham, March 18, 1913, YPEP, box 15, folder 241.

39. Grosvenor to Bingham, December 31, 1912, NGS, 11-15, 73F2.

40. Grosvenor to Bingham, December 23, 1912, NGS, 11-15, 73F2.

41. Grosvenor to Bingham, March 18, 1913, YPEP, box 15, folder 241.

42. For this, he felt that readers would want to know how Bingham found Machu Picchu and wouldn't have the *Harper's Magazine* article at hand, and therefore wouldn't appreciate the "great personal achievement."

43. Grosvenor to Bingham, April 7, 1913, YPEP, box 15, folder 242.

44. Ibid.

45. Grosvenor to Bingham, March 18, 1913, YPEP, box 15, folder 241.

46. Grosvenor to Bingham, March 19, 1913, NGS, 11-15, 73F2.

47. Grosvenor to Bingham, April 7, 1913, YPEP, box 14, folder 242. Grosvenor did this for the subsequent articles as well. He was particularly critical of the 1916 article.

48. Grosvenor to Bingham, April 3, 1913, NGS, 11-15, 73F2.

49. Bingham to Grosvenor, April 14, 1913, YPEP, box 15, folder 242. Grosvenor had praised the narrative, but wanted to improve it for the magazine's readers.

50. Grosvenor edited the text, but sometimes not to Bingham's liking. "Personally I should not have used the word 'wedges,' but that is a matter of opinion and it is your opinion and not mine that counts in this paragraph. We have no evidence either for or against the use of wedges, and it seems reasonable to suppose that they would use them" (Bingham to Grosvenor, May 14, 1913, NGS, 11-15, 73F3).

51. Control over images was difficult. If foreign newspapers or magazines, for example, printed the pictures, it was difficult to pinpoint copyright infringement. Any US newspaper could copy the image from a foreign newspaper without a line of credit. Consequently, the National Geographic Society was adamant about not allowing the images to circulate before their publication in its magazine.

52. Grosvenor to Bingham, May 2, 1913, YPEP, box 15, folder 243.

53. Ibid.

54. Grosvenor to Bingham, April 7, 1913, YPEP, box 15, folder 242.

55. R. Poole 2004. Early on, Alexander Graham Bell criticized Grosvenor about the lack of continuity between the text and the images.

56. Stephen Greenblatt has suggested that possession is grounded in the power

of wonder (1991, 83). He writes that "the marvelous stands for the missing caravels laden with gold; it is—like the ritual of possession itself—a word pregnant with what is imagined, desired, promised" (73).

57. A set of albums was eventually presented to Grosvenor (Bingham to Kodak, January 15, 1913, YPEP, box 14, folder 214).

58. The National Geographic Society sent the albums to Gill Engravers in New York to work up the images to be published. The society maintains the set of albums.

59. Grosvenor to Bingham, April 7, 1913, YPEP, box 15, folder 242. There are also 8 pencil drawings, 1 map, 1 contour drawing, and 1 still life of ceramic vessels. It appears that there are more than 16 panoramic photographs and fewer than 244 illustrations.

60. For a list of scientific articles associated with the expeditions, see the biography by Alfred Bingham (1989).

61. Grosvenor to Bingham, March 1, 1913, YPEP, box 15, folder 241. The publishing of the monograph was a source of contention between Grosvenor and Bingham. Eventually, the society published *Inca Land* (1922), but the negotiations, contracts, and publication process were not as easy as Bingham felt they ought to have been.

62. Grosvenor to Bingham, February 15, 1913, YPEP, box 15, folder 240.

63. Bingham to Grosvenor, February 22, 1912, YPEP, box 15, folder 240. Maps were important to Bingham's scientific goals. Early in the 1912 expedition, Bingham wrote Gannett about the importance of making a larger-scale map than he had originally planned: "The more I study the Cuzco basin the more I become convinced of its great importance historically, archaeologically and geologically, and I believe that the very first thing that I ought to do is to make a map upon which our future discoveries can really be located (July 11, 1912, NGS, 11-15, 73F2).

64. Bingham to Grosvenor, May 12, 1913, YPEP, box 15, folder 243. Bingham had written Grosvenor earlier about including Bumstead's map as a special insert (February 22, 1913, YPEP, box 15, folder 240).

65. Grosvenor to Bingham, May 14, 1913, YPEP, box 15, folder 243. A small map was included as a reference guide for the reader of the "Wonderland" edition. Some of the other maps were included in scientific publications such as the *American Journal of Science*.

66. The National Geographic Society originally cultivated members from the Washington, DC, power structure. Presidents, dignitaries, and senators joined the society and attended its annual white-tie dinners. National Geographic became a household name when its subscription base began to grow; Grosvenor actively pursued members through blank subscription forms inserted into each edition and a direct-mail campaign (R. Poole 2004). Although new members had to be recommended to the society, they were, with very few exceptions, almost always accepted.

67. This schism plagued Bingham. In 1915 he commented to Grosvenor about an article that was published in the *Sunday Star*: "[The article] appreciates so fully the work that I have been trying to accomplish. I wish it might be given greater publicity, for there are a good many scientists who seem to feel that our work

is pictorial rather than scientific, and who do not appreciate how hard we have worked to make the pictures tell a true story in an artistic manner" (Bingham to Grosvenor, February 5, 1915, YPEP, box 16, folder 260).

68. The National Geographic Society started with 209 members. The print run for the magazine in September 1912 was 135,000. By May of the following year, the number of copies had grown to 225,000, an increase of 67 percent in eight months (Grosvenor to Hadley, May 5, 1913, YPEP, box 15, folder 243).

69. Grosvenor to Bingham, YPEP, box 16, folder 260.

70. By 1916, the print run of *National Geographic* totaled 475,000 copies, and a page of advertising cost $350. Grosvenor predicted that by the end of 1916, the run would reach 575,000 copies (Grosvenor to Bingham, YPEP, box 16, folder 260).

71. Grosvenor to Bingham, May 5, 1913, YPEP, box 15, folder 243.

72. Grosvenor to Bingham, April 7, 1913, YPEP, box 15, folder 242. Bingham's 1916 article in *National Geographic* included a panorama foldout of Sacsayhuaman, printed at a cost of $4,000. To justify the expense, Grosvenor reflected that he had spent a long time rearranging and editing the article (Grosvenor to Bingham, June 12, 1916, NGS, 11-15, 73F6).

73. A. Bingham 1989.

74. Bingham to Grosvenor, October 13, 1913, NGS, 11-15, 73F3.

75. Following publication, there were constant requests to republish photographs from the article (La Gorce to Bingham, October 3, 1913, YPEP, box 15, folder 245). In January 1914, Grosvenor felt that newspapers and media were not giving enough attention to the story, so he wanted to reannounce Yale's findings. Although Bingham was irritated with this decision, National Geographic distributed press releases and more coverage of the expedition, and its findings were published again in national papers.

76. See correspondence between Bingham and La Gorce dated September 16 and October 3, 1913, YPEP, box 15, folder 245.

77. Bingham to Eastman, October 27, 1913, YPEP, box 14, folder 220.

78. Kodak to Bingham, April 5, 1912, YPEP, box 14, folder 211.

79. Thomas H. Griffin for Eastman Kodak to Bingham, July 11, 1914, YPEP, box 14, folder 224.

80. Grosvenor to Bingham, January 8, 1917, YPEP, box 16, folder 266. Grosvenor felt this exhibition would arouse public interest (Grosvenor to Bingham, December 17, 1914, NGS, 11-15, 73F4). The exhibition, which included 200 images, was meant to give a general idea of the character of the collection. The photographs were drawn from the 1,000 pictures of Peruvian Indian types, 3,000 pictures of ruins, over 1,000 pictures representing the manners and customs of the Peruvian mountaineers, and 4,000 of topography, physiography, and geology.

81. Bingham had to borrow the photographs semipermanently from National Geographic (Bingham to Grosvenor, January 10, 1917, YPEP, box 16, folder 266). Grosvenor could lend about one hundred.

82. In 1961, a "panoramic display" of expedition photographs was still on permanent exhibit at Yale's Peabody Museum (Bingham to Giesecke, April 18, 1961, AAG, AG-0140). Fifty enlargements of Bingham's photographs were on display at the Instituto Cultural Peruano Norteamericano in Lima (Giesecke to Bingham, December 14, 1961, AAG, AG-0140). Expedition images continue to be published.

When the news of Peru's suit against Yale University was publicized (2005–2008), images were used as graphic art to accompany the story. The *New York Times* had an online slide show of some of the best-known images. In 2005, Yale installed reproductions of photographs and made postcards of some of them. National Geographic's website offers a searchable database of some of the photographs.

83. H. Bingham 1913b.

84. Laborers accompanying the expedition are pictured in the two images of the expedition crossing the Apurímac River.

85. Bingham 1913b, 426.

86. Ibid., 436.

87. Ryan 1997; Edwards 1990; Pinney 1990.

88. In his work on the British Empire and photography, James R. Ryan (1997) also notes the collapse of home and away performed through the photograph.

89. See the article by Glenn Willumson (2004) for a discussion of albums as both narrative and performance.

90. Anderson 1991.

91. Vazquez 2004; Findlay 1998; Hulme 1983; Shumway 1991.

92. Suescun Pozas 1998; Rubenstein 1998; Beezley 1989.

93. Tenorio-Trillo 2003; Andermann and Rowe 2005; Applebaum, Macpherson, and Rosemblatt 2003.

94. Tenorio-Trillo 2003, 66.

95. Ibid., 60.

96. See D. Poole 1997, 1998, 2004, 2005.

97. In her work on Figueroa Aznar, Deborah Poole suggests that photography was not considered an art because of its reliance on the mechanical (D. Poole 1991, 1997). Photography's novel technology relegated it to the field of science rather than art. Although Jorge Coronado (2009) suggests that such a strong bifurcation was not necessarily the case in Cuzco, the photographic burden of representation as artistic or scientific was with photography since its invention. For a discussion of photography as a burden of representation, see the study by Tagg (1988).

98. Benedict Anderson argued that one effect of the sheer reproducibility of prints is that they may eventually produce a "logoization" of the map or image for the nation. Pictorial symbols come to speak metonymically about the nation. Furthermore, these symbolic speech acts—in which images stand in for the nation—are so deeply embedded in the national imagination that very few citizens are aware of their historicity or artificiality (Anderson 1991, 182).

99. Gell 1997.

100. Mirzoeff 2006. In an examination of the photographic representations of Maya subjects presented at the Summer Fair during the 1930s and 1940s in Guatemala, Walter Little argues that there was no singular or homogenous representation of the Mayas such as the "Maya woman" (2008, 645). Rather, a wide range of subject matter was depicted in the photographs, in contrast to the typical images found in publications today (639). The consolidation of archetypal images of the "Maya woman" occurred over time, through the consumptive practices of tourists (654). As Little points out, such representations have significant consequences for Maya women and men today.

101. At the time of the Yale expeditions, photography was quite popular in Peru.

A quick examination of any periodical from the period shows many advertisements for Kodak as well as for studio photography. Bingham's arrival in 1911 was documented with a photograph in *Variedades* (December 9) of a ceremonial wreath hanging on the statue of Raimondi in the Plaza Italia.

102. Flores Noriega 1980.

103. J. Prado Ugarteche to Bingham, August 19, 1913, YPEP, box 9, folder 109.

104. Along with Peru's daily newspapers, other publications printed information about the expedition from the 1913 "Wonderland" issue. *Peru To-Day*, an English-language magazine targeting the expatriate and business community in Peru, summarized the *National Geographic* article in its July 13 edition: "A more extended review of the findings of the Yale Expedition will appear in our next issue but in the meantime the thanks and gratitude of the Republic are most surely due to the little group of American archaeologists who have brought the hieroglyphics of such a gigantic lesson out of the wilderness and forgotten past."

105. The magazine abruptly ended publication, so it is impossible to know how it would have continued to cover the issue.

106. The last issue of the magazine was published on November 16, 1913, when the editor and founder, Manuel Moral, died (Flores Noriega 1980). The first issue was dated January 7, 1909. The additional issues that carried Bingham's article, all from 1913, were dated August 27, September 10, September 24, October 8, October 29, and November 16, at which point the translation ends abruptly.

107. *Ilustración Peruana* 1913a, 170.

108. On the front page of Lima's newspaper *El Comercio* from July 28, 1914, is a full-page photorealist drawing of a Creole planting the flag atop archaeological ruins. The title is "¡Viva la Patria! 1821 to 1914." Printed in a circular stamp in the corner is the date "28 de Julio" (IRA).

109. Cosio 1912.

110. Ibid., 277.

111. The article includes twelve reprinted photographs. In addition to the images of people at the site are close-up shots of the rock walls. Photographs depicting Peruvians celebrating or posing in front of architectural forms were not new. For example, Fernando Garreaud's photos held at the National Library in Lima capture Peruvians around architectural forms.

112. Grosvenor to Bingham, January 14, 1913, YPEP, box 15, folder 239.

113. Mirzoeff 1998; Ryan 1997; Alloula 1986; Pinney 1990.

114. Rice 2014, 79, 117. Worcester was a scientist who participated in two zoological expeditions to the Philippines, eventually becoming a colonial administrator. He wrote five articles for *National Geographic*, and single issues were twice dedicated to his work. His archive contains more than fifteen thousand photographs as well as motion picture footage.

115. Ibid., 107. The accompanying article expounded on race, morality, and economic development.

116. Ryan 1997, 214.

117. The panoramic image is not included.

Chapter 5: Picturing the Miserable Indian for Science

The letter quoted in the chapter epigraph is in NGS, 11-15, 73F5.

1. In addition to providing health services and conducting anthropometry, Ford collected palm and rubber specimens for the US Department of Agriculture.

2. Aleš Hrdlička wrote Bingham on May 14, 1913, before the 1914 expedition to Peru. He encouraged Bingham to return to the country, which, he wrote, was a vast storehouse of facts as well as specimens; he wanted to see at least some US institutions engaged there (YPEP, box 9, folder 100). Hrdlička told Bingham that if he decided to return to Peru, he had information on a number of locales where good collections could be made at moderate expense.

3. Fabian 2010, 208. On one trip to Peru in 1910, he collected 3,400 skulls. Max Uhle helped him, as did the government (Hrdlička 1911). For more on his collections at the Smithsonian, see the account by Feldman (2016).

4. Ferris 1921. Ferris published under his own name, but acknowledged that the fieldwork had been done by Ford. Bingham wanted *National Geographic* to publish the article, but getting Grosvenor to agree was a challenge. Louis Sullivan, assistant curator at the American Museum of Natural History, sent Pliny Goddard, of the same institution, a letter, which was then passed on to Grosvenor. Sullivan stated that Ferris's work, the "most important contribution to South American anthropometry," was detailed and supplemented by "valuable descriptive details" (Sullivan to Goddard, September 2, 1919, NGS, 11-15, 73F5).

5. Ferris 1916. The publication was paid for by *National Geographic*.

6. Stocking 1971; see also Stocking 1968. In 1907 the name of the organization became the Royal Anthropological Institute of Great Britain and Ireland.

7. In his study of the history of archaeology, Bruce Trigger suggests that in the late nineteenth century in Sudan, "archaeological data were no longer interpreted primarily as a record of cultural evolution, but as evidence of the prehistoric existence of various ethnic groups" (1984, 326). Patterns of behavior were associated with specific ethnic groups, which were linked with nationalities, against the idea of "psychic unity" or parallel development. See also Trigger's 2006 study for a specific discussion of Squier's beliefs.

8. Stocking 1971, 372.

9. Ibid., 377.

10. Caspari 2003; Wallis 1995.

11. Fabian 2010, 83.

12. Ibid., 15.

13. Fabian 2010.

14. Fabian 2010.

15. Ford used Hrdlička's method, which necessitated making about fifty measurements and two photographs of each subject. Hrdlička, who was also interested in comparing cranial capacity among native groups, sought skulls that did not exhibit trepanning or other forms of deformation (Hrdlička 1911).

16. Hrdlička 1914, 13.

17. Ibid., 6.

18. Caspari 2003, 67.

19. Ibid.

20. For a discussion of eugenics and scientific racism in Latin America, see the study by Nancy Leys Stepan (1991).

21. For more on the intellectual history of inheritance, see the study by Ted Everson (2007).

22. D. Poole 1997, 63.

23. Ibid., 70.

24. Ibid., 17.

25. Wallis 1995; Edwards 1988, 1990; Pinney 1990, 1992.

26. Bowler 2003.

27. Joseph Barnard Davis and John Thurnam published *Crania Britannica* in 1865. The illustrated book focused on the skulls of the early inhabitants of the British Isles.

28. Wallis 1995; Bernasconi 2001; Cox 2007.

29. Garson and Read 1892; Freire-Marreco and Myres 1912.

30. Urry 1972.

31. Edwards 1988, 241.

32. Physical anthropology began as part of the curriculum for medicine and anatomy. Many physical anthropologists began as medical doctors (Roque 2010, 130).

33. Report on the Peruvian Expedition 1914, NGS, 11-15, 73F4. Bingham wrote, "Our knowledge of the distribution of the ancient tribes and of the gradual formation of the Incan Empire based as it is on unsatisfactory Spanish chronicles, is very limited and uncertain. The historical geography of Peru offers a series of problems of intense interest. They include the origin of Machu Picchu, the relation of the monolithic to the late Incan civilization, the migration of race, and the spread of the ancient civilization. It should be our object to make a map of ancient Peru, showing the location of the early tribes, the growth of the Incan influence, the extent of the Incan Empire, and the steps by which this extent was reached" (Plans for Future Work of Exploration in Peru, NGS, 11-15, 73F5).

34. Ferris 1916, 61; Ferris 1921. Ferris cited Hrdlička's address before the Anthropological Society of Washington on October 28, 1913, in which he listed the "most important problems awaiting solution: (1) the derivation of the Peruvians, (2) the time of their advent into the country, (3) the extension and exact physical characteristics of the Aymara and Quichua, and (4) the genetic relations of the Peruvian to the Argentine and Chilean aborigines" (quoted in Ferris 1916, 59). Hrdlička believed in the Asian origin of the Indian. For more on American anthropology, craniometry, and racial degeneration, see the study by David Hurst Thomas (2001).

35. Ferris 1916, 64.

36. Ibid. Bingham's 1916 article concludes with: "The Indians of the highlands have the purest blood and are much more attractive than those of the montana or slopes. Bronze skinned, of medium height, but with huge chest expansion and wonderful leg development, some of the men of the highlands present a striking appearance. Those of the lowlands, although lighter in color, are generally more ill-favored and lack the ruggedness of features possessed by those of pure blood" (473).

37. Ferris 1916, 65; Ferris 1921, 3.

38. Ford spent time in Washington, DC, with Hrdlička, who trained him in measuring and recording. He noted that he spent "eight or more hours daily in the attics of the Smithsonian building among the hundreds of skulls and tons of old bones (Ford manuscript, n.d., 18, NGS, 11-15, 73F5).

39. YPEP, box 25, folder 20.

40. Nelson journal, attributed to image 3690–3691, YPEP, box 26, folder 27.

41. H. Bingham 1913b, 561.

42. Ferris notes that there were forty-one different measurements taken on the 1912 expedition, and eighteen on the 1915 expedition (1921, 3). Elsewhere the number is calculated at thirty-six.

43. Nelson quoted in Ferris 1916, 61; see also Bingham 1913b, 561; Bingham to Grosvenor, March 20, 1913, NGS, 11-15, 73F2. While most were frightened, a few wanted to have their image taken. Ford was fond of the Machiganga, whom he felt were cooperative; he writes about a person who brought him new subjects. People posed for him and were fascinated by the instruments. He notes that the "sphygometer," which he thought measured handgrip strength, was of particular interest (Ford manuscript, 32, NGS, 11-15, 73F5). The dynamometer was actually the instrument used to measure grip strength.

44. The 1913 article also tells of one subject who "strenuously objected and refused the coin given" (H. Bingham 1913b, 562).

45. Ford quoted in H. Bingham 1916, 472.

46. In other places, such as Puquira and Arma, he didn't take measurements, because of a smallpox outbreak.

47. Ford quoted in H. Bingham 1916, 471.

48. Ibid., 472.

49. Deborah Poole (1997) and Jorge Coronado (2009) suggest that technology was generally suspect in the Andes during this period.

50. Ferris 1921, 7.

51. Alphonse Bertillon was a French criminologist who developed a system of measurements to identity criminals. Measurements focused mainly on the head and face but also included things like the length of the middle finger and the length of left foot. The system also involved taking frontal and profile photographs of the subject. For more on Bertillon and forensic technologies, see the website of the National Library of Medicine, nlm.nih.gov/visibleproofs/galleries/technologies/index.html.

52. Additional photographs of women were also taken (without measurements), bringing the total to 433 photographs.

53. The intake sheet doesn't specify whether these measurements were in millimeters or centimeters. From Ferris's published works, most of the measurements appear to refer to millimeters, but sometimes he also uses centimeters.

54. The lettering is not entirely legible. For example, it is not clear what "5-6-4" referred to.

55. Ferris 1921, 7.

56. D. Poole 1997.

57. Ibid., 137.

58. Ferris 1921, 16.

59. Ibid., 18.

60. Ibid., 33.

61. Ibid., 8.

62. Ibid., 41.

63. Ferris 1916, 71.

64. Ferris 1921, 8.

65. Ibid.

66. Ibid.

67. Ferris estimated brain weight from stature. For males, the formula was height in centimeters × 7; for females, stature × 7 × $^{30}/_{31}$. To calculate comparison values, he used the "Gladstone formula," which was more complicated: brain weight in grams = length of skull × breadth of skull × height of skull (all measured in centimeters) divided by 2.806.

68. Instances of goiter were found to be frequent in the Patallacta area. Ferris noted, "It is the prevailing idea of the natives that goiters are produced by drinking glacier water" (1921, 9). The connection between goiter production and a lack of iodine was hypothesized in 1813. In the 1830s, a French chemist working in the Andes advocated an iodine-rich salt to prevent goiter. For more on the history of iodine deficiency and thyroid enlargement, see Leung, Braverman, and Pearce 2012. In 1922, Switzerland began a national iodized salt program. It is unclear whether people with goiters who were photographed by the teams were treated and whether the thyroid enlargements were the result of iodine deficiency.

69. Cartmill and Smith 2009.

70. Ferris notes that most likely they were "mixed Spanish," but because of uncertainty he used the general term.

71. Mary Weismantel suggests that technologies like measuring are affiliated with whiteness. Numbers, letters, and other types of documentation are often viewed as "weapons" in the Andes (2001, 196).

72. Ferris 1916, 65.

73. Ferris 1921, 3.

74. Ibid., 28.

75. He was also unsure about the way hand measurements were taken (ibid., 19–20).

76. Eaton 1916, 85.

77. Ferris 1921, 39.

78. Ibid., 23.

79. Ibid., 33.

80. Gilbert Grosvenor wrote Bingham: "The point for us to consider now is how to make these valuable measurements of Dr. Ford's available for the advancement of science. I am tempted to offer them to Dr. Ferris, but I doubt whether he would care to handle them, particularly as his report on the 1912 measurements, which was completed a year ago has not yet been published, a delay due in part to the editor of Amer Anthro [American Anthropologist]" (February 29, 1916, YPEP, box 16, folder 260).

81. Ryan 1997.

82. Ryan (1997) argues that the external as a manifestation of the interior and one's moral constitution was beginning to be questioned. Instead, Ryan shows that

an ethnographic picturesque played a prominent role in teaching academic subjects such as geography by conjoining race and place.

83. Maxwell 1999.

84. In contrast, women's bodies have been shown to be a privileged site for writing empire (Stoler 2003; Alloula 1986; Abu-Lughod 2013).

85. In this sense they are similar to cartes de visite.

86. Ferris 1921, 92.

87. See the studies by Brian Dippie (1991) and Susan Krouse (1990) for more on the vanishing Indian.

88. Ford cited in Ferris 1921, 63.

89. Locals thought that the oriental sore was caused by a spider bite. The native remedy was derived from the bark of a specific tree.

90. Salomon 1985; Thurner 2003; de la Cadena 2000. In 1916, Cook concluded: "As a race, it may be assumed that the Megalithic people were ancestor of the modern Quichuas, or at least of the same stock, for there is nothing to show that the human type was different in ancient times . . . [The] general result of such studies (burials) tends to show that the modern Quichuas, the Incas conquered by the Spaniards, and the pre-Inca or Megalithic people were all of the same race and practiced the same arts, including the art of agriculture" (1916, 464).

91. Nicholas Mirzoeff has suggested that images can act as a "key terrain of violence" (2006, 37).

92. The title of this section refers to a passage in Edmund Heller's journal: "Their [Quechua speakers'] explanation of our desire to carry away skulls is that on getting them to the United States we can make them talk and thus we can acquire information about buried treasure" (YPEP, box 27, folder 47). In one sense, this was true.

93. Heald report, 7, YPEP, box 25, folder 24. In this report, Heald wrote about jumping from his horse and knocking "the rebellious one down" (6).

94. Joseph Little, Bingham's assistant on the 1912 expedition, had a slightly different observation about the curiosities in their midst. His report described an Indian village, located on the lands of a hacienda, where approximately three thousand people lived (Little report, 1912, YPEP, box 26, folder 26). Little lamented that the conditions were "semi-feudal," with workers receiving wages of ten cents of gold per day, which he noted, was typically returned to the hacienda owner at week's end through the purchase of merchandise and beverages. Little referred to the wages as "starvation stipends" and the practice as disguised debt peonage that made it possible for less than 5 percent of the ruling class to control all of the lands. Little's concern, however, was not so much for the subjection of people to slave-like conditions, but rather about a system that enhanced the possibility of communism taking root: "This chasm that separates naked poverty from entailed wealth creates in South America the anachronism of de facto dictatorships thinly hidden behind the façade of democracy. It contains all the elements that nourish communism."

95. H. Bingham journal, May 5–6, 1915, YPEP, box 20, folder 33.

96. H. Bingham 1910b, 582.

97. Ibid., 586.

98. C. Miller 1982, 141. Ford felt Quechua speakers were "so absolutely igno-

rant that they cannot be expected to follow advice as to food or even to take medicine as directed" (Ford to his mother, June 20, 1915, NGS, 11-15, 73F5).

99. Bingham to Little, April 26, 1913, YPEP, box 26, folder 26.

100. Bowman 1916, 67. Of Bowman's belief in natural selection and his attribution of people's characteristics to climate, Neil Smith writes: "Even by the standards of the time, this was a fairly blunt environmentally inspired racism" (2004, 74).

101. Bowman 1916, 5. One of the questions Bowman wondered about was the geographic basis of human character and its contribution to political revolutions.

102. N. Smith 2004, 26.

103. Bingham to Hardy, October 10, 1914, YPEP, box 11, folder 143.

104. Ibid.

105. Bingham to Hardy, May 6, 1912, YPEP, box 7, folder 58.

106. Kai Hendricksen, the topographer on the 1911 expedition, wrote in his journal that the lack of campsites, the harsh climate, the rugged terrain, and the slow and frightened Indians made work so frustrating that one wished to be elsewhere (YPEP, box 24, folder 3).

107. Osgood Hardy mentions that while at Camp Angostura, part of the property of Carmen Vargas, the team had a run-in with a group of Quechua speakers. The group, according to Hardy's recollection, carried stones and canes and threatened Hardy and the topographer, Albert Bumstead, demanding to know what they were hunting. The crew members raised their voices, spoke in broken Spanish, and explained who they were and what they were doing. Hardy, with some irony, notes that the Quechua speakers had no idea what they were saying. Explaining that they had governmental support, Hardy showed the group a map. When those explanations did not work, Hardy threatened the men with his gun, "and everyone became more pleasant" (Osgood Hardy journal, June–December 1912, YPEP, box 19, folder 22).

108. In addition to the threat of violence from guns and physical abuse, sickness could have also played a role. Outbreaks of smallpox and typhoid fever were observed by many team members in their journals. Bingham's assistant on the 1912 expedition, Paul Bestor, for example, wrote that entire villages had been abandoned because of sickness.

109. Eaton report, 1912, YPEP, box 24, folder 10.

110. Ibid.; Eaton 1916.

111. Eaton 1916, 48.

112. Heald's report recounts an episode involving Tomás, his assistant and the manager of the other workers. On one reconnaissance trip, Tomás had a horrible nightmare and woke up crying and pleading. This had happened before on the trip, and the repetition of the nightmare scared the other workers. In the nightmare, a huge "black animal with sharp teeth had seized him [Tomás] by the arm and was dragging him to the cliffs which were on one side of the city to throw him over" (Heald report, YPEP, box 25, folder 23). Heald dismissed the dream as nonsense, but noted in his report that the others were frightened and wanted to return home.

113. Wardlow 2002.

114. Many of Bingham's favorite images were hand-tinted by W. C. Ives in New Haven, Connecticut, and used in his illustrated lectures.

115. These images appear to have never been published.

116. Mirzoeff 2006.

117. Appadurai 1988; Foucault 1977.

118. Barthes 1981.

119. Edwards 1999, 75.

120. Sontag 2004.

121. Tucker and Campt 2009, 3.

Chapter 6: The Politics of Seeing

The letter quoted in the first chapter epigraph is found in YPEP, box 6, folder 35. For the second epigraph, see Leon 1934, ix.

1. In 2010, Susan Leigh Star sought to clarify what she and James Griesemer meant when they developed the term "boundary object." The first aspect of boundary objects is that, like all objects, they are subject to interpretive flexibility. Second, boundary objects are both shared and flexible, allow groups to work without consensus, are subject to reflection and tailoring, and thus are "the stuff of action" (Star 2010, 603). Star and Griesemer (1989, 393) suggest that the creation and management of boundary objects is key to "maintaining coherence across intersecting social worlds."

2. Salvatore 2016.

3. Bingham to Hadley, October 26, 1912, YPEP, box 7, folder 71.

4. Cosio 1915.

5. April 13, 1916, YPEP, box 13, folder 191.

6. Cañizares-Esguerra 2006.

7. Although on the face of it this is similar to many utopian projects in Peru (Flores Galindo 2010, 48; Beauchesne and Santos 2011), what makes it less utopian, at least from the perspective of Flores Galindo, is the lack of a counterhegemonic vision. I thank Juan Carlos Calligros for helping me understand this difference.

8. George Stocking writes about the "empire-building" and "nation-building" traditions within Euro-American anthropologies. The first is directed toward "dark-skinned others" in an overseas empire, and the other is concerned with cultural nationalism within its borders (1982, 172). Something similar takes place in this conflict.

9. Callon 1999, 283.

10. Latour 1987.

11. Star and Griesemer 1989.

12. This decree articulated that antiquities were the property of the nation "because they belong to the glory which derives from them" (Tello quoted in Burger 2009, 96).

13. Mould de Pease 2000, 142; Mould de Pease 2003, 2005.

14. Heaney 2010, 115. A recap of the law was published in *El Diario* on September 2, 1911, by Leguía (BN). The law required that although all objects per-

tained to the state, duplicates could be requested for removal for scientific study; unique objects could only be photographed; and licensed excavations would require a governmental representative to oversee and verify the collecting. The law in effect helped facilitate Bingham's collecting by offering a verification of true scientific behavior. This updated law was known and translated into English and sent to the US State Department on September 26, 1911, and received on October 26, 1911 (NA, 823.927).

15. For a discussion of the subversion of Western hegemony and intellectual decolonization, see the works by Walter Mignolo (2000, 2005, 2011).

16. Beasley-Murray 2010, 212.

17. Ibid., 215.

18. García Canclini 2002.

19. Gänger 2014, 6.

20. In his analysis of the Centenario in Mexico City in 1910, Mauricio Tenorio-Trillo examines how Mexican scientists sought to produce modern science and a cosmopolitan nation, and thus were integral to rewriting national history (1996, 102). The Porfiriato demonstrated a strong Hispanism that was constantly "adapted and accommodated to indigenismo, indianismo and pro-mestizaje" (102). Mexican scientists demonstrated a "pragmatic mimetism" and adopted concerns and ideas of their North American counterparts, but reworked them through political utility (Tenorio-Trillo 1999, 1169). Tenorio-Trillo concludes that social science was "not mere cultural imperialism but a multifarious global exchange within a bipolar postwar environment"(1187).

21. Elizabeth Boone (1993) demonstrates that knowledge was thought to be embodied in objects, especially if there were no written records.

22. Argentina also relied on an indigenous population to craft a national identity. Carolyne Larson (2015) demonstrates that like their Peruvian counterparts, Argentinian elites selected useful elements of indigeneity to articulate a unique national identity based on ethnicity. Thus, Creoles became heirs to the past, transforming particular artifacts as stand-ins for national authenticity. Science aided in articulating this subjectivity.

23. Tantalean 2014. An article from *El Comercio* dated July 11, 1911, discusses the laws.

24. Daggett 2009, 11. The first national history museum was established in 1836 (Tantalean 2014).

25. Gänger 2014, 158. Uhle also helped establish the collections at the University of California, Berkeley (Rowe 1954).

26. This was not an uncommon position among those claiming a scientific outlook. Hrdlička was concerned about the way that remains from graves were repackaged and sold for commercial purposes. This "heterogeneous mass" was not useful for pursuing scientific knowledge, and he advocated keeping all remains together (Hrdlička 1911, 12). Later he wrote: "The writer must repeat again what he wished to accentuate in his former report that, due to the lack of scientific supervision of the vast majority of the excavations practiced in Peru to the present date, the actual archaeological collections from that country in the museums are little more than so many curiosities, which for the most part it is impossible to refer either to any definite people or period" (Hrdlička 1914, 57). He called for

the Peruvian government to assist anthropological investigations before it was too late.

27. Daggett 2009, 16.

28. Tantalean 2014, 41.

29. He became a mentor to Peruvian archaeologists, many from rural Peru (Burger 2009, 80).

30. He amassed fifteen thousand skulls and mummies (Daggett 2009, 11).

31. Tello was a friend of the son of Ricardo Palma, who was director of the National Library. Palma took Tello under his wing, ultimately introducing him to Lima's intellectual elite (Daggett 2009).

32. Quoted in Burger 2009, 71.

33. In "The Defense of Archaeological Heritage," Tello writes that archaeology is a specialized science and that those who excavate without proper training produce "enormous and irreparable damage to the national historical heritage" (quoted in Burger 2009, 91). These sites were considered a rich archive of the "race to which we belong—whose history is ours and whose civilization is intimately linked to ours." It was the duty of Peruvians to treat the materials accordingly, because they were the "most valuable heritage of the nation" (92). Echoing Dixon's words to Bingham in 1911, Tello stated that to excavate a site is to destroy it, and so care must be taken.

34. Tantalean 2014, 52. Ricardo Salvatore suggests that intellectual and scientific experts in Peru worked under the frame of imperial connections. Such entanglement revealed the ambivalence of the postcolonial situation (2008, 382).

35. Daggett 2009, 18. Throughout his career, Tello was accused of theft, often by his archrival, Gutiérrez (31).

36. Tello demonstrated that Peruvian civilization was the result of autochthonous development rather than, as Uhle suggested, diffusionism from Central America or Asia (Burger 2009, 67).

37. Tellingly, a skull that Tello offered to the Leguía government was sold to Harvard after Leguía rejected it for financial reasons (Daggett 2009).

38. Tello and Xesspe 1967.

39. Tello 1977.

40. Gänger 2009, 707; Gänger 2014; Méndez 1995.

41. Natalia Majluf points out that as early as 1791, the study of Incan society through archaeology was part of an emerging Creole identity. By the time of independence, the specificity of Incan history had been replaced by distant origins (2005, 272). Visual representations that had once been symbols of political legitimacy were subsequently converted into adornments and national illustrations.

42. Gänger 2009, 703; Castro-Klarén 2003.

43. Castro-Klarén 2003, 194.

44. Gänger 2014, 37. A Peruvian archaeological society was founded in 1868.

45. The conflict over objects and commercialism was larger than Bingham. For example, in a letter to the prefect in Cuzco, the commercial house of Emmel Brothers wrote that it didn't do anything illegal with respect to archaeological remains (April 24, 1912, AGN, Prefectura 1821–1956). Contests over the commercial sale of archaeological objects were a Pan-American phenomenon (Batalla 1996).

46. Gänger 2014, 155.

47. Tantalean 2014, 150; Gänger 2009, 712. In his analysis of the politics of science around collecting, Glenn Penny suggests that early twentieth-century practitioners relied on internationally sanctioned science for legitimacy. Nonetheless, newly independent states began to close their borders to outside ethnologists, who came to be considered foreign nationals rather than members of scientific communities (2002, 115).

48. Bingham to Taft, February 12, 1912, YPEP, box 6, folder 34; see also Charles Hilles, secretary to Taft, to Huntington Wilson, acting secretary of state, February 15, 1912, NA, 823.927/1. Bingham communicated with Grosvenor, too, about his plans. On February 13, 1912, he wrote Grosvenor that he wasn't sure whether it would be "wise or practicable" to do any digging that summer. He was still thinking about his plans and considering what would produce the best results. On February 23, he wrote Grosvenor about the plans for securing a concession and permission to remove materials. He wrote that he would do his best to "persuade the politicians in Lima that this is an enterprise of a purely scientific character and not intended to exploit commercially any of Peru's wonderful archaeological possessions" (Bingham to Grosvenor, February 13 and 23, 1912, NGS, 11-15, 73F1). Two weeks later, he followed up that he didn't think that securing permission would be a problem, but asked Grosvenor to keep the matter quiet (March 1, 1912, NGS, 11-15, 73F1).

49. Bingham to Taft, February 12, 1912, YPEP, box 6, folder 34.

50. Bingham to Schaefer, February 22, 1912, YPEP, box 6, folder 36. Bingham also asked Schaefer whether he should bring letters of backing from American financial institutions and learned societies, or whether the support of Yale and the US government would be sufficient. Louis Schaefer was one of fourteen managers who shared in the profits of W. R. Grace (Clayton 1985, 255).

51. Schaefer to Bingham, March 15, 1912, YPEP, box 6, folder 37.

52. Schaefer to Ballen, February 15, 1912, YPEP, box 6, folder 34.

53. The letter from Schaefer set up a code that allowed Ballen and Schaefer to communicate quickly by telegraph about whether the climate was amenable to a concession. The codes were as follows: OEMOB 1—Think that the prospects are favorable of getting the concession for Professor Bingham, and advise his coming here in June; OEMPH 2—Think the prospects are favorable for getting Professor Bingham the concession, but do not think that he should come here at this time; OEMRY 3—Do not think that the prospects are favorable for getting Professor Bingham the concession. In a letter dated April 19, Schaefer told Bingham that he had received a telegram from Ballen in Peru with "OEMYL" (which he thought must have been a typo), meaning that the time was favorable for Bingham to arrive in Peru (Schaefer to Bingham, April 19, 1912, YPEP, box 6, folder 38).

54. Huntington Wilson to H. Clay Howard, US minister in Lima, dispatch no. 44, February 26, 1912, NA, 823.927/1. The correspondence includes a copy of a request from Taft stating that an informal inquiry be made to the government of Peru.

55. Howard to Richard Flournoy, US State Department, February 28, 1912, NA, 823.927/2.

56. Letter to Howard, most likely from Taft, March 1912, NA, 823.927/2.

57. Wilson to Howard, February 26, 1912, MRE, Embassy Correspondence. Wilson enclosed the following letters: Bingham to Taft, February 12, 1912; Hilles to Wilson, February 15, 1912; and Taft to Howard, March 2, 1912, requesting support for Bingham and the concession.

58. Howard to Bingham, April 1, 1912; Wilson to Bingham, April 8, 1912, YPEP, box 6, folder 42.

59. Wilson to Bingham, April 8, 1912, YPEP, box 6, folder 42, emphasis added; see also NA, 823.927/4; and NA, 823.927/9. Correspondents also included the president's secretary Charles Hilles and the US legation in Peru (see, for example, two letters to Charles Hilles and Bingham, April 13, 1912, NA, 823.927/6).

60. Leguía's first term ended on September 24, 1912.

61. Wilson to Bingham, April 13, 1912, YPEP, box 6, folder 45.

62. H. Clay Howard to Taft, April 1, 1912, YPEP, box 6, folder 42.

63. Howard to Taft, April 1, 1912, NA, 823.927/11.

64. Bristol to Bingham, April 19, 1912, YPEP, box 6, folder 48.

65. Bingham to Wilson, April 11, 1912, YPEP, box 6, folder 44.

66. Bingham to Hadley, April 24, 1912, YPEP, box 6, folder 51.

67. Bingham to Hadley, April 26, 1912, YPEP, box 6, folder 52.

68. Bingham to Schaefer, April 29, 1912, YPEP, box 6, folder 53.

69. Bingham to Wilson, April 29, 1912, YPEP, box 6, folder 53; see also NA, 823.927/12.

70. Bingham to Taft, May 3, 1912; to Schaefer, May 1, 1912; to Woodward, May 2, 1912; to Wilson, May 2, 1912, YPEP, box 7, folder 55. In a letter to Schaefer dated May 13, 1912, Bingham refers to Ballen's work as strategic for "entering into the enemy's camp" to get them interested in the concession (YPEP, box 7, folder 62).

71. For example, in the letter sent to President Taft on May 3 regarding the concession, Bingham writes about the traffic in the Panama Canal. Given that the expedition was setting sail in the next month with seventy boxes of food and other supplies, Bingham asked for a special privilege allowing expedited review and passage of the expedition's materials. Bingham also wrote Leguía on May 3, 1912, apprising him of the expedition's pending arrival and plans, and requesting special treatment at the customs houses in Callao and Mollendo (YPEP, box 7, folder 56).

72. Wilson to Bingham, May 11, 1912, YPEP, box 7, folder 61. Two days earlier, Bingham wrote Hadley of Yale that Peru wanted to put the expedition "under obligation of friendship for her." He thought inserting a clause stipulating that the concession would lapse after two years if no work were done would help ensure the agreement (Bingham to Hadley, May 8, 1912, YPEP, box 7, folder 58).

73. Wilson to Bingham, May 11, 1912, NA, 823.027/14.

74. Nine boxes of osteological material were sent to Yale on July 13, 1912, through Lomellini & Co. (YPEP, box 7, folder 68).

75. Bingham to Morkill, July 14, 1912, YPEP, box 7, folder 68.

76. Bingham to Howard, July 14, 1912, YPEP, box 7, folder 68.

77. According to Howard, Bingham admitted his mistake and regretted not spending the sixty days in Lima to secure the bill's passage (Howard to Knox, November 13, 1912, NA, 823.927/29a).

78. Hadley to Bingham, August 21, 1912, YPEP, box 7, folder 68.

79. The attorney, Leguía's cousin, was also the attorney for the Peruvian Corporation.

80. The contract specified that finds would be divided between the Peruvian government and Yale. Peru would get first choice, then Yale, and so on. The contract also stated that Peru had a right to be acquainted with all studies (dispatch no. 151, August 31, 1912, NA, 823.927/20).

81. Howard wrote a lengthy letter to Wilson on August 31, explaining what had transpired, how Bingham had been largely absent, and how he couldn't remember the attorney's name. Howard didn't know the precise terms of what had been agreed upon, but felt something needed to be done, since no bill had yet been submitted.

82. Leguía quoted in Howard to Wilson, August 31, 1912, NA, 823.927/20.

83. Howard to Wilson, August 31, 1912, NA, 823.927/19.

84. Ibid.

85. Bingham to Hadley, October 4, 1912, YPEP, box 7, folder 70.

86. The Instituto Histórico was in charge of gathering and conserving materials related to national history, supporting historical works about Peru, making recommendations to the government about disseminating works of the historical sciences, conserving national monuments of archaeological or artistic character, and supervising the administration of the museums and archives (Hampe Martinez 1998, 126).

87. Bingham referred to a meeting with the "Society for the prevention of Cruelty to Ruins" (Bingham to Hadley, October 4, 1912, YPEP, box 7, folder 70). Christopher Heaney notes that this was the Society to Protect Monuments, the organization that had influenced the previous year's decree (2010, 142). In 1912, Luis Valcárcel, in support of Billinghurst, traveled to Lima and worked with the Pan-American Student Congress to pass laws against looting.

88. Bingham to Hadley, October 4, 1912, YPEP, box 7, folder 70.

89. A series of correspondence in the National Archives details the controversy. Thomas Barbour, secretary of the Peabody Museum faculty, and A. M. Tozzer, an assistant professor of anthropology at Harvard, expressed their concern and indignation over the proposed arrangement, along with several others, including W. H. Holmes of the National Museum (Smithsonian), Clements Markham, A. L. Kroeber, and two professors from Germany; see Barbour and Tozzer to secretary of state, November 14, 1912, 823.927/23; Barbour and Tozzer to secretary of state, December 10, 1912, 823.927/28; Barbour and Tozzer to secretary of state, undated, 823.927/26; Walcott to secretary of state, November 6, 1912, 823.927/21. The situation escalated, and Grosvenor and President Hadley of Yale weighed in (Hadley to Grosvenor, November 19, 1912, 823.927/24; see also Hadley to Secretary of State Knox, November 18, 1912, 823.927/25A). Letters were sent to Peruvian contacts, including the US legation and Albert Giesecke, regarding how Harvard was "greatly stirred up by this" (Rowe to Giesecke, November 22, 1912, AAG, file AG-1302). Some US citizens were opposed to Bingham's concession (YPEP, box 8, folders 77 and 95).

90. Teodoro Hampe Martinez (1998) refers to Larrabure y Unanue as a coastal hacendado. Larrabure y Unanue was president of the institute from 1905 to 1916

and a member of the Academias Españoles de la Lengua y la Historia. He was also president of the Ateneo in Lima, a literary club, and an ambassador in Argentina. Larrabure y Unanue's father was born in France in the Pyrenees, and he himself was born in Lima in 1844. His first work, *Historia del Descubrimiento y Conquista del Perú*, was lost in a fire in 1895 (Larrabure y Unanue 1934). Like Leguía, he thought industrialization was a key to modernizing Peru. In 1906, he wanted an international law code for the Americas that would promote free navigation, rapid steam lines, a Pan-American railroad, banks, and agreements for trade and treaties (Larrabure y Unanue 1906).

91. Bingham to Hadley, October 7, 1912, YPEP, box 7, folder 70.

92. Concern over the concession continued for several months in the United States as Harvard and others wrote the State Department for updates on it. Grosvenor even wrote Alfreda Bingham on November 18, 1912, saying that unless the "Yale Corporation gets busy, the contemplated concession which your husband so desires may be lost" (NGS, 11-15, 73F2).

93. Larrabure y Unanue 1906.

94. Ibid., 125.

95. Gänger 2014, 203.

96. Larrabure y Unanue 1906, 129.

97. Polar 1906, 146.

98. A May 1912 article in *Peru To-Day* discussed the sale and exportation of prehistoric Incan and colonial relics, urging the government to take action and enforce the law. On September 9, 1913, Gutiérrez de Quintanilla published an article in *La Nación* reminding the public of the legality of Bingham's actions. He had given a talk to the Sociedad Geográfica on December 24, 1911, discussing the need to respect the human dignity of the indigenous ancestors.

99. Bingham to Hadley, October 14, 1912, YPEP, box 7, folder 70.

100. Billinghurst announced his campaign tardily and requested a postponement of the elections. Leguía denied his request, infuriating Billinghurst's supporters, who promptly organized a general strike of the 1912 election. The required one-third of the possible votes was not cast, and the election was decided by Congress; Leguía and Billinghurst eventually struck a deal. Billinghurst would appoint Leguía's brother vice president, and Leguía would urge his supporters to cast their votes for Billinghurst (Klarén 2000). Billinghurst's presidency lasted eighteen months, until he was overthrown and replaced by Óscar Benavides.

101. The period between 1895 and 1919 has been described as an aristocratic republican period when the Limeño oligarchy vied for state power (Klarén 2000; Cotler 1978a). During this period, Peru had nine presidents.

102. General correspondence, October 26, 1912, YPEP, box 7, folder 71. Billinghurst later said that he thought Bingham too hasty in his decision to remove the concession from Congress. The following year, Bingham received word that Billinghurst was inclined to support another expedition to Peru and grant a concession (Bingham to Morkill, December 8, 1913, YPEP, box 9, folder 118).

103. The agreement was signed on October 31, 1912, and the news was published in Lima's *El Comercio* on November 5 (YPEP, box 7, folder 71). Hadley wrote the secretary of state in November, saying that Yale would be satisfied with simply getting export permits for material collected over the last few months (Arthur

Hadley to Philander C. Knox, November 21, 1912, NA, 823.927/25). Morkill assisted in the negotiations.

104. Gutiérrez de Quintanilla 1921.

105. *St. Louis Post* clipping, MRE. A year later, Pezet wrote about Bingham's portrayal of Peru in his illustrated talk for *American Archaeology*. Nonetheless, on February 15, 1915, Pezet asked for an arrangement for the 1915 expedition that would be similar to the one used in 1912, since Bingham had done so much for the country (Embassy Correspondence, MRE).

106. Bingham's letter, dated February 12, 1913, from New Haven, Connecticut, was printed in the March issue of *Peru To-Day*, accompanied by a letter from the editor (H. Bingham 1913c). In the letter, Bingham states that he previously published a response about the exclusivity clause in mid-November in *El Comercio*.

107. Giesecke, who had been trying to interest the University of Pennsylvania in helping establish such a place, wrote Bingham to see whether Yale would be interested (Giesecke to Bingham, April 9, 1913, YPEP, box 8, folder 92; see also folder 98).

108. Bingham to Mr. Carroll, Archaeological Institute of America, YPEP, box 9, folder 98.

109. Although the institute did not materialize initially, a similar project with a transnational center for investigation was revived in 2007, becoming a reality in 2011. Part of the agreement for Yale's return of artifacts in 2011 was the establishment of a joint study center for Yale University and the Universidad Nacional de San Antonio Abad del Cuzco in Cuzco.

110. Bingham's scrapbook has clippings from newspapers such as *La Crónica*, *El Sol*, *La Prensa-Lima*, and *El Comercio-Cuzco*, along with many miscellaneous unmarked clippings.

111. Noel 1912a, 372.

112. Noel 1913, 531, 532.

113. Ibid, 531. Larrabure y Unanue's comment was originally published in the *West Coast Leader*, October 31, 1912.

114. H. Bingham 1912f, 2. Bingham's letter to *El Comercio* was sent to the State Department, along with a translated newspaper article from *El Comercio* dated November 4, 1912, explaining that although Yale hadn't been in strict compliance with the law, Bingham had been given permission through December 19, because the law was mainly to prevent commercial speculation (NA, 823.927/29a).

115. Later he wrote that rather than being suspected of having secret commercial plans, he should have received accolades and honors for his scientific work (H. Bingham 1915a).

116. Gutiérrez de Quintanilla criticized Uhle for the disorder in which he left the National Museum and for failing to produce a catalogue. Julio Tello in turn critiqued Gutiérrez for not valuing Uhle's archaeological collections (Kaulicke 1998; Daggett 2009).

117. Burns and Skidmore 1979. Salvatore (2016) refers to him as an antiquarian.

118. Larson 2004.

119. Patterson 1995a.

120. García 2005. Gutiérrez de Quintanilla and Julio Tello were often at odds. Gutiérrez would call Tello "de indio," and Tello would call Gutiérrez "de español"

(Burger 2009; Tantalean 2014). For more on the relationship between Tello and Valcárcel, see the article by Prieto (2010).

121. Interview with Gutiérrez de Quintanilla (Roger 1917, 4).

122. Gutiérrez de Quintanilla 1913, 4. All translations are the author's. Julio Tello believed that the problems of Peru were rooted in conquest and colonization (Patterson 1995a).

123. Gutiérrez de Quintanilla 1913, 4.

124. Mexican *indigenismo* differs from Peru's in this way. Miguel Gamio of Mexico promoted an ethnicized model to forge a sense of patria, or national identity, and select examples of handicrafts and popular art were counted as authentic expressions of Mexicanidad and indigeneity (López 2010, 112; see also Batalla 1996).

125. Liisa Malkki (1992) argues that references to soil, what she refers to as arborization, are a persistent and pervasive discourse in national imaginings.

126. De la Cadena 2000; Larson 2004; Appelbaum, Macpherson, and Rosenblatt 2003.

127. Larson 2004.

128. Ibid.

129. Gänger 2014, 235.

130. De la Cadena 1998. José Tamayo Herrera (1980) finds seeds of indigenist ideology in the 1908 UNSAAC rebellion. He argues that *indigenismo* is a reflection of class and ethnicity and that it is an ideology of *mestizaje* and intellectuals that has existed in various forms since the colonial period. Machu Picchu, he believes, reinforced a neo-Incan enthusiasm.

131. De la Cadena 2000, 228; D. Poole 1997; García 2005; Coronado 2009.

132. De la Cadena 2000, 327.

133. María Elena García suggests that the movement's racist discourse relied on the notion of the "Indian problem," even as it emphasized indigenous education and miscegenation to strengthen Peru (2005, 67).

134. Salomon 1985. Local intellectuals focused on describing the Andean countryside, and writing and studying the Incan past and its history (D. Poole 1997, 182).

135. Critics of *indigenismo* have referred to it as taking Indians and putting them into laboratories, as an analysis of the indigenous from a dominant class perspective, as ethnocide, and as an appropriation and suppression of indigenous cultures for nation building that reinforces Indians' subaltern status (Becker 1995).

136. Valcárcel 1927.

137. His ideas evolved; see Valcárcel 1981. Ricardo Salvatore (2008) notes that Valcárcel criticized Julio Tello for using indigeneity as political trampoline. Tello, having been trained at Harvard, was an Indian out of place. Both Valcárcel and José Carlos Mariategui "espoused a doctrine of geographical purity, maintaining that only those Indians who remained in their 'natural' rural environment were worthy of admiration" (Weismantel and Eisenman 1998, 133; see also de la Cadena 1998). See the study by Mary Douglas (1966) for a theoretical discussion on matters of place.

138. Coronado 2009, 7.

139. Coronado 2009, 9. José Carlos Mariategui drew on European socialist

ideas to critique Peruvian society and craft a vision for a future wherein indigenous subjects would be brought in as politically and economically equivalent subjects. For an example of Indian elites in another context combining nationalism and indigeneity, see the study by Gregory Grandin (2000).

140. Coronado 2009, 165.

141. Portocarrero 2015.

142. De Rivero and von Tschudi 1951. According to Mark Thurner (2003), the first edition was published in Lima in 1941.

143. Thurner 2006, 397.

144. Ibid., 399; Cañizares-Esguerra 2002.

145. Albert Giesecke, for example, wasn't opposed to excavating, but wanted the objects to remain within Peruvian territory (Salvatore 2008). Yale examined bones excavated by Giesecke and Romualdo Aguilar near Pacaritambo (*El País*, September 20, 1912, CBC).

146. Noel 1912b, 73. By 1912 the sale and exportation of Incan, prehistoric, and colonial relics had increased, and the government was encouraged to take action. In one news article, action was directed toward bishops, reminding them of the 1911 law.

147. These included notices of their arrival and an article by Bingham on the ascent of Mount Coropuna.

148. Cosio 1914, 24.

149. Cosio 1914.

150. Thurner 2010; Cañizares-Esguerra 2002.

151. Thurner 2010, 165.

152. See Coronado 2009, 18.

153. See Coronil 2011.

154. For example, the illustrated daily *La Crónica* published images of Machu Picchu from *National Geographic* on December 8, 1913, but did not mention the concession or Bingham's 1912 conflict with the government. *La Crónica* published a series on the ruins of Machu Picchu and Cuzco, each fully illustrated; see, for example, the issues of December 8, 13, and 16, 1913, and February 3, 1915. *La Prensa* published a lengthy article about "the marvelous Incan ruins of Cuzco," along with a "detailed account of the 1912 expedition by professor Mr. Hiram Bingham" (February 28, 1915). The article focuses on climbing Huayna Picchu, the significance of the site (including a section on the three windows), and the reasons why Machu Picchu was an archaeological treasure.

155. Bingham to Grosvenor, June 22, 1915, YPEP, box 15, folder 256.

156. The institute, formed in 1913, was charged with monitoring and conserving the historic monuments of the area. The IHC was to study Peruvian history and advise the government on the best ways to conserve and protect archaeological remains. It was also supposed to study the folklore of Cuzco. The president of the IHC was Luis Valcárcel. José Gabriel Cosio was also a member. Valcárcel, although critical of Bingham at the time, eventually praised his work. For example, in a letter to the editor of the newspaper *La Prensa*, Valcárcel sought to clarify rumors about Yale removing materials and shipping them through Bolivia (June 15, 1975, LEV).

157. H. Bingham 1915a, 5.

158. Bingham to Grosvenor, June 22, 1915, YPEP, box 15, folder 256.

159. H. Bingham 1915a.

160. Bingham to IHC, n.d., YPEP, box 11, folder 159.

161. Osgood Hardy journal, June 15, 1915, YPEP, box 22, folder 46.

162. Bingham 1915a.

163. Their landlord was the *gobernador* of Ollantaytambo.

164. Salvatore refers to this as the "ritual restoration of sovereignty" (2016, 89). The event was also noted in the journals of Bingham and Erdis and in Ford's letters home. In a letter to his mother, he said that the inspector who had been appointed would not come to Ollantaytambo because he hadn't been paid. He wrote that their every movement was watched (August 5, 1915, NGS, 11-15, 73F5). Bingham's report noted that a box of bones and sherds was taken, and that they were accused of removing the objects of significant value.

165. Osgood Hardy journal, June 15, 1915, YPEP, box 22, folder 46.

166. Heaney (2012) suggests that the conflict in 1915 came about because they did not share information or collaborate with local scholars.

167. In a letter to Cosio, Bingham stated that they did not touch the stone and had photographic evidence to prove it (Bingham to Cosio, September 26, 1913, YPEP, box 9, folder 112).

168. Cosio 1915, 10.

169. Heaney (2012) suggests that noteworthy objects were hidden from Cosio and were not included in the inventory.

170. This is confirmed elsewhere (Gutiérrez de Quintanilla 1921).

171. Bingham 1915a. On June 5, 1915, *La Crónica* had published a formal denunciation of Bingham by the prefect of Cuzco, dated May 28, stating that the North American team had sent relics from Machu Picchu to the United States.

172. Bingham also listed the financial figures that the National Geographic Society and Yale University offered as support.

173. Bingham 1915a, 9.

174. Palomino 1915.

175. Palomino 1915, 9.

176. April 13, 1916, YPEP, box 13, folder 191.

177. W. R. Grace to Bingham, July 3, 1916, YPEP, box 13, folder 198.

178. The sherds, he said, would be hardly worth paying the freight on if they had to return them. Most of the sherds that had been collected were left in Ollantaytambo at their headquarters.

179. Bingham to Grosvenor, February 21, 1916, YPEP, box 16, folder 260.

180. Gutiérrez de Quintanilla 1916.

181. Ibid., 7.

182. Mould de Pease 2003, 154–162.

183. Ibid., 162–170.

184. Gutiérrez de Quintanilla 1921. In 1922, Gutiérrez de Quintanilla published *El Manco Capac, de la Arqueolojía Peruana: Julio C. Tello contra Emilio Gutiérrez de Quintanilla*, accusing Julio Tello, the former director of the National Museum, of selling skulls and other antiquities to foreign collectors.

185. It bothered Gutiérrez that the objects he had signed for had not been returned in a timely manner, and that other collections seemed to have been shipped

without passing through the proper channels. Citing a telegram in which Bingham wrote that he had not yet shipped the collections of minerals, bones, animals, birds, and plants, Gutiérrez wondered what had happened to these pieces.

186. Gutiérrez de Quintanilla 1921, 213. Gutiérrez refers to a priest who purportedly saw the mules and verified that the contents contained a valuable gold idol.

187. Gutiérrez de Quintanilla 1921, 276.

188. Ibid., 289.

189. Ibid., 285.

190. Ibid., 286.

191. Ibid., 292. Such sentiment was resurrected by Mariana Mould de Pease in the early 2000s and by Eliane Karp in 2008, suggesting again that the struggle over modernity and equivalence continues (see, for example, Mould de Pease 2003).

192. Bingham to Holmes, January 7, 1913, YPEP, box 8, folder 76.

193. Bingham to Grosvenor, November 28, 1916, YPEP, box 16, folder 265.

194. Grosvenor to Bingham, November 29, 1916, YPEP, box 16, folder 265.

195. Grosvenor to Bingham, December 29, 1915, YPEP, box 15, folder 258.

196. Bingham to Grosvenor, January 20, 1916, YPEP, box 16, folder 259.

197. Upon returning to Yale, Bingham continued to teach before enlisting in the US Air Force in 1917 to become an aviator during World War I. He was elected Connecticut's lieutenant governor in 1923, and then governor in 1925, a post he held for less than twenty-four hours, since he immediately ran for the US Senate in a special election and won. His reputation was tarnished when he was censured by the Senate for allowing a lobbyist, who was also on his staff, to sit in on a closed committee meeting.

198. Cañizares-Esguerra 2002, 207.

199. Thurner 2010.

200. Breglia 2006.

201. I am grateful to Juan Carlos Callirgos for this last point.

Conclusion: Artifact

1. For more on early guidebooks in Peru, see the articles by Mendoza (2009) and Flores Najar (1994).

2. Sociedad de Propaganda del sur del Perú 1921, 1. Bingham said that Cuzco was the most ancient pueblo of the Americas and that its history was more interesting than any other.

3. Ibid., 45. The book referred to Machu Picchu as the place "discovered and examined scientifically by the members of the Peruvian Expedition of 1912."

4. Dina Berger writes that the tourism industry in Mexico, established in the early twentieth century, helped usher in ideas of modernity, economic development, and nation building. Tourism offered growth opportunities and the chance to participate in global capitalism (2006, 3).

5. Grosvenor wrote Bingham in 1949 congratulating him but wondered whether or not making Machu Picchu accessible to automobile traffic might "take away much of the impressiveness of that extraordinary site which you discovered

and first revealed to the world" (Grosvenor to Bingham, June 6, 1949, NGS, 11-15, 73F8).

6. November 6, 1936, LEV. In the 1930s, a number of letters were written about the lack of maintenance of the site, its abandonment, and the need for adequate funds to properly conserve and develop it (January 24, 1932, and September 18, 1933, 3-11, LEV; May 16, 1930, E-006, 009, LEV).

7. Paul Schwikher to Luis E. Valcárcel, December 29, 1952, LEV. On March 14, 1955, Giesecke wrote Bingham about building a larger hotel at the site. Raising funds could potentially be secured through private stock investment in hotel ownership (AAG, file AG-0140). Bingham had previously written that improved access and a better hotel would increase visitation to Machu Picchu. Bingham also commented that after speaking with Archer Huntington, founder of the Hispanic Society of America, restoration would not make the ruins more attractive and that efforts should focus instead on conservation or preservation (Bingham to Giesecke, January 17, 1955, AAG, file AG-0140). Bingham apparently had published a favorable editorial in *El Comercio* agreeing with Cosio about the need for preservation rather than restoration (see Giesecke to Bingham, April 2, 1955, AAG, file AG-0140).

8. Mendoza 2009, 34.

9. Gade 2016, 161.

10. *El Comercio*, July 4, 2016, 9.

11. See, for example, the images held at the CBC: Machupichu, Tres Ventanas, 1930, CAB00678; Grupo en Machupichu 1925, CAB00030; Grupo en Machupichu 1940, CAB00106.

12. 1955, CBC, SAL00055.

13. Martin to Valcárcel, February 11, 1932, LEV.

14. September 2, 1958, Coronet Instructional Films, LEV.

15. *Caretas*, 1953, no. 45.

16. See the work of Pellegrino Luciano (2006, 2011) for a discussion of conservation and its impact on local residents.

17. Acurio is Peru's most celebrated chef and exponent of Peruvian cuisine. He owns restaurants worldwide, and his flagship restaurant, Astrid y Gastón, was rated one of the top fifty restaurants in the world by San Pellegrino in 2016 (theworlds50best.com/list/1-50-winners).

18. Grosvenor to Manuel de Freyre, minister of Peru, November 23, 1918, NGS, 11-15, 73F7.

19. Eduardo Higginson, consul general to the United States, to Grosvenor, October 26, 1920, NGS, 11-15, 73F8.

20. Bingham to Grosvenor, November 1, 1920, NGS, 11-15, 73F8.

21. Grosvenor to Higginson, November 3, 1920, NGS, 11-15, 73F8.

22. Hiram Bingham Jr. to Giesecke, May 2, 1961, AAG, file AG-0141.

23. Bingham Jr. to Giesecke, February 8, 1962, AAG, file AG-0141.

24. Some of the materials had already been returned (Lubow 2007).

25. Lucy Salazar and Richard Burger (2016, 91) suggest that public interest grew as a result of Yale's traveling exhibition of Machu Picchu materials developed in the late 1990s.

26. See correspondence between the Peruvian Embassy in the United States

and its US counterpart in Lima regarding conversations with Richard Levin, president of Yale, held at the Ministerio de Relaciones Exteriores, May 17, 2005.

27. Eduardo Ferrero Costa, Peruvian ambassador to the US, communication labeled "very urgent," July 26, 2005, MRE. The new plan included the following points: suspending dialogue with Yale temporarily; presenting a formal letter from the Peruvian embassy, requiring the return of all objects; searching for North American support through diplomatic channels or private associations familiar with the topic; carrying out a public campaign to denounce Yale in the international press and other media; and taking diplomatic action with North American authorities, including meetings with the executive and legislative branches of the US government.

28. Ferrero correspondence, February 22, 2006, MRE.

29. The committee consisted of two members elected by Peru, two members elected by Yale, and one member to be agreed on by both parties. The committee was charged with making an inventory of the collections and establishing criteria for dividing them. In addition, the committee negotiated the details of the return of the objects, including the establishment of time lines and locations.

30. Peruvian representatives met with the attorney and former professor of art law Barbara T. Hoffman at a conference on sustainable culture in 2006. She encouraged them to continue with negotiations, arguing that reaching an amicable agreement was far more desirable than opting for a more litigious, and thus riskier and more expensive, route.

31. The MOU was signed by agents of Yale University and Peru and was intended to "create a model for the ongoing collaborative stewardship of materials that are of historical importance to Peru and Yale, and of cultural importance to the people of Peru and the world."

32. Memorandum of Understanding 2007, 1.

33. Ibid.

34. Ibid.

35. The MOU specified that the museum and research center would act as a "suitable memorial acknowledging the life and work of Hiram Bingham" (3).

36. The MOU defined "museum quality" as those materials in the collection that "are suitable for and capable of being displayed in a museum exhibition" (2). Specifically, they were objects taken from the inventory that had been supplied to the ad hoc committee.

37. The MOU specified that not all items would be returned at the same time. Instead, Yale would acknowledge Peru's title to all the excavated objects in exchange for having usufruct rights to research the collection in Cuzco, with museum-quality objects to be returned once the research center was in operation.

38. A state official told the author that building a museum in the spirit of the Getty Museum was something Peru should do to demonstrate its capabilities as a nation.

39. Karp went on to say that Yale refused to acknowledge Peru's sovereign right over the objects and that the MOU reflected a colonial way of thinking by a modern academic institution. She suggested that Yale had deliberately stalled negotiations when her spouse, Alejandro Toledo, was in power, because of his indigenous

identity. Waiting for a new Peruvian president who was hostile to indigenous matters would favor Yale in the negotiations.

40. The op-ed was published in Lima's *El Comercio* on February 25, though it was not as prominently displayed.

41. Needham 2008.

42. In March 2008, the International Council on Monuments and Sites conference was held in Lima. As part of the conference, the INC official Maria Elena Cordova and Luis Lumbreras subjected the MOU to a thorough analysis. After fifteen detailed pages of protest, Lumbreras and Cordova concluded that Peru needed to follow its own laws and its own constitution, with the Peruvian Congress's participation, before agreeing to any MOU with Yale University.

43. In addition, an open letter was addressed to President Alan García. Signed on March 7, 2008, the letter stated: "The 'Machu Picchu Collection' of this university and others, like the vast Max Uhle collection at UC Berkeley, *should* be returned to Peru. . . . Lamentably, although the ownership over this patrimony by Peru is *clearly* recognized in the MOU, this agreement reflects an arrogant and prejudicial attitude on the part of Yale, denying Peru its moral and legal right to decide with sovereignty, without conditions or tutelage, the future of the complete collection." Signatories included scholars from the United States, Peru, and France.

44. See, for example, *Diario El Sol* (Cuzco), March 22, 2008: "In Spite of the Specialist's Critiques—Government: Yale Will Return All the Pieces"; *El Diario del Cuzco*, April 4, 2008: "They Will Repatriate Incan Pieces of Yale"; *El Diario del Cuzco*, May 5, 2008: "UNESCO Supports Peru (Says Yale Should Return Objects)"; *La Republica*, May 11, 2008: "Yale Should Comply with the Law and with Their Word"; *El Comercio*, June 19, 2008: "Yale Shows the Pieces but Does Not Assure That They Are Going to Return Them"; *El Comercio*, June 19, 2008: "National Geographic Asks Yale University to Return All the Objects of Machu Picchu."

45. In the complaint, Peru stated: "These artifacts belong to Peru and its people and are central to the history and heritage of the Peruvian nation. Yale is wrongfully, improperly, and fraudulently detaining this property and has refused its return. The property in question is composed of centuries-old Incan materials—mummies, skulls, bones and other human remains, pottery, utensils, ceramics, objects of art and other items ('artifacts')—which were excavated from Cuzco, Machu Picchu, and the surrounding areas by agents of the University (Republic of Peru v. Yale University [2008])." For support, the document drew on UNESCO treaties and multinational agreements, including the 1970 UNESCO Convention on the Means of Prohibiting and Preventing the Illicit Import, Export, and Transfer of Ownership of Cultural Property and the 1972 UNESCO Convention Concerning the Protection of the World Cultural and Natural Heritage, to justify Peru's claim. Peru filed fourteen causes of action and sought damages in excess of $75,000. The amount, which may seem insignificant, is a standard minimum figure.

46. Glenn 2009, 2.

47. Salazar and Burger 2016.

48. Ibid.

49. Ibid.

50. Levin 2011.

51. The celebration did not take place on July 24, the day Bingham sighted Machu Picchu, but in early July, marking the week in 2007 when Machu Picchu was designated a modern wonder of the world.

52. "Yale and UNSAAC Create Center to Promote Study of Machu Picchu and Inca Culture," *Yale News*, February 11, 2011, news.yale.edu/2011/02/11/yale-and-unsaac-create-center-promote-study-machu-picchu-and-inca-culture.

53. This was closed the two times I visited.

54. Olmos is a Mexican American actor perhaps best known for his role as a detective in the hit television series *Miami Vice*.

55. In the original exhibition, these photographs enveloped the display of artifacts.

56. In the video clip, Protzen says that these are subjective decisions and that tourists should be informed about the modifications. In addition, Protzen dispels myths about the use of metal to quarry rocks, instead suggesting that the Incas at Machu Picchu used stones to quarry the rocks.

57. It was not clear where the explanations came from.

58. Bermudez Zamalloa 2012.

59. Kersel and Luke state that Yale directed the entire exhibition and display, including the paint color of the walls. They question the support of local interests (2015, 76).

60. Aguilar 2011, 9.

61. Che did visit Machu Picchu, though not on his motorcycle; see the excellent volume edited by Drinot (2010) on Che and his travels.

62. Marcel Velaochaga, interview with the author, November 28, 2007.

63. Quoted in Planas 2007.

64. Each insertion into global pop culture is big news in Peru. The Superman story was front-page news in *El Comercio*, Lima's largest daily newspaper.

65. That year, Indiana Jones was found chasing skulls in Cuzco in *Indiana Jones and the Kingdom of the Crystal Skull*.

66. Planas 2007.

67. Velaochaga interview.

68. Planas 2007.

69. Interview by author, May 23, 2008.

70. Mitchell 2005.

Reference List

Abu-Lughod, L. 2013. *Do Muslim Women Need Saving?* Cambridge, MA: Harvard University Press.

Achim, M. 2014. "Skulls and Idols: Anthropometrics, Antiquity Collections, and the Origin of American Man, 1810–1850." In *Nature and Antiquities: The Making of Archaeology in the Americas,* edited by P. Kohl, I. Podgorny, and S. Gänger, 23–46. Tucson: University of Arizona Press.

Adorno, R. 2000. *Guaman Poma: Writing and Resistance in Colonial Peru.* Austin: University of Texas Press.

Aguilar, V. R. 2011. Introduction to *Machu Picchu: Catálogo de la colección,* 9–10. Lima: US Embasssy.

Alloula, M. 1986. *The Colonial Harem.* Minneapolis: University of Minnesota Press.

Andean Air. 2011. "One Million Tourists Visit Machu Picchu in 2011." *Andean Air Mail and Peruvian Times,* November 20, 2011. http://www.peruviantimes.com /20/one-million-tourists-visit-machu-picchu-in-2011/14250.

Andermann, J., and W. Rowe, eds. 2005. *Images of Power: Iconography, Culture, and the State in Latin America.* Oxford: Berghahn.

Anderson, B. 1991. *Imagined Communities: Reflections on the Origin and Spread of Nationalism.* London: Verso.

Appadurai, A. 1988. *The Social Life of Things: Commodities in Cultural Perspective.* Cambridge: Cambridge University Press.

———. 1996. *Modernity at Large: Cultural Dimensions of Globalization.* Minneapolis: University of Minnesota Press.

Appelbaum, N., A. S. Macpherson, and K. A. Rosemblatt. 2003. "Racial Nations." In *Race and Nation in Modern Latin America,* edited by N. Appelbaum, A. S. Macpherson, and K. A. Rosemblatt, 1–31. Chapel Hill: University of North Carolina Press.

Arnold, B. 1990. "The Past as Propaganda: Totalitarian Archaeology in Nazi Germany." *Antiquity* 64, no. 244: 464–478.

Asad, T. 1995. *Anthropology and the Colonial Encounter.* New York: Humanity.

Axel, B. K. 2002. *From the Margins: Historical Anthropology and Its Futures.* Durham, NC: Duke University Press.

Bandelier, A. 1910. *The Islands of Titicaca and Koati*. New York: Hispanic Society of America.

Banta, M., and C. M. Hinsley. 1986. *From Site to Sight: Anthropology, Photography, and the Power of Imagery*. Cambridge, MA: Peabody Museum Press.

Barad, K. 1998. "Agential Realism: Feminist Interventions in Understanding Scientific Practices." In *The Science Studies Reader*, edited by M. Biagioli, 1–11. New York: Routledge.

Barnes, B., and D. Bloor. 1982. "Relativism, Rationalism and the Sociology of Knowledge." In *Rationality and Relativism*, edited by M. Hollis and S. Lukes, 21–47. Oxford: Blackwell.

Barnhart, T. A. 2005. *Ephraim George Squier and the Development of American Anthropology*. Lincoln: University of Nebraska Press.

Barringer, T., and T. Flynn, eds. 1998. *Colonialism and the Object: Empire, Material Culture, and the Museum*. London: Routledge.

Barthes, R. 1981. *Camera Lucida: Reflections on Photography*. Translated by Richard Howard. London: Jonathan Cape.

Batalla, G. B. 1996. *México Profundo: Reclaiming a Civilization*. Austin: University of Texas Press.

Beasley-Murray, J. 2010. "Vilcashuamán: Telling Stories in Ruins." In *Ruins of Modernity*, edited by J. Hell and A. Schönle, 212–231. Durham, NC: Duke University Press.

Beauchesne, K., and A. Santos. 2011. *The Utopian Impulse in Latin America*. New York: Palgrave Macmillan.

Becker, M. 1995. "Indigenismo and Indian Movements in Twentieth-Century Ecuador." Paper presented at the Latin American Studies Association, Washington, DC, September 28–30.

Beezley, W. H. 1989. *Judas at the Jockey Club, and Other Episodes of Porfirian Mexico*. Lincoln: University of Nebraska Press.

Benjamin, W. (1955) 1969. *Illuminations: Essays and Reflections*. Translated by Harry Zohn. Edited by Hannah Arendt. New York: Schocken.

Berger, D. 2006. *The Development of Mexico's Tourism Industry: Pyramids by Day, Martinis by Night*. New York: Palgrave Macmillan.

Berger, D., and A. G. Wood, eds. 2010. *Holiday in Mexico: Critical Reflections on Tourism and Tourist Encounters*. Durham, NC: Duke University Press.

Berger, J. 1972. *Ways of Seeing*. Harmondsworth, UK: Penguin.

Bermudez Zamalloa, B. 2012. "Exposición arqueologíca de la Casa Concha, apología a Hiram Bingham." *Diario El Sol*, 1.

Bernasconi, R. 2001. *Race*. Malden, MA: Blackwell.

Bhaba, H. 1994. *The Location of Culture*. New York: Routledge.

Biagioli, M. 1993. *Galileo, Courtier: The Practice of Science in the Culture of Absolutism*. Chicago: University of Chicago Press.

Bingham, A. 1989. *Portrait of an Explorer: Hiram Bingham, Discoverer of Machu Picchu*. Ames: Iowa State University Press.

———. 1996. *The Tiffany Fortune, and Other Chronicles of a Connecticut Family*. New York: Abeel and Leet.

Bingham, H. 1909. *The Journal of an Expedition Across Venezuela and Colombia,*

1906–1907: An Exploration of the Route of Bolívar's Celebrated March of 1819 and of the Battle-Fields of Boyacá and Carabobo. New Haven, CT: Yale Publishing Association.

———. 1910a. "Causes of Lack of Political Cohesion in South America." *American Political Science Review* 4, no. 4: 508–515.

———. 1910b. "On Certain Characteristics of the South Americans of To-Day." *Popular Science Monthly* 77 (December): 582–589.

———. 1910c. "The Ruins of Choqquequirau." *American Anthropologist*, 12, no. 4: 505–525.

———. 1911. *Across South America: An Account of a Journey from Buenos Aires to Lima by Way of Potosí.* New York: Houghton Mifflin.

———. 1912a. "The Discovery of Pre-historic Human Remains near Cuzco, Peru." *American Journal of Science* 33: 297–305.

———. 1912b. "Exploration in Peru." *National Geographic*, April, 417–423.

———. 1912c. "Preliminary Report of the Yale Peruvian Expedition." *Bulletin of the American Geographical Society* 44: 20–26.

———. 1912d. "A Search for the Last Incan Capital." *Harper's Magazine* 125: 695–705.

———. 1912e. "Vitcos, the Last Inca Capital." *Proceedings of the American Antiquarian Society* 22: 135–196.

———. 1912f. Letter to the editor. *Peru To-Day.*

———. 1913a. "The Discovery of Machu Picchu." *Harper's Magazine* 126: 709–719.

———. 1913b. "In the Wonderland of Peru." *National Geographic*, April, 387–573.

———. 1913c. Letter to the editor: "The Yale Expedition." *Peru To-Day*, March, 643–645.

———. 1914. "Economic Futures of the West Coast of South America." *Bulletin of the American Manufacturers Export Association*, February 1, n.p.

———. 1915a. Letter to the editor. *La Crónica*, July 5.

———. 1915b. "The Story of Machu Picchu: The National Geographic Society–Yale University Explorations in Peru." *National Geographic*, February, 172–217.

———. 1915c. "Types of Machu Picchu Pottery." *American Anthropologist* 17, no. 2: 257–271.

———. 1916. "Further Explorations in the Land of the Incas." *National Geographic*, May, 431–473.

———. 1918. "Building America's Air Army." *National Geographic*, January, 48.

———. 1922. *Inca Land: Explorations in the Highlands of Peru.* Washington, DC: National Geographic Society.

———. 1930. *Machu Picchu: A Citadel of the Incas.* Washington, DC: National Geographic Society.

———. 1952. *Lost City of the Incas: The Story of Machu Picchu and Its Builders.* London: Weidenfeld and Nicolson.

Bingham, W. 1989. *Hiram Bingham: A Personal History.* Boulder, CO: Bin Lan Zhen Publishers.

Blanchard, P. 1991. *Markham in Peru: The Travels of Clements R. Markham, 1852–1853.* Austin: University of Texas Press.

Boardman, A. 2010. "The US-Mexican War and the Beginnings of American

Tourism in Mexico." In *Holiday in Mexico: Critical Reflections on Tourism and Tourist Encounters*, edited by D. Berger and A. G. Wood, 21–53. Durham, NC: Duke University Press.

Bonavio, D., and R. Ravines, eds. 1970. *Arqueología Peruana: Precursores*. Lima: Casa de la Cultura Perú.

Boone, E., ed. 1993. *Collecting the Pre-Columbian Past*. Washington, DC: Dumbarton Oaks Research Library and Collection.

Bowler, P. J. 2003. *Evolution: The History of an Idea*. Berkeley: University of California Press.

Bowman, I. 1916. *The Andes of Southern Peru*. New York: Holt.

Breglia, L. 2006. *Monumental Ambivalence: The Politics of Heritage*. Austin: University of Texas Press.

Brives, C. 2013. "Identifying Ontologies in a Clincial Trial." *Social Studies of Science* 43, no. 3: 397–416.

Bueno, C. 2010. "Teotihuacán: Showcase for the Centennial." In *Holiday in Mexico: Critical Reflections on Tourism and Tourist Encounters*, edited by D. Berger and A. G. Wood, 54–76. Durham, NC: Duke University Press.

Bulletin of the Pan American Union. 1914. Summary of "The Economic Future of the West Coast of South America," a speech by Hiram Bingham. Vol. 38 (January–June): 229–235.

Burger, R., ed. 2009. *The Life and Writings of Julio C. Tello: America's First Indigenous Archaeologist*. Iowa City: University of Iowa Press.

Burger, R., and L. Salazar, eds. 2003. *The 1912 Yale Peruvian Scientific Expedition Collections from Machu Picchu: Human and Animal Remains*. New Haven, CT: Yale University Press.

———, eds. 2004. *Machu Picchu: Unveiling the Mystery of the Incas*. New Haven, CT: Yale University Press.

———, eds. 2012. *The 1912 Yale Peruvian Scientific Expedition Collections from Machu Picchu: Metal Artifacts*. New Haven, CT: Yale University Press.

Burns, E. B., and T. Skidmore. 1979. *Elites, Masses, and Modernization in Latin America, 1850–1930*. Austin: University of Texas Press.

Callirgos, J. C. 2007. "Reinventing the City of the Kings: Postcolonial Modernizations of Lima, 1845–1930." PhD diss., University of Florida.

Callon, M. 1999. "Some Elements of a Sociology of Translation: Domestication of the Scallops and the Fishermen of Saint Brieuc Bay." In *The Science Studies Reader*, edited by M. Biagioli, 67–83. New York: Routledge.

Cañizares-Esguerra, J. 2002. *How to Write the History of the New World: Histories, Epistemologies, and Identities in the Eighteenth-Century Atlantic World*. Palo Alto, CA: Stanford University Press.

———. 2006. *Nature, Empire, and Nation: Explorations of the History of Science in the Iberian World*. Palo Alto, CA: Stanford University Press.

Cannizzo, J. 1989. *Into the Heart of Africa*. Toronto: Royal Ontario Museum Press.

———. 1998. "Gathering Souls and Objects: Missionary Collections." In *Colonialism and the Object: Empire, Material Culture, and the Museum*, edited by T. Barringer and T. Flynn, 153–166. London: Routledge.

Cartmill, M., and F. H. Smith. 2009. *The Human Lineage*. New York: Wiley-Blackwell.

Caspari, R. 2003. "From Types to Populations: A Century of Race, Physical Anthropology, and the American Anthroplogical Association." *American Anthropologist* 105, no. 1: 63–74.

Castañeda, Q. 1996. *In the Museum of Maya Culture: Touring Chichen Itza*. Minneapolis: University of Minnesota Press.

Castro-Klarén, S. 2003. "The Nation in Ruins: Archaeology and the Rise of the Nation." In *Beyond Imagined Communities: Reading and Writing the Nation in Nineteenth-Century Latin America*, edited by S. Castro-Klarén and J. C. Chasteen, 161–195. Washington, DC: Woodrow Wilson Center Press.

Certeau, M. de. 1984. *The Practice of Everyday Life*. Translated by Steven Rendell. Berkeley: University of California Press.

Chakrabarty, D. 2000. *Provincializing Europe: Postcolonial Thought and Historical Difference*. Princeton, NJ: Princeton University Press.

Chambers, D. W., and R. Gillespie. 2000. "Locality in the History of Science: Colonial Science, Technoscience, and Indigenous Knowledge." In *Nature and Empire: Science and the Colonial Enterprise*, edited by R. MacLeod, 221–240. Ithaca, NY: Cornell University Press.

Chavez, L. 2000. *Covering Immigration: Popular Images and the Politics of the Nation*. Berkeley: University of California Press.

Chervin, A. 1908. *Anthropologie bolivienne*. Paris: Imp. Nationale.

Cieza de León, P. (1553) 1999. *The Discovery and Conquest of Peru*. Translated by A. Cook and D. Cook. Durham, NC: Duke University Press.

Clayton, L. 1985. *Grace: W. R. Grace & Co., The Formative Years, 1850–1930*. Ottawa, IL: Jameson.

———. 1999. *Peru and the United States: The Condor and the Eagle*. Athens: University of Georgia Press.

Coe, B. 1988. *Kodak Cameras: The First Hundred Years*. Cincinnati: Seven Hills.

Conn, S. 1998. *Museums and American Intellectual Life, 1876–1926*. Chicago: University of Chicago Press.

Cook, O. F. 1916. "Staircase Farms of the Ancients." *National Geographic*, May, 474–533.

Coronado, J. 2009. *The Andes Imagined: Indigenismo, Society, and Modernity*. Pittsburgh: University of Pittsburgh Press.

Coronil, F. 2011. "The Future in Question: History and Utopia in Latin America (1989–2010)." In *Business as Usual: The Roots of the Global Financial Meltdown*, edited by C. Calhoun and G. Derluguian, 231–264. New York: New York University Press.

———, ed. 2004. "Can the Subaltern See? Photographs as History." Special issue, *Hispanic American Historical Review* 84, no. 1.

Cosio, J. G. 1912. "Una Excursión a Machu Piccho." *Revista Universitaria* 1, nos. 2 and 3: 1–25.

———. 1913. "Informe Elevado." *Revista Universitaria* 2, no. 5: 2–34.

———. 1914. "Expedición científica de la Universidad de Yale en el Cusco." *Boletín Sociedad Geográfica de Lima*, 10–24.

———. 1915. "Sobre las excavaciones en el Cusco." *La Crónica*, July 20.

Cotler, J. 1978a. *Clases, Estado y Nación en el Perú*. Lima: Instituto de Estudios Peruanos.

———. 1978b. "A Structural-Historical Approach to the Breakdown of Democratic Institutions: Peru." In *The Breakdown of Democratic Regimes*, edited by J. J. Linz and A. Stepan, 178–206. Baltimore: Johns Hopkins University Press.

Cox, A. 2007. "Purifying Bodies, Translating Race: The Lantern Slides of Sir Everard im Thurn." *History of Photography*, October, 348–365.

Craib, R. B. 2004. *Cartographic Mexico: A History of State Fixations and Fugitive Landscapes*. Durham, NC: Duke University Press.

Crary, J. 1990. *Techniques of the Observer: On Vision and Modernity in the Nineteenth Century*. Cambridge, MA: MIT Press.

Crimp, D. 1993. "On the Museum's Ruins." In *The Anti-Aesthetic: Essays on Postmodern Culture*, edited by H. Foster, 43–56. Seattle: Bay Press.

Cueto, M. 1994. *Missionaries of Science: The Rockefeller Foundation and Latin America*. Bloomington: Indiana University Press.

Cukierman, H. 2014. "Who Invented Brazil?" In *Beyond Imported Magic: Essays on Science, Technology, and Society in Latin America*, edited by E. Medina, I. da Costa Marques, and C. Holmes, 27–46. Cambridge, MA: MIT Press.

Daggett, R. 2009. "Julio Tello: An Account of His Rise to Prominence in Peruvian Archaeology." In *The Life and Writings of Julio C. Tello: America's First Indigenous Archaeologist*, edited by R. Burger, 7–54. Iowa City: University of Iowa Press.

Daston, L., ed. 2000. *Biographies of Scientific Objects*. Chicago: University of Chicago Press.

Daston, L., and P. Galison. 1992. "The Image of Objectivity." *Representations* 40: 82–128.

———. 2007. *Objectivity*. Brooklyn: Zone.

Daston, L., and E. Lunbeck. 2011. *Histories of Scientific Observation*. Chicago: University of Chicago Press.

Davis, J. B., and J. Thurnam. 1865. *Crania Britannica: Delineations and Descriptions of the Skulls of the Aboriginal and Early Inhabitants of the British Islands: With Notes of Other Remains, Vol. 2*. London.

de la Cadena, M. 1998. "Silent Racism and Intellectual Superiority." *Bulletin of Latin American Research* 17, no. 2: 143–164.

———. 2000. *Indigenous Mestizos: The Politics of Race and Culture in Cuzco, Peru, 1919–1991*. Durham, NC: Duke University Press.

de Molina, C. (1573) 2011. *Account of the Fables and Rites of the Incas*. Translated by B. Bauer. Austin: University of Texas Press.

de Molina, C., and J. de Acosta. (1590) 2002. *Natural and Moral History of the Indies*. Translated by J. Mangan. Durham, NC: Duke University Press.

de Rivero, M., and J. J. von Tschudi. 1851. *Antigüedades Peruanas*. Lima: Impr. Imperial de la Corte y del Estado.

Derrida, J. 2002. "The Archive Market: Truth, Testimony, Evidence." In *Echographies of Television*, edited by J. Derrida and B. Steigler, 82–99. Cambridge: Polity.

Didion, J. 1983. *Salvador*. New York: Random House.

Dippie, B. W. 1991. *The Vanishing American: White Attitudes and US Indian Policy*. Lawrence: University of Kansas Press.

Dirks, N., ed. 1992. *Colonialism and Culture*. Ann Arbor: University of Michigan Press.

d'Orbigny, A. D. 1839. *L'Homme Américain (de l'amérique méridionale) Considéré Sous Ses Rapports Physiologiques et Moraux*. Paris: Pitois-Levraultet.

Douglas, M. 1970. *Purity and Danger: An Analysis of Concepts of Pollution and Taboo*. New York: Penguin.

Drinot, P., ed. 2010. *Che's Travels: The Making of a Revolutionary in 1950s Latin America*. Durham, NC: Duke University Press.

Dumit, J. 1997. "A Digital Image of the Category of the Person: PET Scanning and Objective Self-Fashioning." In *Cyborgs and Citadels: Anthropological Interventions in Emerging Sciences and Technologies*, edited by G. L. Downey and J. Dumit, 83–102. Santa Fe, NM: School of American Research Press.

———. 2004. *Picturing Personhood: Brain Scans and Biomedical Identity*. Princeton, NJ: Princeton University Press.

Eaton, G. 1916. "Collection of Osteological Material from Machu Picchu." Supplement to *Memoirs of the Connecticut Academy of Arts and Sciences* 5 (May): 3–96.

Edwards, E. 1988. "Representation and Reality: Science and the Visual Image." In *Australia in Oxford*, edited by H. Morphy, 27–45. Oxford: Pitt Rivers Museum, University of Oxford.

———. 1990. "Photographic 'Types': The Pursuit of a Method." *Visual Anthropology* 3, no. 23: 241–247.

———, ed. 1992. *Anthropology and Photography, 1860–1920*. New Haven, CT: Yale University Press, in association with the Royal Anthropological Institute.

———. 1999. "Photographs of Objects of Memory." In *Material Memories: Design and Evocation*, edited by M. Kwint, C. Breward, and J. Aynesley, 221–236. Oxford: Berg.

———. 2001a. "Photography and the Performance of History." *Kronos: Southern African Histories* 27 (November): 15–29.

———. 2001b. *Raw Histories: Photographs, Anthropology, and Museums*. Oxford: Berg.

———, ed. 2004. *Photographs, Histories, Objects: On the Materiality of Images*. New York: Routledge.

———. 2009. "Photography and the Material Performance of the Past." *History and Theory* 48, no. 4: 130–150.

———. 2012. "Objects of Affect: Photography beyond the Image." *Annual Review of Anthropology* 41: 221–234.

Edwards, E., C. Gosden, and R. Phillips, eds. 2006. *Sensible Objects: Colonialism, Museums, and Material Culture*. Oxford: Berg.

Edwards, E., and J. Hart. 2004. "Introduction: Photographs as Objects." In *Photographs, Histories, Objects: On the Materiality of Images*, edited by E. Edwards and J. Hart, 1–15. New York: Routledge.

Everson, T. 2007. *The Gene: A Historical Perspective*. Westport, CT: Greenwood.

Fabian, A. 2010. *The Skull Collectors: Race, Science, and America's Unburied Dead*. Chicago: University of Chicago Press.

Feldman, J. 2016. "'Miserable San Damian—But What Treasures!': The Life of Aleš Hrdlička's Peruvian Collection." *History and Anthropology* 27, no. 2: 230–250.

Ferris, H. B. 1916. "The Indians of Cuzco and Apurímac." *Memoirs of the American Anthropological Association* 3, no. 2 (April–June): 55–148.

————. 1921. "Anthropological Studies on the Quichua and Machiganga Indians." *Transactions of the Connecticut Academy of Arts and Sciences* 25 (April): 1–92.

Findlay, E. 1998. "Love in the Tropics: Marriage, Divorce, and the Construction of Benevolent Colonialism in Puerto Rico, 1898–1910." In *Close Encounters of Empire: Writing the Cultural History of US–Latin American Relations*, edited by G. M. Joseph, C. LeGrand, and R. Salvatore, 139–172. Durham, NC: Duke University Press.

Finlay, M. 2009. *Growing American Rubber: Strategic Plants and the Politics of National Security*. New Brunswick, NJ: Rutgers University Press.

Flores Galindo, A. 1987. "In Search of an Inca." In *Resistance, Rebellion, and Consciousness in the Andean Peasant World, 18th to 20th Centuries*, edited by S. Stern, 193–210. Madison: University of Wisconsin Press.

————. 2010. *In Search of an Inca*. Translated by W. Hiatt, C. Aguirre, and C. Walker. Cambridge: Cambridge University Press.

Flores Najar, E. 1994. "Notas para la historia del turismo en el Cusco." *Revista del Instituto Americano de Arte* 14: 209–227.

Flores Noriega, E. P. 1980. *"La Ilustración Peruana" y su contribución al periodismo en el Perú*. Thesis, Escuela Nacional de Bibliotecarios. Lima: Biblioteca Nacional.

Flores Ochoa, J. 1996. "Buscando los Espíritus del Ande: Turismo Místico en el Qosqo." In *La Tradición Andina en Tiempos Modernos, Senri Ethnological Reports* 5: 9–29. Edited by Hiroyasu Tomoeda and Luis Milliones. Osaka: National Museum of Ethnology.

Foucault, M. 1972. *The Archaeology of Knowledge and the Discourse on Language*. Translated by A. M. Sheridan Smith. London: Tavistock.

————. 1974. *The Order of Things: An Archaeology of the Human Sciences*. New York: Vintage.

————. 1977. *Discipline and Punish: The Birth of the Prison*. Translated by Alan Sheridan. New York: Vintage.

Freire-Marreco, B., and J. L. Myres. 1912. *Notes and Queries on Anthropology*. 4th ed. London: Royal Anthroplogical Institute.

Gade, D. 2016. *Spell of the Urubamba: Anthropogeographical Essays on an Andean Valley in Space and Time*. New York: Springer.

Gänger, S. 2009. "Conquering the Past: Post-War Archaeology and Nationalism in the Borderlands of Chile and Peru, c. 1880–1920." *Society for Comparative Studies in Society and History* 51, no. 4: 691–714.

————. 2014. *Relics of the Past: The Collecting and Study of Pre-Columbian Antiquities in Peru and Chile, 1837–1911*. Oxford: Oxford University Press.

Gänger, S., P. Kohl, and I. Podgorny. 2014. "Nature in the Making of Archaeology in the Americas." In *Nature and Antiquities: The Making of Archaeology in the Americas*, edited by P. Kohl, I. Podgorny, and S. Ganger, 3–20. Tucson: University of Arizona Press.

García, M. E. 2005. *Making Indigenous Citizens: Identities, Education, and Multicultural Development in Peru*. Palo Alto, CA: Stanford University Press.

García Canclini, N. 2002. *Transforming Modernity: Popular Culture in Mexico*. Translated by L. Lozano. Austin: University of Texas Press.

Garson, J., and C. Read, eds. 1892. *Notes and Queries on Anthropology*. 2nd ed. London: Anthropological Institute.

Gell, A. 1997. *Art and Agency: Towards a New Anthropological Theory*. Oxford: Clarendon.

Ginzburg, C., ed. 1986. *Clues, Myths, and the Historical Method*. Baltimore: Johns Hopkins University Press.

Glenn, D. 2009. "Peru v. Yale: A Battle Rages over Machu Picchu." *Chronicle of Higher Education*, A1.

Goldgar, A. 1995. *Impolite Learning: Conduct and Community in the Republic of Letters, 1680–1750*. New Haven, CT: Yale University Press.

Golinski, J. 1998. *Making Natural Knowledge: Constructivism and the History of Science*. Chicago: University of Chicago Press.

Gootenberg, P. 1988. *Between Silver and Guano: Commercial Policy and the State in Post-Independence Peru*. Princeton, NJ: Princeton University Press.

———. 2008. *Andean Cocaine: The Making of a Global Drug*. Chapel Hill: University of North Carolina Press.

Gosden, C. 2004. *Archaeology and Colonialism: Cultural Contact from 5000 BC to the Present*. Cambridge: Cambridge University Press.

Gosden, C., and C. Knowles. 2001. *Collecting Colonialism: Material Culture and Colonial Change*. Oxford: Berg.

Grandin, G. 2000. *The Blood of Guatemala: A History of Race and Nation*. Durham, NC: Duke University Press.

Greenblatt, S. 1991. *Marvelous Possessions: The Wonder of the New World*. Chicago: University of Chicago Press.

———, ed. 1993. *New World Encounters*. Berkeley: University of California Press.

Gündüz, R. 2001. *El Mundo Ceremonial de los Huaqueros*. Lima: Editorial Universitaria.

Gutiérrez de Quintanilla, E. 1913. "El saqueo de las huacas." *La Nación*, September 9.

———. 1916. "Riqueza Arqueológica Peruana." *La Prensa*, January 8.

———. 1921. *Memoria del Director del Museo de Historia Nacional*. Lima: Taller Tipográfico del Museo.

———. 1922. *El Manco Capac, de la Arqueolojía Peruana: Julio C. Tello (Señor de Huarochirí) contra Emilio Gutiérrez de Quintanilla Autor de este Folleto*. Lima.

Hampe Martínez, T. 1998. "Max Uhle y los origenes del Museo de Historia Nacional." In *Max Uhle y el Perú Antiguo*, edited by P. Kaulicke, 123–158. Lima: Fondo Editorial de la Pontificia.

Haraway, D. 1989. *Primate Visions: Gender, Race, and Nature in the World of Modern Science*. New York: Routledge.

———. 1991. "Situated Knowledges: The Science Question in Feminism and the Privilege of Partial Perspective." *Feminist Studies* 14, no. 3: 575–599.

———. 1997. *Modest_Witness@Second_Millennium. FemaleMan©_Meets_Onco-Mouse™: Feminism and Technoscience*. New York: Routledge.

Hardy, O. 1914. "Cuzco and Apurimac: A Report on the Commercial and Industrial Outlook of South Central Peru." *Bulletin of the American Geographical Society* 46, no. 7.

Hayden, C. 2003. *When Nature Goes Public: The Making and Unmaking of Bioprospecting in Mexico*. Princeton, NJ: Princeton University Press.

Heaney, C. 2010. *Cradle of Gold: The Story of Hiram Bingham, a Real-Life Indiana Jones, and the Search for Machu Picchu*. New York: Palgrave Macmillan.

———. 2012. *Las Tumbas de Machu Picchu: La Historia de Hiram Bingham y la Búsqueda de las Últimas Ciudades de los Incas*. Lima: PUCP.

Hecht, S. 2013. *The Scramble for the Amazon and the "Lost Paradise" of Euclides da Cunha*. Chicago: University of Chicago Press.

Heidegger, M. (1936) 2002. "The Origin of the Work of Art (1935–1936)." In *Off the Beaten Track*, edited by J. Young and Kenneth Haynes, 1–56. Cambridge: Cambridge University Press.

Hinsley, C. M. 1985. "From Shell-Heaps to Stelae: Early Anthropology at the Peabody Museum." In *Objects and Others: Essays on Museums and Material Culture*, edited by G. W. Stocking, 49–75. Madison: University of Wisconsin Press.

Hooper-Greenhill, E. 1992. *Museums and the Shaping of Knowledge*. New York: Routledge.

———. 2000. *Museums and the Interpretation of Visual Culture*. New York: Routledge.

Hrdlička, A. 1911. "Some Results of Recent Anthropological Exploration in Peru." *Smithsonian Miscellaneous Collections* 56, no. 16: 1–32.

———. 1914. "Anthropological Work in Peru in 1913, with Notes on the Pathology of the Ancient Peruvians." *Smithsonian Miscellaneous Collections* 61, no. 18: 1–128.

Huhtamo, E. 2013. *Illusions in Motion: Media Archaeology of the Moving Panorama and Related Spectacles*. Cambridge, MA: MIT Press.

Hulme, P. 1983. *Colonial Encounters: Europe and the Native Caribbean, 1492–1797*. London: Methuen.

Ilustración Peruana. 1911. "Vistas del Peru." Vol. 3, no. 88 (June 7): 1097.

———. 1912a. Untitled article. Vol. 4, no. 144 (July 10).

———. 1912b. "Machu-piccho = Cuzco." Vol. 4, no. 152 (November 13): 257–288.

———. 1913a. "Charlas Quincenales." Vol. 5, no. 7 (July 16): 170.

———. 1913b. "Ruinas de la Antigua Ciudad Incaica, Machu Picchu—En la Maravillosa Tierra del Perú." Vol. 5, no. 7 (July 16), 171–176.

Ivy, M. 1995. *Discourses of the Vanishing: Modernity, Phantasm, Japan*. Chicago: University of Chicago Press.

Jacobsen, N. 1988. "Free Trade, Regional Elites, and the Internal Market in Southern Peru, 1895–1932." In *Guiding the Invisible Hand: Economic Liberalism and the State in Latin American History*, edited by J. L. Love and N. Jacobsen, 145–176. New York: Praeger.

———. 1993. *Mirages of Transition: The Peruvian Altiplano, 1780–1930*. Berkeley: University of California Press.

Jordanova, L. 1989. *Sexual Visions: Images of Gender in Science and Medicine between the Eighteenth and Twentieth Centuries*. Madison: University of Wisconsin Press.

———. 2000. *Defining Features: Scientific and Medical Portraits, 1660–2000*. London: Reaktion.

Juan, J., and A. Ulloa. (1748) 1964. *A Voyage to South America*. Abridged ed. Translated by J. Adams. New York: Knopf.

Kaulicke, P., ed. 1998. *Max Uhle y El Perú Antiguo*. Lima: PUCP.

Kersel, M., and C. Luke. 2015. "Civil Societies? Heritage Diplomacy and Neo-

Imperialism." In *Global Heritage: A Reader*, edited by L. Meskell, 70–93. West Sussex, UK: Wiley Blackwell.

Keys, D. 2008. "Inca City: Who Found Machu Picchu?" *Independent*, June 2.

Klarén, P. 1973. *Modernizaton, Dislocation, and Aprismo: Origins of the Aprista Party, 1870–1932*. Austin: University of Texas Press.

———. 2000. *Peru: Society and Nationhood in the Andes*. Oxford: Oxford University Press.

Knauft, B., ed. 2002. *Critically Modern: Alternatives, Alterities, Anthropologies*. Bloomington: Indiana University Press.

Kohl, P. 1998. "Nationalism and Archaeology: On the Constructions of Nations and the Reconstructions of the Remote Past." *Annual Review of Anthropology* 27: 223–246.

Kohl, P., and C. Fawcett. 1994. "Archaeology in the Service of the State." In *Nationalism, Politics, and the Practice of Archaeology*, edited by P. Kohl and C. Fawcett, 3–20. Cambridge: Cambridge University Press.

Kohl, P., I. Podgorny, and S. Gänger, eds. 2014. *Nature and Antiquities: The Making of Archaeology in the Americas*. Tucson: University of Arizona Press.

Krouse, S. A. 1990. "Photographing the Vanishing Race." *Visual Anthropology* 3, nos. 2–3: 213–233.

Kuhn, A. 1985. *The Power of the Image: Essays on Representation and Sexuality*. New York: Routledge.

Kuhn, T. 1962. *The Structure of Scientific Revolutions*. Chicago: University of Chicago Press.

Larrabure y Unanue, E. 1906. "Instalación solemne el 29 de Julio de 1905." *Revista Histórica* 1: 122–139.

———. 1934. *Manuscritos y Publicaciones de Eugenio Larrabure y Unanue*. Vol. 3. Lima: Imprenta Americana.

Larson, B. 2004. *Trials of Nation Making: Liberalism, Race, and Ethnicity in the Andes, 1810–1910*. Cambridge: Cambridge University Press.

Larson, C. 2015. *Our Indigenous Ancestors: A Cultural History of Museums, Science, and Identity in Argentina, 1877–1943*. University Park: Pennsylvania State University Press.

Latour, B. 1987. *Science in Action*. Cambridge, MA: Harvard University Press.

———. 1993. *We Have Never Been Modern*. Cambridge, MA: Harvard University Press.

Latour, B., and S. Woolgar. 1986. *Laboratory Life: The Construction of Scientific Facts*. Princeton, NJ: Princeton University Press.

Law, J. 1992. "Notes on the Theory of the Actor-Network: Ordering, Strategy and Heterogeneity." *Systems Practice* 5: 179–193.

———. 1999. "After ANT: Complexity, Naming, and Typology." In *Actor Network Theory and After*, edited by J. Law and J. Hassard, 1–14. Oxford: Blackwell.

Law, J., and M. E. Lien. 2013. "Slippery: Field Notes in Empirical Ontology." *Social Studies of Science* 43, no. 3: 363–378.

León, J. M. 1934. Introduction to Eugenio Larrabure y Unanue, *Manuscritos y Publicaciones de Eugenio Larrabure y Unanue*. 3 vols. 1:vii–xii. Lima: Imprenta Americana.

Leung, A., L. Braverman, and E. Pearce. 2012. "History of US Iodine Fortification and Supplementation." *Nutrients* 4, no. 11: 1740–1746.

Levin, R. C. 2011. Introduction to *Machu Picchu: Catálogo de la colección*, 10–11. Lima: US Embassy.

Levi-Strauss, C. 1966. *The Savage Mind*. Chicago: University of Chicago Press.

Little, W. 2008. "A Visual Political Economy of Maya Representations in Guatemala, 1931–1944." *Ethnohistory* 55, no. 4: 633–663.

Löfgren, O. 1999. *On Holiday: A History of Vacationing*. Berkeley: University of California Press.

López, R. 2010. *Crafting Mexico: Intellectuals, Artisans, and the State after the Revolution*. Durham, NC: Duke University Press.

López Lenci, Y. 2004. *El Cusco, paqarina moderna: Cartografía de una modernidad e identidades en los Andes peruanos (1900–1935)*. Lima: Fondo Editorial Universidad Nacional Mayor San Marcos.

López-Ocón, L. 1995. "El nacionalismo y los orígenes de la Sociedad Geográfica de Lima." In *Saberes Andinos: Ciencia y Tecnología en Bolivia, Ecuador y Perú*, edited by M. Cueto, 109–125. Lima: IEP.

Lubow, A. 2007. "The Possessed." *New York Times*, June 24.

Luciano, P. 2006. "Neoliberalism, Heritage Conservation, and the Resulting Dispossession at Machu Picchu, a Protected Area in the Peruvian Andes." *Applied Anthropology* 26, no. 1: 26–36.

———. 2011. "Where Are the Edges of a Protected Area? Political Dispossession in Machu Picchu, Peru." *Conservation and Society* 95, no. 1: 35–41.

Lutz, C., and J. L. Collins. 1993. *Reading "National Geographic."* Chicago: University of Chicago Press.

MacQuarrie, K. 2007. *The Last Days of the Incas*. New York: Simon and Schuster.

Majluf, N. 2000. "Photographers in Andean Visual Culture." *History of Photography* 24, no. 2: 91–100.

———. 2005. "De la rebelión al museo: Genealogías y retratos de los incas, 1781–1900." In *Los Incas, Reyes del Perú*, edited by T. Cummins, G. Ramos, E. Phipps, J. Estenssoro, L. Wuffarden, and N. Majluf, 254–320. Lima: Banco del Credito.

Majluf, N., and L. E. Wuffarden. 2001. "El primer siglo de la fotografía, Perú 1842–1942." In *El primer siglo de la fotografía, Perú 1842–1942: La Recuperación de la Memoria*, edited by N. Majluf and L. E. Wuffarden, 20–133. Lima: Fundación Telefónica y Museo de Arte de Lima.

Malkki, L. 1992. "National Geographic: The Rooting of Peoples and the Territorialization of National Identity among Scholars and Refugees." *Cultural Anthropology* 7, no. 1: 24–44.

Markham, C. 1856. *Cuzco: A Journey to the Ancient Capital of Peru*. London: Chapman and Hall.

———. 1862. *Travels in Peru and India while Superintending the Collection of Chinchona Plants and Seeds in South America*. London: J. Murray.

———. 1892. *A History of Peru*. Chicago: Sergel.

———. (1910) 1969. *The Incas of Peru*. New York: AMS Press.

Mathewson, C. H. 1915. "A Metallographic Description of Some Ancient Peruvian Bronzes from Machu Picchu." *American Journal of Science* 190, no. 240: 525–616.

Maurer, K. 2009. "Archeology as Spectacle: Heinrich Schliemann's Media of Excavation." *German Studies Review* 32, no. 2: 303–317.

Maxwell, A. 1999. *Colonial Photography and Exhibitions: Representations of the Native and the Making of European Identities.* Leicester, UK: Leicester University Press.

McCray, P. 2006. *Giant Telescopes: Astronomical Ambition and the Promise of Technology.* Cambridge, MA: Harvard University Press.

McElroy, K. 1977. "The History of Photography in Peru in the Nineteenth Century, 1839–1876." PhD diss., University of New Mexico.

———. 1985. *Early Peruvian Photography: A Critical Case Study.* Ann Arbor: University of Michigan Research Press.

Medina, E., I. da Costa Marques, and C. Holmes, eds. 2014. *Beyond Imported Magic: Essays on Science, Technology, and Society in Latin America.* Cambridge, MA: MIT Press.

Memorandum of Understanding. 2007. "Memorandum of Understanding between the Government of Peru and Yale University." September 14.

Méndez, C. 1995. *Incas Sí, Indios No: Apuntes Para el Estudio del Nacionalismo Criollo en el Perú.* Lima: Instituto de Estudios Peruanos.

Mendoza, Z. 2009. "Tourism, Folklore, and the Emergence of Regional and National Identities." In *Cultural Tourism in Latin America: The Politics of Space and Imagery,* edited by M. Baud and A. Ypeij, 23–44. Boston: Brill.

Mignolo, W. 2000. *Local Histories / Global Designs: Coloniality, Subaltern Knowledges, and Border Thinking.* Princeton, NJ: Princeton University Press.

———. 2005. *The Idea of Latin America.* London: Blackwell.

———. 2011. *The Darker Side of Western Modernity: Global Futures, Decolonial Options.* Durham, NC: Duke University Press.

Miller, C. 1982. *Fathers and Sons: The Bingham Family and the American Mission.* Philadelphia: Temple University Press.

Miller, D., and P. Reill. 1996. *Visions of Empire: Voyages, Botany, and Representations of Nature.* Cambridge: Cambridge University Press.

Miller, G. R. 2003. "Food for the Dead, Tools for the Afterlife: Zooarchaeology at Machu Picchu." In *The 1912 Yale Peruvian Scientific Expedition Collections from Machu Picchu: Human and Animal Remains,* edited by R. Burger and L. Salazar, 1–64. New Haven, CT: Yale University Press.

Miller, R. 1976. "The Making of the Grace Contract: British Bondholders and the Peruvian Government, 1885–1890." *Journal of Latin American Studies* 8, no. 1: 73–100.

Mirzoeff, N. 1998. "Photography at the Heart of Darkness: Herbert Lang's Congo Photographs, 1909–1915." In *Colonialism and the Object: Empire, Material Culture, and the Museum,* edited by T. Barringer and T. Flynn, 167–187. New York: Routledge.

———. 2006. "Invisible Empire: Visual Culture, Embodied Spectacle, and Abu Ghraib." *Radical History Review* 95 (Spring): 21–44.

Mitchell, W. J. T. 2005. *What Do Pictures Want? The Lives and Loves of Images.* Chicago: University of Chicago Press.

Mol, A. M. 2003. *The Body Multiple: Ontology in Medical Practice.* Durham, NC: Duke University Press.

Moreyra, C. P. 1997. "La Peruvian Corporation." *Revista del Archivo General de la Nación* 16: 307–318.

Mould de Pease, M. 2000. "Apuntes interculturales para la historia inmediata de Machu Picchu: Las funciones de Hiram Bingham and Albert Giesecke." *Revista del Archivo Histórico del Cusco* 15: 133–147.

———. 2001. "Un día en la vida peruana de Machu Picchu: Avance de historia intercultural." *Revista Complutense de Historia de América* 27: 257–279.

———. 2003. *Machu Picchu y el Código de Ética de la Sociedad de Arqueología Americana*. Lima: Pontificia Universidad Catolica del Peru.

———. 2005. "Machu Picchu: Un rompecabezas para armar." *Revista Andina* 41: 199–220.

Mulligan, T., and D. Wooters, eds. 1999. *Photography from 1839 to Today: George Eastman House, Rochester, NY*. New York: Taschen.

Muniz, C. n.d. "Chronology of Machu Picchu." Unpublished paper.

Murphy, E., D. Cohen, C. Bhimull, F. Coronil, M. Patterson, and J. Skurski, eds. 2011. *Anthrohistory: Unsettling Knowledge, Questioning Discipline*. Ann Arbor: University of Michigan Press.

Mytelka, A. 2009. "Judge Transfers Peru's Lawsuit against Yale to a Connecticut Court." *The Ticker* (blog), *Chronicle of Higher Education*, July 30.

Needham, P. 2008. "Inca Inventory Review Underway." *Yale Daily News*, March 3.

New York Herald. 1911. "Explorers Find a City That Was." December 22.

Noel, J. 1912a. "Valuable Scientific Expedition." *Peru To-Day*. Vol. 4, no. 7 (October): 372–373.

———. 1912b. "Dr. Bingham's Valuable Work." *Peru To-Day*. Vol. 4, no. 9 (December): 475–476.

———. 1913. "The Yale Scientific Expedition." *Peru To-Day*. Vol. 4, no. 10 (January): 531–532.

Orlove, B. 1994. "The Dead Policemen Speak: Power, Fear, and Narrative in the 1931 Molloccahua Killings (Cusco)." In *Unruly Order: Violence, Power, and Cultural Identity in the High Provinces of Southern Peru*, edited by D. Poole, 63–95. Boulder, CO: Westview.

Owens, C. 1991. *Beyond Recognition: Representation, Power, and Culture*. Berkeley: University of California Press.

Pagden, A. 1993. *European Encounters with the New World: From Renaissance to Romanticism*. New Haven, CT: Yale University Press.

Palomino, E. 1915. "La comisión Bingham en Machu Picchu: Informe al instituto histórico del Cusco." *La Crónica*, July 5.

Parker, W. B. 1919. *Peruvians of Today*. Lima: Southwell.

Patterson, T. C. 1995a. "Archaeology, History, *Indigenismo*, and the State in Peru and Mexico." In *Making Alternative Histories: The Practice of Archaeology and History in Non-Western Settings*, edited by P. R. Schmidt and T. C. Patterson, 69–86. Santa Fe, NM: School of American Research.

———. 1995b. "Power Relations and State Formation." In *Power Relations and State Formation and Disintegration of a Pre-Capitalist State*, edited by T. C. Patterson and C. Gailey, 1–26. Washington, DC: American Anthropological Association.

Penny, H. G. 2002. *Objects of Culture: Ethnology and Ethnographic Museums in Imperial Germany*. Chapel Hill: University of North Carolina Press.

Pickering, A. 1999. "The Mangle of Practice: Agency and Emergence in the Sociology of Science." In *The Science Studies Reader*, edited by M. Biagioli, 372–393. New York: Routledge.

Pillsbury, J. 2012. *Past Presented: Archaeological Illustrations and the Ancient Americas.* Washington, DC: Dumbarton Oaks Research Library and Collection.

———. 2014. "Finding the Ancient in the Andes: Archaeology and Geology, 1850–1890." In *Nature and Antiquities: The Making of Archaeology in the Americas*, edited by P. Kohl, I. Podgorny, and S. Gänger, 47–68. Tucson: University of Arizona Press.

Pimental, J. 2001. *Viajeros Científicos: Tres Grandes Expediciones al Nuevo Mundo.* Madrid: Nivola Editores.

Pinney, C. 1990. "Classification and Fantasy in the Photographic Construction of Caste and Tribe." *Visual Anthropology* 3: 259–288.

———. 1992. "The Parallel Histories of Anthropology and Photography." In *Anthropology and Photography, 1860–1920*, edited by E. Edwards, 74–95. New Haven, CT: Yale University Press, in association with the Royal Anthropological Institute.

Planas, E. 2007. "Machu Pictures." *El Comercio*, November 4.

Podgorny, I. 2009. *El Sendero del Tiempo y de las Causas Accidentales: Los Espacios de la Prehistoria en la Argentina, 1850–1910.* Rosario, Argentina: Prohistoria.

Podgorny, I., and M. Lopes. 2008. *El Desierto en una Vitrina: Museos e Historia Natural en la Argentina 1810–1890.* Mexico City: Limusa.

Polar, J. 1906. "Instalación solemne el 29 de Julio de 1905." *Revista Histórica* 1: 122–139.

Poole, D. 1992. "Figueroa Aznar and the Cusco *Indigenistas*: Photography and Modernism in Early Twentieth-Century Peru." *Representations* 38 (Spring): 39–75.

———, ed. 1994. *Unruly Order: Violence, Power, and Cultural Identity in the High Provinces of Southern Peru.* Boulder, CO: Westview.

———. 1997. *Vision, Race, and Modernity: A Visual Economy of the Andean Image World.* Princeton, NJ: Princeton University Press.

———. 1998. "Landscape and the Imperial Subject: US Images of the Andes, 1859–1930." In *Close Encounters of Empire*, edited by G. Joseph, C. LeGrand, and R. Salvatore, 107–138. Durham, NC: Duke University Press.

———. 2004. "An Image of 'Our Indian': Type Photographs and Racial Sentiments in Oaxaca, 1920–1940." In "Can the Subaltern See? Photographs as History," special issue, *Hispanic American Historical Review* 84, no. 1: 37–82.

———. 2005. "An Excess of Description: Ethnography, Race, and Visual Technologies." *Annual Review of Anthropology* 34: 159–179.

Poole, R. M. 2004. *Explorers House: "National Geographic" and the World It Made.* New York: Penguin.

Portocarrero, G. 2015. *La Urgencia por Decir "Nosotros": Los Intelectuales y la Idea de Nación en el Perú Republicano.* Lima: Fondo Editorial, PUCP.

Pratt, M. L. 1992. *Imperial Eyes: Travel Writing and Transculturation.* London: Routledge.

Prescott, W. H. 1862. *The Conquest of Peru.* London: Routledge, Warne, and Routledge.

Prieto, G. 2010. "Dos Forjadores de la Ciencias Sociales en el Perú: Sus Publicaciones y Confrontaciones." *Arqueología y Sociedad* 22: 1–34.

Pupio, M. A. 2005. "Coleccionistas de objetos históricos, aqueológicos, y de ciencias naturales en museos municipales de la provincia de Buenos Aires en la década de 1950." *Manguinhos* 12 (supplement): 205–209.

Ranney, E. 2000. "New Light on the Cusco School." *History of Photography* 24, no. 2: 113–120.

Rapp, R. 1999. *Testing Women, Testing the Fetus: The Social Impact of Amniocentesis in America*. New York: Routledge.

Ravines, R., ed. 1970. *100 Años de Arqueología en el Perú*. Lima: Instituto de Estudios Peruanos.

———. 1982. *Panorama de la Arqueología Andina*. Lima: Instituto de Estudios Peruanos.

Reid, D. 2002. *Whose Pharaohs? Archaeology, Museums, and Egyptian National Identity from Napoleon to World War I*. Berkeley: University of California Press.

Rice, M. 2014. *Dean Worcester's Fantasy Islands: Photography, Film, and the Colonial Philippines*. Ann Arbor: University of Michigan Press.

Riviale, P. 2000. *Los Viajeros Franceses en Busca del Perú Antiguo (1821–1914)*. Lima: Fondo Editorial de la Pontificia Universidad Católica del Perú.

Rodriguez, J. 2013. "Beyond Prejudice and Pride: The Human Sciences in Nineteenth and Twentieth Century Latin America." *Isis* 4, no. 4: 807–817.

Roger, G. 1917. "Los Olvidados con Gutiérrez de Quintanilla." *Revista de Actualidades*, July 7, no. 2: 4–5.

Romero, C. 1909. "Informe sobre las Ruinas de Choquequirau." *Revista Histórica* 4:3–19.

Romero, S. 2008. "Was a Lost City Ever Lost?" *New York Times*, December 7.

Roque, R. 2010. *Headhunting and Colonialism: Anthropology and the Circulation of Human Skulls in the Portuguese Empire, 1870–1930*. New York: Palgrave Macmillan.

Rowe, J. H. 1954. *Max Uhle, 1856–1954: A Memoir of the Father of Peruvian Archeology*. Berkeley: University of California Press.

Rubenstein, A. 1998. *Bad Language, Naked Ladies, and Other Threats to the Nation: A Political History of Comic Books in Mexico*. Durham, NC: Duke University Press.

Ryan, J. 1997. *Picturing Empire: Photography and the Visualization of the British Empire*. London: Reaktion.

Safier, N. 2008. *Measuring the New World: Enlightenment Science and South America*. Chicago: University of Chicago Press.

Said, E. 1978. *Orientalism*. New York: Pantheon.

Salazar, L., and R. Burger. 2016. "The Machu Picchu Solution: A New Approach to Cultural Patrimony Disputes." In *Finding Solutions for Protecting and Sharing Archaeological Heritage Resources*, edited by A. P. Underhill and L. Salazar, 87–102. New York: Springer.

Salomon, F. 1985. "The Historical Development of Andean Ethnology." *Mountain Research and Development* 5, no. 1: 79–98.

Salvatore, R. 1998. "The Enterprise of Knowledge: Representational Machines of Informal Empire." In *Close Encounters of Empire: Writing the Cultural History of*

US–Latin American Relations, edited by G. Joseph, C. LeGrand, and R. Salvatore, 69–106. Durham, NC: Duke University Press.

———. 2003. "Local versus Imperial Knowledge: Reflections on Hiram Bingham and the Yale Peruvian Expedition." *Nepantla* 4, no. 1: 67–80.

———. 2006. "Imperial Mechanics: South America's Hemispheric Integration in the Machine Age." *American Quarterly* 58, no. 3: 662–691.

———. 2008. "Tres Intelectuales Peruanos: Conexiones Imperiales en la Construcción de una Cultural Nacional." In *Intelectuales y Poder: Ensayos en Torno a la República de las Letras en el Perú e Hispanoamérica (Siglos XVI–XX)*, edited by C. Aguirre and C. McEvoy, 353–384. Lima: Instituto Francés de Estudios Andinos.

———. 2016. *Disciplinary Conquest: US Scholars in South America, 1900–1945*. Durham, NC: Duke University Press.

Savoy, G. 1970. *Antisuyo: The Search for the Lost Cities of the Amazon.* New York: Simon and Schuster.

Schmidt, P. R., and T. C. Patterson, eds. 1995. *Making Alternative Histories: The Practice of Archaeology and History in Non-Western Settings.* Santa Fe, NM: School of American Research.

Scorer, J. 2014. "Andean Self-Fashioning: Martín Chambi, Photography, and the Ruins at Machu Picchu." *History of Photography* 38, no. 4: 379–397.

Sekula, A. 1983. "The Invention of Photographic Meaning." In *Thinking Photography*, edited by V. Burgin, 84–109. London: Macmillan.

———. 1986. "The Body and the Archive." *October* 39 (Winter): 3–64.

Sellen, A. T. 2012. "Nineteenth-Century Photographs of Archaeological Collections." In *Past Presented: Archaeological Illustration and the Ancient Americas*, edited by J. Pillsbury, 207–230. Washington, DC: Dumbarton Oaks Research Library and Collection.

Shapin, S. 1984. "Pump and Circumstance: Robert Boyle's Literary Technology." *Social Studies of Science* 14, no. 4: 481–520.

Shapin, S., and S. Schaffer. 1985. *Leviathan and the Air-Pump: Hobbes, Boyle, and the Experimental Life*. Princeton, NJ: Princeton University Press.

Shumway, N. 1991. *The Invention of Argentina*. Berkeley: University of California Press.

Silverman, H. 2002. "Touring Ancient Times: The Present and the Presented Past in Contemporary Peru." *American Anthropologist* 104, no. 2: 881–902.

Smith, K. 2005. "Looting and the Politics of Archaeological Knowledge in Northern Peru." *Ethnos* 72, no. 2: 149–170.

Smith, N. 2004. *American Empire: Roosevelt's Geographer and the Prelude to Globalization*. Berkeley: University of California Press.

Sociedad de Propaganda del Sur del Perú. 1921. *Guía General del Sur del Perú*. Cuzco: Libreria Imprenta HG Rozas.

Sommer, D. 1991. *Foundational Fictions: The National Romances of Latin America*. Berkeley: University of California Press.

Sontag, S. 2004. *Regarding the Pain of Others*. New York: Picador.

Spivak, G. 1988. "Can the Subaltern Speak?" In *Marxism and the Interpretation of Culture*, edited by C. Nelson, 271–316. Urbana: University of Illinois Press.

Squier, E. G. 1877. *Peru: Incidents of Travel and Exploration in the Land of the Incas.* New York: Harper and Brothers.

Star, S. 2010. "This is Not a Boundary Object: Reflections on the Origin of a Concept." *Science, Technology, and Human Values* 35, no. 5: 601–617.

Star, S., and J. P. Griesemer. 1989. "Institutional Ecology, 'Translations' and Boundary Objects: Amateurs and Professionals in Berkeley's Museum of Vertebrate Zoology, 1907–39." *Social Studies of Science* 19, no. 3: 387–420.

Stepan, N. L. 1991. *"The Hour of Eugenics": Race, Gender, and Nation in Latin America.* Ithaca, NY: Cornell University Press.

Stocking, G., Jr. 1968. *Race, Culture, and Evolution: Essays in the History of Anthropology.* New York: Free Press.

———. 1971. "What's in a Name?" *Man* 6, no. 3: 369–390.

———. 1987. *Victorian Anthropology.* New York: Free Press.

Stoler, A. L. 2003. *Carnal Knowledge and Imperial Power: Race and the Intimate in Colonial Rule.* Berkeley: University of California Press.

Suescun Pozas, M. 1998. "From Reading to Seeing: Doing and Undoing Imperialism in the Visual Arts." In *Close Encounters of Empire: Writing the Cultural History of US–Latin American Relations,* edited by G. Joseph, C. LeGrand, and R. Salvatore, 525–556. Durham, NC: Duke University Press.

Tagg, J. 1988. *Burden of Representation: Essays on Photographies and Histories.* Basingstoke, UK: Macmillan.

Tamayo Herrera, J. 1980. *Historia del Indigenismo Cuzqueño, Siglos XVI–XX.* Lima: Instituto Nacional de la Cultura.

———. 1981. *Historia Social del Cuzco Republicano.* Lima: Editorial Universo.

Tantalean, H. 2014. *Peruvian Archaeology.* Walnut Creek, CA: Left Coast Press.

Taussig, M. 1993. *Mimesis and Alterity: A Particular History of the Senses.* New York: Routledge.

Tello, J. C. 1977. *La Investigación Científica.* Lima: Universidad Nacional de San Marcos.

Tello, J. C., and T. Mejia Xesspe. 1967. *Historia de los Museos Nacionales del Perú: 1892–1946.* Lima: Museo Nacional de Antropología y Arqueología.

Tenorio-Trillo, M. 1994. *Mexico at the World's Fair: Crafting a Modern Nation.* Berkeley: University of California Press.

———. 1996. "1910 Mexico City: Space and Nation in the City of the Centenario." *Journal of Latin American Studies* 28, no. 1: 75–104.

———. 1999. "Stereophonic Scientific Modernisms: Social Science between Mexico and the United States, 1880s–1930s." *Journal of American History* 86, no. 3: 1156–1187.

———. 2003. "Essaying the History of National Images." In *After Spanish Rule: Postcolonial Predicaments of the Americas,* edited by M. Thurner and A. Guerrero, 58–88. Durham, NC: Duke University Press.

Theroux, P. (1979) 1989. *The Old Patagonian Express: By Train through the Americas.* New York: Mariner.

Thomas, D. H. 2001. *Skull Wars: Kennewick Man, Archaeology, and the Battle for Native American Identity.* New York: Basic Books.

Thomson, H. 2002a. Introduction to H. Bingham, *Lost City of the Incas: The Story of Machu Picchu and Its Builders.* New York: Sterling.

———. 2002b. *Machu Picchu and the Camera*. Bassingbourn, UK: Penchant.

Thurner, M. 2003. "Peruvian Genealogies of History and Nation." In *After Spanish Rule: Postcolonial Predicaments of the Americas*, edited by M. Thurner and A. Guerrero, 141–175. Durham, NC: Duke University Press.

———. 2006. "After Colonialism and the King: Notes on the Peruvian Birth of 'Contemporary History.'" *Postcolonial Studies* 9, no. 4: 393–420.

———. 2010. *History's Peru: The Poetics of Colonial and Postcolonial Historiography*. Gainesville: University of Florida Press.

Thurner, M., and A. Guerrero, eds. 2003. *After Spanish Rule: Postcolonial Predicaments in the Americas*. Durham, NC: Duke University Press.

Traweek, S. 1988. *Beamtimes and Lifetimes: The World of High Energy Physicists*. Cambridge, MA: Harvard University Press.

Trever, L. 2012. "The Uncanny Tombs in Martínez Compañón's *Trujillo del Perú*." In *Past Presented: Archaeological Illustration and the Ancient Americas*, edited by J. Pillsbury, 107–142. Washington, DC: Dumbarton Oaks Research Library and Collection.

Trigger, B. 1984. "Alternative Archaeologies: Nationalist, Colonialist, Imperialist." *Man* 19: 355–370.

———. 2006. *A History of Archaeological Thought*. Cambridge: Cambridge University Press.

Trigo, B. 2005. "Walking Backwards to the Future: Time, Travel, and Race." In *Science and the Creative Imagination in Latin America*, edited by E. Fishburn and E. L. Ortiz, 24–43. London: Institute for the Study of the Americas.

Tsing, A. 2005. *Friction: An Ethnography of Global Connection*. Princeton, NJ: Princeton University Press.

Tucker, J. 1997. "Photography as Witness, Detective, and Imposter: Visual Representation in Victorian Science." In *Victorian Science in Context*, edited by B. Lightman, 378–408. Chicago: University of Chicago Press.

———. 2006. *Nature Exposed: Photography as Eyewitness in Victorian Science*. Baltimore: Johns Hopkins University Press.

Tucker, J., and T. Campt. 2009. "Entwined Practices: Engagements with Photography in Historical Inquiry." *History and Theory* 48, no. 4: 1–8.

Turkle, S., ed. 2007. *Evocative Objects: Things We Think With*. Cambridge, MA: MIT Press.

Urry, J. 1972. "*Notes and Queries on Anthropology* and the Development of Field Methods in British Anthropology." In *Proceedings of the Royal Anthropological Institute of Great Britain and Ireland*, 45–57. London: Royal Anthropological Institute of Great Britain and Ireland.

———. 1991. *The Tourist Gaze: Leisure and Travel in Contemporary Societies*. Thousand Oaks, CA: Sage.

Valcárcel, L. 1927. *Tempestad en los Andes*. Lima: Editorial Universo, S.A.

———. 1981. *Memorias*. Lima: Instituto de Estudios Peruanos.

Vázquez, O. E. 2004. "A Better Place to Live: Government Agency Photography and the Transformations of the Puerto Rican Jíbaro." In *Colonialist Photography: Imag(in)ing Race and Place*, edited by E. M. Hight and G. D. Sampson, 281–315. London: Routledge.

Vilela, S., and J. C. de la Puente. 2014. *El Último Secreto de Machu Picchu: ¿Tiene*

Dueño la Ciudadela de los Incas? New York: Penguin Random House Grupo Editorial.

Villela, K. D. 2012. "Beyond Stephens and Catherwood: Ancient Mesoamerica as Public Entertainment in the Early Nineteenth Century." In *Past Presented: Archaeological Illustration and the Ancient Americas*, edited by J. Pillsbury, 143–172. Washington, DC: Dumbarton Oaks Research Library and Collection.

Wallis, B. 1995. "Black Bodies, White Science: Louis Agassiz's Slave Daguerreotypes." *American Art* 9, no. 2: 38–61.

Wardlow, H. 2002. "'Hands-up'-ing Buses and Harvesting Cheese-Pops: Gendered Mediation of Modern Disjuncture in Melanesia." In *Critically Modern: Alternatives, Alterities, Anthropologies*, edited by B. Knauft, 144–174. Bloomington: Indiana University Press.

Weismantel, M. 2001. *Cholas and Pishtacos: Stories of Race and Sex in the Andes*. Chicago: University of Chicago Press.

Weismantel, M., and S. Eisenman. 1998. "Race in the Andes: Global Movements and Popular Ontologies." *Bulletin of Latin American Research* 17, no. 2: 121–142.

Wiener, C. 1880. *Pérou et Bolivie*. Paris: Librairie Hachette.

Willumson, G. 2004. "Making Meaning: Displaced Materiality in the Library and Art Museum." In *Photographs, Objects, Histories: On the Materiality of Images*, edited by E. Edwards and J. Hart, 65–83. New York: Routledge.

Wolf, E. 1989. *Europe and the People without History*. Berkeley: University of California Press.

Wulf, A. 2015. *The Invention of Nature: Alexander von Humboldt's New World*. New York: Knopf.

Zevallos Quiñones, J. 1994. *Huacas y Huaqueros en Trujillo durante el Virreynato (1535–1835)*. Trujillo, Peru: Editora Normas Legales.

Index

Page numbers in *italics* refer to illustrations.

Abu Ghraib, 133
Across South America: An Account of a Journey from Buenos Aires to Lima by Way of Potosí (Bingham), 10, 12–13, 77
Agassiz, Louis, 116
Aguas Calientes, 2, *166*, 166
Aguilar, Victor Raúl, 170, 174
Alaskan Eskimo, 121–122
Alvarez, Anacleto, 57–58, 131
Amundsen, Roald, 34
Anderson, Benedict, 103
Andes of Southern Peru, The (Bowman), 130
Anthropological Institute of Great Britain and Ireland, 115–116
"Anthropological Measurements for Field Use" (chart), 119
Anthropological Society of London, 116
anthropometry, 15, 21, 51, 73–74, 111, 115–128, 132–134, 179
Antigüedades Peruanas (de Rivero and von Tschudi), 7, 62, 153–154
Apurímac River, 13, 95–96
Archaeological Institute of America, 149
arriero (muleteer), 30, 44–45
Arteaga, Melchor, 15, 164
Axel, Brian, 19

Bakula, Cecilia, 170
Ballen, Mr., 39, 137, 143, 146, 148
Banard, Otto, 42, 43
Bandelier, Adolph, 8, 28, 116
Beasley-Murray, Jon, 140
Bell, Alexander Graham, 88
Bermudez Zamalloa, Bertha, 173–174
Berns, Augusto, 17, 18
Bestor, Paul, 44, 82
Billinghurst, Guillermo, 148, 150
Bingham, Hiram: and anthropometry, 115–119, 123, 128–132; and archaeological collecting, 49–66; Bingham Family Papers, 25; and camera technology, 69–85; and Cosmos Club, 4, 25; early expeditions, 9–12; and expeditionary science, 3–6; Hiram Bingham with his camera, 70; and *Ilustración Peruana*, 104–113; influence of, 164–181; influences on, 7–8; and mapmaking, 4–5, 13–15, 20–21, 32–36, 51, 53, 56, 73–74, 89–93, 95, 142, 150; and *National Geographic Magazine*, 86–101, 110–113; and 1911 Peruvian expedition, 12–15; and Peruvian law and conditions, 137–163; and scientific discoveries, 16–19, 65–66, 68–69; and Yale University, 137–163

Bingham, Hiram, books of: *Across South America: An Account of a Journey from Buenos Aires to Lima by Way of Potosí*, 10, 12–13, 77; *Inca Land*, 17, 63; *Journal of an Expedition Across Venezuela and Colombia, 1906–1907, The*, 10; *Lost City of the Incas*, 17, 69

Bingham, Hiram, correspondence of, 25–28, 44–48; with Farabee, 29–33, 35–36, 44; fund-raising and supplies, 33–37, 42–48; with Giesecke, 28–30, 32–33, 36; with Leguía, 37–40; with Markham, 29–36; with Marsters, 29–31, 33, 44; and networks, 47–48; and political support, 37–41

Bingham, Hiram, photographs of: "Altar of the Chief Temple of Machu Picchu, The," *99*; "Best type of Indian Workman: Southern Peru, The," *97*, *100*; "Bird's-Eye View of Machu Picchu (During Clearing) and the Urubamba Canon," 96, *96*; "Cheerful Workman From Cuzco, A," *97*; "Collecting the Skeletal Remains of the Ancient Inhabitants: Machu Picchu," *99*; "Excavating at Machu Picchu," *99*; "Good Mule Road in Southern Peru, A," *98*; "Large Burial Cave: Machu Picchu, A," *99*; "Ruins of the Ancient Inca Capital, Machu Picchu, The," *84*, 84

Bingham Jr., Hiram, 167

Boas, Franz, 121

Boletín de la Sociedad Geográfica de Lima (Bulletin of the Geographic Society of Lima), 154

Bolívar, Simón, 9–10, 142

Bowman, Isaiah, 44–45, 57, 130

Bristol, John, 144

Bueno, Christina, 61

Bumstead, Albert, 93

Burger, Richard, 170, 172

Cabrera brothers, *165*, 165

Caceres, Eduardo, 157

Caceres, J., 38

Callon, Michel, 139

cameras. *See* Cirkut (panorama) camera; Eastman Kodak; Panoram camera

Cañizares-Esguerra, Jorge, 162

Caretas (magazine), 166

Carrasco Escalante, Fabián, 15

cartography. *See* maps and mapmaking

Castro-Klarén, Sara, 142

Certeau, Michel de, 75

Chambi, Martín, 84, 113, 127, 165

charla (chat), 107

Charnay, Claude Joseph Désiré, 72

Chervin, Arthur, 121, 124

Choqquequirau, 1, 12–13, 28–29, 33–35, 38, 157

Cirkut (panorama) camera, 81

collections and collecting, 49–66; animals, 49, 50, 59; antiquities, 49–51, 61; books, 49, 51; incentivizing and coercion, 56–61; looting and grave robbing, 49, 61–65, 131; personnel, 53–56; practices and prospecting, 49–65; and scientific discovery, 65–66; shipping objects, 38, 41, 43, 53, 55, 58, 61, 139, 155, 156; skeletal remains, 50–52, 54–56, 58–61, 64–66

Coronado, Jorge, 153

Cosio, José Gabriel, 17, 18, 107–110, 138, 154–155, 157, 162

Creole, 9, 109, 111, 138–139, 142, 152–153, 155, 162–163

Cuzco: A Journey to the Ancient Capital of Peru (Markham), 8

Cuzqueña/o, 107, 132, 138, 153, 174

Darwin, Charles, 8

Daston, Lorraine, 3, 72

de la Cadena, Marisol, 152

de Milhau–Harvard Expedition, 31

de Rivero, Mariano Eduardo, 7, 62, 153–155

Derrida, Jacques, 18
Desiderata in Exploration (Markham), 30
Didion, Joan, 65
Dixon, Roland, 28, 53–54, 141
d'Orbigny, Alcide, 121
Duque, Alberto, 31–32, 44–45

Eastman, George, 74, 75, 81
Eastman Kodak, 20, 26, 36, 45, 70, 80–82, 92, 94, 164, 178; 3A Special, 75, 76, 114; Panoram camera, 73–76, *84*
Eaton, George, 44, 49, 55, 58–59, 62, 122, 131
Edwards, Elizabeth, 72, 87
enganche (labor recruitment system), 12
Erdis, Ellwood, 58–61, 64, 79, 138–139, 156, 159–160
ethnography: ethnographic picturesque, 125, 127, 133; salvage ethnography, 50–51; and science, 7
Ethnological Society of London, 116
Evocative Objects: Things We Think With (Turkle), 47
expeditionary science, 3–12, 26, 37, 99. *See also* scientific exploration and expeditions

Fabian, Ann, 116
Farabee, William Curtis, 29–33, 35–36, 44, 53–54, 141
Ferris, Harry Burr, 115, 118, 121–128
Ferro, Mariano, 57
Foote, Harry, 44
Ford, David, 79, 114–115, 118–119, *120*, 124–129, 132
Fuentes, Tomás, 58

Galindo, Alberto Flores, 14
Galison, Peter, 72
gamonal/es (political power system), 12
Gänger, Stefanie, 140
García, Alan, 171

Gell, Alfred, 104
Geographic Society of Lima, 9, 154, 158
Giesecke, Albert, 17, 19, 28–30, 32–33, 36, 51, 107, 148–149, 153, 164, 167
Gliddon, George, 116
gobernador (governor), 57
Grace, William Russell. *See* W. R. Grace & Co.
Gras, Enrico, 166
grave robbing, 49, 61–65, 131
Gregory, Herbert, 33, 34, 44
Griesemer, James, 139
Grosvenor, Gilbert, 30, 86, 88–90
Guevara, Victor, 157
Guía General del Sur del Peru, 164
Gündüz, Réna, 62
Gutiérrez de Quintanilla, Emilio, 151–155, 159–162

Haddon, A. C., 72
Hadley, Arthur, 40, 145–146, 148
Hardy, Osgood, 15, 44, 130–131, 156
Harkness, Ed, 34, 42–43
Hart, Janice, 87
Hasbrouck, J. J., 44, 60
Heald, K. C., 57, 64, 129
Heaney, Christopher, 140
Heidegger, Martin, 18
Heller, Edmund, 79
Hendriksen, Kai, 38, 44–45, 93
History of Peru, A (Markham), 8
Holmes, William Henry, 161
Hotchkiss, Henry, 42, 43
Hotchkiss, Stuart, 28, 42–43
Howard, H. Clay, 144, 146–147
Howe, Ernest, 32
Hrdlička, Aleš, 115–116, 118–119, 124, 141, 161
huaca (sacred house), 61
huaquero/s (relic or treasure hunters), 52, 61–63, 66, 141
Huarmiwañusqa (Dead Woman's Pass), 1
Huayna Picchu, 1–2, 91, 113, 114, 175, 179

Humboldt, Alexander von, 7, 65, 109, 117

Ilustración Peruana (periodical), 21, 86–87, 94, 104–111
Imagined Communities (Anderson), 103
Imperial Eyes: Travel Writing and Transculturation (Pratt), 65
Inca Land (Bingham), 17, 63
Incas, The (instructional film), 165–166
Incas of Peru, The (Markham), 8
indigenismo movement, 51, 113, 152–155, 162, 177
informe (report), 33, 147
infrastructure, 5, 8, 18, 44, 46
Instituto Histórico, 147–148
Instituto Histórico del Cusco (IHC), 156–158
Intihuatana, 16, 154, 157, 173
Islands of Titicaca and Koati, The (Bandelier), 8, 28
Ives, W. C., 78

Journal of an Expedition Across Venezuela and Colombia, 1906–1907, The (Bingham), 10

Karp, Eliane, 169–170
Keith, Minor C., 42, 43
Kipling, Rudyard, 50
Kodak. *See* Eastman Kodak

La Condamine, Charles de, 6–7, 65
La Crónica (periodical), 86, 149, 157
La Gorce, John Oliver, 92
Lake Parinacochas, 14, 30, 34–36
La Nación (periodical), 149, 151
Lanius, Paul Baxter, 42, 43
Larrabure y Unanue, Eugenio, 137, 147
Latour, Bruno, 26, 139
Leguía, Augusto, 13, 28, 37–40, 129, 141, 143–144, 146–148, 164
León, J. Matías, 137
letters and letter writing. *See* Bingham, Hiram, correspondence of
Leviathan and the Air-Pump (Shapin and Schaffer), 63

Levin, Richard, 171
Lévi-Strauss, Claude, 47
Limeño (male resident of Lima), 151, 153
Linnaeus, Carolus, 61
Little, Joseph, 44, 130
Lizárraga, Agustín, 16–17
Lomellini, Cesar, 13, 40–41
Lost City of the Incas (Bingham), 17, 69
"lost city" trope, 18, 63–65, 101
Lunbeck, Elizabeth, 3

Machiganga Indians, 115, 127–128
Machu Picchu: cost to visit, 2; contestations of "discovery," 16–19; history of, 2; panoramic photography of, 73–76, 83–85, 90–96, 101, 106–108; and tourism, 1–2, 17, 19, 69, 111–112, 150, 151, 162, 164–167, 169, 173, 176–178; as UNESCO World Heritage Site, 2, 112, 168. *See also* Yale Peruvian Expeditions
Machu Picchu (documentary), 166
Machu Picchu 100 Years: A Glimpse of the Expedition That Astonished the World (exhibition), 85
Machu Picchu: A Lost City Uncovered; Photographs from the Hiram Bingham Expeditions, 1911–1915 (exhibition), 85
Manco Capac, 13
Manco Inca, 4
maps and mapmaking, 4–5, 13–15, 20–21, 32–36, 51, 53, 56, 73–74, 89–93, 95, 142, 150
Marín, José, 59
Markham, Clements, 7–9, 11, 15, 25, 29–36
Marsters, V. F., 29–31, 33, 44
Martin, Dorothea Knox, 165
Maurer, Kathrin, 75
Means, James, 42, 43
Means, Philip Ainsworth, 44
measurements. *See* anthropometry
Memoirs of American Anthropological Association (Nelson), 115

Memorandum of Understanding (MOU), 168–170
Méndez, Cecilia, 142
mestizaje (miscegenation), 153
Mirzoeff, Nicholas, 104, 133
modernity, 5–6, 11, 37, 52, 63, 65, 84, 105, 115, 117, 138, 140, 151–155, 160, 162, 178
Morkill, W. L., 43–44, 146
Morton, Samuel, 116
Mould de Pease, Mariana, 17–18, 139–140
Mount Coropuna, 14, 28, 30, 33–36, 74, 89

National Geographic Magazine, 52, 64, 73, 132, 157, 162, 178; "Wonderland of Peru" issue, 20–21, 83, 85–101, 104–112, 115, 155
National Geographic Society, 14–15, 21, 26, 30, 42, 44, 73–74, 82, 110–111, 125, 167; and "Wonderland of Peru" magazine issue, 85–88, 90–91, 94
national identity, 6, 9, 22, 104, 141, 152, 155, 171
nationalism, 18, 26, 37, 46, 52, 112, 137–138, 141–142, 148, 153, 159–160, 168
National Museum (Lima), 39, 138–139, 141, 151, 153
National University of San Antonio Abad of Cuzco (Universidad Nacional de San Antonio Abad del Cusco), 28, 170–171, 174
Nelson, Luther T., 77, 86, 115, 118–119, 124; Quechua "types" photographs, 101, *102*
North Pole, 33
Nuñez Valdivia, Juan José, 13, 29

Old Patagonian Express, The (Theroux), 65
Ollantaytambo, 15, 31–32, 120, 154, 156
Olmos, Edward James, 172
On the Origin of the Species (Darwin), 8
Orientalism (Said), 3

Other and Othered, 3, 71, 125, 128
Owens, Craig, 18

Pachacuti, 2
Pachakuteq, 171
Palomino, Enrique, 158
Panama-Pacific International Exposition, 94
Panoram camera, 73–76. *See also* Eastman Kodak
Paz Soldan, Mariano, 13
Peabody Museum (Harvard University), 31, 36, 147
Peabody Museum of Natural History (Yale University), 170, 172, 178
Pérou et Bolivie (Wiener), 16
Peru: Incidents of Travel and Exploration in the Land of the Incas (Squier), 7
Peru: independence, 138, 161, 164; and infrastructure, 5, 8, 18, 44, 46; and injunction to halt excavation, 137, 139, 156–161; and Memorandum of Understanding (MOU), 168–170; Ministry of Culture (formerly National Institute of Culture), 1, 170, 178; and Yale attempts at concessions, 137–155
Peruanization, 17
Peru To-Day (periodical), 86, 94, 149–150, 154
Peruvian Corporation, 43–44, 146
Pezet, Federico Alfonso, 148
Písac, 154
Planas, Enrique, 177
Polar, Jorge, 148
Poole, Deborah, 63, 103, 117
Pratt, Mary Louise, 65
Protzen, Jean-Pierre, 173

racialization, 9, 12, 18, 50–51, 66, 130, 132–133
racial purity, 118
Raimondi, Antonio, 13, 30, 32
Revista Universitaria (periodical), 107, 157
Rice, Hamilton, 9–10
Richarte, Torvis, 58

Rios, Dionysius, 120–121
Rockefeller Foundation, 46
Rodman, Amy Oakland, 173
Romero, Carlos, 13, 28, 32, 33, 147
Rowe, John, 29
Ryan, James, 112, 125, 127

Sacsayhuaman, 154, 167
Said, Edward, 3
Salas, David, 165, *166*
Salazar, Lucy, 170, 172
salonniers (ones who frequent salons),
  61
Salvador (Didion), 65
Salvatore, Ricardo, 5, 46, 138
San Martín, José de, 9
Schaefer, Louis, 42, 43, 143, 145
Schaffer, Simon, 63, 72
Schapiro, Meyer, 18
Scheftel, Herbert, 42
Schliemann, Heinrich, 75
science and technology studies (STS),
  3–6, 52
Science in Action (Latour), 139
scientific exploration and expeditions:
  criticism of, 137–163; expeditionary
  science, 3–12, 26, 37, 99; funding
  for, 33–37, 42–48; and "lost city"
  trope, 18, 63–65, 101. *See also* Yale
  Peruvian Expeditions
Secret of the Incas, The (film), 165
Sellen, Adam, 72
Shapin, Steven, 63, 72–73
Smith, Huntington, 25, 33–36, 62
Smith, Kimbra, 62
Smithsonian Institution, 115, 147, 161
Smith-Worthington, 36
South Pole, 33–34
Squier, Ephraim George, 7–9, 11, 78
Stanford, Edward, 32
Steward, Julian, 29
Stocking, George, 115
Star, Susan Leigh, 139
Strathern, Marilyn, 104

Taft, William Howard, 38, 40,
  142–145

Tello, Julio C., 28, 116, 141
Tempestad en los Andes (Valcárcel), 153
Temple of the Moon, 2
Tenorio-Trillo, Mauricio, 103
Teotihuacán, Mexico, 61
Theroux, Paul, 65
Tiahuanaco, 78
Tiwanaku ruins, 9
Toledo, Alejandro, 167–168, 170
Torontoy, 45, 154
Torres Strait expedition, 72
tourism, 1–2, 17, 19, 69, 111–112, 150,
  151, 162, 164–167, 169, 173, 176–178
Travels in Peru and India (Markham),
  7–8
Túpac Inka Yupanki, 171
tupu (pin), 51, 60
Turkle, Sherry, 47
typologizing, 73, 117, 126–127

Uhle, Max, 29, 141, 151
Unanue, José Hipólito, 155
UNESCO World Heritage Site, 2,
  112, 168
United Fruit Company, 43, 44
UNSAAC. *See* National University of
  San Antonio Abad of Cuzco
UNSAAC-Yale International Center
  for the Study of Machu Picchu and
  Inca Culture, 171–173
Unveiling the Mystery of the Incas (exhi-
  bition), 169, 174
Urteaga, Horacio, 104
Urubamba Canyon/Valley, 13, 16,
  31–33, 35, 40, 44–45, 50, 74, 96,
  105–106, 120–121
utopia, 2, 14, 21, 73, 110, 113, 152–155

Valcárcel, Luis, 153, 156, 165
Van Gogh, Vincent, 18
Vargas, Carmen, 129
Velaochaga, Marcel, 175–179
Vilcabamba, 13, 15, 33–35, 44–45, 49
Vilcas, 140
Vision, Race, and Modernity (Poole),
  103
Vitcos, 4, 28, 90–91

Voltaire, 27–28
von Hassel, J. M., 17–18
von Tschudi, Johann Jakob, 7, 153

Waltham Watch Company, 36
Wardlow, Holly, 131
Wellcome Photographic Exposure Record and Diary, 76
Wiener, Charles, 16, 31
Wilson, Huntington, 143–145
Winchester Repeating Arms, 36
Woolgar, Steve, 26
Worcester, Dean, 111
W. R. Grace & Co., 38, 43, 45, 143, 145–146

Yale Peruvian Expeditions, 2, 12–15; and anthropometry, 114–134; and collecting, 49–66; and correspondence, 25–48; and expeditionary science, 3–6, 16–17; and *Ilustración Peruana*, 103–113; and National Geographic Society, 86–102, 110–113; and photography, 69–85; and Yale-Peruvian concessions conflicts, 137–164
Yale University: and Memorandum of Understanding (MOU), 168–170; and Peruvian concession attempts, 137–155; and Peruvian injunction again excavation, 137, 139, 156–161; Sterling Library, 25; *Unveiling the Mystery of the Incas* (exhibition), 169, 174
yanaconaje (sharecropping), 12
Yucay: A Romance in Early Peru (Martin), 165

Zedillo, Ernesto, 170